Microsoft Dynamics NAV 2013 Application Design

Second Edition

Customize and extend your vertical applications with Microsoft Dynamics NAV 2013

Marije Brummel

[PACKT] enterprise 🞕
PUBLISHING   professional expertise distilled

BIRMINGHAM - MUMBAI

Microsoft Dynamics NAV 2013 Application Design
Second Edition

First published: June 2010

Second edition: September 2014

Production reference: 3100822

Published by Packt Publishing Ltd.
Livery Place
35 Livery Street
Birmingham B3 2PB, UK.

ISBN 978-1-78217-036-5

www.packtpub.com

Cover image by Pratyush Mohanta (tysoncinematics@gmail.com)

Credits

Author
Marije Brummel

Reviewers
Danilo Capuano
Alex Chow
Stefano Demiliani
Tony Hemy
Daniel Rimmelzwaan

Acquisition Editor
Nikhil Karkal

Content Development Editor
Poonam Jain

Technical Editor
Shashank Desai

Project Coordinator
Mary Alex

Proofreaders
Simran Bhogal
Maria Gould
Ameesha Green

Indexers
Hemangini Bari
Priya Sane
Tejal Soni

Graphics
Sheetal Aute
Ronak Dhruv
Valentina D'silva
Disha Haria

Production Coordinators
Kyle Albuquerque
Aparna Bhagat
Melwyn D'sa
Adonia Jones
Manu Joseph
Nilesh R. Mohite
Komal Ramchandani
Alwin Roy
Nitesh Thakur
Shantanu N. Zagade

Cover Work
Manu Joseph

Foreword

Most books on Microsoft Dynamics NAV are about the tooling and the platform, but this book is different. It describes the building blocks, the code, and the metadata patterns that the application is made up of. The foundation for the patterns was created many years ago when we developed the first versions of Microsoft Dynamics NAV. Since then, they have been reused over and over again by us and every developer in the partner channel through the copy-paste mechanism. However, it was not until Marije and her friends in PRS, Gary and Waldo, rediscovered the patterns and started to write books, blog, teach, and speak at conferences that they became well known. Over time, this has evolved into a larger effort in collaboration with the Microsoft Dynamics NAV developer community, which has improved the overall quality of customization projects and reduced the implementation time. This book is important because it describes the patterns that are most used and explores how to leverage them when you modify Microsoft Dynamics NAV to suit industry-specific needs. It also contains examples on how to create add-ons and other enhancements that are easily upgraded. Everything is based on Marije's extensive experience of designing Microsoft Dynamics NAV implementations over almost two decades and expresses Marije's dedication to the Microsoft Dynamics NAV product and the various passionate people in the Microsoft Dynamics NAV community.

Michael Nielsen
Director of Engineering for NAV at Microsoft

Marije Brummel is the person other Microsoft Dynamics NAV experts go to when they have a really hard problem to solve. In this book, Marije shares the knowledge she has gained over the past two decades. In my own work as a Microsoft Dynamics NAV consultant/developer and as an author (writing three texts on programming in different versions of Microsoft Dynamics NAV), I've had the opportunity to draw on Marije's expertise many times. By reading this book, you now have a chance to do the same.

I've known Marije since we met at TechEd in Boston in 2006. Marije was already an accomplished analyst and developer—an expert in Microsoft Dynamics NAV and an MVP. Marije had been invited to that conference by Microsoft to help represent Microsoft Dynamics NAV to the other attendees who were technical experts. Since then, Marije has gained considerable experience and broadened his knowledge, particularly in the areas of business application problem solving using Microsoft Dynamics NAV.

Microsoft Dynamics NAV is a very special business software product. Included in the product is a set of IDE tools designed for the development of business applications and tailored to Microsoft Dynamics NAV. This makes it easier to create enhancements to fit the needs of specific businesses. As an integrated, full-featured ERP system, Microsoft Dynamics NAV includes functionalities for accounting, order processing, inventory control, manufacturing, distribution, service management, materials planning, and asset management. This book provides you with examples on how to choose from and apply these in a variety of business situations.

Each new version of Microsoft Dynamics NAV has delivered both new application functionalities and new technical capabilities. Upcoming versions are becoming more compatible with the cloud, mobile users, and various user interface devices. Each of these new capabilities expands the types of business applications to which Microsoft Dynamics NAV can be appropriately applied. With a worldwide-installed base already of well over 1,000,000 users, we know the uses of Microsoft Dynamics NAV are only limited by how creatively we apply our knowledge. Read on, let Marije expand your knowledge, and then use your own creativity to apply Microsoft Dynamics NAV to the needs of your businesses.

David Studebaker
Co-author, Programming Microsoft Dynamics NAV 2013

About the Author

Author, programmer, consultant, project manager, presenter, evangelist, salesperson, and a trainer. **Marije Brummel** has worked for Partners, ISVs, End Users, Master VARs, and Microsoft across the globe in more than 25 countries.

It's next to impossible to find someone as widely and deeply experienced as Marije in the Business Central community. She has received numerous awards including the Microsoft MVP award and the NAVUG All-Star. She was chair of the Dynamics Credentialling committee and authored the official Microsoft Exam materials. She did both onsite and online readiness sessions for Microsoft when the product went through major changes, such as moving from two-tier to three-tier and the introduction of extensions.

Her biggest passion is changing the world for the better in every way possible. One of her biggest achievements was the introduction of Design Patterns into the Business Central community. She is the go-to girl when it comes to performance troubleshooting and upgrade challenges. Technologies such as the Azure stack and Web frameworks don't hold secrets in regards to Business Central.

Marije has written many books and countless blog articles and YouTube videos, which influenced almost every person and project involved with Business Central. At home, she enjoys the outdoors with her dog and tries to spend as much time as possible with her kids and family. She likes shopping and traveling.

Acknowledgments

After I wrote my first book about application design in Microsoft Dynamics NAV, a lot has happened because of the book. I co-initiated Partner-Ready Software and worked closely together with Microsoft to improve the awareness of the great way Dynamics NAV is designed. This has been an amazing journey working together with some of the best people I've met in my professional life.

One of the best results is the awareness of design patterns in the application. In a team, more than 50 patterns have been documented.

I tried my best to implement the patterns in this book. A lot of the patterns were already there in the first edition. In this book, the patterns come together as applications, which give end users a great ERP system to use every day.

Since my previous book, my son Daan was born in 2010. The other kids, Josefien, Wesley, and Saskia, got older too, and I hope that one day they will understand the books and the beauty of software architectures. I'd like to thank them and my wife, Dionel, for giving me the freedom to explore my creativity, writing down my thoughts, and travel the world to share them. Because of my job, I have the opportunity to raise my kids in a great place where they can grow up in peace and become great people. I am very thankful for that.

A lot of people have helped me in writing and publishing this book, and I would like to thank them all for their help and patience as I am aware I am not always easy to work with.

Software architecture is more than database tables and code lines. Like any architecture, every piece should be well balanced and fit together in the complete structure. Unlike buildings and infrastructure, software is a lot more abstract, and the architecture is harder to see from outside. Together with Gary Winter, Eric Wauters, and Vjeko Babic, we have created a framework of patterns and best practices on how to put software together that is easy to understand, maintain, and upgrade, which are the cornerstones in applications such as Microsoft Dynamics NAV.

Special thanks go to David and Karen Studebaker. I met them in 2006 at TechEd in Boston, USA. Their help has been invaluable in bringing structure to my business and personal life. They have a very special place in my heart.

About the Reviewers

Danilo Capuano is a software engineer with over 8 years' experience. He lives in Naples, Italy, where he earned a degree in Computer Science. He currently works as a consultant on Microsoft Dynamics NAV in an IT company where he also completed the MCTS certification. You can refer to his website at www.capuanodanilo.com and his Twitter handle is @capuanodanilo.

Alex Chow has been working with Microsoft Dynamics NAV, formerly Navision, since 1999. Over the years, Alex has conducted hundreds of implementations across multiple industries. His customers range from $2 million a year small enterprises to $500 million a year multinational corporations.

Over the course of his Dynamics NAV career, he has often been designated as the primary person responsible for the success and failure of a Dynamics NAV implementation. The fact that Alex is still in the Dynamics NAV business means that he's been pretty lucky so far. His extensive career in the Dynamics NAV business is evidence of his success rate and expertise.

With a background of implementing all the functions and modules in and outside of Microsoft Dynamics NAV, Alex has encountered and resolved the most practical to the most complex requirements and business rules. Through these experiences, he has learned that sometimes you have to be a little crazy to have a competitive edge.

Believing that sharing these experiences and knowledge would benefit the Dynamics NAV community, Alex writes about his journey at www.dynamicsnavconsultant.com. He is also the founder of AP Commerce, Inc. (www.apcommerce.com), a full service Dynamics NAV service center founded in 2005. In addition, Alex has written a book about Dynamics NAV titled *Getting Started with Dynamics NAV 2013 Application Development*, *Packt Publishing*.

Alex lives in Southern California with his beautiful wife and two lovely daughters. He considers himself as the luckiest man in the world.

Stefano Demiliani is a Microsoft Certified Solution Developer (MCSD), MCAD, MCTS on Microsoft Dynamics NAV; MCTS on SharePoint; MCTS on SQL Server; and an experienced expert on other Microsoft-related technologies.

He has a Master's degree in Computer Engineering from Politecnico di Torino.

He works as a senior project manager and solution developer for EID (`http://www.eid.it`), a company of the Navlab group (`http://www.navlab.it`) and one of the biggest Microsoft Dynamics groups in Italy. His main activity is architecting and developing enterprise solutions based on the entire stack of Microsoft technologies (Microsoft Dynamics NAV, Microsoft SharePoint, and .NET applications in general).

He has written many articles and blogs on different Microsoft-related topics, and he's frequently involved in consulting and teaching. He has worked with Packt Publishing in the past for other books related to Microsoft Dynamics NAV.

You can get more details and keep in touch with him by reaching him at `http://www.demiliani.com` or via Twitter, `@demiliani`.

Tony Hemy has been deeply rooted in Microsoft Dynamics NAV from the age of 16. He started as an enthusiastic apprentice and now, more than a decade later, is an accomplished software development manager for Encore Business Solutions. Over the years, he has architected and customized Microsoft Dynamics NAV solutions for global organizations such as Warner Brothers and Viacom, earning an outstanding reputation and a role as the technical reviewer for two books published on Dynamics NAV. Tony has also served more than 5 years as a reserve soldier with the British Army, where he expanded not only his technical skills, but also the personal skills that have attributed to his disciplined work ethic and his determination to always do things right.

Tony's hands-on development experience with Microsoft Dynamics has given him an exceptional ability to help clients define the proper requirements that enable them to achieve their objectives. He has delivered extended capabilities through every version, every module, and every feature of Dynamics NAV, building thousands of unique configurations along the way. Tony also oversees software development, where he manages and mentors a talented development team and facilitates the best practices and standards that ensure clients receive the highest quality solutions and services. Tony is well traveled, well rounded, and well liked for his personable nature and "no shortcuts" approach, whether he is writing complex code or coaching his team.

Daniel Rimmelzwaan was born and raised in the Netherlands and moved to the USA at the end of 1999 to be with his new American wife. In Holland, he worked as a Microsoft Access and VBA developer. When looking for a job as a VB developer in the USA, he was introduced to Navision by a VB recruiter and was intrigued by the simplicity of its development tools. He decided to accept the job offer as a Navision developer with the firm intention to continue looking for a real developer job.

Almost 15 years later, a couple of stints with Microsoft's partner channel, a few years as a freelancer, Daniel is still working with NAV. He currently works with KCP Dynamics Group, an international partner that provides services to customers all over the world, and he is enjoying his career more than ever.

Daniel has had the opportunity to work in a wide variety of roles such as developer, analyst, designer, team lead, project manager, consultant, and more. Although he has a versatile experience with all things related to NAV, his main focus is designing custom solutions and business analysis.

Ever since he started working with NAV, Daniel has been an active member of the online communities for NAV, such as `http://mibuso.com/`, `http://dynamicsuser.net/`, and the online forums managed by Microsoft. For his contributions to these online communities, Daniel received his first of ten consecutive Microsoft Most Valuable Professional awards in July 2005, which was just the second year that the MVP award was given out for NAV. The MVP award is given out by Microsoft to independent members of technology communities around the world and recognizes people that share their knowledge with other members of the community.

Daniel lives with his wife and two kids in Arizona in the USA.

www.PacktPub.com

Support files, eBooks, discount offers, and more

For support files and downloads related to your book, please visit www.PacktPub.com.

Did you know that Packt offers eBook versions of every book published, with PDF and ePub files available? You can upgrade to the eBook version at www.PacktPub.com and as a print book customer, you are entitled to a discount on the eBook copy. Get in touch with us at service@packtpub.com for more details.

At www.PacktPub.com, you can also read a collection of free technical articles, sign up for a range of free newsletters and receive exclusive discounts and offers on Packt books and eBooks.

http://PacktLib.PacktPub.com

Do you need instant solutions to your IT questions? PacktLib is Packt's online digital book library. Here, you can search, access, and read Packt's entire library of books.

Why subscribe?

- Fully searchable across every book published by Packt
- Copy and paste, print, and bookmark content
- On demand and accessible via a web browser

Free access for Packt account holders

If you have an account with Packt at www.PacktPub.com, you can use this to access PacktLib today and view 9 entirely free books. Simply use your login credentials for immediate access.

Instant updates on new Packt books

Get notified! Find out when new books are published by following @PacktEnterprise on Twitter or the *Packt Enterprise* Facebook page.

Table of Contents

Preface

In 1997, the company I worked for was looking to replace their MS-DOS-based software package. We were very fortunate in finding Navision Financials 1.1 as a software package that supported the upcoming Windows platform and was flexible enough to be implemented, supporting our demands.

Even though the standard functionality was nowhere near what we have today, the structure of the application design was simple and solid and has not changed since then.

In the years after that, more companies embraced Navision as their answer to the changing demands in the market, and many vertical solutions that still exist today started their life cycle. With the acquisition of Navision by Microsoft, the interest of new partners grew into the channel we know today.

Microsoft Dynamics NAV offers a unique development experience that can only be fully used once you understand how the standard application parts are designed.

When properly licensed, everyone can change how the application works. With this great possibility comes great responsibility as this means that we can also easily break important business logic.

This results in a unique need for a designer of applications that run inside Microsoft Dynamics NAV to know more about the application without going into deep functional details.

The balance in this book will be between learning and understanding how the standard application features of Microsoft Dynamics NAV are designed, and how to use this knowledge when designing our own solutions. The area between understanding the application functionality and technical design is very thin.

In this book, we will make both changes to the standard application and create new solutions. We will also discuss how Microsoft Dynamics NAV can work with other applications.

What this book covers

Chapter 1, Introduction to Microsoft Dynamics NAV, will introduce you to Microsoft Dynamics NAV. We will briefly talk about the history of the application and talk about the concepts. We will cover some of the basic design patterns such as Number Series and Navigation. Then we will discuss the data model principles used by Microsoft Dynamics NAV using master data, journals, and ledger entries covered by documents.

Chapter 2, A Sample Application, will implement the theory you learned in the first chapter in a sample application. The goal of this chapter is to better understand how Journals and Ledger entries work throughout the system, and how to create your own Journal application. You will learn how to reverse engineer the standard application to learn from it and apply this to your own customizations. We will integrate the application with relationship management and sales in Microsoft Dynamics NAV, and extend Navigation and Dimensions for our solution.

Chapter 3, Financial Management, will explore how the financial management part of the application can be used and how it is designed. This is the heart of Microsoft Dynamics NAV. You will learn important concepts such as VAT and TAX, posting groups, closing dates, entry application, and financial data analysis. We will make some changes in the core application, adding new information to the general ledger, and learn how to integrate financial management into our add-on solution.

Chapter 4, Relationship Management, will help you to analyze the sales data in our system and be more productive towards your customers. We will explore the unique design of this part of the application and integrate this with the sample application we created in *Chapter 2, A Sample Application*.

Chapter 5, Production, will show us how to set up Microsoft Dynamics NAV for production companies. These companies are at the start of the supply chain. We will discuss the assembly management and manufacturing. Item Costing and Item Tracking are the key elements when using this part of the application. We will look at the planning worksheet, and how to create production orders using Make-to-Order and Make-to-Stock policies. We will reverse engineer the Inventory Profile Offsetting codeunit and see how this leads to planning and purchase orders. At the end of this chapter, we will look at ten ways to customize production for vertical industries.

Chapter 6, Trade, will discuss the relationship between sales, inventory management, and purchasing, and how warehousing can be involved using different levels of complexity. Without sales, most companies will not survive. We will learn how reservation entries are used in the system from a technical perspective.

Chapter 7, Storage and Logistics, will design and build a solution for planning routes for shipments, a feature that is not available in Microsoft Dynamics NAV. We will design a solution that can be used by trading companies not only for their own shipments but also for storage companies. The solution is seamlessly integrated with the Dynamics NAV product. We will extend the Journal knowledge that we learned in *Chapter 2, A Sample Application* and *Chapter 3, Financial Management*, with new document structures we learned in *Chapter 5, Production* and *Chapter 6, Trade*.

Chapter 8, Consulting, will discuss how to implement the Job functionality using four example jobs, and extend jobs with an issue registration and timesheet application using resource groups and calculations. The Jobs functionality in Microsoft Dynamics NAV can be compared to an add-on solution. It was designed outside financial management and trade but is still integrated into the product.

Chapter 9, Interfacing, will discuss how to design a rock solid business-to-business interface. In the last decade, interfacing has become a crucial part of designing and implementing ERP systems. We will show you which technologies are available to use for interfacing and how these technologies are implemented in the standard product. We will discuss all the built-in interfaces with other Microsoft applications such as Office, SharePoint, BizTalk, and Exchange.

Chapter 10, Application Design, will focus on the concepts of application design and how they apply to Microsoft Dynamics NAV. We will focus on design to use, maintain, support, upgrade, perform, and analyze. This includes concepts for the user interface, version management, and the development methodology.

Appendix, Installation Guide, will cover installation procedures associated with objects of Dynamics NAV.

What do you need for this book

To successfully follow the examples in this book, you will need the following:

- The Microsoft Dynamics NAV 2013 product CD to install the application.
- A full developer's license, which can be obtained by being registered or register as a Microsoft Dynamics NAV partner. Alternatively, most of the example code can be explored using a demo license, which can be downloaded from MSDN.

- Microsoft Office and SQL Server Management Studio for the interface examples in *Chapter 9, Interfacing*.

The *Appendix, Installation Guide,* describes how to install these prerequisites.

Who this book is for

Basically, this book is for:

- NAV consultants and developers
- Designers of business applications
- Application managers at end users
- Business owners and influencers

This book assumes that you have a basic understanding of business management systems, application development, with a working knowledge of Microsoft Dynamics NAV or another ERP system.

Conventions

In this book, you will find a number of styles of text that distinguish between different kinds of information. Here are some examples of these styles and an explanation of their meaning.

Code words in text, database table names, folder names, filenames, file extensions, pathnames, dummy URLs, user input, and Twitter handles are shown as follows: "We need to copy the `CreateVendor` function."

A block of code is as follows:

```
Currency Code - OnValidate()
IF "Currency Code" <> xRec."Currency Code" THEN
IF NOT JobLedgEntryExist THEN
CurrencyUpdatePlanningLines
ELSE
ERROR(Text000,FIELDCAPTION("Currency Code"),TABLECAPTION);
```

When we wish to draw your attention to a particular part of a code block, the relevant lines or items are set in bold:

```
UpdateSquashPlayer()
WITH SquashPlayer DO BEGIN
GET(ContBusRel."No.");
xRecRef.GETTABLE(SquashPlayer);
NoSerie := "No. Series";
```

```
TRANSFERFIELDS(Cont);
"No." := ContBusRel."No.";
"No. Series" := NoSerie;
MODIFY;
RecRef.GETTABLE(SquashPlayer);
ChangeLogMgt.LogModification(RecRef,xRecRef);
END;
```

New terms and **important words** are shown in bold. Words that you see on the screen, in menus or dialog boxes for example, appear in the text like this: "We can add functions in the **Globals** menu."

[Warnings or important notes appear in a box like this.]

[Tips and tricks appear like this.]

Where to find the screens in this book

Most of the screens in the book were created using the Windows Client with Microsoft Dynamics NAV 2013 Release 2. Wherever possible and necessary, the Role Center that was used is mentioned. Some chapters had new or modified Role Centers.

To find a screen, type the name in the search window on the upper-right corner of **Role Center**, as shown in the following screenshot. This will lead you there and tell where to find it in the menu.

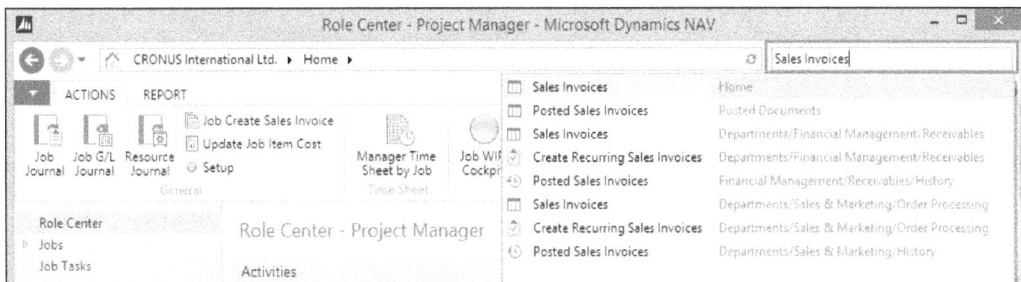

Search window

Screenshots

All the screenshots in this book are taken from Windows client, which was introduced with Microsoft Dynamics NAV 2013 Release 2.

For most the images, the **Action Pane** and **FactBox Pane** were turned off to save space. This can be done using the **Customize** option on each page.

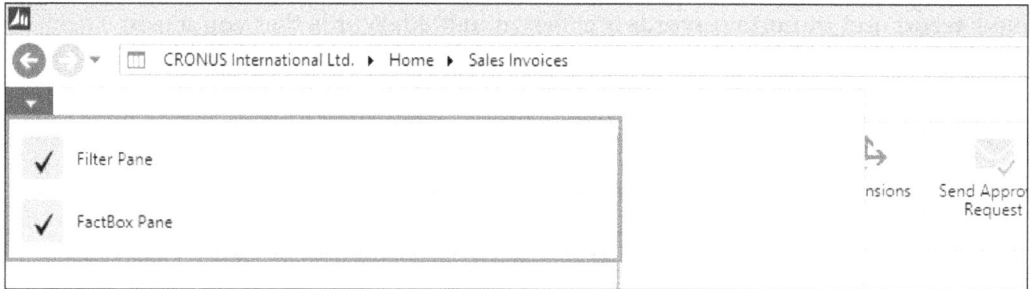

Customize option

How to read the application schemas

Most of the chapters in this book have schemas to clarify the flow of data though the system. They are specially designed for this book.

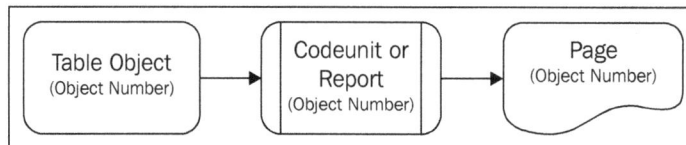

To read the schemas, follow the arrows. Wherever possible, the functional areas are grouped using boxes. Some schemas might have more starting and ending points as this is how the application is designed. Multiple master data tables are processed using normalized business logic.

Number and date punctuation

This book is written by a Dutch author, which means that all the number and date formatting is done in Dutch formats, for example 1.000,00 instead of 1,000.00 and 18-10-10 for October 18, 2010.

Reader feedback

Feedback from our readers is always welcome. Let us know what you think about this book—what you liked or may have disliked. Reader feedback is important for us to develop titles that you really get the most out of.

To send us general feedback, simply send an e-mail to feedback@packtpub.com, and mention the book title through the subject of your message.

If there is a topic that you have expertise in and you are interested in either writing or contributing to a book, see our author guide on www.packtpub.com/authors.

Customer support

Now that you are the proud owner of a Packt book, we have a number of things to help you to get the most from your purchase.

Errata

Although we have taken every care to ensure the accuracy of our content, mistakes do happen. If you find a mistake in one of our books—maybe a mistake in the text or the code—we would be grateful if you would report this to us. By doing so, you can save other readers from frustration and help us improve subsequent versions of this book. If you find any errata, please report them by visiting http://www.packtpub.com/support, selecting your book, clicking on the **errata submission form** link, and entering the details of your errata. Once your errata are verified, your submission will be accepted and the errata will be uploaded to our website, or added to any list of existing errata, under the Errata section of that title.

Piracy

Piracy of copyright material on the Internet is an ongoing problem across all media. At Packt, we take the protection of our copyright and licenses very seriously. If you come across any illegal copies of our works, in any form, on the Internet, please provide us with the location address or website name immediately so that we can pursue a remedy.

Please contact us at copyright@packtpub.com with a link to the suspected pirated material.

We appreciate your help in protecting our authors, and our ability to bring you valuable content.

Questions

You can contact us at questions@packtpub.com if you are having a problem with any aspect of the book, and we will do our best to address it.

1
Introduction to Microsoft Dynamics NAV

Once upon a time; this is how fairytales often start and even though the story of Microsoft Dynamics NAV is everything but a fairytale, it sure has some magic.

With more than 100,000 installations, it is one of the most popular ERP packages in the mid-market. In this book, we will go through the magic of the Dynamics NAV application. We'll see how Dynamics NAV will give better information on how our business is doing and provide a better insight where processes can be optimized or need to be changed.

In this chapter, we'll discuss the basic principles of the Microsoft Dynamics NAV application, how it's structured, and why. After reading this chapter, you will have a better understanding of what to expect when implementing and designing for Microsoft Dynamics NAV.

Versions and history

At the time of publishing this book, Microsoft Dynamics NAV 2013R2, is the most recent version of the product. When the Windows version was first introduced in 1995, the product was called Navision Financials 1.0. The Danish software company that originally developed the product, Navision Software A/S, was not yet acquired by Microsoft and it was a revolution. It was a full Windows product and had all basic functionality that small companies needed. It is important to understand that the original version was targeted at smaller companies.

Since then, we have had many (20+) versions. All new versions contained new functionality and with it the product has become more mature and suitable for bigger companies as well. This was especially empowered with the support of the Microsoft SQL Server platform, allowing more concurrent users to work in the same application areas.

Until Version 5.0, the technology of the product did not change. The original intention of Microsoft was to release a new technology platform together with new functional changes. This turned out to be a very difficult task so they decided to split the technology into two releases. Version 5.0 contained new functionality and improvements while Version 2009, or 6.0, which is the technical release number, was a technology release.

The technical challenge was to migrate from the old C++ platform to .NET and to move from a two tier to a three tier technology. This was also the first release with a drastic change in the user interface. Microsoft Dynamics NAV 2009 contains an entirely new user interface, the Role Tailored Client, which is built new from the ground up — the existing (classic) user interface is the same with no changes. During this migration process, all application functionality was frozen although small improvements and bug fixes were made in 2009 SP1.

With Microsoft Dynamics NAV 2013, we have entered a new era where the transformation is complete. The product is converted to .NET and even supports limited use of DotNet Interoperability directly from the C/AL programming language. The classic user interface is discontinued as is the native database.

This book supports functionality from the 2013 release although most concepts relate back to the older versions.

What is this book about

The title of the book is Microsoft Dynamics NAV 2013 Application Design. What does application design mean? And what does it mean in Microsoft Dynamics NAV 2013?

Microsoft Dynamics NAV 2013 is a complete ERP package, but unlike other ERP packages, it has a design capable of providing an open structure and a development platform. The idea is to provide 80 percent of the solution out of the box and allow the other 20 percent to be designed by qualified business application developers.

The partner channel is a unique part of Microsoft Dynamics NAV. From the moment Navision was introduced, company management decided that it would only make sense to have an indirect selling model and to let the resellers (called partners) have the availability to change the product and add new functionalities.

This book is about both the 80 percent and the 20 percent. We'll see that the percentages differ per industry where it is applied. Some industries have close to a 100 percent fit while others have a need for an 80 percent development.

So there is a very thin line in this book between using the standard application and designing changes and expanding the product. Although this is not a development book, we'll dive into code and objects in almost every chapter.

Reading this chapter will be more than enough to understand the code but if you want to know more, we highly recommend reading *Programming Microsoft Dynamics NAV 2013, David A. Studebaker, Christopher D. Studebaker, Packt Publishing.*

This book is not a manual for Microsoft Dynamics NAV 2013. It will give you a clear idea of how the structure of the application is laid out and about its possibilities. We do not want to replace or rewrite the Microsoft documentation but rather want to provide ideas that you might not have thought about.

Setup versus customization

In Microsoft Dynamics NAV, the line between implementing and developing is very thin. Where you would perform a lot of setup in other ERP packages, you'll see that it often makes more sense in Dynamics NAV to make a change with the development tools.

The standard package is very complete in its functionality but does not support all industries. It is more a framework for partners to work with. In this book, we will explain this framework and what philosophy it is built on. Understanding this philosophy is critical to knowing how to expand the functionality.

However, expanding the functionality means customizing the application. Do end users in 2013 still want customized applications? Mostly, they will say they don't want their software customized, but in the next breath, they will say that the software should change to match their way of doing business, and that they should have to change their business to fit the software.

This is why Microsoft pushes their partners to create horizontal and vertical solutions on top of the standard product and release these solutions as products with their own versions as if they were a part of the standard applications. This way of using the partner channel is a unique concept that has proven to be very successful and make Microsoft Dynamics NAV useable in almost any industry.

Most companies, however, have such a unique way of working that they will always require more or less customized solutions. The total cost of ownership depends on the level of customizations and how these customizations are designed.

The key is in knowing when to do a setup and when to do a customization. Only a solid understanding of the application will help you determine which is correct.

After reading this book, you will know how to design your application best to have a good balance between cost of ownership and functionality.

The beauty of simplicity

As discussed earlier, the application is designed to be expanded and changed by external partners. When this partner program was created, a decision was made that partners could only do a proper job if the application was completely open for them to add and change. This philosophy is very important to understand when you first start implementing or changing Microsoft Dynamics NAV.

Partners can change all business logic in the application. They can add new fields to tables and create their own tables. The only thing they cannot do is delete fields from the tables in the base application.

As you can see, Microsoft Dynamics NAV is an extremely flexible and open product with a lot of freedom. But with freedom comes responsibilities. In Dynamics NAV, you are responsible for the housekeeping in your system.

Horizontal versus vertical solutions

Because of this open system, partners have created thousands of smaller and larger changes to the system. Some of these changes were bundled into new functional pieces and called add-ons. These add-ons are often solutions that change Dynamics NAV into a product for a specific industry rather than a generic ERP system. Other add-ons are specific features that can be used in all industries such as EDI or workflow. Microsoft calls the industry specific add-ons verticals and the generic add-ons horizontals.

Open source

Even though Dynamics NAV has an open source for their partners, it does not come fully equipped with a development environment like most developers are used to. It has a customization tool that lets you customize the application like you would customize another ERP system with settings. This customization tool is a basic tool that is nice to work with but misses some development features such as version control or IntelliSense. This makes it more difficult to keep track of your changes. We will discuss how to use Team Foundation Server for Object Versioning in *Chapter 10, Application Design*.

Design patterns

When customizing Microsoft Dynamics NAV, you can use proven concepts in the application. These proven concepts are called design patterns. There are three types of design patterns.

Architectural patterns

Architectural patterns are the main data processes and table structures. Examples are master data, singleton tables, documents, and posting and archiving processes.

Design patterns

Although this is the name that people use for the entire concept, design patterns are reusable elements to solve specific problems, such as number series and blocked entity.

Implementation patterns

Different development techniques are called implementation patterns. Examples are proxy, façade, temporary datasets, and hooks.

APIs

Application programming interfaces (**APIs**) are reusable blocks of code that generally do not change. They are as important to know to work with Dynamics NAV as .NET libraries are to work in C#. Within Microsoft Dynamics NAV, we have several building blocks that are reused but not changed. Examples are address formatting and the navigate page.

Structure of this book

This book will cover most functional elements of Dynamics NAV in a number of vertical industries. We will do this in a supply chain matrix. The specific industries we will look at are fashion, automotive, medicines, food, and furniture. For production and trade, we will look at the general process, and we will see how consultancy and distribution companies help in this process.

The following diagram shows how this book is structured:

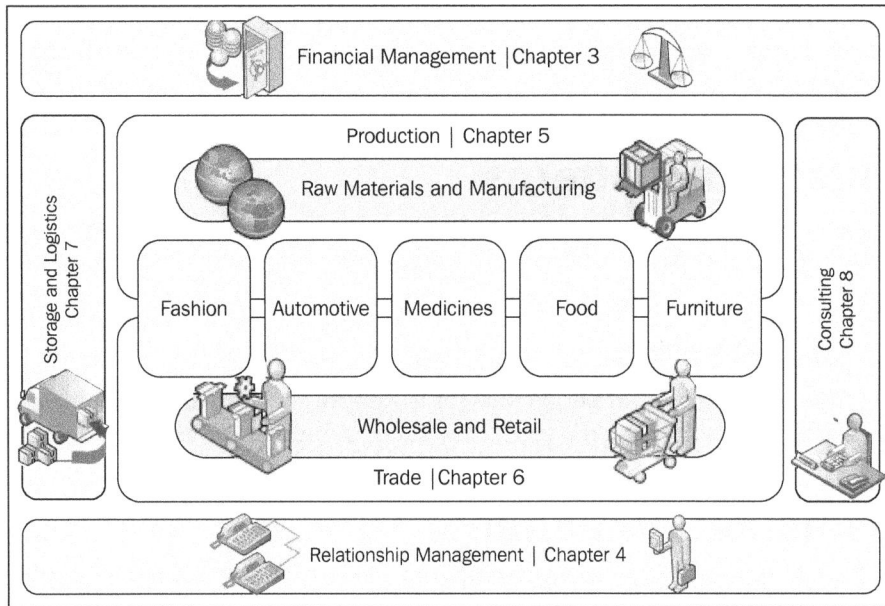

For all these industries, we will look at what parts of the standard product can be utilized and where we need vertical solutions. We'll discuss how these vertical solutions will interface with the standard package or maybe even change the behavior of the standard product.

Two parts of the product, however, are so general in their use and usability for all industries that we'll discuss them in their own chapter. These are **Financial Management** and **Relationship Management**.

To emphasize the strength of the vertical concept, we'll design and create a vertical solution for a distribution company.

Now, we will look at some of the basic concepts of the application.

The Role Tailored concept

With the NAV 2009 release, Microsoft marketing decided to introduce the concept of Role Tailored ERP. Until now, most ERP systems were module driven, meaning the application has an area for finance, CRM, sales, purchasing, and so on. The access to the individual modules was separated. A purchaser needs to switch to sales in order to see the sales orders.

Most people in a company have specialized tasks that the ERP system should support. In a classic ERP interface, the users would have to decide themselves the location of the parts that they need. This has changed with the introduction of the Role Tailored concept.

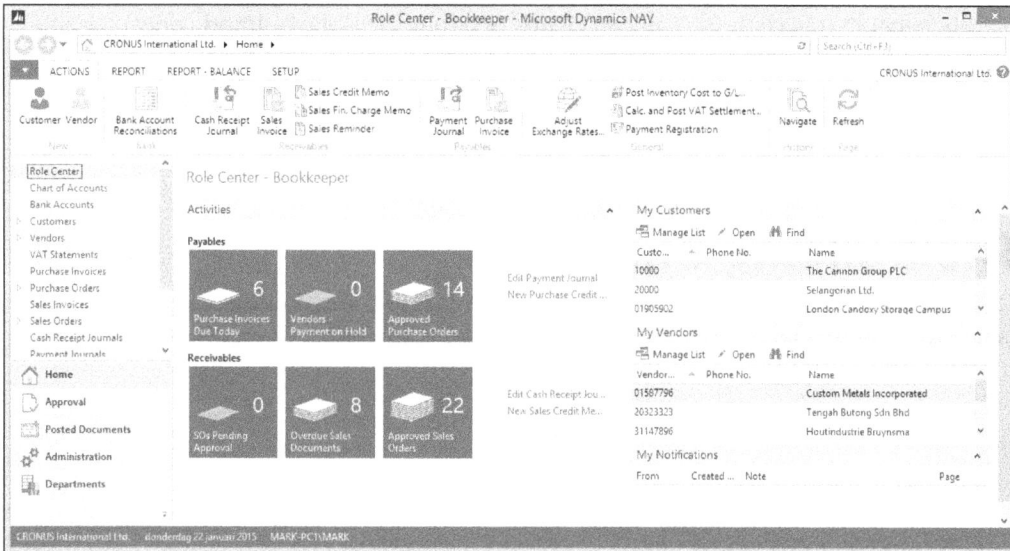

This screenshot shows a purchasers' Role Center. As you can see, all information for this person in the organization is in one place and usable in a workflow-like way. Also, the **Sales Orders** are accessible from the **Main Menu** window. It is completely different to the menu found in Version 5.0 or before.

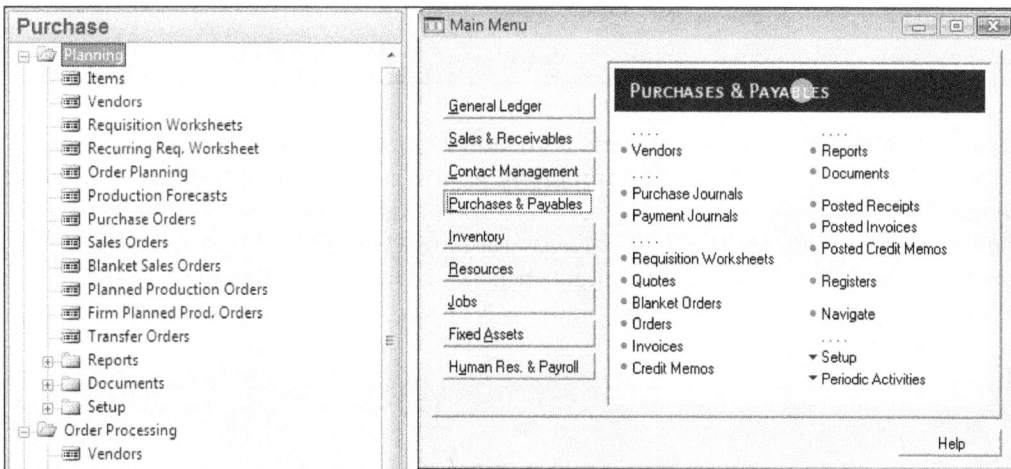

However, the Role Tailored concept is not new. Dynamics NAV partners have been implementing it for many years. In the classic menu, as seen in the preceding screenshot, it was extremely easy to create new menus and most companies implemented their own menus per role. When the Microsoft Outlook style menu was introduced in Version 4.0, end users could create shortcut Menu Suites, which also quickly became role centers. You can clearly see that the Role Tailored concept is like coming home for Dynamics NAV.

In Microsoft Dynamics NAV 2013, the Windows Client is no longer referred to as the Role Tailored Client as it was in Version 2009. All available clients are Role Tailored.

The building blocks

To understand the development examples in this book, we will discuss some of the basic building blocks of Microsoft Dynamics NAV 2013.

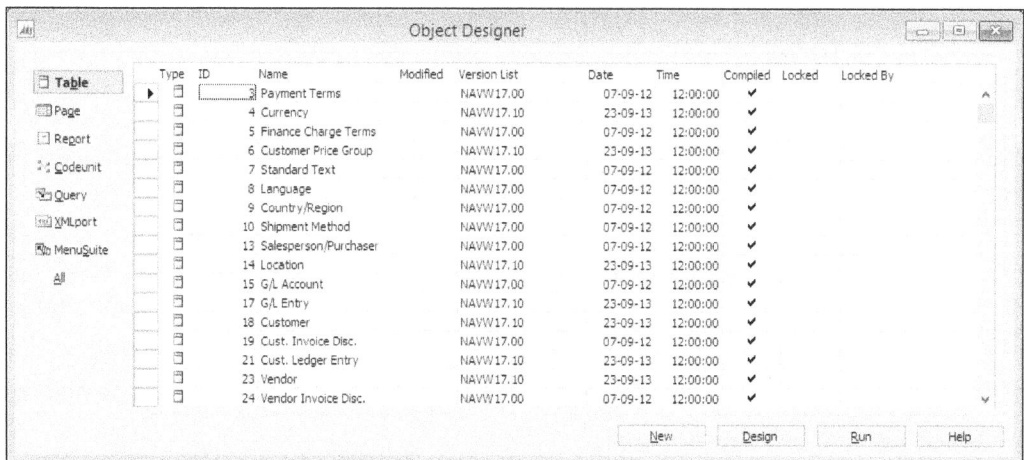

Like all database applications, it starts with tables. They contain all the information displayed in a structured way. It is important to understand that the tables of Microsoft Dynamics NAV are not completely normalized. The tables are structured in the way the user interface works. This makes it easy for nontechnical people to understand the data model. We'll discuss the unique structure of the application in *Chapter 2, A Sample Application.*

Tables, however, not only contain data, but they contain business logic as well. As they are structured like the functionality in the database, tables contain simple functions like address validation and more complex functions for VAT and discount calculation.

Whenever functionality gets more complex or can be shared across the application, it is better to move them to the codeunit object. These are containers of business logic for a special purpose. Tables can also be used as a class without storing data. This allows more structured programming.

For the user interface, there are two object types: reports and pages. Reports are originally intended to be printed on paper but with the current status of technology, they are more and more used as information dashboards, combining management information with drill-through possibilities.

As the tables are structured in the way the application works, the pages are bound to one table. For people new to this concept, it sometimes takes a while to get used to this.

The Menu Suite defines the way the navigation is structured when people leave their Role Centers and go to the department pages. The Menu Suite is used for the **Search** window.

The last object type is an external interface object. XML ports make it possible to import and export data in and out of the system.

Query objects are introduced in Microsoft Dynamics NAV 2013 and allow developers to define SQL Server SELECT statements on the metadata level that can be used in C/AL code. It is possible to join multiple tables into one query. Query objects can also be exposed as OData web services.

For this book, the table and page objects are the most important to understand. Most of this book, however, can also be applied to older versions but then forms should be applied wherever this book addresses pages.

Tables as user interface and business logic

The table object in Microsoft Dynamics NAV is very important. Since it is not normalized, it contains a lot of information about how the database works.

For example, the Job Card (88) is built on one table, the Job (167). This table contains all the fields required for this screen.

In a traditional development environment, this screen would have a transaction `GetJobData` and `UpdateJobData`. These transactions would read the information from the database, map them to the screen, and save the information in the database if the user is finished. However, in Microsoft Dynamics NAV, all fields that are displayed in the interface are stored in one table. This makes it possible for the screen to have built-in triggers to get the data and update the database.

The table object then contains the business logic required for this document. Let's have a look at some of the fields in this table:

E.. Field No.	Field Name	Data Type	Length	Description
✔ 61	Bill-to City	Text	30	
✔ 63	Bill-to County	Text	30	
✔ 64	Bill-to Post Code	Code	20	
✔ 66	No. Series	Code	10	
✔ 67	Bill-to Country/Region Code	Code	10	
✔ 68	Bill-to Name 2	Text	50	
▶ ✔ 117	Reserve	Option		
✔ 1000	WIP Method	Code	20	
✔ 1001	Currency Code	Code	10	
✔ 1002	Bill-to Contact No.	Code	20	
✔ 1003	Bill-to Contact	Text	50	
✔ 1004	Planning Date Filter	Date		

Table 167 Job - Table Designer

In the preceding screenshot, we can see a lot of fields such as **WIP Method**, **Currency Code**, and so on, which are required for a job.

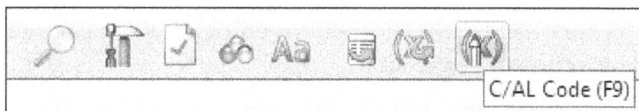

C/AL Code (F9)

When we click on the **C/AL Code** icon and we focus on currency code, we get the following result:

```
Currency Code - OnValidate()
IF "Currency Code" <> xRec."Currency Code" THEN
  IF NOT JobLedgEntryExist THEN
    CurrencyUpdatePlanningLines
  ELSE
    ERROR(Text000,FIELDCAPTION("Currency Code"),TABLECAPTION);
```

This contains business logic that gets executed every time something happens with this field. In this case, the currency factor is recalculated and updated in the sales lines.

So the tables in Microsoft Dynamics NAV are not just data containers, they are the foundation for both the business logic and the application workflow.

Dynamics NAV in throughout supply chain

The Dynamics NAV product is used almost everywhere in the business supply chain. This is mainly because it is a highly customizable ERP system. Dynamics NAV is used in the classical supply chain companies, such as manufacturing plants, wholesale companies, and in retail with or without many changes. But with an add-on, the product is also used in transportation companies or in the recycling industry.

In order to understand this better, it is important to know how companies work. A company is a person or a group of persons using materials and resources to deliver a product or a service to other companies or end consumers. A group of companies working together is called a supply chain. Dynamics NAV can be used in all these companies, although it is traditionally used in companies with five to 250 concurrent users.

In order to serve this process, Dynamics NAV has a list of the following basic modules:

- **Financial management**: Traditionally, this was used in companies to comply with federal regulations of bookkeeping. For entrepreneurs starting their business, this is usually the part they least like. However, good bookkeeping can give a clear view on the company's wellbeing and support strategic decisions with good financial information.

- **Inventory**: Every company that grows will reach a certain point where it is no longer possible to handle inventory without a system. Keeping too much inventory is very expensive. A good inventory system can help you keep your stock as efficient as possible.

- **Relationship management (RM)**: When it comes to people, a company is not only dealing with customers and vendors. RM will help you keep track of every company and person your company is dealing with.

- **Sales**: The sales process is usually the place where businesses make money. The system will help you keep track of orders that your customers place.

- **Purchasing**: The purchasing department is usually split in two pieces. One piece is the purchasing of goods the company needs for itself. This facility management can grow into a business of its own at large companies. The other purchasing part is buying the materials and resources you need for your sales process. For some trading companies, this can even be a drop shipment process where you never have the purchased goods in house.

- **Warehouse management**: Warehouses are getting bigger and bigger, making the need for a system that supports the picking and put-away process even greater. This is usually tightly connected to the sales and purchase process.

- **Manufacturing**: When you make products yourself, you need a system that helps you create a new item from one or more purchased materials and resources.

- **Jobs**: In some companies, the process of delivering a service is so complex that it requires its own administration process. Time and billing is usually a very important process for these companies.

- **Service management**: This supports the service process handling warranty and necessary periodical maintenance of your items.

Some basic design patterns

Microsoft Dynamics NAV has some basic design patterns that are reused throughout the application and are necessary to understand the concepts of this book.

Number series

Databases need unique records. The application has two ways of making this happen.

Some tables have automatic incremental numbering that cannot be influenced. These are often accounting tables that have auditable purposes. Examples of these tables are G/L entries, G/L registers, and VAT entries.

The other way is using a flexible alphanumeric code. In some setup tables, users are free to create their own numbers like in the location table but most of the time, number series functionality is used. These can be influenced by the end user depending on their access rights. Let's have a closer look at them:

Code	Description	Starting ...	Ending No.	Last Date ...	Last No. ...	Defa...	Man...	Date...
A-BLK	Assembly Blanket Orders	A00001	A01000		A00000	✔	✔	☐
A-ORD	Assembly Orders	A00001	A01000		A00000	✔	✔	☐
A-ORD+	Posted Assembly Orders	A00001	A01000		A00000	✔	✔	☐
A-QUO	Assembly Quote	A00001	A01000		A00000	✔	✔	☐
BANK	BANK	B010	B990			✔	✔	☐
CAMP	Campaign	CP0001	CP9999			✔	✔	☐
CASHFLOW	Cash Flow	CF100001			CF100001	✔	✔	☐
CONT	Contact	CT000001	CT100000	1-1-2014	CT000141	✔	✔	☐
CUST	Customer	C00010	C99990			✔	✔	☐

Users can define their own numbering, usually starting with an alphanumeric character. Numbering can be done automatically, manually, or a combination of the two. Numbers can have a starting date and incremental number. This way you can number your Sales Invoices SI11-0001. SI means Sales Invoice, 11 means 2011, and 0001 is the incremental number.

For example, number series can be linked to each other making it possible to have a different number series for national and international customers.

Extended text

Most master data tables in Microsoft Dynamics NAV have two description fields, but it is possible to add extra text.

The text can be defined for all languages in the system and made valid for a specific period.

We can enable or disable using the text for most documents available in the system, so we can have some long text for the **Sales Quote** and some shorter text for the **Sales Invoice**, as shown in the following screenshot:

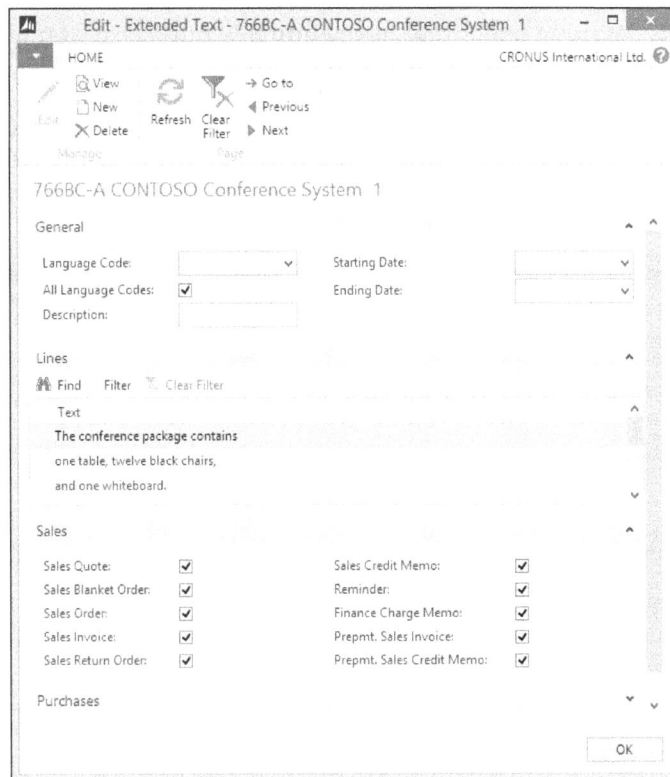

Navigate

The main reason Microsoft Dynamics NAV consultants like you to use numbers like SI11-0001 is because of the **Navigate** functionality. This functionality makes it possible to find all information in the database linked to this document. If you name your Sales Invoice 110001 and your Purchase Invoice the same, the system would not be able to find the information at a detailed level.

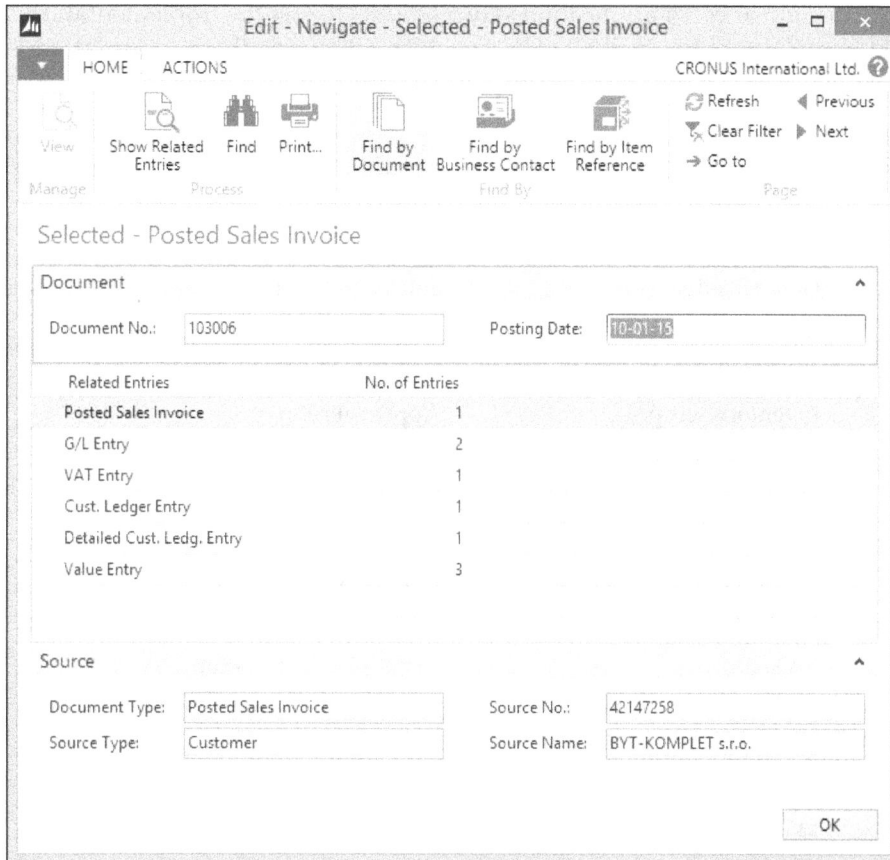

When navigating to **Posted Sales Invoice 103006** in the CRONUS Demo database, we get all the information that is linked to this number.

Navigation shows both documents and entries. Using the **Show** option, we can drill down into the records and go even deeper into the information. Navigation is present at most pages that show posted transactions and historical data.

Setup tables

An ERP application can be used in many different ways and to make it work in the way we want, we need to set it up correctly. We already discussed that Dynamics NAV has far less setup than other ERP packages and is more likely to be changed, but nonetheless there is setup work to do.

Every part of the application has its own setup table. There are also some application-wide or cross-application setup tables. During the implementation, we need to make sure to touch all of these tables. Changing these setups after the implementation should be done with great care.

The setup tables use the singleton table design pattern. The following table shows all Microsoft Dynamics NAV setup tables grouped by type:

Specific setup tables	Application-wide setup tables
General ledger setup	Source code setup
Sales & receivables setup	Change log setup
Purchases & payables setup	SMTP mail setup
Inventory setup	Approval setup
Resources setup	Job queue setup
Jobs setup	Online map setup
Marketing setup	Interaction template setup
Human resources setup	Employee portal setup
Production schedule setup	Notification setup
FA setup	Order promising setup
Nonstock item setup	BizTalk management setup
Warehouse setup	
Service Mgt. setup	
Manufacturing setup	

When we open a setup from the application, we see some options, including the numbering we discussed earlier:

Posting groups

Microsoft Dynamics NAV is very flexible in its posting to the **General Ledger**. This is set up in posting groups. These form a matrix that is filtered out by the application.

Most application areas have one or more posting group tables:

- Customer posting group
- Vendor posting group
- Inventory posting group
- Job posting group
- Gen. business posting group
- Gen. product posting group
- Bank account posting group
- VAT business posting group
- VAT product posting group
- FA posting group

> We'll discuss posting groups in more detail in
> *Chapter 3, Financial Management*.

Pricing

When it comes to pricing and discounts, Microsoft Dynamics NAV has a very simple yet effective way of calculating.

All sales and purchase prices are stored in four simple tables:

- 7002 – Sales Price
- 7004 – Sales Line Discount
- 7012 – Purchase Price
- 7014 – Purchase Line Discount

The system finds the appropriate price by filtering down in these tables. The narrower the filter, the more likely the price is applied.

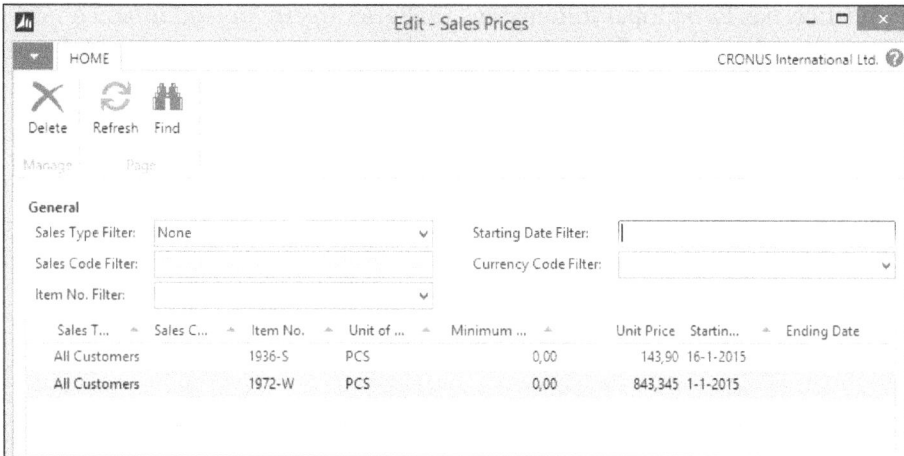

For example, the normal price of item **1972-W** on the item card is 97,480, but from **1-1-2011** it is **843,345**.

The filtering is done in codeunits Sales Price Calc. Mgt. (7000) and Purch. Price Calc. Mgt. (7010). We'll discuss this structure in *Chapter 2*, *A Sample Application*, where we will also create such a structure for our own application.

Dimensions

Throughout the application, an unlimited number of dimensions can be used to analyze the data. These dimensions are inherited from master data tables.

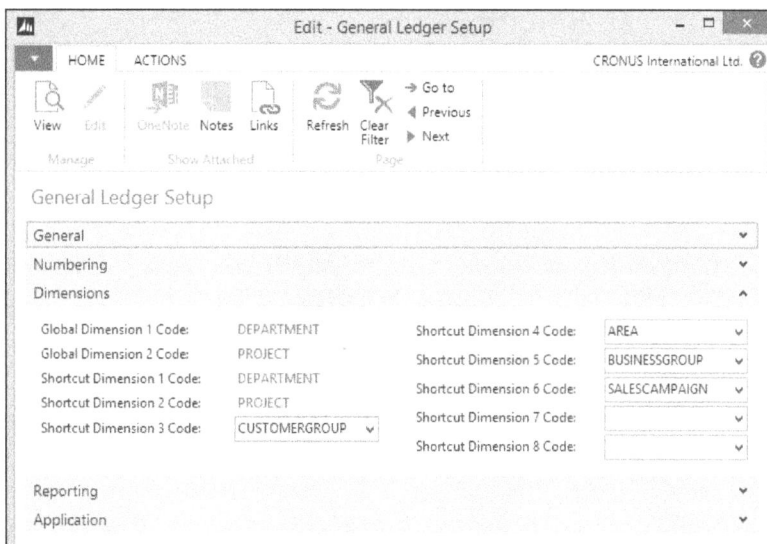

The application has two global dimensions that are directly posted into each transaction. Six other dimensions can be defined as shortcut dimensions to be directly used in journals and documents. An unlimited number of additional dimensions can be added but need to be accessed with additional effort.

101005 - John Haddock Insurance Co.

General

No.:	101005	...	Document Date:	8-1-2015
Sell-to Customer No.:	30000		Requested Delivery Date:	
Sell-to Customer Name:	John Haddock Insurance Co.		External Document No.:	
Sell-to City:	Manchester		Salesperson Code:	PS
Posting Date:	23-1-2015		Status:	Released
Order Date:	8-1-2015			

Lines

Line ▾   Functions ▾   Order ▾   Find   Filter   Clear Filter

Department Code	Project Code	Customergroup Code	Area Code	Businessgr...	Salescampa...	Shortcut Dimension 7 Code	Shortcut Dimension 8 Code
SALES		MEDIUM	30	HOME			

The preceding screenshot shows how Global and Shortcut Dimensions can be used in a **Sales Document**.

Microsoft Dynamics NAV has built in OLAP possibilities. It allows us to create cubes to be analyzed within the application or in SQL Server analysis services.

View - Analysis View List

HOME   ACTIONS   CRONUS International Ltd.

New | Edit | Edit Analysis View | Email as Attachment | Show as List | OneNote | Refresh
| View | Update | Microsoft Excel | Show as Chart | Notes | Clear Filter
| Delete | | | | Links | Find

New   Manage   Process   Send To   View   Show Attached   Page

Analysis View List ▾

Type to filter (F3)   Code

No filters applied

Code	↑	Name	Account ...	Incl...	Last Date ...	Dimensio...	Dimensio...	Dimensio...	Dimensio...
CAMPAIGN		Campaign Analysis (Retail)	G/L Account	☐	23-9-2013	SALESCA...	AREA	BUSINESS...	SALESPERS...
CASHFLOW		Analysis of cash receipts	Cash Flow ...	☐	23-9-2013	DEPARTM...	AREA		
CUSTOMER		Customer Group Analysis	G/L Account	☐	23-9-2013	AREA	CUSTOME...		
DEPTEXP		Departmental Expenses	G/L Account	☑	23-9-2013	DEPARTM...			
REVENUE		Sales Revenue	G/L Account	☑	23-9-2013	AREA	DEPARTM...	PROJECT	

Although the cubes can be updated real time during posting, it is highly recommended to update them periodically in a batch. Also, the number of dimensions has an impact on the performance of the system.

Dimensions were redesigned in Microsoft Dynamics NAV 2013. The redesign has a huge impact on application performance and can reduce database size up to 30 percent.

Architectural design patterns

Microsoft Dynamics NAV has some specific architectural design patterns principles that are very important to understand before you can create your own structure. The building blocks are layered and reused and rely on each other in order to secure data integrity.

Master data

The data model starts with master data. There are three types or levels of master data. They are all used in transactions. We differentiate supplemental, normal, and subsidiary master data.

Examples of supplemental data are currencies, locations, and payment terms. They often do not use a number series but allow us to create our own unique codes.

Examples of master data are G/L Accounts, customers, vendors, items, resources, and fixed assets. They are numbered using number series and have their own journal structure.

An example of a supplemental table is the item vendor table.

Journals

Every transaction starts with a journal. Each journal can contain a number of sub-transactions that are treated by the system as one. This way the system is able to check, for example, whether the integrity of the system is maintained after the transaction is completed.

The following diagram shows how a journal is structured. **PK** means **Primary Key**, which is the unique identifier of the table:

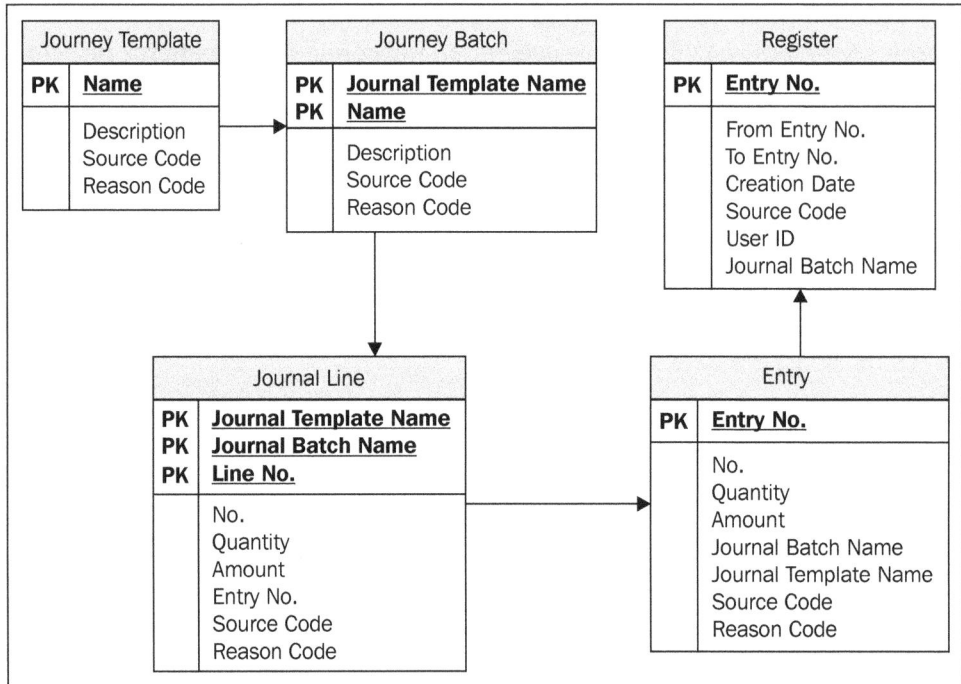

Journey Template	
PK	**Name**
	Description
	Source Code
	Reason Code

Journey Batch	
PK	**Journal Template Name**
PK	**Name**
	Description
	Source Code
	Reason Code

Register	
PK	**Entry No.**
	From Entry No.
	To Entry No.
	Creation Date
	Source Code
	User ID
	Journal Batch Name

Journal Line	
PK	**Journal Template Name**
PK	**Journal Batch Name**
PK	**Line No.**
	No.
	Quantity
	Amount
	Entry No.
	Source Code
	Reason Code

Entry	
PK	**Entry No.**
	No.
	Quantity
	Amount
	Journal Batch Name
	Journal Template Name
	Source Code
	Reason Code

Every journal can contain one or more templates with one or more batches, allowing multiple users to have multiple templates and batches. A journal line has a source number field that refers to, for example, the G/L Account number or the item number we are changing. When we post the journal, the changes are stored in the entry table and all the lines. For the journal, a register is maintained allowing auditors to check if the transactions are consistent.

The general ledger

To see how this works in the application, we can go to the **Chart of Accounts** and the **General Journals**, as shown in the following screenshot:

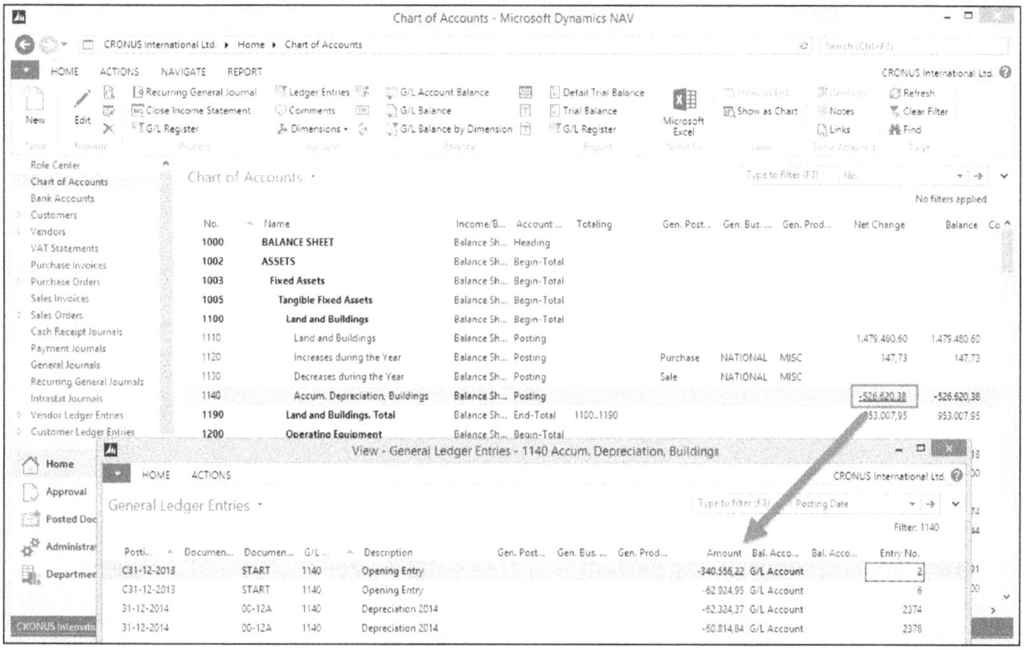

If we select **G/L Account 1140** and drill down, we will see the details of this record.

These are created through journals, so let's open a journal:

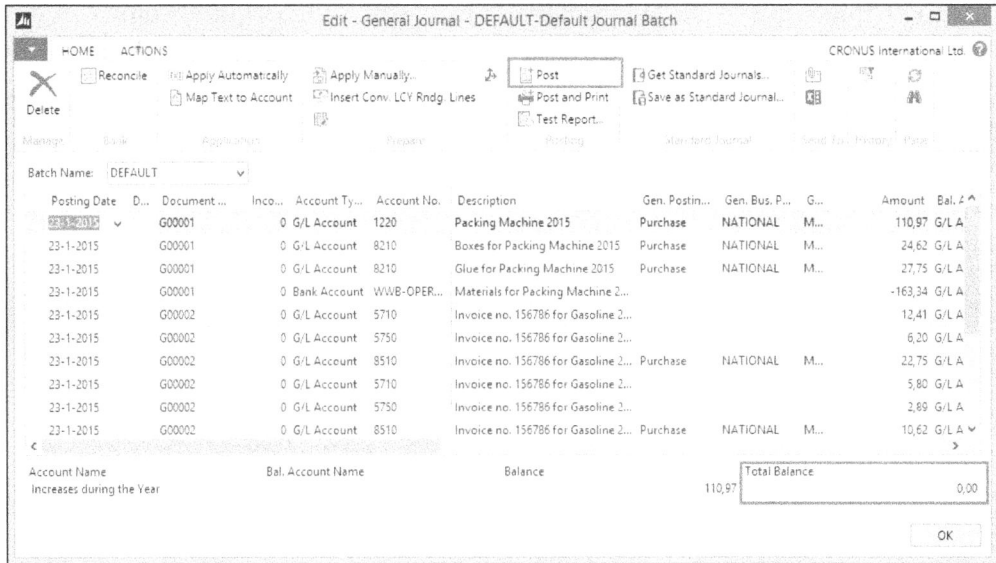

This journal contains two documents on the same posting date and the balance is zero. When we post this journal, the system will create the ledger entries and a register.

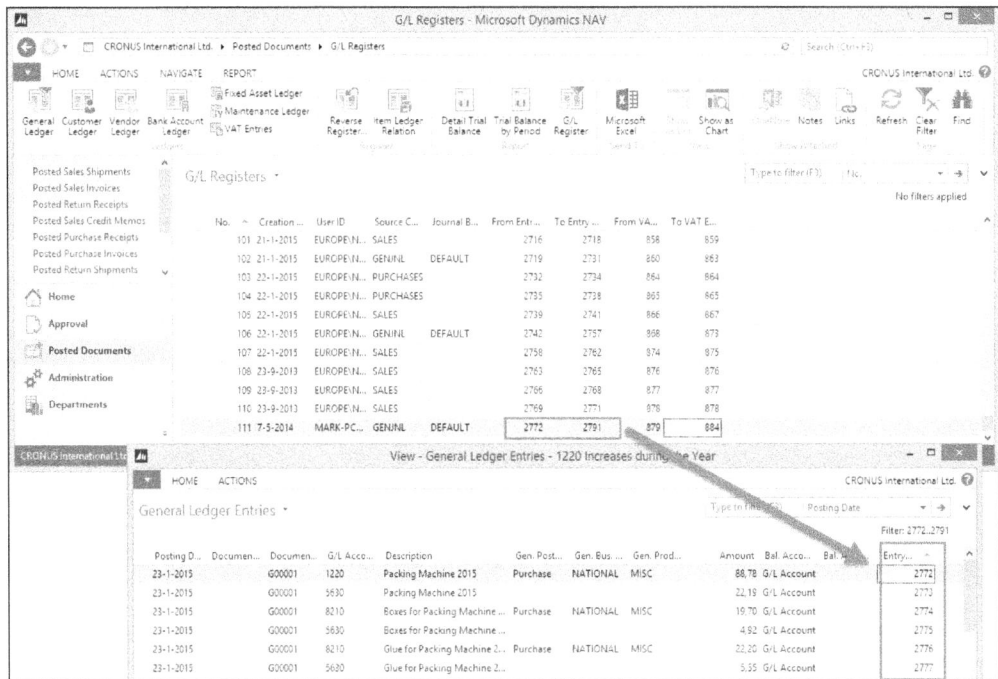

This is the basic building block for Dynamics NAV. Everything in Dynamics NAV is built on top of a journal, registers, and entries.

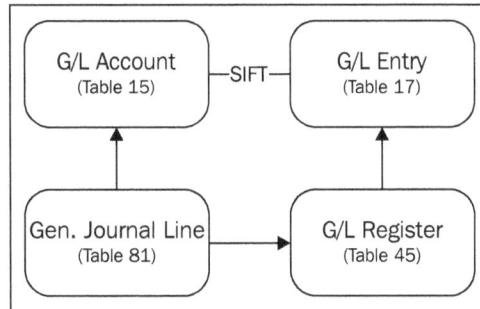

Balancing

In any ERP system, totaling and balancing is crucial, and whether you are totaling the general ledger, customer payments, or inventory, it is important to know the balance of each account, customer, or item.

Traditionally, this requires calculating these balances and deciding a place to store the totals and subtotals. In Dynamics NAV, the system has built-in technology that will handle balancing and totaling for you.

This built-in technology is called **Sum Index Field Technology** (**SIFT**). For Dynamics NAV, it is the key feature to its success.

The way it works is that, as a developer, you define your totaling on an index level. By associating the totaling fields with a key, the system knows that it has to maintain the totals for you.

In the original proprietary database, this technique was built in and invisible for the user, but in the SQL Server database, we can see how this works.

If we go in the CRONUS database and open the **G/L Entry** table with its keys, we see this information, as shown in the following screenshot:

Let's take key number two as an example. The key contains the fields G/L Account number and posting date. If we take a closer look at the **SumIndexFields** column, we see the following fields listed:

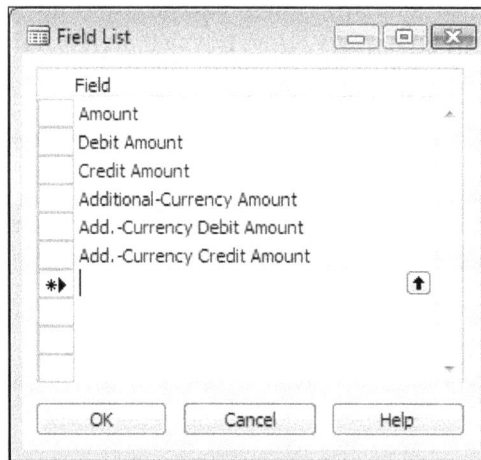

Notice that these are all fields of type decimal. This is mandatory for SumIndexfields.

> From the SQL Server Management studio, you can see the generated data from the SumIndexField definition. Each key with SumIndexField generates a view in the database. In older versions (prior to 5 SP 1), the SumIndexFields are saved in tables.

So, now we know that we do not have to worry about maintaining the totals, we can spend our time on what's really important.

Flow fields and flow filters

As discussed earlier, screens in Microsoft Dynamics NAV are built directly on one table. These table definitions contain all fields including the totals. However, these totals are not real database fields.

This can be illustrated by comparing the table definition in Microsoft Dynamics NAV to the table definition in SQL Server:

The fields **Date Filter (28)** to **Budgeted Amount (33)** are not actual fields in the database. They are helper fields to show data on screen.

Flow filters can have seven types; Sum, Average, Exist, Count, Min, Max, and Lookup and contain a query to the database. For example, Balance at Date (31) shows the following:

```
Sum("G/L Entry".Amount
    WHERE (G/L Account No.=FIELD(No.),
           G/L Account No.=FIELD(FILTER(Totaling)),
           Business Unit Code=FIELD(Business Unit Filter),
           Global Dimension 1 Code=FIELD(Global Dimension 1 Filter),
           Global Dimension 2 Code=FIELD(Global Dimension 2 Filter),
           Posting Date=FIELD(UPPERLIMIT(Date Filter))))
```

This creates the sum of the field amount in the G/L Entry table (17) filtering on **G/L Account**, **G/L Account No.**, **Business Unit Code**, **Global Dimension 1 & 2 Code**, and **Posting Date**.

Some of these filters are actual fields in the G/L Account table, but others are flow filters. Non-existing fields can be used as a runtime filter to limit the results of the query.

We will use and discuss more of these flow filters and flow fields later in this book.

More journals and entries

So now that we know how a journal works, it might be interesting to build a posting diagram of Dynamics NAV. Dynamics NAV has a number of journals, registers, and entries built on top of each other.

The following table shows the most important journals, registers, and entries:

Journals	Registers	Entries
Gen. Journal Line (81)	G/L Register (45)	G/L Entry (17)
Item Journal Line (83)	Item Register (46)	Cust. Ledger Entry (21)
Res. Journal Line (207)	Resource Register (240)	Vendor Ledger Entry (25)
Job Journal Line (210)	Job Register (241)	Item Ledger Entry (32)
		Job Ledger Entry (169)
		Res. Ledger Entry (203)
		VAT Entry (254)
		Bank Account Ledger Entry (271)

Please notice that when you look in the database, you'll find more of these tables, but these are the main building blocks.

Each journal is responsible for creating its own entries but may run another journal if that is required. For example, an Item Journal may generate G/L entries if required using a General Journal and a Job Journal may create Item Ledger Entries using the Item Journal.

We already discussed the G/L Entry table, which is used to store the basic financial information. This is the basic administration table.

The other entry tables are sub ledger tables. They store redundant information but have extra information for their specific use. A total of a sub ledger should always balance with the G/L. We'll see how that works in *Chapter 3, Financial Management*. Here are some more tables:

- The Customer and Vendor Ledger Entry tables are used to store specific information about the accounts receivables. They are linked to Customer and Vendor master data tables.

- The VAT Entry table stores specific information to make registration easier. Most companies do monthly or quarterly VAT registrations with one or more governmental agencies. VAT is different in many countries and could be different from what this book describes in localized country systems.

- The bank account entries should show exactly what transactions we do on our bank accounts.

The logistical part of the ERP package is handled by the Item Journal. Every item that is purchased, produced, or sold is handled though this journal. Services are handled through the Resource Journal. A resource can either be a person or a piece of equipment like a lift.

The Job Journal is an umbrella overlaying the entire application. It allows you to group transactions making it easier to analyze cost and profit for larger projects.

Posting schema

When we combine all this information in a schema, we can create the following basic Microsoft Dynamics NAV posting schema:

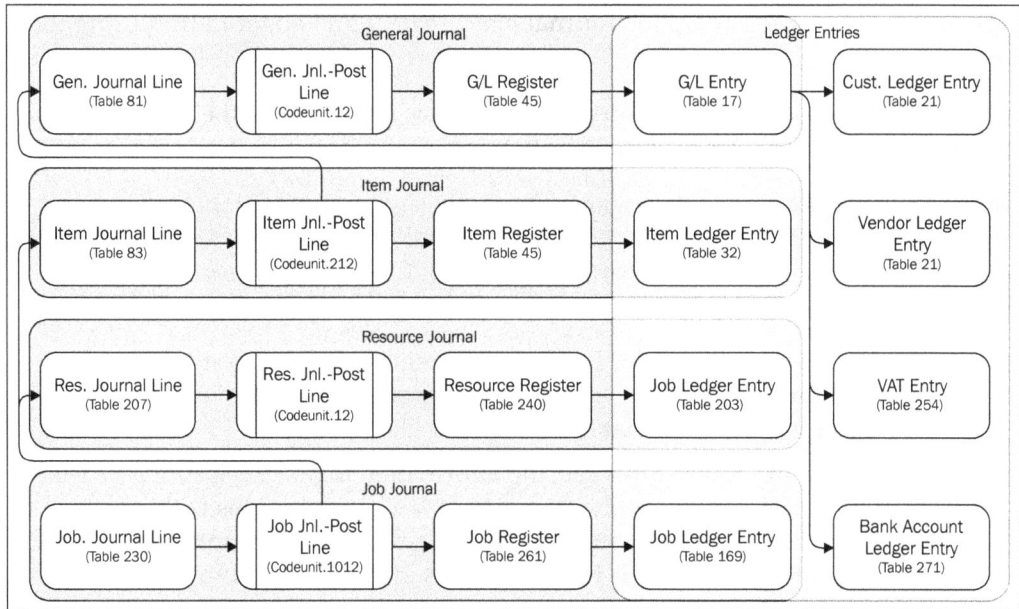

Here you can clearly see which journal is responsible for creating what entry. An entry table is always maintained by one process.

The **General Journal** is the heart of the application where the basic financial information is created in the ledger entries. All the basic information is in the G/L Entry table which is grouped in the G/L Register, which is then always balanced. The **Customer**, **Vendor**, **VAT**, and **Bank Account Ledger** entries are sub tables that always refer to a G/L register. We can never create one of these entries without touching this part of the application.

Sub and detailed entries

When an entry is created, its basic structure should not be changed for audit ability. This is why most entries in Microsoft Dynamics NAV have sub or detailed entries.

The **Customer** and **Vendor Ledger Entry** have details for application, unrealized loss and gain, various discounts, and corrections. This way, we are able to keep track of what happens with an entry without changing the original information.

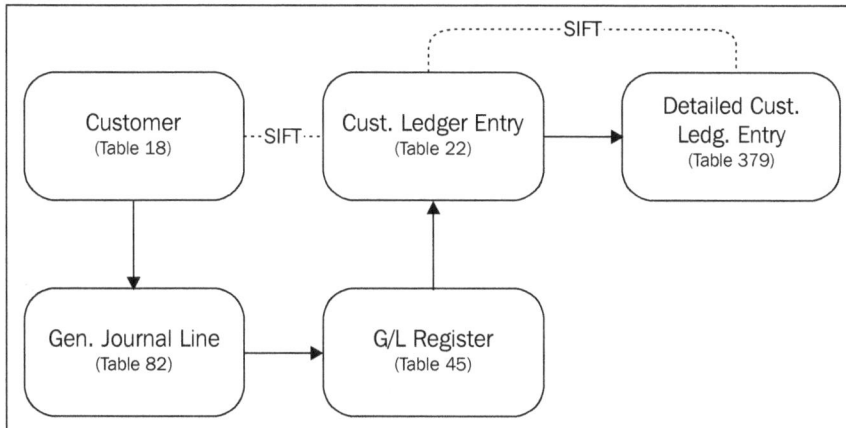

The Item Ledger Entries have a wide variety of sub entries depending on what you are doing with the items.

One of the most important tables in Microsoft Dynamics NAV is the Value Entry table. Each Item Ledger Entry has one or more of these. This table is the soft bridge between the inventory and the financial part of the application.

Warehouse entries enable moving items within our organization without touching the basic inventory or financial application.

Combining the journals into processes

The journal and entry tables make it possible for us to do the basic balancing in our company but people in companies are not used to working with journals.

Traditionally, companies work with documents. This was also the case before ERP applications were introduced. A sales representative would travel through the country with a paper order block and then come back to the back office. The back office then ships the orders with shipping documents and invoices.

Microsoft Dynamics NAV supports working with documents. Traditionally, we divide the documents in sales and purchasing documents but the later versions of Microsoft Dynamics NAV also have warehouse documents. Other supported documents are reminders and service documents.

Document structure

A document in Microsoft Dynamics NAV always has a header and lines. The header contains the basic information about the transaction, such as shipment dates, addresses, and payment terms.

The lines contain information about what is sold or purchased. This can be a variety of G/L Accounts, items, and resources.

A document can have different stages depending on the type of the transaction. A quote is a typical starting point in the sales or purchasing process. When a quote is approved, it can be promoted to an order, which is then shipped and invoiced. The process can be also reversed via a return order resulting in a credit memo.

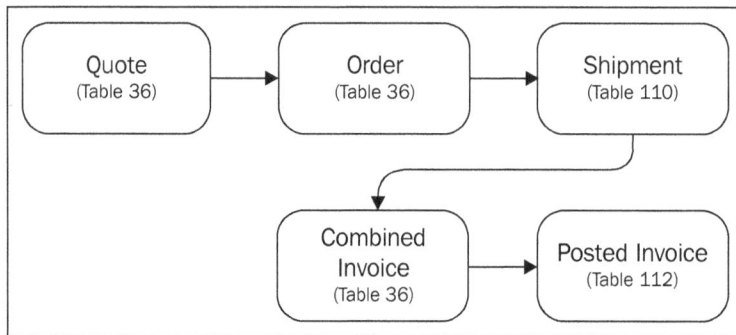

Document transactions

Transactions in the database can be started via documents. When a document is processed, the necessary journals are automatically populated. For example, when an order is shipped, the goods leave the warehouse, then an Item Journal is created and posted to handle this. When the invoice is posted, a General Journal is generated to create G/L Entries and a Customer or Vendor Ledger Entries.

Other patterns

The previously discussed pattern with journals and documents is by far the most important transaction structure. But Microsoft Dynamics NAV also has other structures as well.

The three most important other patterns are CRM, jobs, and manufacturing. These areas are all umbrella structures for other processes.

Relationship management

Microsoft Dynamics NAV RM helps you to maintain master data and analyze transactional data. It is both at the very start of the data process and at the end.

We have already seen the customer, vendor, and bank master data records. But what if a vendor is also a customer, or vice versa. We don't want to maintain the same data twice. We might also want to keep extra information such as contact persons and the interests of our customers and vendors. We'll see more of that in *Chapter 4*, *Relationship Management*.

There is also a need to analyze the data we have created with the document and journal structure.

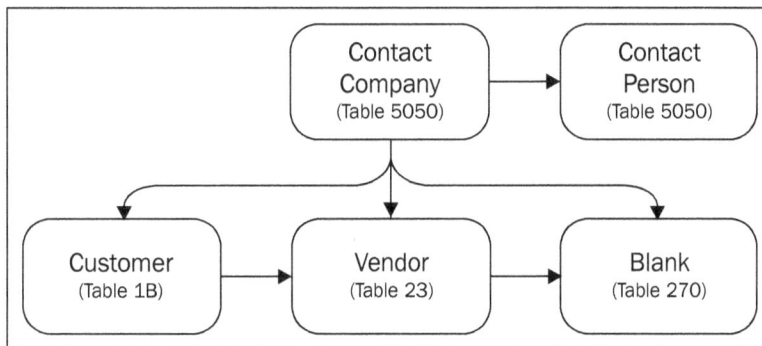

Jobs

Sometimes, a project can be more comprehensive than just a purchase and/or a sales document. A project can take from several weeks to over a year and requires multiple documents.

The job structure in Dynamics NAV allows you to handle this. Every document and journal transaction can be attached to a job, making it easy to analyze profit and loss and even schedule your jobs.

The jobs module also allows you to do a calculation before you start the project and balance this calculation throughout the process.

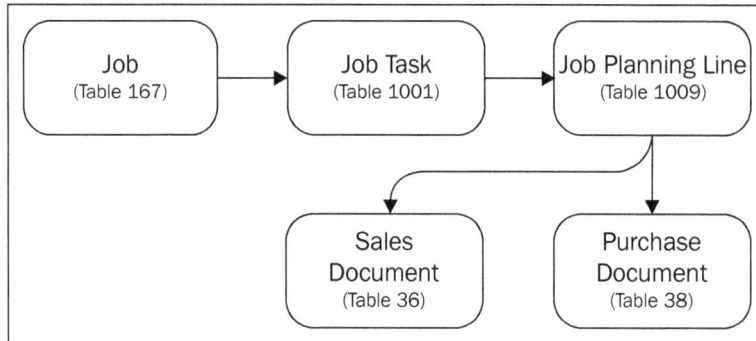

Manufacturing

When you produce your own items, you have different needs in your ERP process than when you only purchase the items you sell.

The manufacturing module of Microsoft Dynamics NAV allows you to handle this process. Basically what it does is create an item out of one or more other items and resources.

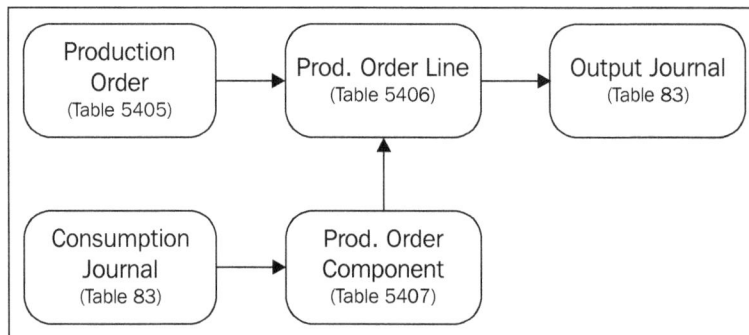

Summary

In this chapter, we have covered the basic structure of Microsoft Dynamics NAV. We talked about the design philosophy, application objects, and the unique table structure. We discussed the Role Tailored Concept and its reflection to older versions of the product. We talked about some basic functions of the product-like number series and application setup. We also talked about the important basic posting structure and the way SIFT works. We discussed how the document structure overlays the journal structure and how the umbrella structure is on top of that.

In the next chapter, we will look at a sample industry application and its effect on the standard functionality.

2
A Sample Application

Let's create a structure of our own in Microsoft Dynamics NAV. To do this, we must think of something that is not already available in the standard package but can be built on top of it.

For our example application, we will run a squash court. Running a squash court is simple to understand but something we cannot do without changing and expanding the product. In order to define our changes, we first need to make a fit-gap analysis.

After this chapter, you will have better understanding on how to reuse the framework of the Microsoft Dynamics NAV application. We will show how to reverse engineer the application and to study its functionality by going into the application code.

For this example, some new and changed objects are required. The *Appendix*, *Installation Guide*, describes where to find the objects and how to install and activate them.

In the first part, we will look at how to reverse engineer the standard application to look at and learn how it works and how to reuse the structures in our own solutions.

In the second part of the chapter, we will learn how to use the journals and entries in a custom application.

Lastly, we will look at how to integrate our solution with the standard application; in our case, sales invoicing.

Fit-gap analysis

When we do a fit-gap analysis, we look at the company's processes and define what we can and cannot do with the standard package. When a business process can be handled with the standard software we call this a **Fit**. When this cannot be done it's called a **Gap**. All gaps have to be either developed or we need to purchase an add-on.

However, even when something could be done with standard software features it does not necessarily mean that doing this is wise. The standard application should be used for what it is designed for. Using standard features for something else might work in the current version but if it changes in a new version it might no longer fit. For this reason it is better to design something new instead of wrongly using standard features.

Designing a squash court application

The basic process of a squash court company is renting the courts to squash players; both members and non-members. There is a reservation and invoicing process handling different rates for members and non-members.

Although this could be implemented using items as squash courts and customers as players, this would be a typical example of using standard features wrongly. Instead of doing this, we will look at how items and customers are designed and use this to create a new squash court application.

Designing a specific application using standard NAV features is a matter of **total cost of ownership (TCO)**. If only one customer would use this solution, it would be better to use the standard application in a creative way. However, if we deploy the design from this chapter on a multi-tenant architecture and let thousands of companies run it, it would be economically possible to make the best application for the job. Keep this in mind each time you make a decision to design.

Look, learn, and love

To determine the design for this application, we will first look at the parts of the standard application, which we can use to learn how they work. We will use this knowledge in our own design.

In Microsoft Dynamics NAV, customer and vendor master data are maintained using **relationship management (RM)**. For our solution, we will create a new master data for squash players being the business part of the application. This will also be integrated with RM.

To design the squash court, we will look at the design of items in the standard package. The squash court will be the product part of our application with a journal to create reservation entries, which we can invoice.

For this invoicing process, we will use and integrate with the sales part of Microsoft Dynamics NAV.

Drawing the table and posting schema

After we have decided on the design of our application, we can draw the tables and post the routines as we did in the previous chapter. This will clarify the design for others and guide us through the development process.

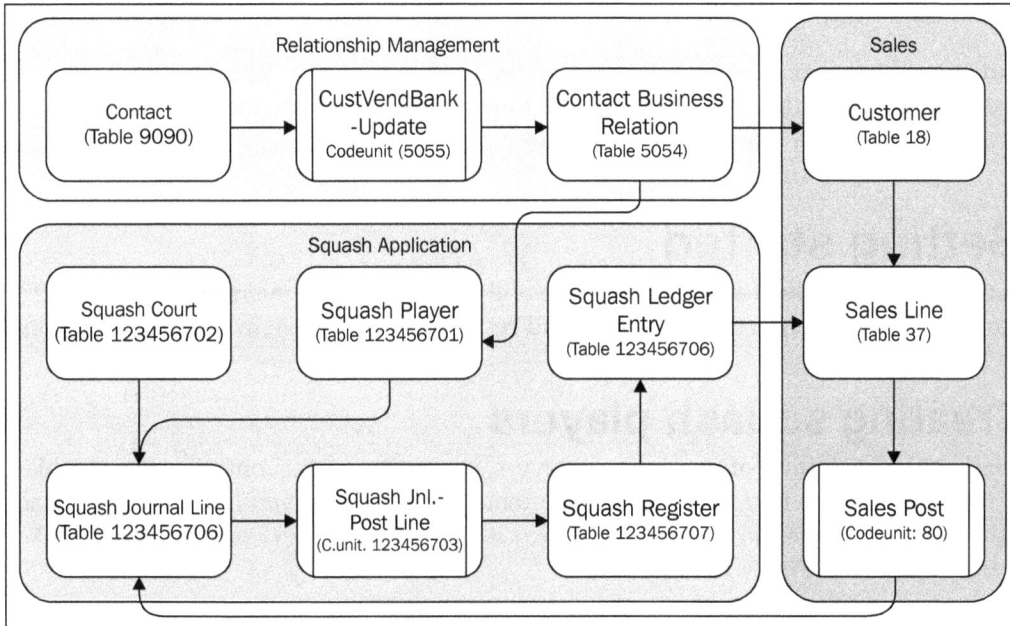

In the preceding diagram, the objects in **Relationship Management** and **Sales** are standard objects that we will possibly need to modify. The objects for the **Squash Application** are new objects but based on similar objects in the standard application.

The project approach

In order to keep track of our project, we'll cut the changes into smaller tasks. The first task will be to do the changes in relationship management to be able to create a squash player from a contact. The second part is to create squash courts. The reservation and invoice processes are part three and four.

Interfacing with the standard application

In our schema, we can see that we have two processes where we need to work on the standard Microsoft Dynamics NAV processes, which are **Relationship Management** and **Sales**.

Design patterns

To create the squash court application, we can use proven design patterns. This will limit the risk of our development's success and make it easy to communicate with others who are familiar with the patterns.

Examples of the patterns we will use are master data, number series, and journals.

Not everything that you need will be documented in patterns. Sometimes it is necessary to innovate. If you do this, it is important to still imagine your design as a pattern and document it for future use.

Getting started

In the first part of the design process, we will look at how to reverse engineer the standard application in order to learn and reuse the knowledge in our own solution.

Creating squash players

For the administration of our squash players, we use the data from the contact table. In the standard product, it is possible to create a customer or vendor with the contact data. We require the same functionality to create squash players so let's have a look at how this is done by Microsoft.

Open **Contact Card** and try to find this function, as shown in the following screenshot:

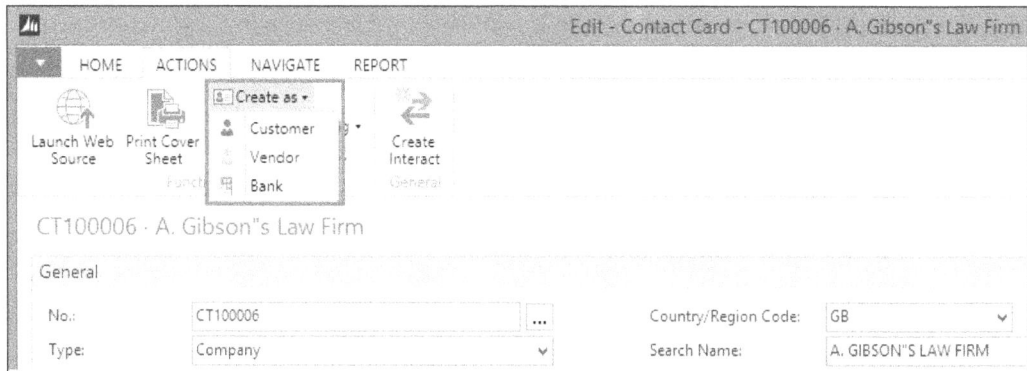

We want a function like this for our squash players. So let's get in and see what it does. For this, we need to design the page and look at the actions. The page number in this case is **5050**, which we can find by clicking on **About this Page** in the top-right corner of the page, as shown in the following screenshot:

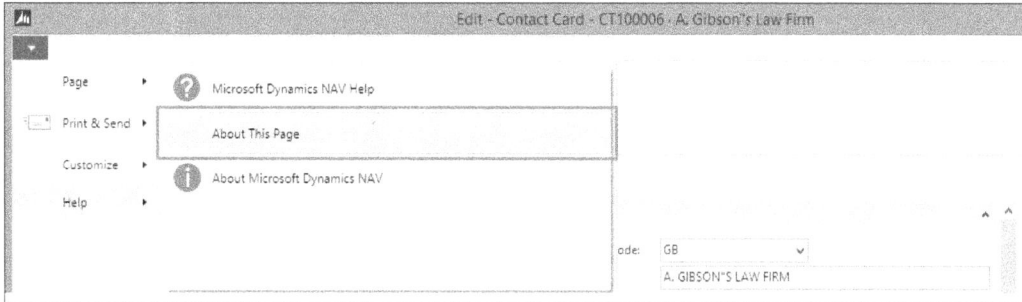

This option can be very useful to find information about the fields that are not on the page, the filters, or the source table.

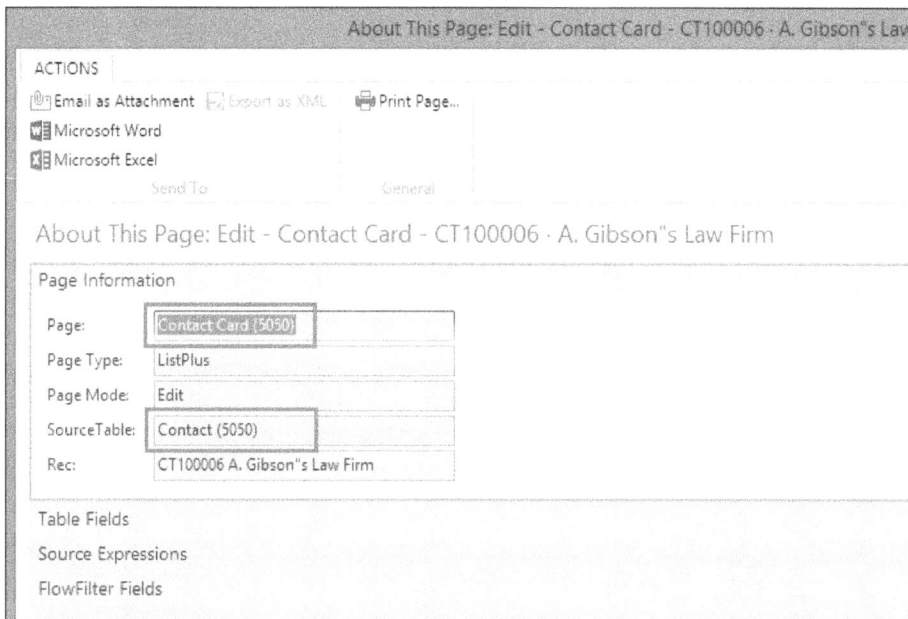

To open the page, we need to open **Object Designer** in **Development Environment** (*Shift + F12*), as shown in the following screenshot:

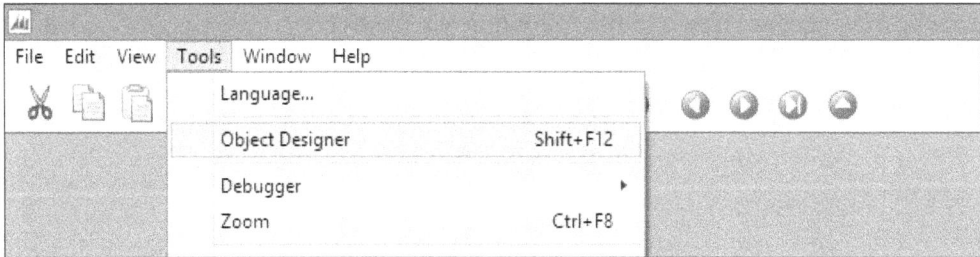

Here, we can find **5050 Contact Card** in **Page**:

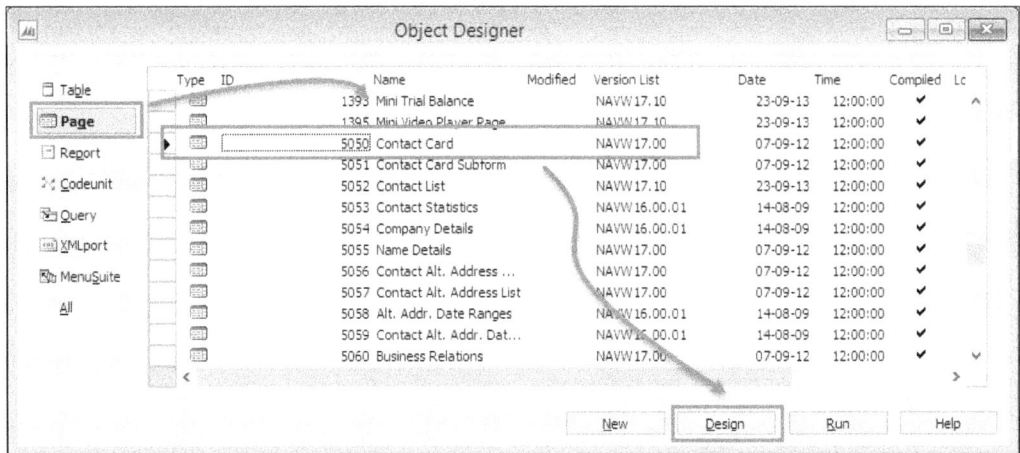

We are looking for **Actions** on this page. They are kind of difficult to find if you are unfamiliar with **Page Designer**. To open **Actions**, the cursor should be on the blank line below the last populated line. Then click on the right mouse button and **Actions** or select **Actions** from the **View** drop-down menu.

E.. Type	SubType		Name	Caption

Table shown with Copy, Paste, Clear, Copy Previous, New, Delete, Hide Column, Show Column..., Go To Definition..., Control Actions, C/AL Code, Properties menu items.

Fields visible:
- Field ... <No. of Mailin... <No. of Mailing Groups>
- Field ... <No. of Busine... <No. of Business Relations>
- Field ... <No. of Indust... <No. of Industry Groups>
- Field ... <No. of Job R... <No. of Job Responsibilities>
- Field ... <Organization... <Organizational Level Code>
- Field ... <Exclude from... <Exclude from Segment>
- Group Group <Control1907... **Foreign Trade**
- Field <Currency Co... <Currency Code>
- Field <Territory Cod... <Territory Code>
- Field <VAT Registra... <VAT Registration No.>
- Container FactBoxAr... <Control190000... <Control1900000007>
- Part System <RecordLinks> <RecordLinks>
- Part System <Notes> <Notes>
- Field

Preview Help

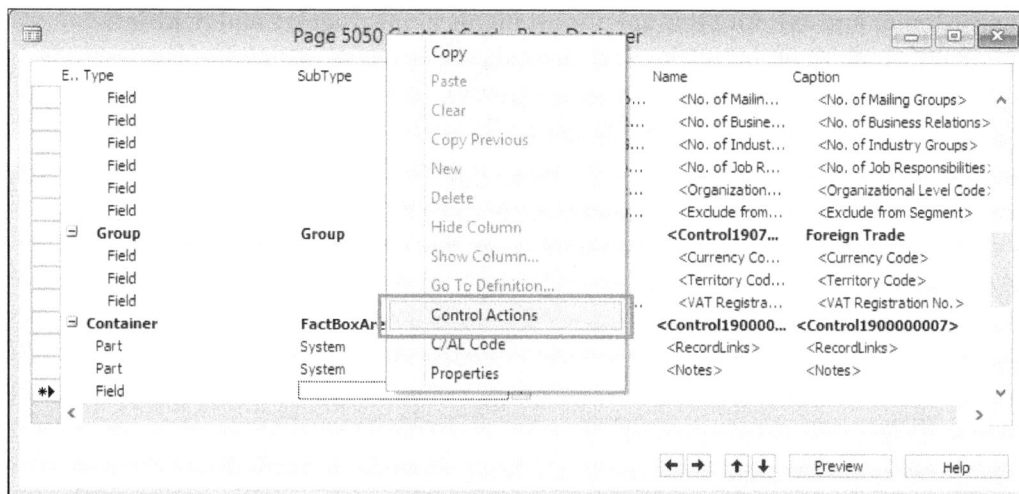

Alternatively, you can also use the **Preview** option from the **View** drop-down menu to find the action.

Now, we are in the **Action Designer** and we can search for the **Create as** option. To see what it does, we need to go into the C/AL code by pressing *F9* or by selecting **C/AL Code** from the **View** drop-down menu:

C/AL Code (F9)

CreateVendor versus CreateCustomer

In Microsoft Dynamics NAV, there is a small difference between creating a customer and a vendor from a contact. When creating a customer, the system will ask us to select a customer template. The **Vendor** option does not have that. To keep things simple, we will look at and learn from the Vendor function in this chapter.

The customer and vendor table are almost identical in structure and fields are numbered similarly in both tables. This is called transaction mirroring between sales and purchasing, which we will discuss further in *Chapter 6, Trade*. We will mirror our new table in a similar way to the other Microsoft Dynamics NAV tables.

The C/AL code in **Action** tells us that when clicking on the **Menu** option, the function CreateVendor in the contact table is started. To copy this feature, we need to create a new function, CreateSquashPlayer. Let's keep that in mind while we dive further in this code.

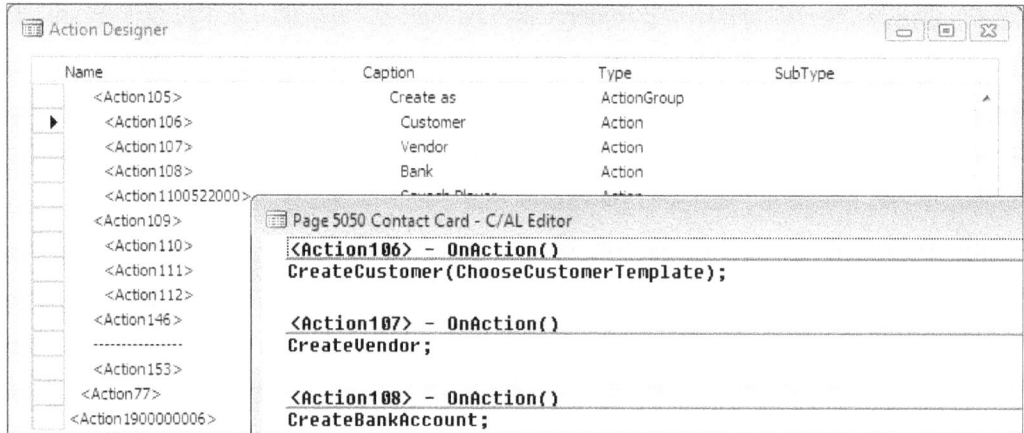

Open the contact table (5050) and search for the function CreateVendor. You can find functions in a table by going into the C/AL code (*F9*) from anywhere in the table designer, and by using the **Find [Ctrl+F]** function, as shown in the following screenshot:

Reverse engineering

We need to reverse engineer this code in order to see what we need to create for our CreateSquashPlayer function. We will look at each part of the C/AL code in order to decide whether we need it or not.

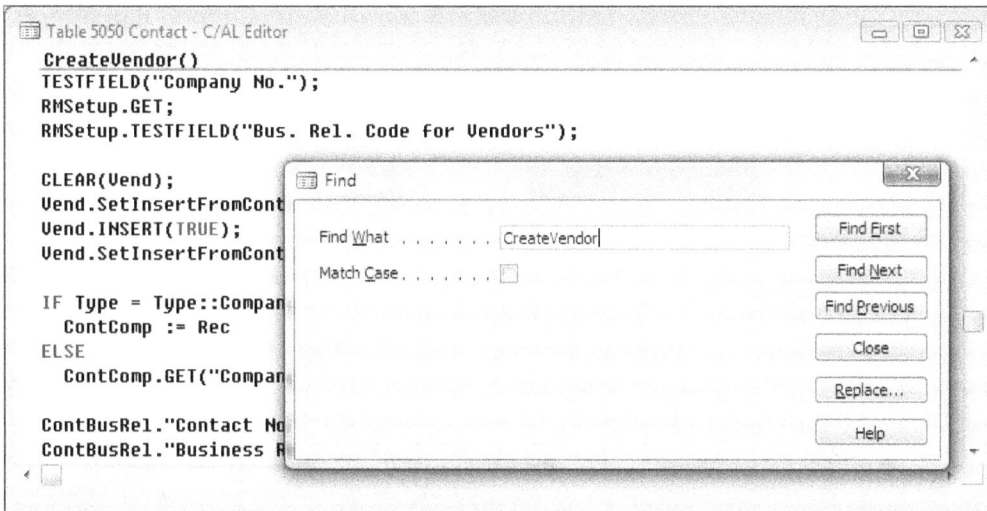

What does the following piece of code do?

```
TESTFIELD("Company No.");
```

This tests the current record for a valid `Company No`. If this fails, we cannot continue and the end user gets a runtime error.

```
RMSetup.GET;
RMSetup.TESTFIELD("Bus. Rel. Code for Vendors");
```

This reads the `Marketing Setup` table from the system and tests whether the `Bus. Rel. Code for Vendors` is valid. We need a new code for squash players here, which will be added as a new field to the setup table:

```
CLEAR(Vend);
Vend.SetInsertFromContact(TRUE);
Vend.INSERT(TRUE);
Vend.SetInsertFromContact(FALSE);
```

Here, the `Vendor` table is cleared and a function is called within that table, then a new record is inserted in the database while activating the necessary business logic. Then the same function is called again with another parameter. Since the `Vendor` table is what we are copying, we will write down that we might need a similar function as `SetInsertFromContact`:

```
IF Type = Type::Company THEN
   ContComp := Rec
ELSE
   ContComp.GET("Company No.");
```

This code checks whether the current contact is a company. If so, it populates the `ContComp` variable with this record. If not, it populates `ContComp` with the company our current contact is related to:

```
ContBusRel."Contact No." := ContComp."No.";
ContBusRel."Business Relation Code" := RMSetup."Bus. Rel. Code for
Vendors";
ContBusRel."Link to Table" := ContBusRel."Link to Table"::Vendor;
ContBusRel."No." := Vend."No.";
ContBusRel.INSERT(TRUE);
```

The `ContBusRel` function refers to the table Contact Business Relation (5054) and is a linking table in the Microsoft Dynamics NAV data model. Technically, a contact can be connected to multiple customers and vendors although this does not make sense. This table is populated here. Let's write down that we need to look into this table and see if it needs changes:

```
UpdateCustVendBank.UpdateVendor(ContComp,ContBusRel);
```

`UpdateCustVendBank` is an external codeunit that is used with the function `UpdateVendor`. We might need a copy of this function for our Squash players.

```
MESSAGE(Text009,Vend.TABLECAPTION,Vend."No.");
```

The preceding code gives a message box for the end user that the record is created with the new number. Now, we have a number of things on our to-do list:

1. Create a master data table that looks like the `Vendor` table.

2. We need to copy the `CreateVendor` function.

3. Look at the `Contact Business Relation` table and the `CustVendBank-Update (5055)` codeunit.

Let's look at the latter to learn something important before we start with the first:

```
UpdateVendor()
WITH Vend DO BEGIN
  GET(ContBusRel."No.");
  xRecRef.GETTABLE(Vend);
  NoSerie := "No. Series";
  PurchaserCode :=  Vend."Purchaser Code";
  TRANSFERFIELDS(Cont);
  "No." := ContBusRel."No.";
  "No. Series" := NoSerie;
  Vend."Purchaser Code" := PurchaserCode;
  MODIFY;
```

```
    RecRef.GETTABLE(Vend);
    ChangeLogMgt.LogModification(RecRef,xRecRef);
END;
```

This code synchronizes the contact table with the vendor table. It does that by using the TRANSFERFIELDS function. This function transfers all fields with the same number from one table to another. This means that we cannot be creative with our field numbering. For example, in the contact table, the **Name** field is number **2**. If we were to use a different number for the **Name** field, TRANSFERFIELDS would not copy the information.

Using this information, our table should look like this:

Notice that we use field **19** for our **Squash Player** specific field. This is because field **19** was used for **Budgeted Amount** in the vendor table. We can therefore safely assume that Microsoft will not use field **19** in the contact table in future.

An alternative approach for this if we wanted to be even safer is to add the fields that are specific to our solution as fields in our add-on number series. In our case, it would be 123.456.700.

> You can copy and paste fields from one table to another table. Note that table relations and C/AL code in the OnValidate and OnLookup trigger is copied as well. If the table we want to create is similar to an existing table, we could also use the **Save As** option from the **File** drop-down menu.

The next step is to add some business logic to the table. We want this table to use number series functionality just like the vendor table. This requires some standard steps:

1. First we create the setup table. A number series is defined in a setup table. As the **Squash Court** module will be quite sophisticated, we'll create our own.

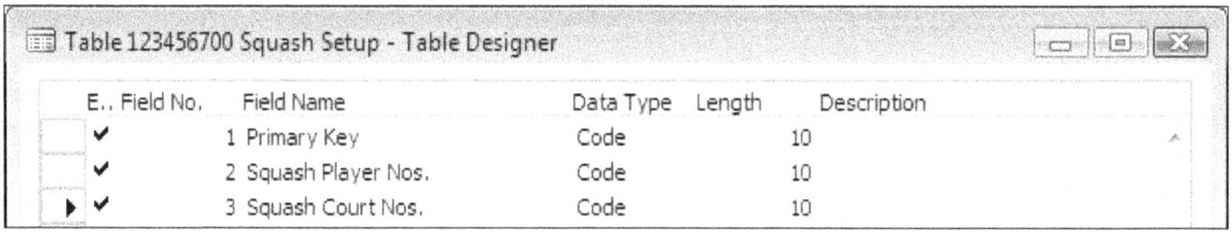

On MSDN, you can watch a video about the singleton pattern at http://msdn.microsoft.com/en-us/dynamics/nav/dn722393.aspx.

A setup table always has a single **Primary Key** field, as shown in the preceding screenshot, and the necessary setup fields. This table is designed to only have one single record.

2. Then, we create a link to the number series. Our **Squash Player** table is now required to have a link to the number series. We can copy this field from the vendor table and can make a table relation to the **No. Series** table, as shown in the following screenshot:

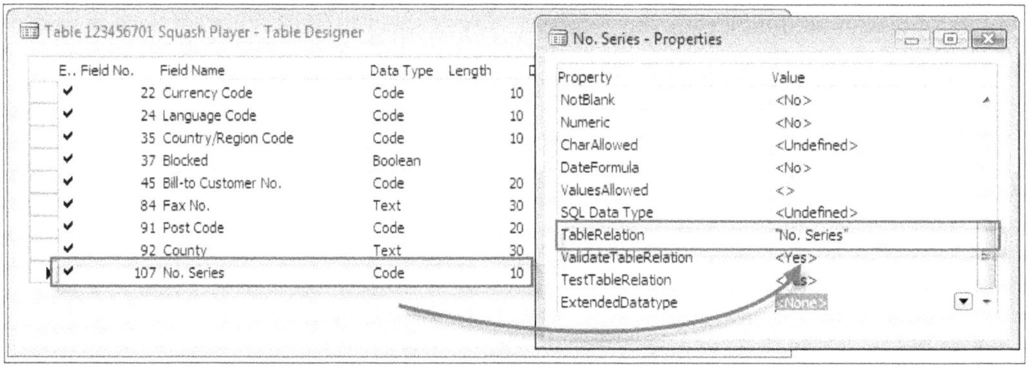

3. Now, we add the C/AL business logic to our table, but first we need to define the variables that are required. These are our new **Squash Setup** table and the **Number Series Management** codeunits.

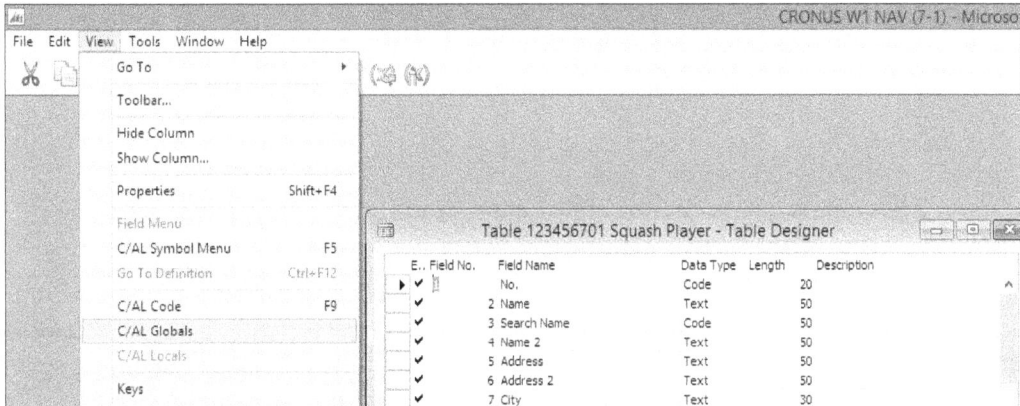

We can define the variables in the specially created **C/AL Globals** menu.

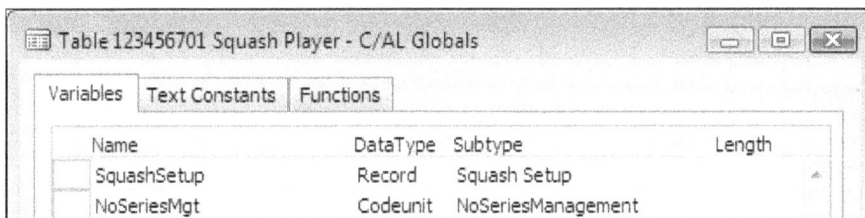

It is highly recommended to use the Microsoft naming standard, which allows you to copy and paste a lot of code and makes it easier for others to read your code.

Number Series require three places of code. This code makes sure that the business logic of the Number Series functionality is always followed:

1. The following code goes into the `OnInsert` trigger. It populates the `No.` field with the next value of the Number Series:

```
OnInsert()
IF "No." = '' THEN BEGIN
  SquashSetup.GET;
```

```
SquashSetup.TESTFIELD("Squash Player Nos.");
NoSeriesMgt.InitSeries(SquashSetup."Squash Player Nos.",
  xRec."No. Series",0D,"No.","No. Series");
END;
```

2. The `OnValidate` trigger of the `No.` field tests when a user manually enters a value if that is allowed:

```
No. - OnValidate()
IF "No." <> xRec."No." THEN BEGIN
  SquashSetup.GET;
  NoSeriesMgt.TestManual(SquashSetup."Squash Player Nos.");
  "No. Series" := '';
END;
```

3. Lastly, we create a new `AssistEdit` function. This function is for readability and others reading your code afterwards. The code is used in the page or form and allows users to switch between linked number series:

```
AssistEdit() : Boolean
SquashSetup.GET;
SquashSetup.TESTFIELD("Squash Player Nos.");
IF NoSeriesMgt.SelectSeries(SquashSetup."Squash Player Nos.",
  xRec."No. Series","No. Series")
THEN BEGIN
  NoSeriesMgt.SetSeries("No.");
  EXIT(TRUE);
END;
```

When the Number Series are in place, we can make the necessary change in the Contact Business Relation table.

In this table, we need to add the possibility to link squash players to contacts. This is done in the **Properties** window of **Table Designer** that can be accessed by pressing (*Shift* + *F4*) or by using the **Properties** option from the **View** drop-down menu, as shown in the following screenshot:

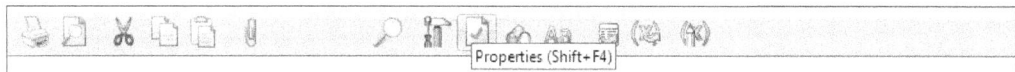

First, we add the **Squash player** option to the **Link to Table** field, as shown in the following screenshot:

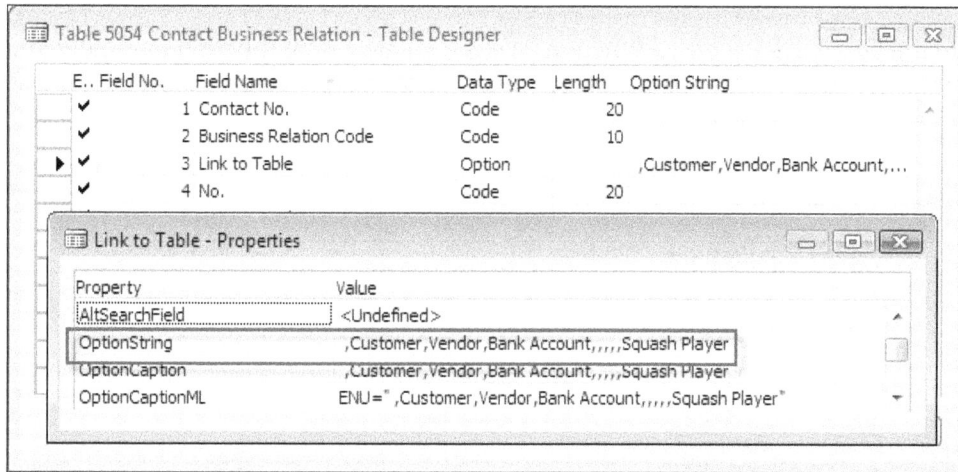

> Options are converted to SQL Integer data types. Make sure to add some blank options so when Microsoft releases other functionality we are not impacted. Changing the integer value of an existing option field requires a lot of work.

Then, we create a table relation with our new table, as shown in the following screenshot:

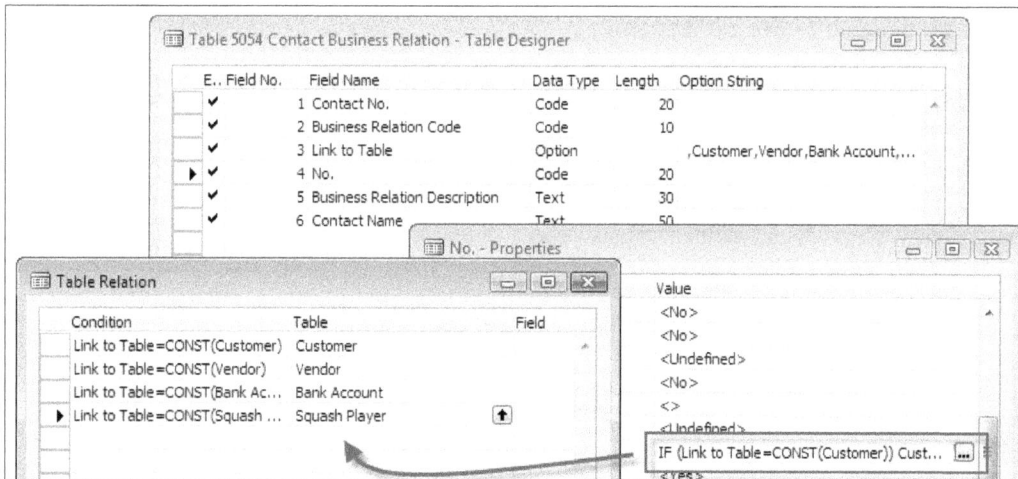

The next step is to expand the **CustVendBank-Update** codeunit with a new `UpdateSquashPlayer` function. This is a copy of the `UpdateVendor` function that we discussed before. We can add functions in the **Globals** menu.

There are two ways to copy a function. We can create a new function manually and copy the C/AL code and variables, or we can select a function from the list and use copy and paste and then rename the function.

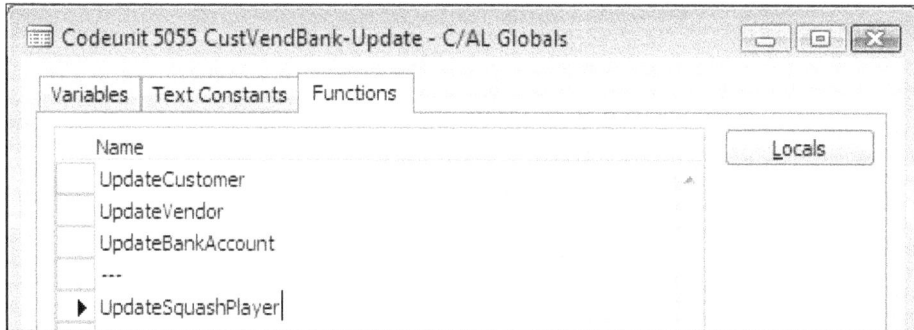

When you add the - - - line to the function, others can see that it is not a Microsoft function. You can also include the project name like - - -Squash. This also makes the code easier to upgrade or to merge with other code.

This code also requires a new global variable, `SquashPlayer`:

```
UpdateSquashPlayer()
WITH SquashPlayer DO BEGIN
  GET(ContBusRel."No.");
  xRecRef.GETTABLE(SquashPlayer);
  NoSerie := "No. Series";
  TRANSFERFIELDS(Cont);
  "No." := ContBusRel."No.";
  "No. Series" := NoSerie;
  MODIFY;
  RecRef.GETTABLE(SquashPlayer);
  ChangeLogMgt.LogModification(RecRef,xRecRef);
END;
```

The final piece of preparation work is to add the **Bus. Rel. Code for Squash Players** field to the **Marketing Setup** table, as shown in the following screenshot:

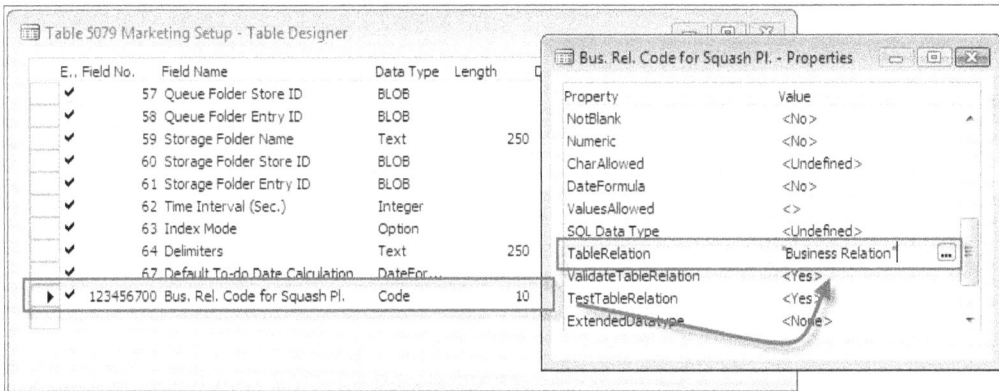

> We use the same numbering in our fields as in our objects. This makes it easier in the future to see what belongs to what if more functionality is added.

With all this preparation work, we can now finally go ahead and make our function in the contact table (5050) that we can call from the user interface:

```
CreateSquashPlayer()
TESTFIELD(Type, Type::Person);

RMSetup.GET;
RMSetup.TESTFIELD("Bus. Rel. Code for Squash Pl.");

CLEAR(SquashPlayer);
SquashPlayer.INSERT(TRUE);

ContBusRel."Contact No." := Cont."No.";
ContBusRel."Business Relation Code" :=
  RMSetup."Bus. Rel. Code for Squash Pl.";
ContBusRel."Link to Table" :=
  ContBusRel."Link to Table"::"Squash Player";
ContBusRel."No." := SquashPlayer."No.";
ContBusRel.INSERT(TRUE);

UpdateCustVendBank.UpdateSquashPlayer(Cont,ContBusRel);

MESSAGE(Text009,SquashPlayer.TABLECAPTION,SquashPlayer."No.");
```

Please note that we do not need the `SetInsertFromContact` function. This function enables users to create a new vendor first and create a contact using the vendor information. We do not want to support this method in our application.

Now, we can add the function to the page and test our functionality:

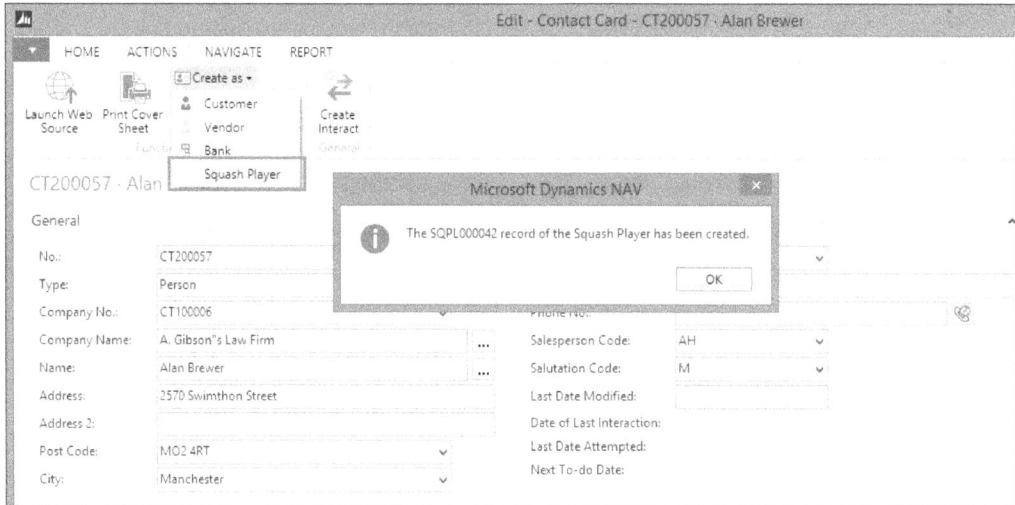

Designing a journal

Now, it is time to start on the product part of the squash application. In this part, we will no longer reverse engineer in detail. We will learn how to search in the standard functionality and reuse parts in our own software.

For this part, we will look at resources in Microsoft Dynamics NAV. Resources are similar to using as products as items but far less complex making it easier to look and learn.

Squash court master data

Our company has 12 courts that we want to register in Microsoft Dynamics NAV. This master data is comparable to resources so we'll go ahead and copy this functionality. Resources are not attached to the contact table like the vendor/squash player tables. We need the number series again so we'll add a new number series to our Squash Setup table.

The **Squash Court** table should look like this after creation:

E.. Field No.	Field Name	Data Type	Length	Description
✔ 1	No.	Code	20	
✔ 2	Description	Text	50	
✔ 3	Search Description	Code	50	
✔ 107	No. Series	Code	10	

Table 123456702 Squash Court - Table Designer

Chapter objects

With this chapter some objects are required. A description of how to import these objects can be found in the *Appendix, Installation Guide*.

Type	ID	Name	Modified	Version List	Date	Time	Compiled	Lc
	123456700	Squash Role Center	✔	Chapter2-4	07-05-14	17:49:19	✔	
	123456701	Squash Setup	✔	Chapter2-4	07-05-14	21:14:36	✔	
	123456702	Squash Ledger Entries	✔	Chapter2-4	07-05-14	18:43:49	✔	
	123456703	Squash Journal Templ...	✔	Chapter2-4	17-12-01	12:00:00	✔	
	123456704	Squash Journal Templ...	✔	Chapter2-4	17-12-01	12:00:00	✔	
	123456705	Squash Activities	✔	Chapter2-4	02-01-10	20:11:15	✔	
	123456706	Squash Journal	✔	Chapter2-4	07-05-14	18:44:22	✔	
	123456707	Squash Jnl. Batches	✔	Chapter2-4	28-12-09	21:40:50	✔	
	123456708	Squash Registers	✔	Chapter2-4	08-06-01	12:00:00	✔	
	123456709	Recurring Squash Jnl.	✔	Chapter2-4	07-05-14	18:45:32	✔	
	123456710	Squash Players	✔	Chapter2-4	18-04-10	17:21:35	✔	
	123456711	Squash Player Card	✔	Chapter2-4	18-04-10	17:22:54	✔	
	123456712	Squash Courts	✔	Chapter2-4	18-04-10	17:21:59	✔	

Object Designer

After the import process is completed, make sure that your current database is the default database for the Role Tailored Client and run page 123456701, **Squash Setup**.

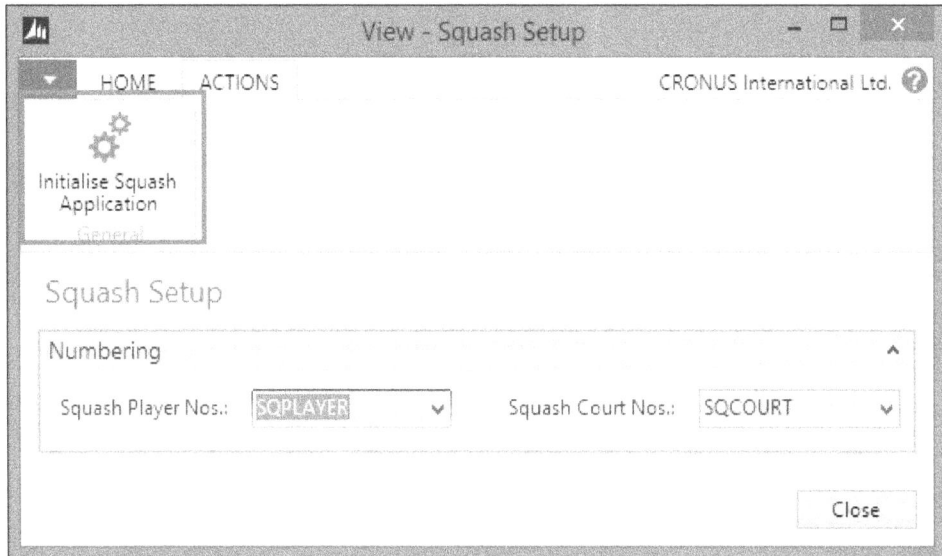

From this page, select the action **Initialize Squash Application**. This will execute the C/AL code in the InitSquashApp function of this page, which will prepare the demo data for us to play with. The objects are prepared and tested in a Microsoft Dynamics NAV 2013 R2 W1 database.

Reservations

When running a squash court, we want to be able to keep track of reservations. Looking at standard Dynamics NAV functionality, it might be a good idea to create a squash player journal. The journal can create entries for reservations that can be invoiced.

A journal needs the object structure. The journal is prepared in the objects delivered with this chapter. Creating a new journal from scratch is a lot of work and can easily lead to making mistakes. It is easier and safer to copy an existing journal structure from the standard application that is similar to the journal we need for our design.

In our example, we have copied the Resource Journals:

Type	ID	Name	Modified	Version List	Date	Time	Compiled	Lc
	123456703	Squash Journal Template	✔	Chapter2-4	07-05-14	17:55:02	✔	
	123456705	Squash Journal Batch	✔	Chapter2-4	05-11-08	12:00:00	✔	
	123456706	Squash Journal Line	✔	Chapter2-4	07-05-14	17:59:45	✔	
	123456707	Squash Register	✔	Chapter2-4	07-05-14	21:40:32	✔	
	123456709	Squash Ledger Entry	✔	Chapter2-4	07-05-14	21:41:24	✔	
	123456701	Squash Journal - Test	✔	Chapter2-4	07-05-14	21:15:44	✔	
	123456702	Squash Register	✔	Chapter2-4	07-05-14	20:39:06	✔	
	123456701	SquashJnlManagement	✔	Chapter2-4	07-05-14	17:47:48	✔	
	123456702	Squash Jnl.-Check Line	✔	Chapter2-4	02-01-10	17:44:53	✔	
	123456703	Squash Jnl.-Post Line	✔	Chapter2-4	07-05-14	21:14:47	✔	
	123456704	Squash Jnl.-Post Batch	✔	Chapter2-4	02-01-10	22:54:30	✔	
	123456705	Squash Jnl.-Post	✔	Chapter2-4	28-12-09	21:12:24	✔	
	123456706	Squash Jnl.-Post+Print	✔	Chapter2-4	28-12-09	21:12:29	✔	
	123456707	Squash Jnl.-B.Post	✔	Chapter2-4	28-12-09	21:12:33	✔	
	123456708	Squash Jnl.-B.Post+Print	✔	Chapter2-4	28-12-09	21:12:38	✔	
	123456709	Squash Reg.-Show Le...	✔	Chapter2-4	28-12-09	21:12:56	✔	
	123456702	Squash Ledger Entries	✔	Chapter2-4	07-05-14	18:43:49	✔	
	123456703	Squash Journal Templ...	✔	Chapter2-4	17-12-01	12:00:00	✔	
	123456704	Squash Journal Templ...	✔	Chapter2-4	17-12-01	12:00:00	✔	
	123456706	Squash Journal	✔	Chapter2-4	07-05-14	18:44:22	✔	
	123456707	Squash Jnl. Batches	✔	Chapter2-4	28-12-09	21:40:50	✔	
	123456708	Squash Registers	✔	Chapter2-4	08-06-01	12:00:00	✔	
	123456709	Recurring Squash Jnl.	✔	Chapter2-4	07-05-14	18:45:32	✔	

Sidebar (Table, Page, Report, Codeunit, Query, XMLport, MenuSuite, All)

> You can export these objects in text format and then rename and renumber the objects to be reused easily. The Squash Journal objects are renumbered and renamed from the Resource Journal.

As explained in *Chapter 1, Introduction to Microsoft Dynamics NAV*, all journals have the same structure. The template, batch, and register tables are almost always the same whereas the journal line and ledger entry table contain function-specific fields. Let's have a look at all of them one by one.

The **Journal Template** has several fields, as shown in the following screenshot:

E..	Field No.	Field Name	Data Type	Length	Description
✔	1	Name	Code	10	
✔	2	Description	Text	80	
✔	5	Test Report ID	Integer		
✔	6	Form ID	Integer		
✔	7	Posting Report ID	Integer		
✔	8	Force Posting Report	Boolean		
✔	10	Source Code	Code	10	
✔	11	Reason Code	Code	10	
✔	12	Recurring	Boolean		
✔	13	Test Report Name	Text	80	
✔	14	Form Name	Text	80	
✔	15	Posting Report Name	Text	80	
✔	16	No. Series	Code	10	
✔	17	Posting No. Series	Code	10	

Table 123456703 Squash Journal Template - Table Designer

Let's discuss these fields in more detail:

- **Name**: This is the unique name. It is possible to define as many templates as required but usually one template per form ID and one for recurring will do. If you want journals with different source codes, you need to have more templates.
- **Description**: A readable and understandable description for its purpose.
- **Test Report ID**: All templates have a test report that allows the user to check for posting errors.
- **Form ID**: For some journals, more UI objects are required. For example, the General Journals have a special form for bank and cash.
- **Posting Report ID**: This report is printed when a user selects **Post** and **Print**.
- **Force Posting Report**: Use this option when a posting report is mandatory.
- **Source Code**: Here you can enter a trail code for all the postings done via this journal.
- **Reason Code**: This functionality is similar to **Source Code**.

- **Recurring**: Whenever you post lines from a recurring journal, new lines are automatically created with a posting date defined in the recurring date formula.

- **No. Series**: When you use this feature the **Document No.** in the journal line is automatically populated with a new number from this Number Series.

- **Posting No. Series**: Use this feature for recurring journals.

The **Journal Batch** has various fields, as shown in the following screenshot:

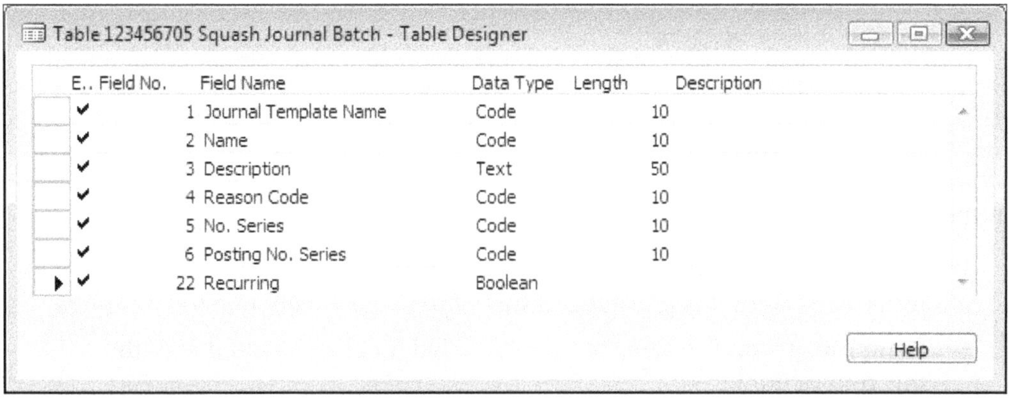

Let's discuss these fields in more detail:

- **Journal Template Name**: The name of the journal template this batch refers to

- **Name**: Each batch should have a unique code

- **Description**: A readable and explaining description for this batch

- **Reason Code**: When populated this **Reason Code** will overrule **the Reason Code** from the **Journal Template**

- **No. Series**: When populated this **No. Series** will overrule the **No. Series** from the **Journal Template**

- **Posting No. Series**: When populated this **Posting No. Series** will overrule the **Posting No. Series** from the **Journal Template**

The **Register** table has various fields, as shown in the following screenshot:

E..	Field No.	Field Name	Data Type	Length	Description
✔	1	No.	Integer		
✔	2	From Entry No.	Integer		
✔	3	To Entry No.	Integer		
✔	4	Creation Date	Date		
✔	5	Source Code	Code	10	
✔	6	User ID	Code	20	
✔	7	Journal Batch Name	Code	10	

Table 123456707 Squash Register - Table Designer — Help

Terms from the **Journal Register** tab that you need to know would be:

- **No.**: This field is automatically and incrementally populated for each transaction with this journal and there are no gaps between the numbers
- **From Entry No.**: A reference to the first ledger entry created is with this transaction
- **To Entry No.**: A reference to the last ledger entry is created with this transaction
- **Creation Date**: Always populated with the real date when the transaction was posted
- **User ID**: The ID of the end user who has posted the transaction

The journal

The journal line has a number of mandatory fields that are required for all journals and some fields that are required for their designed functionality.

In our case, the journal should create a reservation which then can be invoiced. This requires some information to be populated in the lines.

Reservation

The reservation process is a logistical process that requires us to know the number of the squash court, the date, and the time of the reservation. We also need to know how long the players want to play. To check the reservation, it might also be useful to store the number of the squash player.

Invoicing

For the invoicing part, we need to know the price we need to invoice. It might also be useful to store the cost to see our profit. For the system to figure out the proper G/L Account for the turnover, we also need to define a General Product Posting Group. We will see more of how that works later in *Chapter 3, Financial Management*.

Let's discuss these fields in more detail:

- **Journal Template Name**: This is a reference to the current **Journal Template**.
- **Line No.**: Each journal has a virtually unlimited number of lines; this number is automatically incremented by 10000 allowing lines to be created in between.
- **Entry Type**: This is the reservation or invoice.
- **Document No.**: This number can be used to give to the squash player as a reservation number. When the **Entry Type** is **Invoice**, it is the invoice number.
- **Posting Date**: This is usually the reservation date but when the **Entry Type** is **Invoice**, it might be the date of the invoice, which might differ from the posting date in the general ledger.
- **Squash Player No.**: This is a reference to the squash player who has made the reservation.
- **Squash Court No.**: This is a reference to the squash court.

- **Description**: This is automatically updated with the number of the squash court, reservation date, and times, but can be changed by the user.

- **Reservation Date**: This is the actual date of the reservation.

- **From Time**: This is the starting time of the reservation. We only allow whole and half hours.

- **To Time**: This is the ending time of the reservation. We only allow whole and half hours. This is automatically populated when people enter a quantity.

- **Quantity**: This is the number of hours' playing time. We only allow units of 0.5 to be entered here. This is automatically calculated when the times are populated.

- **Unit Cost**: This is the cost to run a squash court for one hour.

- **Total Cost**: This is the cost for this reservation.

- **Unit Price**: This is the invoice price for this reservation per hour. This depends on whether or not the squash player is a member or not.

- **Total Price**: This is the total invoice price for this reservation.

- **Shortcut Dimension Code 1 & 2**: This is a reference to the dimensions used for this transaction.

- **Applies-to Entry No.**: When a reservation is invoiced, this is the reference to the **Squash Entry No.** of the reservation.

- **Source Code**: This is inherited from the journal batch or template and used when posting the transaction.

- **Chargeable**: When this option is used, there will not be an invoice for the reservation.

- **Journal Batch Name**: This is a reference to the journal batch that is used for this transaction.

- **Reason Code**: This is inherited from the journal batch or template and used when posting the transaction.

- **Recurring Method**: When the journal is a recurring journal, you can use this field to determine if the **Amount** field is blanked after posting the lines.

- **Recurring Frequency**: This field determines the new posting date after the recurring lines are posted.

- **Gen. Bus. Posting Group**: The combination of general business and product posting group determines the G/L Account for turnover when we invoice the reservation. The **Gen. Bus. Posting Group** is inherited from the bill-to customer.

- **Gen. Prod. Posting Group**: This will be inherited from the squash player.
- **External Document No.**: When a squash player wants us to note a reference number, we can store it here.
- **Posting No. Series**: When the **Journal Template** has a **Posting No. Series**, it is populated here to be used when posting.
- **Bill-to Customer No.**: This determines who is paying for the reservation. We will inherit this from the squash player.

So now we have a place to enter reservations but we have something to do before we can start doing this. Some fields were determined to be inherited and calculated:

- The time field needs calculation to avoid people entering wrong values
- The **Unit Price** should be calculated
- The **Unit Cost**, **Posting groups**, and **Bill-to Customer No.** need to be inherited
- As the final cherry on top, we will look at implementing dimensions

Time calculation

When it comes to the time, we want only to allow specific start and end times. Our squash court can be used in blocks of half an hour. The **Quantity** field should be calculated based on the entered times and vice versa.

To have the most flexible solution possible, we will create a new table with allowed starting and ending times. This table will have two fields: **Reservation Time** and **Duration**.

The **Duration** field will be a decimal field that we will promote to a **SumIndexField**. This will enable us to use SIFT to calculate the quantity.

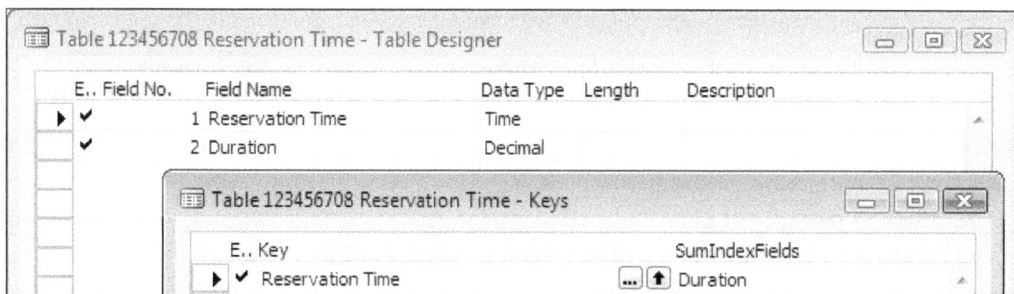

When populated the table will look like this:

The time fields in the squash journal table will now get a table relation with this table. This prevents a user entering values that are not in the table, thus entering only valid starting and ending times. This is all done without any C/AL code and is flexible when times change later.

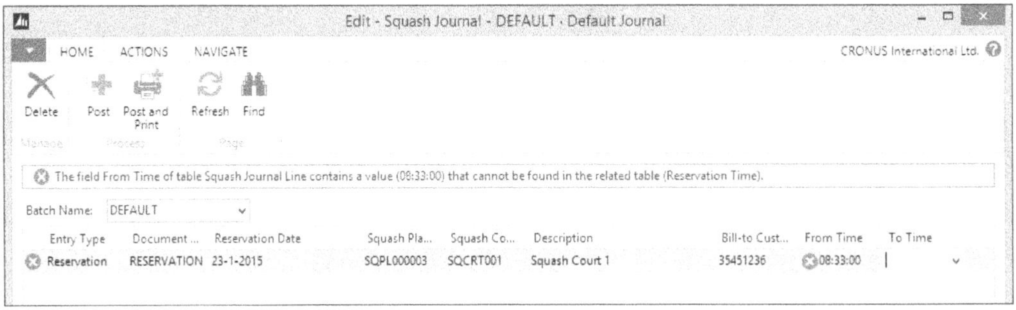

Now, we need some code that calculates the quantity based on the input:

```
From Time - OnValidate()
CalcQty;


To Time - OnValidate()
CalcQty;


CalcQty()
IF ("From Time" <> 0T) AND ("To Time" <> 0T) THEN BEGIN
```

```
    IF "To Time" <= "From Time" THEN
        FIELDERROR("To Time");
    ResTime.SETRANGE("Reservation Time", "From Time",
        "To Time");
    ResTime.FIND('+');
    ResTime.NEXT(-1);
    ResTime.SETRANGE("Reservation Time", "From Time",
        ResTime."Reservation Time");
    ResTime.CALCSUMS(Duration);
    VALIDATE(Quantity, ResTime.Duration);
END;
```

When a user enters a value in the **From Time** or **To Time** fields, the `CalcQty` function is executed. This checks if both fields have a value and then checks whether **To Time** is larger than **From Time**.

Then we place a filter on the **Reservation Time** table. Now, when a user makes a reservation from 8:00 to 9:00, there are three records in the filter making the result of the `Calcsums` (total of all records) of duration 1,5. Therefore, we find the previous reservation time and use that.

This example shows how easy it is to use the built-in Microsoft Dynamics NAV functionality such as table relations and `Calcsums` instead of complex time calculations, which we could have also used.

Price calculation

As discussed in *Chapter 1, Introduction to Microsoft Dynamics NAV*, there is a special technique to determine prices. Prices are stored in a table with all possible parameters as fields and by filtering down on these fields, the best price is determined. If required, extra logic is need to find the lowest (or highest) price, if more prices are found.

To look, learn, and love this part of the standard application, we have used table Sales Price (7002) and codeunit Sales Price Calc. Mgt. (7000), even though we only need a small part of this functionality. This mechanism of price calculation is used throughout the application and offers a normalized way of calculating sales prices. A similar construction is used for purchase prices with the table Purchase Price (7012) and codeunit Purch. Price Calc. Mgt. (7010).

Squash prices

In our case, we have already determined that we have a special rate for members, but let's say we have also a special rate for daytime and evening in winter and summer.

This could make our table look as follows:

E..	Field No.	Field Name	Data Type	Length	Description
✔	1	Squash Court No.	Code	20	
✔	2	Starting Date	Date		
✔	3	Unit Price	Decimal		
✔	4	Member	Boolean		
✔	5	Ending Time	Time		
✔	6	Ending Date	Date		

Table 123456710 Squash Price - Table Designer

We can make special prices for members on dates for winter and summer and make a price valid only until a certain time. We can also make a special price for a court.

This table could be creatively expanded with all kinds of codes until we end up with table Sales Price (7002) in the standard product, which was the template for our example.

Price Calc Mgt. codeunit

To calculate the price, we need a codeunit similar to the standard product. This codeunit is called with a squash journal line record and stores all valid prices in a buffer table and then finds the lowest price if there is any overlap:

```
FindSquashPrice()
WITH FromSquashPrice DO BEGIN
  SETFILTER("Ending Date",'%1|>=%2',0D,StartingDate);
  SETRANGE("Starting Date",0D,StartingDate);

  ToSquashPrice.RESET;
  ToSquashPrice.DELETEALL;

  SETRANGE(Member, IsMember);

  SETRANGE("Ending Time", 0T);
  SETRANGE("Squash Court No.", '');
  CopySquashPriceToSquashPrice(FromSquashPrice,ToSquashPrice);
```

```
    SETRANGE("Ending Time", 0T);
    SETRANGE("Squash Court No.", CourtNo);
    CopySquashPriceToSquashPrice(FromSquashPrice,ToSquashPrice);

    SETRANGE("Squash Court No.", '');
    IF StartingTime <> 0T THEN BEGIN
      SETFILTER("Ending Time",'%1|>=%2',000001T,StartingTime);
      CopySquashPriceToSquashPrice(FromSquashPrice,
        ToSquashPrice);
    END;

    SETRANGE("Squash Court No.", CourtNo);
    IF StartingTime <> 0T THEN BEGIN
      SETFILTER("Ending Time",'%1|>=%2',000001T,StartingTime);
      CopySquashPriceToSquashPrice(FromSquashPrice,
        ToSquashPrice);
    END;
  END;
```

If there is no price in the filter, it uses the unit price from the squash court, as shown here:

```
CalcBestUnitPrice()
WITH SquashPrice DO BEGIN
  FoundSquashPrice := FINDSET;
  IF FoundSquashPrice THEN BEGIN
    BestSquashPrice := SquashPrice;
    REPEAT
      IF SquashPrice."Unit Price" <
        BestSquashPrice."Unit Price"
      THEN
        BestSquashPrice := SquashPrice;
    UNTIL NEXT = 0;
  END;
END;

// No price found in agreement
IF BestSquashPrice."Unit Price" = 0 THEN
  BestSquashPrice."Unit Price" := SquashCourt."Unit Price";

SquashPrice := BestSquashPrice;
```

Inherited data

To use the journal for the product part of the application, we want to inherit some of the fields from the master data tables. In order to make that possible, we need to copy and paste these fields from other tables to our master data table and populate it.

In our example, we can copy and paste the fields from the Resource table (156). We also need to add code to the `OnValidate` triggers in the journal line table.

The squash court table, for example, is expanded with the fields **Unit Code**, **Unit Price**, **Gen. Prod. Posting Group**, and **VAT Prod. Posting Group**, as shown in the preceding screenshot.

We can now add code to the `OnValidate` of the `Squash Court No.` field in the Journal Line table.

```
Squash Court No. - OnValidate()
IF SquashCourt.GET("Squash Court No.") THEN BEGIN
   Description := SquashCourt.Description;
   "Unit Cost" := SquashCourt."Unit Cost";
   "Gen. Prod. Posting Group" := SquashCourt."Gen. Prod. Posting
Group";
   FindSquashPlayerPrice;
END;
```

Please note that unit price is used in the Squash Price Calc. Mgt. codeunit that is executed from the `FindSquashPlayerPrice` function.

Dimensions

In Microsoft Dynamics NAV, dimensions are defined in master data and posted to the ledger entries to be used in analysis view entries. In *Chapter 3, Financial Management*, we will discuss how to analyze the data generated by dimensions. In between that journey they move around a lot in different tables as follows:

- **Table 348 | Dimension**: This is where the main dimension codes are defined.

- **Table 349 | Dimension Value**: This is where each dimension can have an unlimited number of values.

- **Table 350 | Dimension Combination**: In this table, we can block certain combinations of dimension codes.

- **Table 351 | Dimension Value Combination**: In this table, we can block certain combinations of dimension values. If this table is populated, the value `Limited` is populated in the dimension combination table for these dimensions.

- **Table 352 | Default Dimension**: This table is populated for all master data that has dimensions defined.

- **Table 354 | Default Dimension Priority**: When more than one master data record in one transaction have the same dimensions, it is possible here to set priorities.

- **Table 480 | Dimension Set Entry**: This table contains a matrix of all used dimension combinations.

- **Codeunit 408 | Dimension Management**: This codeunit is the single point in the application where all dimension movement is done.

In our application, dimensions are moved from the squash player, squash court, and customer table via the squash journal line to the squash ledger entries. When we create an invoice, we move the dimensions from the ledger entries to the sales line table.

Master data

To connect dimensions to master data, we first need to allow this changing codeunit 408 dimension management.

```
SetupObjectNoList()
TableIDArray[1] := DATABASE::"Salesperson/Purchaser";
TableIDArray[2] := DATABASE::"G/L Account";
TableIDArray[3] := DATABASE::Customer;
. . .
```

```
TableIDArray[22] := DATABASE::"Service Item Group";
TableIDArray[23] := DATABASE::"Service Item";

//* Squash Application
TableIDArray[49] := DATABASE::"Squash Player";
TableIDArray[50] := DATABASE::"Squash Court";
//* Squash Application

Object.SETRANGE(Type,Object.Type::Table);

FOR Index := 1 TO ARRAYLEN(TableIDArray) DO BEGIN
  ...
```

The `TableIDArray` variable has a default number of 23 dimensions. This we have changed to `50`.

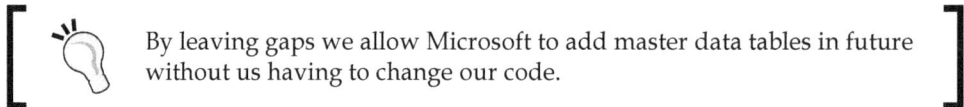

[
By leaving gaps we allow Microsoft to add master data tables in future without us having to change our code.
]

Without this change, the system would return the following error message when we try to use dimensions:

Table ID must not be 123456701 in Default Dimension Table ID='123456701',No.='',Dimension Code=''. (Select Refr...

Next change is to add the **Global Dimension** fields to the master data tables. They can be copied and pasted from other master data tables.

E , Field No.	Field Name	Data Type	Length	Description
16	Global Dimension 1 Code	Code	20	
17	Global Dimension 2 Code	Code	20	
19	Member	Boolean		
22	Currency Code	Code	10	

Table 123456701 Squash Player - Table Designer

When these fields are validated, the `ValidateShortcutDimCode` function is executed as follows:

```
ValidateShortcutDimCode()
DimMgt.ValidateDimValueCode(FieldNumber,ShortcutDimCode);
DimMgt.SaveDefaultDim(DATABASE::"Squash Player","No.",
  FieldNumber,ShortcutDimCode);
MODIFY;
```

Journal

When we use the master data records in the journal table, the dimensions are copied from the default dimension table to the dimension set entry table. This is done using the folowing piece of code that is called from `OnValidate` of each master data reference field:

```
CreateDim()
TableID[1] := Type1;
No[1]  := No1;
TableID[2] := Type2;
No[2]  := No2;
TableID[3] := Type3;
No[3]  := No3;

"Shortcut Dimension 1 Code" := '';
"Shortcut Dimension 2 Code" := '';

"Dimension Set ID" :=
  DimMgt.GetDefaultDimID(TableID,No,"Source Code",
    "Shortcut Dimension 1 Code",
      "Shortcut Dimension 2 Code",0,0);
```

To decide which dimensions to inherit, we should first analyze which master data is used in our Journal that is using default dimensions.

```
Squash Court No. - OnValidate()
CreateDim(
  DATABASE::"Squash Court","Squash Court No.",
  DATABASE::"Squash Player","Squash Player No.",
  DATABASE::Customer,"Bill-to Customer No.");
```

In our case, `Table[1]` is `Squash Player`, `Table[2]` is `Squash Court`, and `Table[3]` is `Customer`. The dimension management codeunit makes sure everything is copied. We can use standard Microsoft Dynamics NAV functions.

Posting

When we post a journal using `Codeunit Squash Jnl.-Post Line (123456703)`, the dimensions are copied using the dimension set ID as follows:

```
Code()

...

SquashLedgEntry."Dimension Set ID" := "Dimension Set ID";

...
```

```
SquashLedgEntry.INSERT;

NextEntryNo := NextEntryNo + 1;
```

This field is also used from our combine invoicing report, which we will create later in this chapter in the **Invoicing** section.

```
CreateLn()
...
SalesLn.INIT;

SalesLn."Dimension Set ID" := "Dimension Set ID";

SalesLn.INSERT(TRUE);
```

The posting process

Our journal is now ready to be posted. We've implemented all business logic, except the posting code.

Type	ID	Name	Modified	Version List
	123456702	Squash Jnl.-Check Line	✔	Chapter2-4
	123456703	Squash Jnl.-Post Line	✔	Chapter2-4
	123456704	Squash Jnl.-Post Batch	✔	Chapter2-4
	123456705	Squash Jnl.-Post	✔	Chapter2-4
	123456706	Squash Jnl.-Post+Print	✔	Chapter2-4
	123456707	Squash Jnl.-B.Post	✔	Chapter2-4
	123456708	Squash Jnl.-B.Post+Print	✔	Chapter2-4

The posting process of a journal in Microsoft Dynamics NAV has several codeunits for the structure:

- `Jnl.-Check Line`: This codeunit checks if the journal line is valid for posting.

- `Jnl.-Post Line`: This codeunit does the actual creation of the ledger entry and register tables and calls other `Jnl.-Post Line` codeunits if necessary to provide the transaction structure in *Chapter 1, Introduction to Microsoft Dynamics NAV*.

- `Jnl.-Post Batch`: This codeunit loops though all journal lines in a journal batch and posts all the lines.

- `Jnl.-Post`: This is the codeunit that is called from the page. It calls the `Jnl.-Post Batch` codeunit and takes care of some user messaging.

- Jnl.-Post+Print: This is the codeunit that is called when you click on **Post + Print**. It does the same as the Jnl.-Post codeunit but with the additional printing of a report defined in the journal template.

- Jnl.-B.Post: This posts all the journal lines that have no errors and marks the ones that have errors.

- Jnl.-B.Post+Print: This does the same as Jnl.-B.Post but with the additional printing of a report defined in the journal template.

Check line

Let's have a look at the check line codeunit. When it comes to testing, Microsoft Dynamics NAV has a simple rule:

Test near, Test far, Do it, Clean up

First, we need to test the field in the journal line table, then read external data tables to check if all is good, and then post the lines and delete the data from the journal table.

It does not make sense to read the G/L setup table from the database if the document no. in our own table is blank, or to start the posting process and error out because the posting date is outside of a valid range. This would cause a lot of unnecessary I/O from the database to the client.

```
RunCheck()
WITH SquashJnlLine DO BEGIN
  IF EmptyLine THEN
    EXIT;

  TESTFIELD("Squash Player No.");
  TESTFIELD("Squash Court No.");
  TESTFIELD("Posting Date");
  TESTFIELD("Gen. Prod. Posting Group");
  TESTFIELD("From Time");
  TESTFIELD("To Time");
  TESTFIELD("Reservation Date");
  TESTFIELD("Bill-to Customer No.");

  IF "Entry Type" = "Entry Type"::Invoice THEN
    TESTFIELD("Applies-to Entry No.");

  IF "Applies-to Entry No." <> 0 THEN
    TESTFIELD("Entry Type", "Entry Type"::Invoice);
```

```
IF "Posting Date" <> NORMALDATE("Posting Date") THEN
  FIELDERROR("Posting Date",Text000);

IF (AllowPostingFrom = 0D) AND (AllowPostingTo = 0D) THEN
  ...
END;

...

IF NOT DimMgt.CheckDimIDComb("Dimension Set ID") THEN
  ...
TableID[1] := DATABASE::"Squash Player";
No[1] := "Squash Player No.";
...
IF NOT DimMgt.CheckJnlLineDimValuePosting(JnlLineDim,
  TableID,No)
THEN
  IF "Line No." <> 0 THEN
    .................
```

In the preceding code, we can clearly see that fields in our table are checked first, and then the date validation, and lastly the dimension checking.

Post line

The actual posting code turns out to be quite simple. The values are checked and then a register is created or updated.

```
Code()
WITH SquashJnlLine DO BEGIN
  IF EmptyLine THEN
    EXIT;

  SquashJnlCheckLine.RunCheck(SquashJnlLine,TempJnlLineDim);

  IF NextEntryNo = 0 THEN BEGIN
    SquashLedgEntry.LOCKTABLE;
    IF SquashLedgEntry.FIND('+') THEN
      NextEntryNo := SquashLedgEntry."Entry No.";
    NextEntryNo := NextEntryNo + 1;
  END;

  IF SquashReg."No." = 0 THEN BEGIN
    SquashReg.LOCKTABLE;
```

```
   IF (NOT SquashReg.FIND('+') OR ... THEN BEGIN
     SquashReg.INIT;
     SquashReg."No." := SquashReg."No." + 1;
     ...
     SquashReg.INSERT;
   END;
END;
SquashReg."To Entry No." := NextEntryNo;
SquashReg.MODIFY;

SquashPlayer.GET("Squash Player No.");
SquashPlayer.TESTFIELD(Blocked,FALSE);

IF (GenPostingSetup."Gen. Bus. Posting Group" <>
  "Gen. Bus. Posting Group") OR
  (GenPostingSetup."Gen. Prod. Posting Group" <>
  "Gen. Prod. Posting Group")
THEN
  GenPostingSetup.GET("Gen. Bus. Posting Group",
    "Gen. Prod. Posting Group");

SquashLedgEntry.INIT;
SquashLedgEntry."Entry Type" := "Entry Type";
SquashLedgEntry."Document No." := "Document No.";
...
SquashLedgEntry."No. Series" := "Posting No. Series";

SquashLedgEntry.INSERT;
```

All the fields are simply moved to the ledger entry table. This is what makes Microsoft Dynamics NAV simple and powerful.

Here, we can clearly see how easy it is to add a field to a posting process. Just add the fields to the journal line, the ledger entry, and add one line of code to the posting process.

Invoicing

The last issue on our to-do list is the invoicing process. For this, we use a part of the standard application.

As explained in *Chapter 1, Introduction to Microsoft Dynamics NAV*, invoicing is done using a document structure with a header and a line table. This has a posting routine that will start the journal transactions.

For our application, we need to create the invoice document and make sure that when posted, it updates our sub administration.

Invoice document

The sales invoice documents in Microsoft Dynamics NAV are stored in the Sales Header (36) and Sales Line (37) tables. We will create a report that will combine the outstanding reservation entries into invoices allowing the user to filter on a specific entry or any other field value in the squash ledger entry table.

Reports in Microsoft Dynamics NAV are not just for printing documents; we can also use its dataset capabilities to start batch jobs.

To enable this, our batch job needs to have a special property, ProcessingOnly, so let's start a blank report and do this.

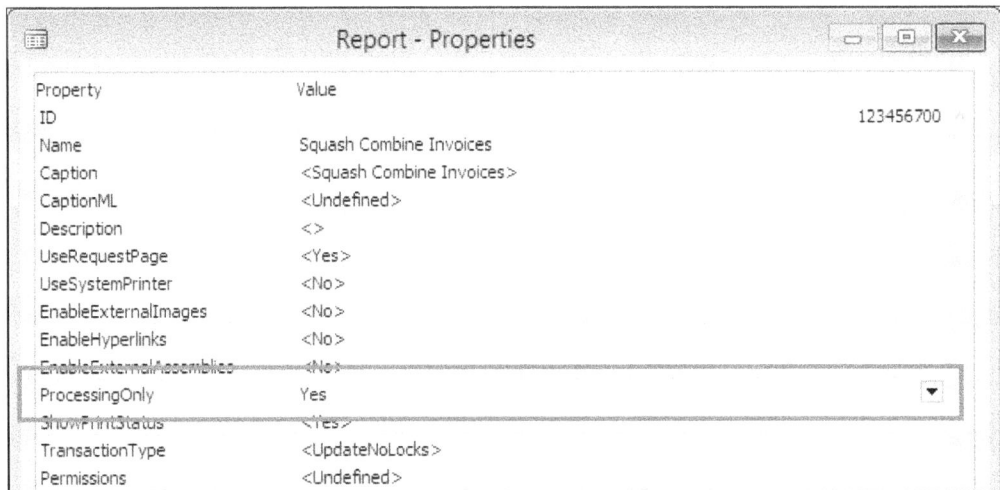

The report will browse through the squash ledger entries filtered on entry type **Reservation** and open **Yes**. The sorting is **Open, Entry Type, Bill-to Customer No.,** and **Reservation Date**. To use sorting, the fields must be defined together as a key in the table definition.

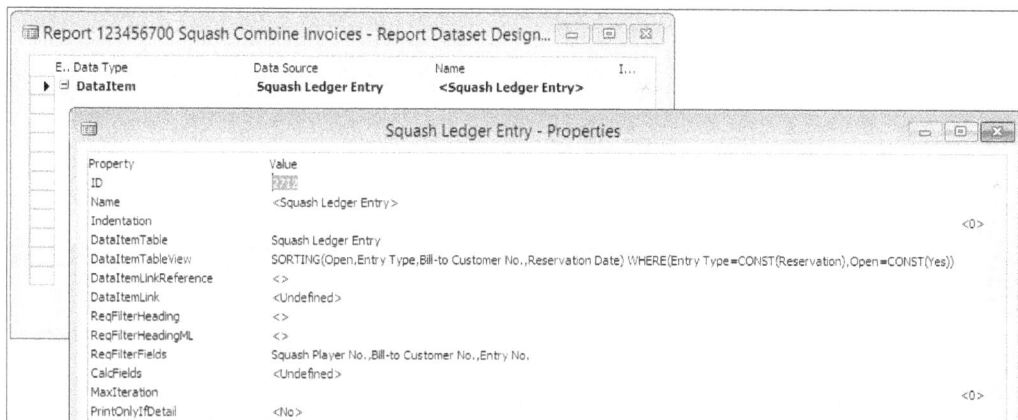

As **Bill-to Customer No.** is the first non-filtered value in the sorting, we can assume that if this value changes, we need a new sales header.

For every squash ledger entry, we will generate a sales line as follows:

```
Squash Ledger Entry - OnAfterGetRecord()
IF "Bill-to Customer No." <> SalesHdr."Bill-to Customer No."
THEN
  CreateSalesHdr;

CreateLn;
```

Sales header

The code to create a sales header is as follows:

```
CreateSalesHdr()
CLEAR(SalesHdr);
SalesHdr.SetHideValidationDialog(TRUE);
SalesHdr."Document Type" := SalesHdr."Document Type"::Invoice;
SalesHdr."Document Date" := WORKDATE;
SalesHdr."Posting Date" := WORKDATE;
SalesHdr.VALIDATE("Sell-to Customer No.",
  "Squash Ledger Entry"."Bill-to Customer No.");
SalesHdr.INSERT(TRUE);

NextLineNo := 10000;
CounterOK := CounterOK + 1;
```

The `SetHideValidationDialog` function makes sure we don't get pop-up messages while validating values. This is a standard function in Microsoft Dynamics NAV, which is designed for this purpose.

The `TRUE` parameter to the `INSERT` statement makes sure that the Number Series are triggered.

Sales line

To create a sales line, we need a minimum of the following code. Please note that we added the field `Applies-to Squash Entry No.` to the sales line table.

```
CreateLn()
WITH "Squash Ledger Entry" DO BEGIN
  GenPstSetup.GET("Gen. Bus. Posting Group",
    "Gen. Prod. Posting Group");
  GenPstSetup.TESTFIELD("Sales Account");

  SalesLn.INIT;
  SalesLn."Document Type" := SalesHdr."Document Type";
  SalesLn."Document No." := SalesHdr."No.";
  SalesLn."Line No." := NextLineNo;
  SalesLn."Dimension Set ID" := "Dimension Set ID";

  SalesLn."System-Created Entry" := TRUE;

  SalesLn.Type := SalesLn.Type::"G/L Account";
  SalesLn.VALIDATE("No.", GenPstSetup."Sales Account");
  SalesLn.Description := Description;

  SalesLn.VALIDATE(Quantity, Quantity);
  SalesLn.VALIDATE("Unit Price", "Unit Price");
  SalesLn.VALIDATE("Unit Cost (LCY)", "Unit Cost");

  SalesLn."Applies-to Squash Entry No." := "Entry No.";
  SalesLn.INSERT(TRUE);

END;
NextLineNo := NextLineNo + 10000;
```

> When you add fields to the sales and purchase document tables, make sure to also add these to the posted equivalents of these tables with the same number. This way you make sure that the information is copied to the historic data. This is done using the TRANSFERFIELDS command. We will discuss these tables in *Chapter 6, Trade*.

Dialog

If the combined invoicing takes some time, it might be good to show the user a process bar. For this, Microsoft Dynamics NAV has a standard structure.

The window shows the bill-to customer no. it is currently processing and a bar going from 1 percent to 100 percent. This is calculated by keeping a counter.

At the end of the process, we show a message telling the user how many invoices were created out of the number of squash ledger entries.

```
Squash Ledger Entry - OnPreDataItem()
CounterTotal := COUNT;
Window.OPEN(Text000);


Squash Ledger Entry - OnAfterGetRecord()
Counter := Counter + 1;
Window.UPDATE(1,"Bill-to Customer No.");
Window.UPDATE(2,ROUND(Counter / CounterTotal * 10000,1));


. . .


Squash Ledger Entry - OnPostDataItem()
Window.CLOSE;
MESSAGE(Text001,CounterOK,CounterTotal);
```

To do this, we need some variables. The **Window** variable is of type **Dialog** whilst **Counter**, **CounterTotal**, and **CounterOK** are integers, as shown in the following screenshot:

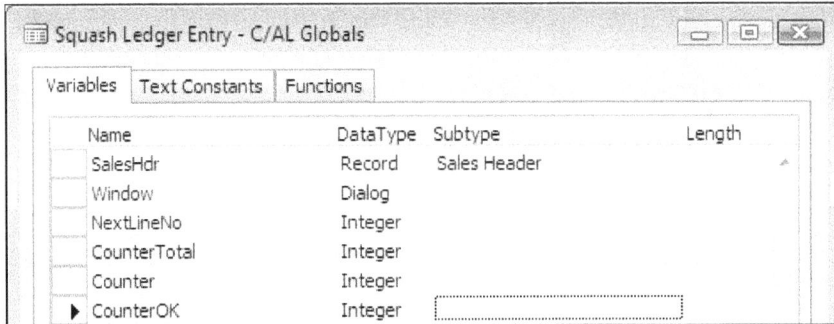

The constant **Text000** has the special values **#1##########** and **@2@@@@@@@@@@@@**. The first allows us to show and update some text; the latter is used to create the process bar.

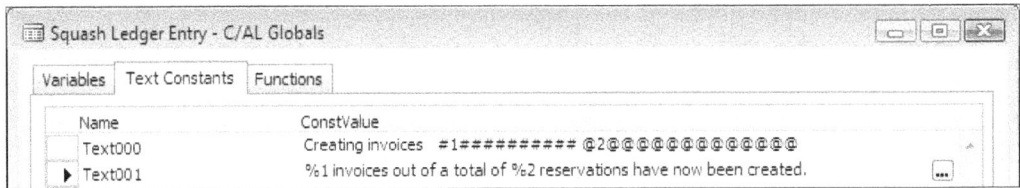

The result will look like what is shown in the following screenshot:

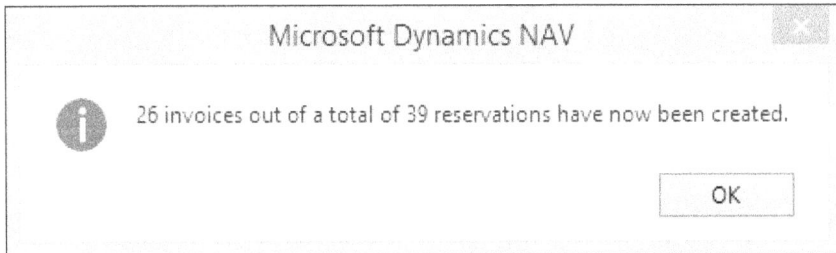

> There is a best practice document about using progress bars in combination with the impact on performance at `http://www.mibuso.com/howtoinfo.asp?FileID=17`.

Posting process

Now, our Sales Invoice is ready so we can start making the necessary changes to the posting process. Posting a sales document is done using a single posting codeunit and some helper objects.

- **Report 297**: This report can be used to post more than one document at the same time with a filter.
- **Codeunit 80**: This is the actual posting routine we are going to change.
- **Codeunit 81**: This codeunit is called from the user interface and has a dialog if the user wants to ship, invoice, or both if the document is an order and a yes/no if the document is an invoice or credit memo.
- **Codeunit 82**: When the user chooses post and print, this codeunit is executed, which does the same as **Codeunit 81** plus printing a report.

So we will make a change to **Codeunit 80**. This codeunit has a specific structure that we need to understand before we go in and make the change.

Analyze the object

The codeunit also has the *Test Near*, *Test Far*, *Do it*, and *Clean up* strategy so the first step is to make sure everything is in place before the actual posting starts. Let's have a look at how this codeunit is structured.

> The Sales-Post codeunit is too long to discuss in detail. We will focus on the most important parts and learning how to read this type of code routine.

This first part does the test near step and a part of the test far step. The Ship, Invoice, and Receive fields are set in codeunit 81 and 82 but checked and completed to make sure.

```
Code()
...
WITH SalesHeader DO BEGIN
  TESTFIELD("Document Type");
  TESTFIELD("Sell-to Customer No.");
  TESTFIELD("Bill-to Customer No.");
  TESTFIELD("Posting Date");
  TESTFIELD("Document Date");
  IF GenJnlCheckLine.DateNotAllowed("Posting Date") THEN
    FIELDERROR("Posting Date",Text045);
```

```
CASE "Document Type" OF
  "Document Type"::Order:
    Receive := FALSE;
  "Document Type"::Invoice:
    BEGIN
      Ship := TRUE;
      Invoice := TRUE;
      Receive := FALSE;
    END;
  "Document Type"::"Return Order":
    Ship := FALSE;
  "Document Type"::"Credit Memo":
    BEGIN
      Ship := FALSE;
      Invoice := TRUE;
      Receive := TRUE;
    END;
END;

IF NOT (Ship OR Invoice OR Receive) THEN
  ERROR(...);

WhseReference := "Posting from Whse. Ref.";
"Posting from Whse. Ref." := 0;

IF Invoice THEN
  CreatePrepaymentLines(...);
CheckDim;
```

The next step is moving the sales header information to the history tables for
shipment, invoice, credit memo, or return receipt header. These sections are
commented like this:

```
// Insert invoice header or credit memo header
IF Invoice THEN
  IF "Document Type" IN ["Document Type"::Order,
    "Document Type"::Invoice]
  THEN BEGIN
    SalesInvHeader.INIT;
    SalesInvHeader.TRANSFERFIELDS(SalesHeader);
```

We will discuss the relation between a sales header and the sales
shipment, sales invoice, sales credit memo, and return receipt in
Chapter 6, Trade.

When this is done, the sales lines are processed. They are also moved to the various posted line tables. This is all part of the *Do it* section of the posting routine.

```
// Lines
InvPostingBuffer[1].DELETEALL;
DropShipPostBuffer.DELETEALL;
EverythingInvoiced := TRUE;

SalesLine.RESET;
SalesLine.SETRANGE("Document Type","Document Type");
SalesLine.SETRANGE("Document No.","No.");
LineCount := 0;
RoundingLineInserted := FALSE;
MergeSaleslines(...);
```

If there is a drop shipment in a purchase order, this is handled here. We will discuss drop shipments in *Chapter 6, Trade*.

```
// Post drop shipment of purchase order
PurchSetup.GET;
IF DropShipPostBuffer.FIND('-') THEN
  REPEAT
    PurchOrderHeader.GET(
      PurchOrderHeader."Document Type"::Order,
      DropShipPostBuffer."Order No.");
```

Then there is a section that creates the financial information in the general journal. We will go deeper into this section in *Chapter 3, Financial Management*.

```
IF Invoice THEN BEGIN
  // Post sales and VAT to G/L entries from posting buffer
  LineCount := 0;
  IF InvPostingBuffer[1].FIND('+') THEN
    REPEAT
      LineCount := LineCount + 1;
      Window.UPDATE(3,LineCount);

      GenJnlLine.INIT;
      GenJnlLine."Posting Date" := "Posting Date";
      GenJnlLine."Document Date" := "Document Date";
```

Then the *Clean up* section starts by calculating remaining quantities, VAT, and deleting the sales header and sales lines if possible.

```
IF ("Document Type" IN ["Document Type"::Order,
  "Document Type"::"Return Order"]) AND
```

```
      (NOT EverythingInvoiced)
  THEN BEGIN
    MODIFY;
    // Insert T336 records
    InsertTrackingSpecification;

    IF SalesLine.FINDSET THEN
      REPEAT
        IF SalesLine.Quantity <> 0 THEN BEGIN
          IF Ship THEN BEGIN
            SalesLine."Quantity Shipped" :=
              SalesLine."Quantity Shipped" +
              SalesLine."Qty. to Ship";
            SalesLine."Qty. Shipped (Base)" :=
              SalesLine."Qty. Shipped (Base)" +
              SalesLine."Qty. to Ship (Base)";
          END;
```

The *Clean up* section ends by deleting the sales document and related information and clearing the variables used.

```
IF HASLINKS THEN DELETELINKS;
DELETE;
...

SalesLine.DELETEALL;
DeleteItemChargeAssgnt;
...

CLEAR(WhsePostRcpt);
CLEAR(WhsePostShpt);
...
CLEAR(WhseJnlPostLine);
CLEAR(InvtAdjmt);
Window.CLOSE;
```

Making the change

The change we are going to make is in the section where the lines are handled:

```
// Squash Journal Line
IF SalesLine."Applies-to Squash Entry No." <> 0 THEN
  PostSquashJnlLn;
```

```
IF (SalesLine.Type >= SalesLine.Type::"G/L Account") AND
   (SalesLine."Qty. to Invoice" <> 0)
THEN BEGIN
   // Copy sales to buffer
```

We will create a new function, `PostSquashJnlLn`. This way we minimize the impact on standard code and when we upgrade to a newer version, we can easily copy and paste our function and only need to change the calling place if required.

> Always try to design for easy upgrading whenever possible. Remember that Microsoft might change this code in newer versions so the more flexible we are and the more we manage to minimize the impact on standard code, the better.

```
PostSquashJnlLn()
WITH SalesHeader DO BEGIN
  OldSquashLedEnt.GET(
    SalesLine."Applies-to Squash Entry No.");
  OldSquashLedEnt.TESTFIELD(Open);
  OldSquashLedEnt.TESTFIELD("Bill-to Customer No.",
    "Bill-to Customer No.");

  SquashJnlLn.INIT;
  SquashJnlLn."Posting Date" := "Posting Date";
  SquashJnlLn."Reason Code" := "Reason Code";
  ...
  SquashJnlLn."Document No." := GenJnlLineDocNo;
  SquashJnlLn."External Document No." := GenJnlLineExtDocNo;
  SquashJnlLn.Quantity := -SalesLine."Qty. to Invoice";
  SquashJnlLn."Source Code" := SrcCode;
  SquashJnlLn."Dimension Set ID" :=
    SalesLine."Dimension Set ID";
  SquashJnlLn.Chargeable := TRUE;
  SquashJnlLn."Posting No. Series" := "Posting No. Series";
  SquashJnlPostLine.RunWithCheck(SquashJnlLn);
END;
```

Our new function first gets the squash ledger entry it applies to and tests if it's still open and the bill-to customer no. has not changed. Then, we populate the squash journal line with the help of the sales line and the old squash ledger entry. Then dimensions are handled and the squash journal line is posted.

> The journal lines are never actually inserted into the database. This is for performance and concurrency reasons. All journal transactions here are handled in the service tier cache. A journal is also never populated using `Validate`. This makes it very clear for you to see what happens.

Now when we post an invoice, we can see that the invoice entries are created:

Navigate

We have now covered everything that is necessary for our squash court application to run but there is one special function of Microsoft Dynamics NAV that needs changing when we add new documents and ledger entries: the `Navigate` function.

The functionality was already discussed in *Chapter 1, Introduction to Microsoft Dynamics NAV*. The object is a single page (344) in the application that requires two changes.

FindRecords

The first function we change is `FindRecords`. This browses through the database finding all possible combinations of document no. and posting date.

```
FindRecords()
...
// Squash Ledger Entries
IF SquashLedgEntry.READPERMISSION THEN BEGIN
```

```
SquashLedgEntry.RESET;
SquashLedgEntry.SETCURRENTKEY("Document No.",
  "Posting Date");
SquashLedgEntry.SETFILTER("Document No.",DocNoFilter);
SquashLedgEntry.SETFILTER("Posting Date",PostingDateFilter);
InsertIntoDocEntry(
  DATABASE::"Squash Ledger Entry",0,
  SquashLedgEntry.TABLECAPTION,SquashLedgEntry.COUNT);
END;
// Squash Ledger Entries

DocExists := FINDFIRST;
```

The function first checks if we have permission to read the squash ledger entry table. If our system administrator does not allow us to see this table, it should not show up.

The filtering is done on the document no. and posting date. When ready, the system inserts the number of found records in the result table.

ShowRecords

The second function to change is ShowRecords. This makes sure we see the squash ledger entries when we click on the **Show** action.

```
ShowRecords()
...
    DATABASE::"Warranty Ledger Entry":
      FORM.RUN(0,WarrantyLedgerEntry);
//* Squash Ledger Entries
    DATABASE::"Squash Ledger Entry":
      FORM.RUN(0,SquashLedgEntry);
    END;
END;
```

Testing

Now when we navigate from an invoice we posted that was generated from our combine invoicing report, we get the following result:

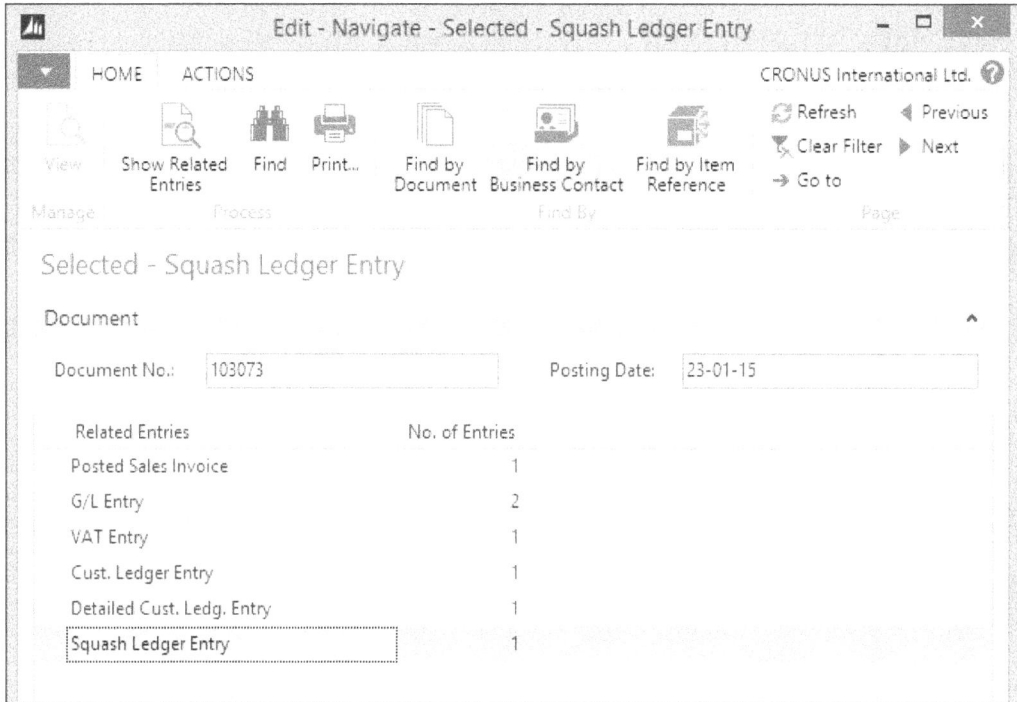

Summary

In this chapter, we created our own vertical add-on application for Microsoft Dynamics NAV. We used similar data model and posting structures and reused parts of the standard application where appropriate but never wrongly used standard features.

We saw how to reverse engineer Microsoft Dynamics NAV code in order to find out what similar standard functionality to copy, paste, and change for our application.

We also found out how a journal and document posting code unit works and how to structure using *Test near*, *Test far*, *Do it*, and *Clean up*.

In the next chapter, we will explore the financial functionality of Microsoft Dynamics NAV and even make some changes to this part of the application.

3
Financial Management

Whether you run a company, a non-profit organization, or an educational institute, doing proper bookkeeping is mandatory and required by the government.

This makes the financial management the most used part of Microsoft Dynamics NAV and the least obvious place to make changes, as federal regulations do not allow much creativity in this part of the application.

The first part of this chapter is all about the look, learn, and love principle that we discussed in the previous chapter. We cannot integrate our application with financial management without knowing the basic functionality and structure of the tool.

In the second part of the chapter, we will look at some examples of how to change or expand the way financial management works.

Lastly, we will look at how to create a posting in the general ledger from a newly designed posting routine.

After reading this chapter, you should be able to set up financial management in a new database and create basic postings to the general ledger and understand how to integrate financial management with your application.

Chart of accounts

A **chart of accounts (COA)** is a list of the accounts used by an organization to define each class of items for which money or the equivalent is spent or received. It is used to organize the finances of the entity and to segregate expenditures, revenue, assets, and liabilities in order to give interested parties a better understanding of the financial health of the entity.

Every financial system starts with a COA and although the numbering might differ from country to country, we all have income statements and balance accounts.

Microsoft Dynamics NAV also has some other special accounts: **Heading**, **Begin-Total**, and **End-Total** accounts.

With these accounts, you can make the COA more readable. The accounts within the total accounts are automatically indented.

Posting accounts

When creating a new posting account, there are several options to choose. Most of them are not mandatory but they make it easier to push the end users to using the correct account while generating entries.

Let's have a look at the options by opening a **G/L Account Card**:

The first and most important decision to make is the type of account to be created. It can be either **Income Statement** or **Balance Sheet**. Income statement accounts are reset to zero every new fiscal year, while balance sheet accounts continue indefinitely. The total of the balance sheet accounts should always match the total of the income statement accounts.

No.	Name	Income/Bal...	Account Ty...	Totaling	Net Change	Balance
99998	Total Income Statement	Income Stat...	Total	6000..9999	-23.095,30	-23.095,30
99999	Total Balance Sheet	Balance Sheet	Total	1000..5997	23.095,30	23.095,30

> You can create two total accounts to check whether the balance in your G/L is accurate. Take a total of all income statements and all balance sheets.

You can also force an account to only accept debit or credit postings. The **No. Of Blank Lines** and **New Page** fields are used when printing reports and have no effect on the system. **Reconciliation Account** is hardly used anymore unless, you do not use sub accounting.

Automatic Ext. Texts creates the extra texts discussed in *Chapter 1, Introduction to Microsoft Dynamics NAV*, automatically when you use this account in a sales or purchasing document.

Direct Posting is a very important option. It is highly recommended to disable this option when an account is used in one of the posting setups. When **Direct Posting** is enabled, an end user can create entries in this account, disrupting the balance between the general ledger and the sub administration. We'll discuss this in more detail later in this chapter.

When you do allow **Direct Posting**, the fields on the **Posting** tab are very important.

Gen. Posting Type determines whether the account is used for purchase and/or sales for the VAT calculation and filtering in the VAT statements. A more detailed VAT specification is determined by the VAT business and product posting group. The general business and product posting groups can be used to automatically populate these fields, when this account is used.

In the **Consolidation** tab, you can populate the consolidation accounts used when consolidating two or more companies. We'll discuss consolidation later in this chapter.

Microsoft Dynamics NAV allows an additional reporting currency to be used. This is an inheritance from the days before the Euro in Europe and was very popular in the years of Euro introduction. Today, it is used by international companies, for example, a company based in the USA with a Dutch Parent company. In the **Reporting** tab, you can determine how you want to handle exchange rate adjustments when using this functionality.

VAT versus sales tax

Microsoft Dynamics NAV allows the calculation of both European VAT and North American Sales Tax. The examples in this book are based on European VAT.

For sales tax, the **Tax Area Code** and **Tax Group Code** fields are used instead of the VAT Business Posting Group and the VAT Product Posting Group.

The entry tables

As discussed in *Chapter 1*, *Introduction to Microsoft Dynamics NAV*, the entries for the general ledger are created in the general journals when you post a sales or purchase document. So, let's have a closer look at this functionality and see what we can do with it.

Sub accounting

In theory, you could run Microsoft Dynamics NAV with just the G/L Entry table, but in accounting, we have invented sub administrations.

Sub administrations are very old. Before computers were invented, people would have cards for all customers and vendors to keep track of their balance. Updating these cards was a manual and time-consuming process with a high probability of making mistakes.

In Microsoft Dynamics NAV, this is taken care of automatically. In the general ledger, we have four sub administrations:

- **Bank**: For every transaction on a bank account, a bank ledger entry is created. The total of all bank ledger entries should match your bank account's balance. It allows you to quickly find payments.

- **Customer**: Whenever you sell something to a customer or a customer pays a customer ledger, an entry is created. It allows you to analyze payment history and send out reminders.

- **Vendor**: When you buy something using a vendor, the system creates a vendor ledger entry. We can use the vendor ledger entries to determine which invoice needs to be paid. The vendor ledger entries are the opposite of the customer ledger entries.

- **VAT/TAX**: These entries help us to easily create clear VAT/TAX statements.

As discussed earlier, it is very important that the total of the sub administration matches the general ledger. For example, when your bank account balance is **2.846,54**, the G/L Account should also have that amount.

For this, you can disable the **Direct Posting** option we discussed earlier.

Working with general journals

When we open a general journal, we can start making transactions. Let's discuss the possibilities.

The most important fields of a general journal are the **Posting Date** and the **Document No**. The total of amounts for each combination of these fields should always be in balance. In other words, all journal lines for any particular combination of **Posting Date** and **Document No.** should always add up to zero.

There are different account types we can post to. When we post directly to a **G/L Account**, it is clear what will happen; a new **G/L Entry** will be created for that amount. When we choose another **Account Type**, the sub administrations will start to work. For example, when we choose **Customer**, a **Customer Ledger Entry** will be created as well as a **G/L Entry**. Which **G/L account** is used is determined by the posting group, which we will discuss later in this chapter.

Here, we also see the **Gen. Posting Type**, **General Business** and **Product Posting** groups and **VAT Business** and **Product Posting** groups come back. These are inherited from the **G/L Account** we discussed earlier, but you can choose a different one if you want.

The VAT options determine the VAT calculation that is done automatically. A VAT entry is created with the VAT amount and additional **G/L Entries** are created.

There are two ways of balancing a general ledger. We can create two lines with the same debit and credit amount or we can use the balance fields.

Let's see some of this in an example. We have made a purchase somewhere at an irregular vendor. All we have is a small cash receipt with the amount and the VAT, which we want to bring into our company.

The amount is 440 including 10 percent VAT, so we want to create the following transaction:

Cost	VAT	Current account
400,00	40,00	440,00

The transaction can also be seen in the following screenshot:

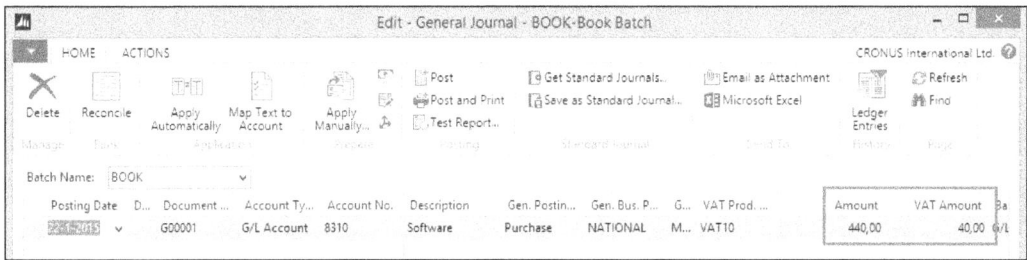

We can see that Microsoft Dynamics NAV calculates the **VAT Amount** and by populating the balance account, we only need one line, which is always in balance.

When we **Navigate** this transaction, we see that we have three **G/L Entries** and one **VAT Entry**.

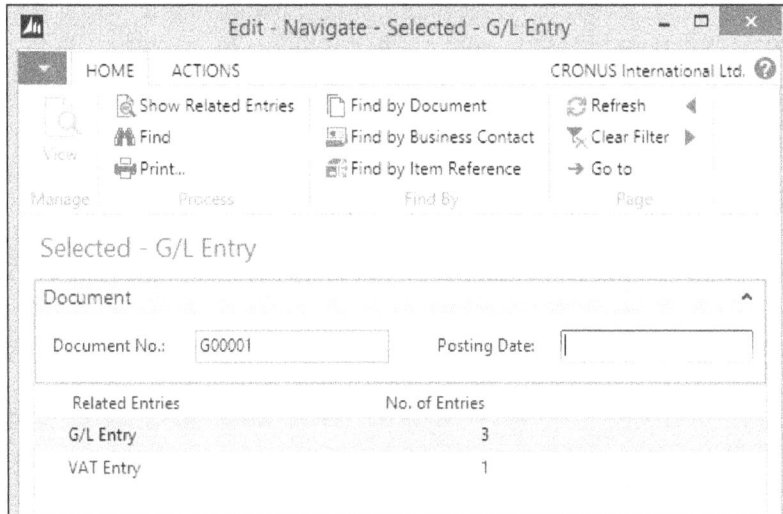

Opening the **G/L Entries** shows the correct amounts.

In another example, we'll create a customer payment via the bank journal.

Entry application

A bank journal is a general journal with a specific page ID. This allows the application to have a different user interface based on the same business logic. A specific feature of a bank journal is the possibility to easily apply payments to invoices.

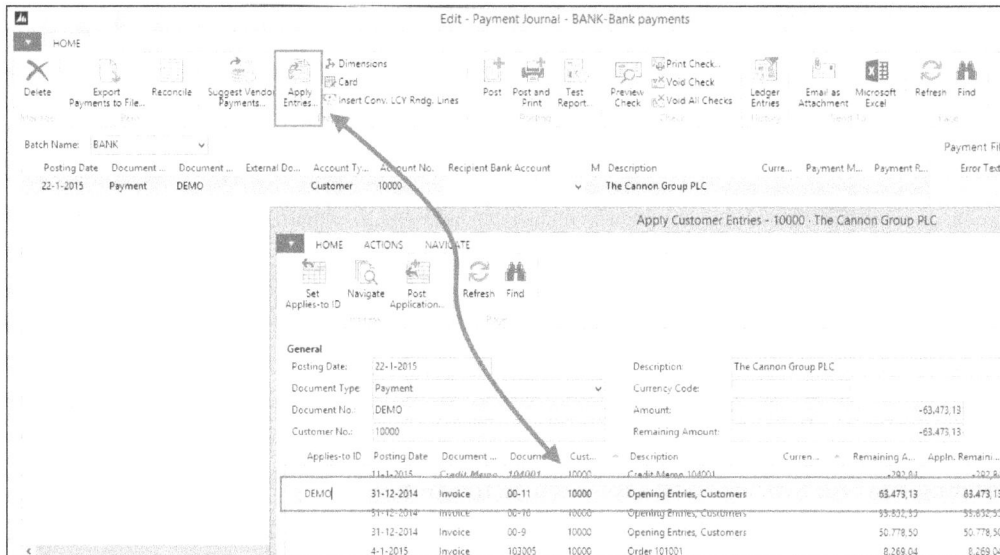

The bank journal does not directly post to a G/L Account but uses other account types. In this case, the **Account Type** is **Customer** and the **Balance Account Type** is **Bank Account**. Instead of a list with G/L Accounts, the **Account No.** field now refers to the **Customers** and the **Balance Account No.** fields refer to the **Bank Account**. The latter is automatically populated from the Journal Batch definition.

We'll use the **Apply Entries** feature to determine which invoice this payment applies to. If we did not do this, the system would not know which invoice is paid.

Another option would be to automatically apply entries, but when a customer decides to skip a payment, the system might get confused, so it is highly recommended to apply entries manually.

When we post this journal and navigate the entries, we see that all necessary sub administrations are updated:

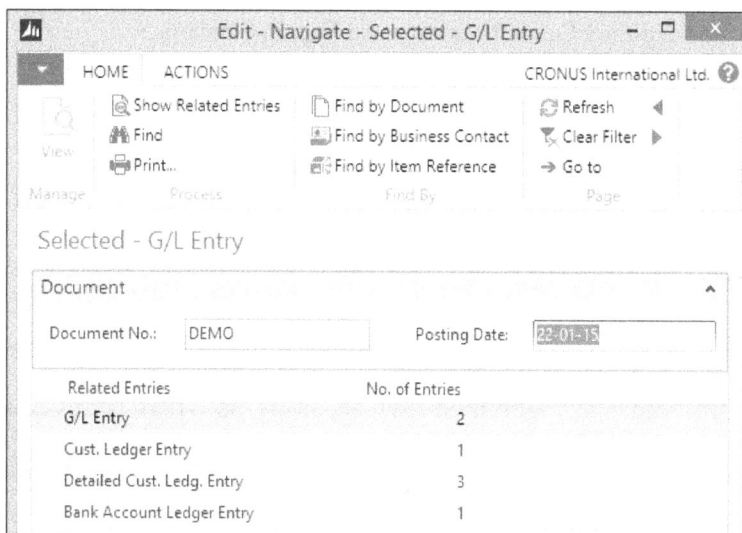

Posting groups

In the previous section, we talked about using customer numbers and bank account numbers as an account number in the general journal. The system can then figure out what G/L Account numbers to use. But how does that work?

This is done using the various posting group matrices. Most application parts that post to the general ledger have their own posting group table. There are two types of posting groups: single layer and matrix layer.

The single layer has direct G/L Account columns and the matrix layer has an additional setup table:

Single layer	Matrix layer
Customer posting group	Gen. business posting group
Vendor posting group	Gen. product posting group
Inventory posting group	VAT business posting group
Job posting group	VAT product posting group
Bank account posting group	Inventory posting setup
FA posting group	

> Each country uses different account schedules and regulations. The G/L Accounts in this book are used for the CRONUS example database. These can be different in each country and implementation.

Let's have a look at **Customer Posting Groups**:

Code	Receivabl...	Service C...	Payment ...	Payment ...	Interest A...	Additiona...	Invoice R...	Debit Cur...	Credit Cu...	Debit Rou...	Credit Ro...	Payment ...	Payment ...
DOMESTIC	2310	6810	9250	9255	9120	9120	9140	9150	9150	9150	9150	9260	9270
EU	2320	6810	9250	9255	9120	9120	9140	9150	9150	9150	9150	9260	9270
FOREIGN	2320	6810	9250	9255	9120	9120	9140	9150	9150	9150	9150	9260	9270

We see three different codes with their own accounts. So where is this code used? Let's open **Customer Card**:

On the **Invoicing** tab, we see the customer posting group. So this is what determines the customer G/L Accounts.

We also see other posting groups on **Customer Card**. There is a **Gen. Bus. Posting Group** and a **VAT Bus. Posting Group**.

In our list, they are matrix layers. So they don't directly point to a G/L Account. When we open **Gen. Bus. Posting Group**, we see this:

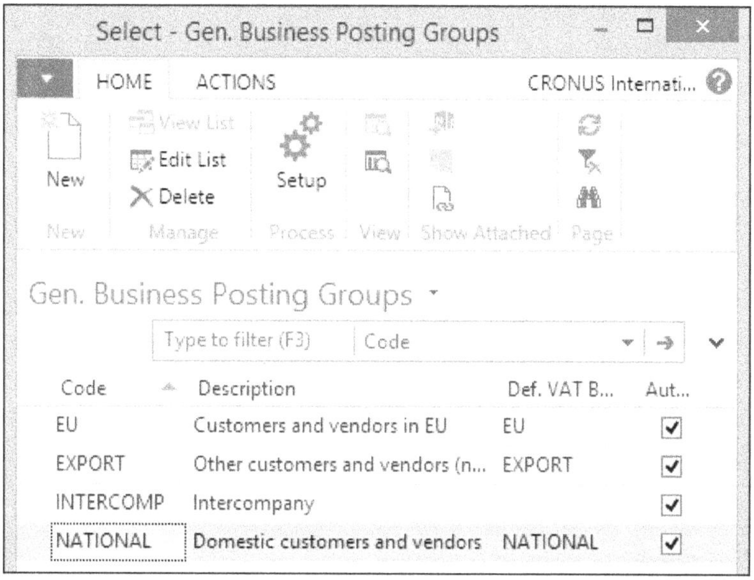

Just a simple table connecting it to a **Default VAT Business Posting Group**. To see where the G/L Accounts are defined, we need to go to the **General Posting Setup**.

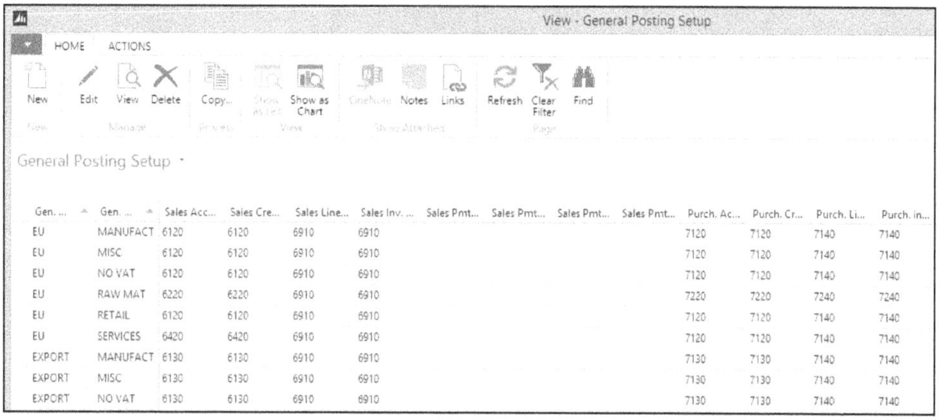

Here we can see that, when combined with a **Gen. Prod. Posting Group**, the G/L Accounts can be determined. So where does the **Gen. Prod. Posting Group** come from? To find out, we need to go to **Item Card**:

Here we can see the same tab, **Invoicing**, with the product posting groups.

Our journey ends here, as we can see the last matrix posting group, **Inventory**. When we open this setup, we see that it is determined by the combination of **Inventory Posting Group** and **Location Code**:

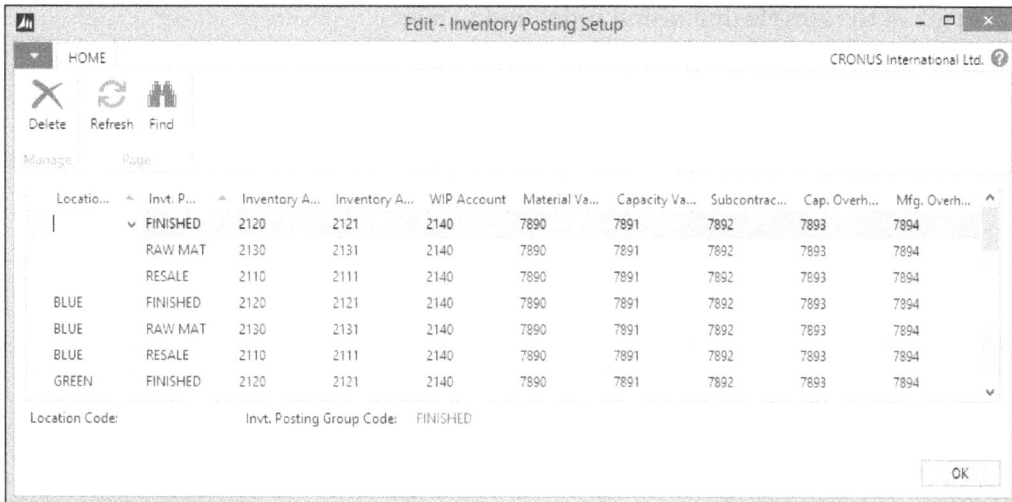

Locatio... ^	Invt. P... ^	Inventory A...	Inventory A...	WIP Account	Material Va...	Capacity Va...	Subcontrac...	Cap. Overh...	Mfg. Overh... ^
	⌄ FINISHED	2120	2121	2140	7890	7891	7892	7893	7894
	RAW MAT	2130	2131	2140	7890	7891	7892	7893	7894
	RESALE	2110	2111	2140	7890	7891	7892	7893	7894
BLUE	FINISHED	2120	2121	2140	7890	7891	7892	7893	7894
BLUE	RAW MAT	2130	2131	2140	7890	7991	7892	7893	7894
BLUE	RESALE	2110	2111	2140	7890	7891	7892	7893	7894
GREEN	FINISHED	2120	2121	2140	7890	7891	7892	7893	7894

Location Code: Invt. Posting Group Code: FINISHED

Dimensions

Apart from the general ledger and sub administrations, Microsoft Dynamics NAV allows a third level of posting. An unlimited number of dimensions can be attached to every posting and used to cross-analyze the system.

> Using more dimensions results in increased database activity during the processing of transactions and a more complex setup of the system. This should be carefully considered during the implementation.

Dimensions originated from the old project code and department code functionality, allowing you to consolidate or differentiate costs and profits. The dimensions are determined via a filtering mechanism. Every master data record can have dimension definitions.

Let's look at the sample dimension codes and values:

			Edit - Dimensions									— □

(screenshot of Microsoft Dynamics NAV "Edit - Dimensions" window)

Dimensions window — HOME ribbon with: New, Edit List, Delete, Map to IC Dim. with Same Code, Dimension Values, Account Type Default Dim., Translations, OneNote, Notes, Links, Refresh, Find. CRONUS International Ltd.

Code	Name	Code Caption	Filter Caption	Description	Bloc...
AREA	Area	Area Code	Area Filter		☐
BUSINESSGR...	Business Group	Businessgroup Code	Businessgroup Filter		☐
CUSTOMER...	Customer Group				
DEPARTMENT	Department				
PROJECT	Project				
PURCHASER	Purchaser				
SALESCAMP...	Sales campaign				
SALESPERSON	Salesperson				

Edit - Dimension Values - AREA · Area — HOME, ACTIONS

Dimension Values

Code	Name	Dimension ...	Totaling
10	**Europe**	Begin-Total	
20	**Europe North**	Begin-Total	
30	Europe North (EU)	Standard	
40	Europe North (Non EU)	Standard	
45	**Europe North, Total**	End-Total	20..45
50	Europe South	Standard	
55	**Europe, Total**	End-Total	10..55

The **Dimension Code Area** has several **Dimension Values**. Here, you can also have total records, just as in the general ledger.

When more than one master data record has the same dimension code with different values, it is able to set priorities. It is also possible to block combination of dimensions to be posted.

Dimensions are a powerful tool for analyzing data and structuring the system to avoid incorrect entries. However, it requires a lot of time and special skills to determine these combinations and maintain the setup.

We'll see more of dimensions as we discuss the reporting possibilities.

Budgeting

Microsoft Dynamics NAV allows budgeting as well. We can create our own budgeting codes. A budgeting code can be a year, or a department, or just some budget we want to try and throw away later.

Budgeting can be done on G/L Accounts but also on any dimension.

The decision of budgeting periods is very important. If you want to compare monthly budgets with real figures, it does not make sense to create a yearly budget. Most companies use monthly budgets. It is also most likely that we want to create budgets for income statement accounts, not for balance sheets.

Importing and exporting budgets to Excel is a very important feature. Here, we can easily copy and paste and, for example, automatically have the same values each month.

Creating budget entries

Budget entries are created by simply entering new amounts in the columns. In previous versions of Microsoft Dynamics NAV, a built-in mechanism would handle the creation of the entry based on deltas between the previous value and the newly entered value.

In Microsoft Dynamics NAV 2009, this was changed from the Role Tailored Client to C/AL Code. The matrix page object that handles the amount is Budget Matrix (9203). This page uses the Matrix Management Codeunit (9200) to simulate the classic built-in algorithms.

Accounting periods

While most companies have accounting periods from January 1 to December 31 divided into months, there can be exceptions to this.

This is supported by Microsoft Dynamics NAV and set up in **Accounting Periods**:

Starting Date	▲ Name	New Fiscal Year	Closed	Date Locked	Inventory Period Closed
1-1-2013	January	✓	✓	✓	☐
1-2-2013	February	☐	✓	✓	☐
1-3-2013	March	☐	✓	✓	☐
1-4-2013	April	☐	✓	✓	☐
1-5-2013	May	☐	✓	✓	☐
1-6-2013	June	☐	✓	✓	☐
1-7-2013	July	☐	✓	✓	☐
1-8-2013	August	☐	✓	✓	☐
1-9-2013	September	☐	✓	✓	☐
1-10-2013	October	☐	✓	✓	☐
1-11-2013	November	☐	✓	✓	☐
1-12-2013	December	☐	✓	✓	☐
1-1-2014	January	✓	☐	✓	☐
1-2-2014	February	☐	☐	☐	☐
1-3-2014	March	☐	☐	☐	☐

We are completely free to set up our own desired posting periods as long as there is a date algorithm.

Edit - Create Fiscal Year

ACTIONS CRON...

Clear
Filter
Page

Options ▲

Starting Date: 1-2-2016

No. of Periods: 12

Period Length: 1M

OK Cancel

A posting period should also be closed when appropriate. When closing a posting period, all Income Statement G/L Accounts are set to zero and the profit/loss is posted to a balance account.

Edit - Close Income Statement

ACTIONS CRONUS International Ltd.

Clear
Filter
Page

Options ▲

Fiscal Year Ending Date: 31-12-2014

Gen. Journal Template: GENERAL

Gen. Journal Batch: DEFAULT

Document No.: CLOSE2014

Retained Earnings Acc.: 9410

Posting Description: Close Income Statement

Close by

Business Unit Code: ☐

Dimensions: ...

Inventory Period Closed: ☐

OK Cancel

When we run this batch, a general journal is populated with the postings. It is not recommended to make changes here.

Closing dates

After closing the income statement, it is still possible to make transactions but with special posting dates called closing dates. When putting a C character in front of the posting date, the system will accept this as a special transaction and allow you to post it.

2013							Closing	2014
Jan.	Feb.	Mar.	...	Okt.	Nov.	Dec.	C31-12-2009	Jan.
Filter: 01-01-2013		..				31-12-2013		
01-01-2013		..					C31-12-2013	
01-01-2013		..						31-01-2014

When filtering on `01-01-2013..31-12-2013`, the system will not include the entries on the closing dates. Filtering on `01-01-2013..C31-12-2013` and `01-01-2013..31-01-2014` will include the entries on the closing dates.

Currencies

Besides having the possibility of the extra reporting currency, every transaction in Microsoft Dynamics NAV can have its own currency. The transaction is transformed into **Local Currency (LCY)** with the current currency exchange rates.

Handling currency is simple, as long as the exchange rates do not change. After that, it can get complex. The exchange rate can change as often as you want but with a maximum of one per day. Before you consider implementing a daily change of exchange rates, you should look at the consequences.

When you change the currency exchange rate, everything in the system gets adjusted, which can lead to a huge number of transactions in your system. Changing the currency exchange rate requires the following two steps:

1. Enter new values. In our case, the new **USD** rate in 2010 is **60**:

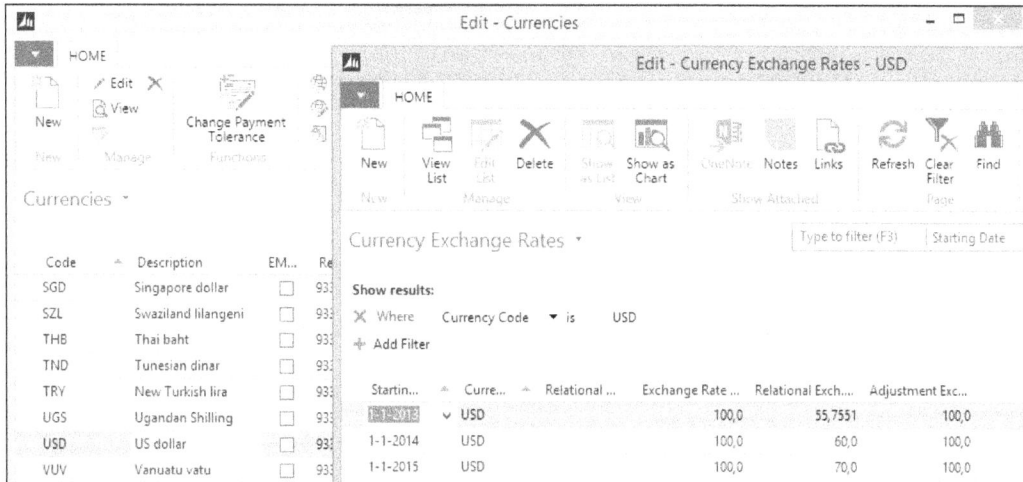

2. Implement the value and generate the entries.

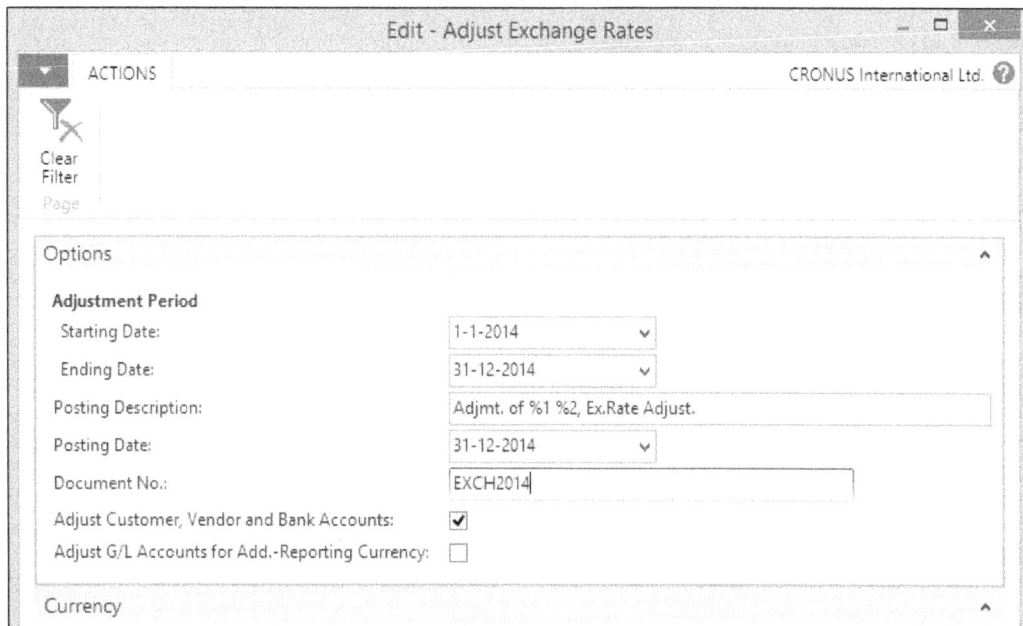

Consolidation

Consolidation means taking (part of) the general ledger of two or more companies together in one consolidated company. To handle consolidation in Microsoft Dynamics NAV, first the consolidation accounts have to be populated in the G/L Accounts. These consolidation accounts have to be valid accounts in the consolidation company.

A consolidation company is a "dummy" company in the database that just exists for consolidation purposes. The consolidation company has a business unit for each consolidated company.

The data can be exported out of the database via an XML or TXT format.

The data is imported via the **Business Unit** list in the consolidation company.

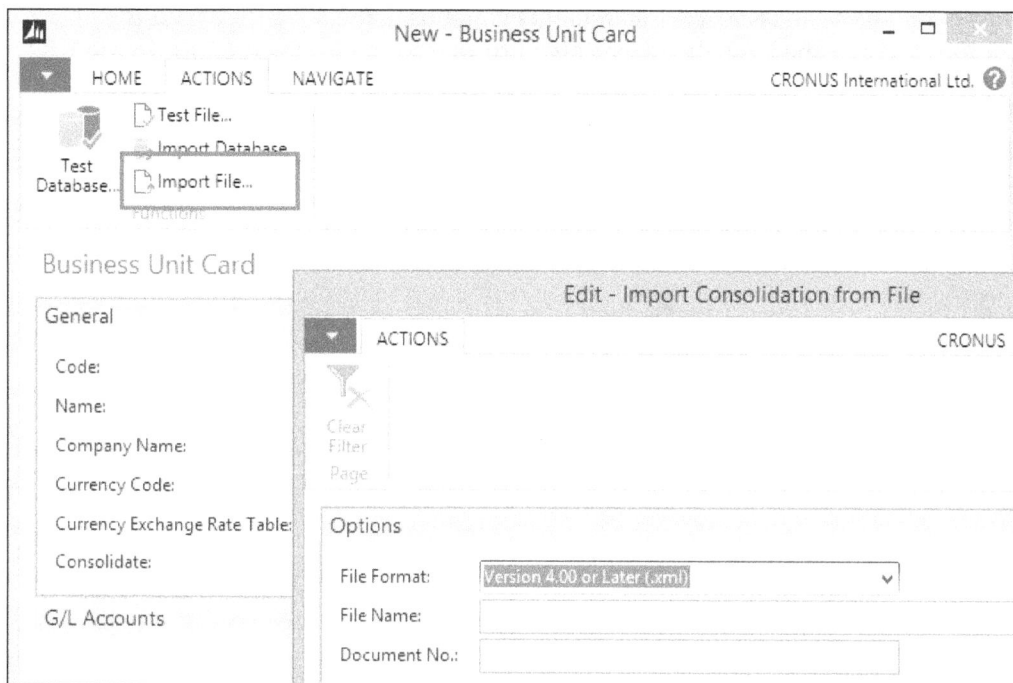

The other option is to import it from within the database with the **Import Database** function.

VAT statement

Most companies can issue VAT statements to get back the VAT they paid to vendors and pay the VAT they've received from customers. This is done in the VAT statement. This is a straightforward list where we can filter on the VAT entries.

Every country has its own VAT statement and many countries have localizations in this application area.

Data analysis

Some companies do bookkeeping because it is mandatory and do very little with the generated information, but there is a lot you can do with the information the system creates.

In bigger companies, using analysis tools is often the only way to get a clear view on the company's assets.

Chart of accounts

The chart of accounts is a reporting tool. The total accounts give a lot of information and by applying limit totals (flow filters), we can narrow down this information.

Chart of Accounts ▾

Show results:

✕ Where   No.   ▾ is   6000..

╪ Add Filter

Limit totals to:

✕ Where   Date Filter   ▾ is   01-01-14..31-12-14

✕ And   Department Filter ▾ is   PROD

╪ Add Filter

No. ▲	Name	Income/B...	Account ...	Totaling	Gen. Bus. ...	Net Change	Balance	Cost Typ...
8130	Repairs and Maintenance	Income St...	Posting		NATIONAL	70.704,92	70.704,92	8130
8190	**Total Bldg. Maint. Expenses**	Income St...	End-Total	8100..8190		89.276,11	89.276,11	
8200	**Administrative Expenses**	Income St...	Begin-Total					
8210	Office Supplies	Income St...	Posting		NATIONAL	19.520,94	19.520,94	8210
8230	Phone and Fax	Income St...	Posting		NATIONAL	2.279,80	2.279,80	8230
8240	Postage	Income St...	Posting		NATIONAL	1.148,92	1.148,92	8240
8290	**Total Administrative Expenses**	Income St...	End-Total	8200..8290		22.949,66	22.949,66	
8300	**Computer Expenses**	Income St...	Begin-Total					
8310	Software	Income St...	Posting		NATIONAL	13.252,52	13.252,52	8310

This example filters on G/L Account no. larger than or equal to 6000 and limits totals to 2014 and Department PROD.

> You can save these views by clicking on the page name **Chart of Accounts** and then **Save View As**. By choosing a name that makes sense like Income Statement 2010 Production, it is easy to find.

Account schedules

For advanced reporting requirements, we can use the account schedules. Like the VAT statement, it allows us to filter on the G/L Entries in this case. We can filter on individual G/L Accounts or use the total filter. If the filter gets complex, we can sum individual rows and hide the source rows. We can also apply up to four dimensions to each account schedule.

The account schedules also let you define your column layout. You can use multiple column layouts per schedule and reuse **Column Layouts** across other schedules.

The column layout can contain formulas and date filters. We can show either the budget or G/L Entries per column.

For very valuable information on how to use account schedules, refer to `http://dynamicsnavfinancials.com/`

Analysis by dimensions

As discussed earlier in this chapter, Microsoft Dynamics NAV allows an unlimited number of dimensions to be posted in the general ledger. To analyze this information, we need to tell the system what to compare. This is done in analysis by dimensions.

Each analysis view gets a unique code. An analysis view can be generated for an ad hoc requirement and thrown away afterwards or be in the system permanently for periodical reporting. Analysis views generate redundant information that can always be discarded and regenerated.

It is recommended to use a copy of the database on a separate system to use with analysis views and to update them during the night.

When updated, the analysis view contains all data within the filters in the analysis view entries. When not properly maintained, this can be a gigantic table with data.

The result of an analysis view can be viewed in a matrix where all values can be used as rows, columns, and filters.

In this example, we view the results of a sales campaign per area and sales person.

The setup

Financial management has a single general ledger setup table, which is important as many of these setup fields will determine how the core of Microsoft Dynamics NAV behaves.

We will discuss the setup options to find out what they do and to explore the possibilities of creating a flexible setup for an application:

- **Allow Posting From** and **Allow Posting To**: These limit the freedom of people to choose posting dates while posting to the general ledger. It is highly recommended to enable this feature to avoid posting dates like 01012090 instead of 01012009.

- **Register Time**: This allows you to create an entry in the time register each time a user logs in and out.

- **Local Address Format** and **Local Cont. Addr. Format**: This refers to how the address should be printed for the local country. In Microsoft Dynamics NAV, it is best practice to leave **Country Code** and **Currency Code** blank for local values.

- **Inv. Rounding Precision (LCY)** and **Inv. Rounding Type (LCY)**: These define how the rounding on your invoices is calculated. **Nearest** is a best practice and allows your customers to easily register your invoice in their system.

- **Allow G/L Acc Deletion Before**: This allows you to clean up closed fiscal years. It is hardly ever used and you should consult your partner before using this feature.

- **Check G/L Account Usage**: This checks whether the G/L Account is used in setup tables before it is deleted.

- **EMU Currency**: This is the currency that has a fixed conversion rate to the Euro in the European Union. The **LCY Code** field is used when printing reports to indicate the companies' local currency.

- **Pmt. Disc. Excl. VAT**: This indicates whether or not VAT is calculated when you apply payment discounts. When you check this field, you need to think about the **Adjust for Payment Disc.** field, as this will recalculate the VAT.

- **Unrealized VAT**: This should only be checked if your company has to deal with this issue. Otherwise, it will lead to unnecessary postings. This is VAT that is only valid when the customer pays the invoice rather than when the invoice is issued.

- **Prepayment Unrealized VAT**: This should only be checked if your company handles **Unrealized VAT** and if you want to implement this for the prepayment features.

- **Max. VAT Difference Allowed**: This field determines the maximum amount of VAT differences. Most of the time, the VAT difference will be not more than 0, 01.

> You can post VAT differences by selecting **FULL VAT** in the **VAT Calculation Type** for the VAT business posting group.

- **VAT Rounding Type**: This determines how the VAT remainder is calculated. It recommended **Nearest**.

- **Bill-to/Sell-to VAT Calc.**: This allows you to change what the source for the VAT business posting group is, whether it is the Bill-to Customer or Sell-to Customer and Pay-to Vendor or Buy-from Vendor.

- **Print VAT specification**: This field allows VAT on your invoices to always be in your local currency.

- **Bank Account Nos.**: This is almost always number series that is manually determined. Most companies have up to 10 bank accounts.

- **Global Dimensions**: This determines which dimensions are posted directly to the G/L Entries and sub administrations. These you can most often use when limiting totals and should be considered carefully.

- **Shortcut Dimensions**: These are easier to access when you enter journals and documents. They can easily be switched later.

- **Additional Reporting Currency**: This is a useful feature for international companies. Remember that it requires extra effort if the exchange rates change. You can change this later but a batch job will start, which might take a long time if you have a large database.

- **VAT Exchange Rate Adjustment**: This makes it possible to recalculate VAT if the reporting currency exchange rates changes. Think about this thoroughly before you activate it. It is most likely to generate information that is difficult to analyze and use.

- **Appln Rounding Precision**: This can be used to allow rounding differences when applying different currencies.

- **Pmt. Disc. Tolerance Warning**: This field when checked, a warning will appear whenever a difference is posted.

- **Pmt. Disc. Tolerance Posting**: This determines if the payment tolerance amount is posted to a special account or to the normal discount account.

- **Payment Discount Grace Period**: This can be used whether you want to be tolerant when people are one or two days late with their payment and still deduct the discount amount.

- **Payment Tolerance Warning**: This option will show a warning whenever there is a tolerance amount posted to the general ledger.

- **Payment Tolerance Posting**: This determines if a special G/L Account is used to post this amount.

- **Payment Tolerance %**: This determines the tolerance percentage. To change this, a batch function is used that updates open entries.

- **Max. Payment Tolerance Amount**: This field sets a maximum value to the amount so an invoice that is issued for 100.000 cannot have a tolerance amount of more than 5.000 if the percentage is set to 5 percent.

Customizing financial management

As financial management is regulated by the government and the standard functionality is already very complete, this application area is unlikely to have many changes, even though we have some examples of where the functionality is changed.

> The examples in this chapter are included in the objects we used in *Chapter 2, A Sample Application*.

Sales line description to G/L Entries

When we post a sales invoice, the system will generate the G/L Entries based on the sales lines. To avoid creating too many entries, they are compacted. This is done using a buffer table, the Invoice Post. Buffer:

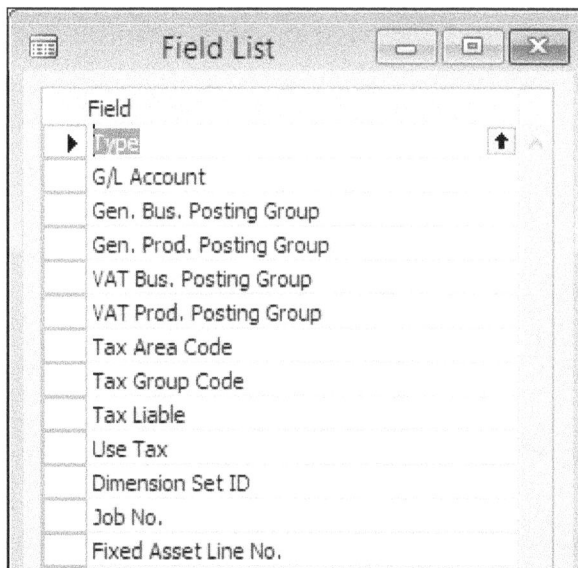

Only for the combination of the preceding listed fields, a G/L Entry record is created. As we can see, the description is not one of these. This results in G/L Entries with the posting description of the sales header, which is often confusing for accountants when looking at the G/L Entries.

As an example, we will generate a sales invoice with one G/L Account line selling one of these books.

When we post this invoice, we will get these G/L Entries. Note that the description has gone.

To change this behavior, we have to change the **Invoice Post. Buffer** table. The description field needs to be part of the unique combination since the grouping is done using a `FIND` command in the `UpdInvPostingBuffer` function in `Sales-Post Codeunit (80)`:

```
UpdInvPostingBuffer()
...
InvPostingBuffer[2] := InvPostingBuffer[1];
IF InvPostingBuffer[2].FIND THEN BEGIN
  InvPostingBuffer[2].Amount :=
    InvPostingBuffer[2].Amount + InvPostingBuffer[1].Amount;
  ...
  InvPostingBuffer[2].MODIFY;
END ELSE
  InvPostingBuffer[1].INSERT;
```

This requires the following two steps:

1. We need to add the description field to the table.

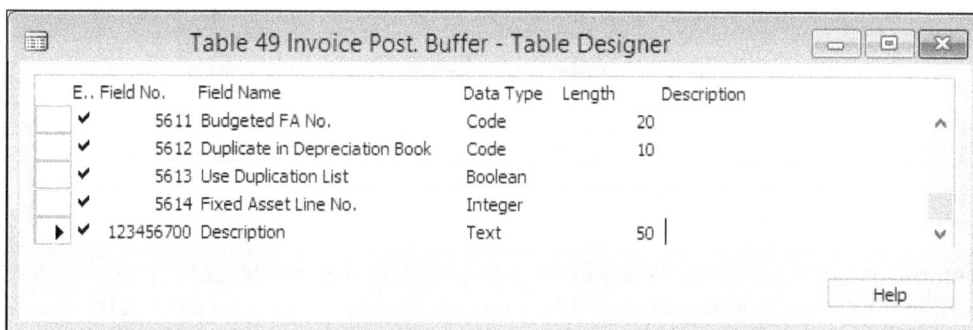

E..	Field No.	Field Name	Data Type	Length	Description
✔	5611	Budgeted FA No.	Code	20	
✔	5612	Duplicate in Depreciation Book	Code	10	
✔	5613	Use Duplication List	Boolean		
✔	5614	Fixed Asset Line No.	Integer		
✔	123456700	Description	Text	50	

2. We need to add this new field to the key.

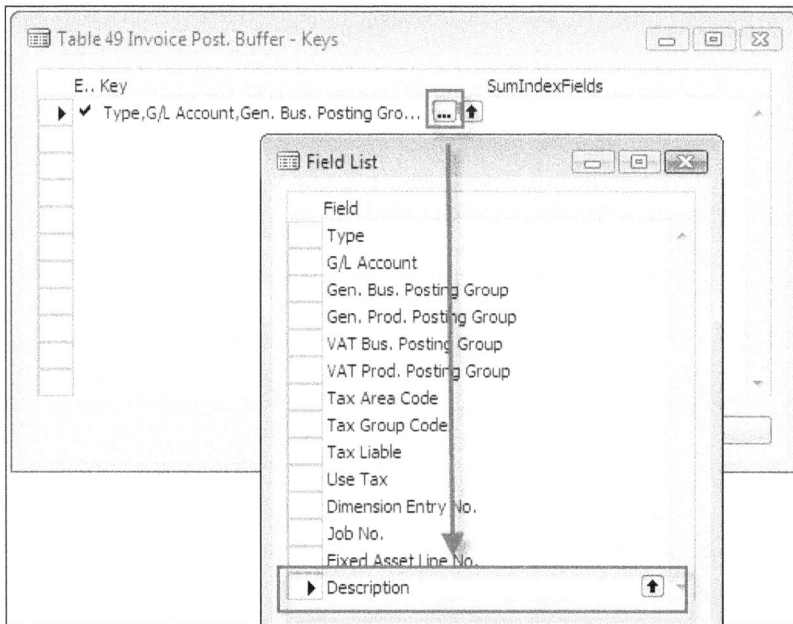

> A key in Microsoft Dynamics NAV can only contain 252 bytes, so be careful not to add too many fields to this table.

When this is done, a change is required in populating the buffer table. This is done in the `PrepareSales` function in the table `Invoice Post. Buffer (49)` itself:

```
PrepareSales()
CLEAR(Rec);
Type := SalesLine.Type;
"System-Created Entry" := TRUE;
...
"Job No." := SalesLine."Job No.";
"VAT %" := SalesLine."VAT %";
"VAT Difference" := SalesLine."VAT Difference";
//* Description >>>
Description := SalesLine.Description;
//* Description <<<
IF Type = Type::"Fixed Asset" THEN BEGIN
  ...
END;
```

The last change we are going to make is in the posting routine of the sales documents. This is the Sales-Post codeunit (80) we discussed in *Chapter 2, A Sample Application*:

```
IF Invoice THEN BEGIN
  // Post sales and VAT to G/L entries from posting buffer
  LineCount := 0;
  IF InvPostingBuffer[1].FIND('+') THEN
    REPEAT
      LineCount := LineCount + 1;
      Window.UPDATE(3,LineCount);

      GenJnlLine.INIT;
      GenJnlLine."Posting Date" := "Posting Date";
      GenJnlLine."Document Date" := "Document Date";
//* Posting Description now from buffer table >>>
//      GenJnlLine.Description := "Posting Description";
      GenJnlLine.Description :=
        InvPostingBuffer[1].Description;
//* Posting Description <<<
      GenJnlLine."Reason Code" := "Reason Code";
```

Instead of the posting description of the sales header, we will now use the new field in the buffer table. When we post the same invoice again, this is the changed result:

This makes it a lot easier to read the general ledger.

> Making this change might cause our system to create more G/L Entries if we have large invoices with different descriptions. Creating extra G/L Entries takes more time during a posting routine, resulting in longer running posting transactions and a larger database.

Extra fields in the G/L Entries

Although the G/L Entry table has a lot of information, some companies want to add extra fields to it and populate these in the posting process.

For this example, we will use the database with the squash court application from *Chapter 2, A Sample Application*. For this business, it might be very useful to have the **Squash Court No.** as a field in the G/L Entries to analyze.

The first step is to add the field to the G/L Entry table and make sure we have a table relation with the source table.

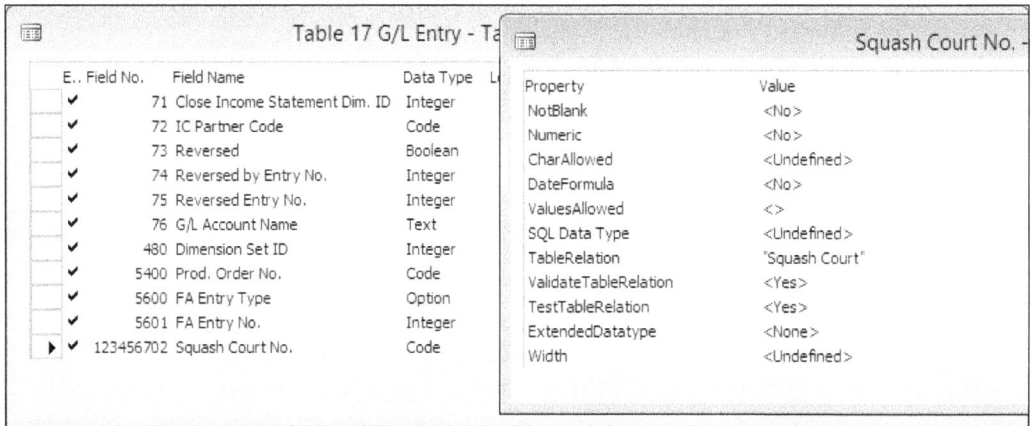

We have learned that the G/L Entries are generated from the general journal so we need to add this field there as well. This can be done with copy and paste.

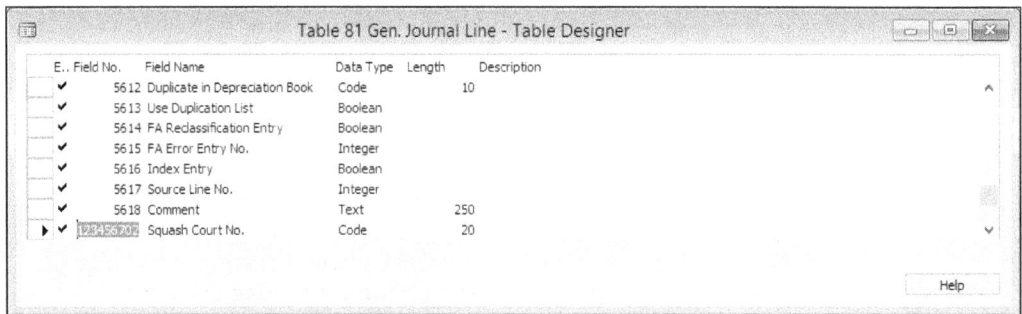

The last step is to make sure we move the information from the journal to the ledger entry table. Like in our sample squash application, this is done in the Gen. Jnl.-Post Line Codeunit (12) only this codeunit has much more code.

We need to find the place where the G/L Entries are created and add our field there. This is done in the `InitGLEntry` function, as follows:

```
InitGLEntry()

...

GLEntry.INIT;
GLEntry."Posting Date" := GenJnlLine."Posting Date";
GLEntry."Document Date" := GenJnlLine."Document Date";
GLEntry."Document Type" := GenJnlLine."Document Type";
GLEntry."Document No." := GenJnlLine."Document No.";

...
GLEntry."Source Code" := GenJnlLine."Source Code";
//* Squash App. >>>
GLEntry."Squash Court No." := GenJnlLine."Squash Court No.";
//* Squash App. <<<
IF GenJnlLine."Account Type" = ...
```

This is all that is required in Microsoft Dynamics NAV to add a field to the financial posting process. Of course, it does not make sense to do this unless we use it, so a logical next step could be to add this new field to the Invoice Post. Buffer table from our previous example.

This shows how easy it is to combine solutions in Microsoft Dynamics NAV.

Integrating with financial management

Although it is not likely to make big changes in financial management, it might be necessary to create G/L Entries in a new posting routine.

In the previous chapter, we already pointed out briefly that during posting transactions in Microsoft Dynamics NAV, the actual journal line records are never really inserted in the database. They are used as temporary containers to hold the data during posting. Doing an actual `INSERT` would require defining a journal template name, journal batch name, and line no. and could cause locking in the database.

Let's create a new codeunit that will create a G/L transaction.

Creating a G/L transaction

After creating the codeunit, we need to set up the two variables that are the minimum requirement to post something to the general ledger.

The preceding screenshot shows two variables:

- **GenJnlLine**: This is a reference to the `General Journal Line table (81)`.

- **GenJnlPostLine**: The `Gen. Jnl.-Post Line Codeunit (12)` creates the G/L Entries, the register, and the other financial entries.

The C/AL code

Creating a new G/L Entry requires some of mandatory fields. All the other fields in the general journal line are either optional for basic entries or mandatory in combination with more advanced postings, as we will find out later.

We will start by writing this code to the `OnRun` trigger, as follows:

```
OnRun()
GenJnlLine.INIT;
GenJnlLine."Posting Date" := WORKDATE;
GenJnlLine.Description := 'Test Entry';
GenJnlLine."Document No." := 'PACKT';
GenJnlLine."Account No." := '6120';
GenJnlLine.Amount := 100;
GenJnlPostLine.RunWithCheck(GenJnlLine);
```

If we execute this C/AL code, we will receive the following error message, which indicates that our transaction will result in an unbalanced chart of accounts:

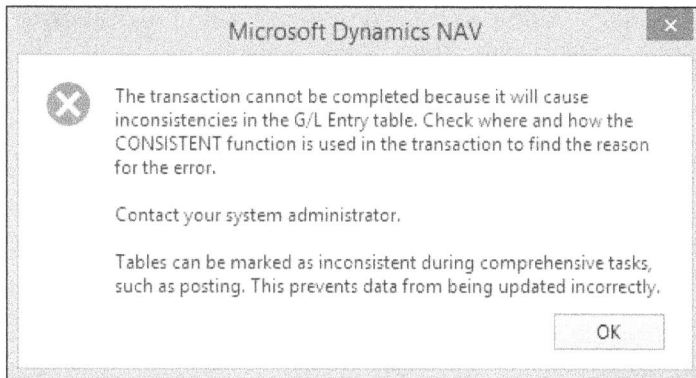

We can fix this by creating a balance transaction for `-100` in the same `OnRun` trigger, as follows:

```
GenJnlLine.INIT;
GenJnlLine."Posting Date" := WORKDATE;
GenJnlLine.Description := 'Test Entry';
GenJnlLine."Document No." := 'PACKT';
GenJnlLine."Account No." := '6120';
GenJnlLine.Amount := -100;
GenJnlPostLine.RunWithCheck(GenJnlLine, TempJnlLineDim);
```

After executing the codeunit, we can navigate on our document no. to see the G/L Entries we created:

This was a very simple example of how to integrate with financial management; let's create a more advanced example.

Advanced entries

We will create a new customer ledger entry with dimensions. To do this, we should change one of the C/AL parts we created to the following code:

```
GenJnlLine.INIT;
GenJnlLine."Posting Date" := WORKDATE;
GenJnlLine.Description := 'Test Entry';
GenJnlLine."Document No." := 'PACKT2';
GenJnlLine."Account Type" := GenJnlLine."Account Type"::Customer;
GenJnlLine."Account No." := '10000';
GenJnlLine.Amount := 100;
GenJnlPostLine.RunWithCheck(GenJnlLine);
```

But when we execute this C/AL code, we receive the following error message:

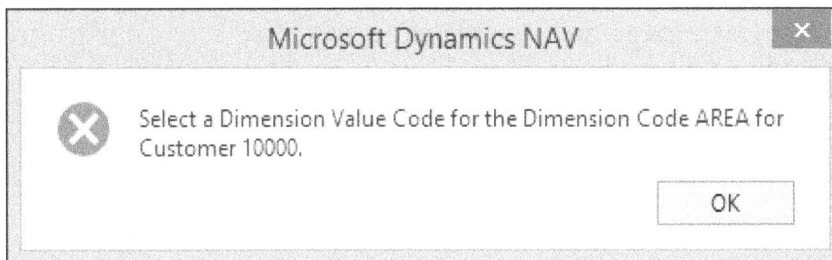

This means we need to implement dimensions. Let's add the following C/AL code to the routine:

```
...
GenJnlLine.Amount := 100;
GenJnlLine."Dimension Set ID" := 3;
GenJnlPostLine.RunWithCheck(GenJnlLine, TempJnlLineDim);
```

This will use dimension set entry 3, which contains the dimensions that are required for this transaction.

> This article on MSDN at http://msdn.microsoft.com/en-us/library/jj552498(v=nav.71).aspx explains how dimension sets are used in the Microsoft Dynamics NAV 2013 architecture.

Now, when we navigate on **PACKT**, we see that the system has created a **Customer Ledger** entry and a **Detailed Cust. Ledg. Entry**.

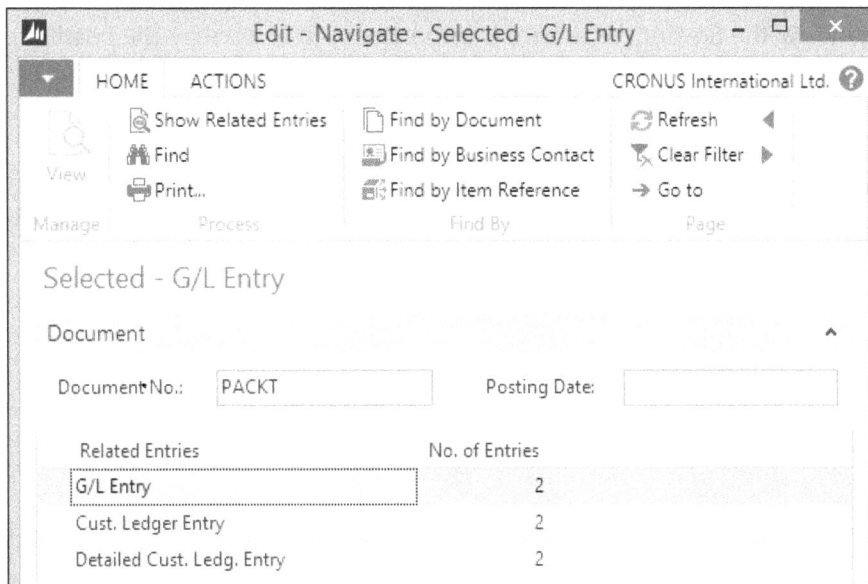

Look, learn, and love

In Microsoft Dynamics NAV, there are many examples of how to integrate with financial management. The following is a list of interesting codeunits that create general journal lines:

- Sales-Post (80)
- Purch.-Post (90)
- Job Calculate WIP (1000)
- CheckManagement (367)
- Sales-Post Prepayments (442)
- Inventory Posting To G/L (5802)
- Serv-Posting Journals Mgt. (5987)

Go ahead and have a look inside these codeunits to learn how Microsoft does the integration.

Summary

In this chapter, we looked at the financial heart of Microsoft Dynamics NAV. Understanding the flow of the entries is important as it is the way the posting groups are set up. It is important to regularly check whether the sub administrations are balanced with the general ledger.

The reporting possibilities offer great insight if the system is set up correctly. Be careful with changing the setup options on a running system.

In the next chapter, we will look at the opposite of this module; relationship management. While the financial management system is strict, relationship management system is flexible and expandable.

4
Relationship Management

Relationship management software is typically a result of what ERP applications have achieved.

In earlier days, everyone had a rolodex on their desk with phone numbers and addresses and salespeople would always know by heart who was a good customer and which customers were always late paying or had bad margins.

The introduction of RM software completely changed that, allowing us to maintain all companies' contacts in a single place and analyze sales data very easily.

Relationship management has been part of Microsoft Dynamics since Version 2.0 and was dramatically changed and improved in Version 3.0. The current Microsoft Dynamics NAV RM software is mostly the same as in that version, except for the Microsoft Outlook integration that keeps changing in every version.

In this chapter, we will deep dive into this module, which is very complete. After reading this chapter, you will have a good understanding of the concepts and how to maintain master data and analyze transaction data.

We will also perform some application changes in the relationship management part.

How companies work

In traditional accounting software, we differentiate customers and vendors as business relations for invoices, but companies have many more relations we would like to register in our system.

Also, a company or person can have multiple relations with our company. The best example is my relationship with Microsoft. As everyone, I use the software so I am a customer, both in my business and personal life. On the other hand, Microsoft hires me to teach workshops and do presentations, which makes me a vendor. As an MVP, I have a totally different relationship with them. They give me an award and invite me to special events and allow me to access the company store. They also ask for my advice in future versions, so to them, I am their consultant.

So one person or company can have different roles in RM. Microsoft Dynamics NAV is able to handle all that while maintaining a single point of data entry and maintenance.

Unlike financial applications, RM is much more flexible. The functionality and rules of financial applications are defined by government regulations and are mandatory for companies to comply with. Companies are not forced to use RM but once implemented, everyone understands the benefits and never want to do without it.

Contacts

The starting point of the RM application is the **Contact** table. This is where we store the address, phone numbers, e-mail addresses, and so on of everyone we know.

When we open the **Contact list**, we see that companies and persons are grouped for an easy overview.

No.	Name	Phone No.	Salespers...	Territory ...	Search N...
CT000136	Blanemark Hifi Shop		JR		BLANEMA...
CT000114	Boybridge Tool Mart		RL	FOREIGN	BOYBRIDG...
CT100141	John Tippett		RL	LND	JOHN TIPP...
CT000117	Busterby Stole og Borde A/S		RL	FOREIGN	BUSTERBY ...
CT000041	BYT-KOMPLET s.r.o.		JR	FOREIGN	BYT-KOM...
CT000004	Candoxy Canada Inc.		JR	FOREIGN	CANDOXY...
CT000050	Candoxy Kontor A/S		JR	FOREIGN	CANDOXY...
CT100232	Ingelise Lang		JR	FOREIGN	INGELISE L...
CT000021	Candoxy Nederland BV		JR	FOREIGN	CANDOXY...
CT100239	Cane Showroom		DC	S	CANE SHO...
CT100125	Andrew Lan		DC	S	ANDREW L...
CT100188	Jane Clayton		DC	S	JANE CLA...
CT100187	Scott Bishop		DC	S	SCOTT BIS...

The cut-off text is not important for reference in this screenshot

As we learned in the previous chapters, a page in Microsoft Dynamics NAV is based on a single table, so that must mean that companies and persons are stored in the same table.

When we open the contact card, we can clearly see that this is the case. The **Type** field indicates whether the contact is a business or a person and whether the person belongs to a company. The **Company No.** field refers to a contact with type **Company**. This is a one-to-many relationship meaning that if a physical person has a relationship with more than one company, he or she needs to be maintained for each company with a relation.

The following screenshot is from the contact card in Microsoft Dynamics NAV:

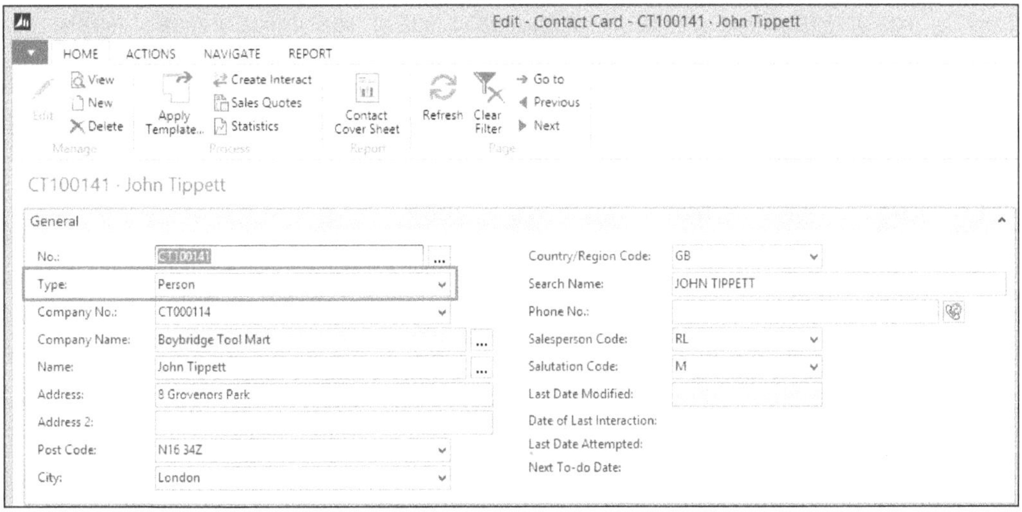

Let's step through the tabs and look at some important fields:

- **No.:** This is a unique key value determined by a Number Series. Companies and persons have the same numbering.

- **Type**: This indicates whether this contact is a person or a company.

- **Company Name**: When the contact is a person and connected to a company, it is automatically populated with that company's name.

- **Name**: This is the name of the contact. If the contact is a person, we can click on the **AssistEdit** button next to the name to open the name details. The name is automatically broken down in to first, middle, and last name depending on the number of words we enter. However, if our contact has a more complex name like "Walter van den Broek", which is typical for Dutch people, the system is unable to break it down.

- **Address**: Enter the street where the contact lives or has an office.

> It is always best practice to enter the postal address here since this will be used on all documents. For a visiting address, use the **Alternative Address** feature.

- **Post Code & City**: These fields are connected via the **Post Code** table and one can populate the other if that table is maintained, which is an optional feature.

> Most companies maintain the **Post Code** table for their country and manually enter the post codes for foreign countries. Most countries offer a post code/city list for sale or as a web service, which will speed up data entry and keep people from entering the wrong master data.

- **Search Name**: This is automatically populated with the **Name** field and lets you search for contacts faster, as you can enter this field instead of the **No.** field when referencing to a contact.

- **(Mobile) Phone, Fax**, and **Telex No.**: This is a reference to the phone and fax numbers of this company. The (mobile) phone field also allows you to start an interaction with this contact.

- **Sales Person**: This is the main salesperson for this contact. If this contact is promoted to a customer, the salespersons' name will be printed on the order form and invoices.

- **Salutation Code**: This special field refers to how this contact should be addressed. The salutation code table allows you to build phrases such as "Dear Mrs. Brown". We'll see more about salutation codes in segments.

- **E-Mail**: This field contains the e-mail address of the contact. By pressing the **E-Mail** button [ ], we can send an e-mail directly.

- **Homepage**: Here is where the URL of the contacts website goes. We can access the website by clicking on the **URL** button [ ].

- **Correspondence Type**: This field is used when we create a Microsoft Word document in an interaction. It indicates whether we send a hardcopy, e-mail, or fax.

- **Currency Code & VAT Registration No.**: When this contact is promoted to a customer or vendor, the currency code and VAT registration no. are inherited from here.

- **Territory Code**: This field can be used in segments to filter on geographic regions.

Salutation codes

When we perform mail merge, we want the letters to start nicely with "Dear Harry" or dear "Mrs. Brown". This can be done using salutation codes.

We can create as many codes as we like but a contact can only use one. This is the list in the CRONUS demo database.

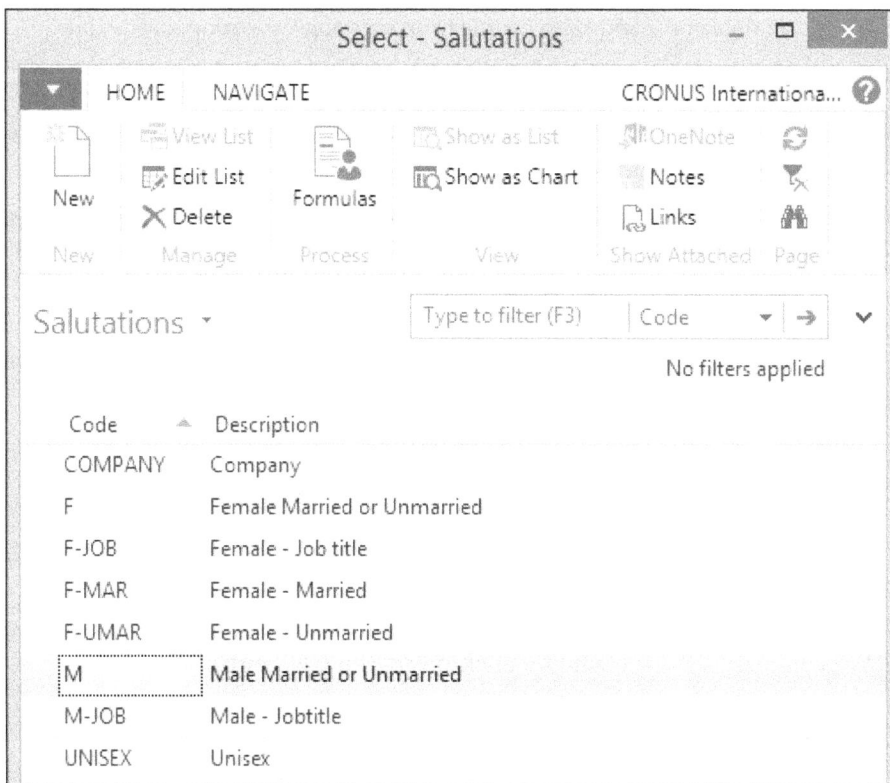

There is one salutation code for companies but most are for persons. When we look at the formulas for **Female Married** or **Unmarried**, we see this screen:

We can enter a formal and informal code. The salutation can have up to five variables pointing to **Job Title**, **First Name**, **Middle Name**, **Surname**, **Initials**, and **Company Name**.

When we look at the result for Karen Friske, it will be "Dear Ms. Karen Friske" or "Hi Karen".

At the end of this chapter, we will look at how to create extra salutation types.

Alternative addresses

Like we said earlier in this chapter, it is best practice to use the address fields in the contact table for the postal address since this will be printed on all documents.

In the **Contact Alt. Address Card** table, we can add as many other addresses to a contact as we want.

Although the codes are not related to anything, it is best practice to have a rule here. Always use the same code for home or office addresses. We can later use this when printing labels or segments.

An alternative address can also have a valid to and valid end date to control which alternative address is currently active.

Relationships with customer and vendor

In *Chapter 2, A Sample Application*, you saw that the contact table is the umbrella data of the customer, vendor, and bank account master data tables.

Each contact of the type **Company** can be promoted as one of these tables. The benefit is that all address information fields have a single place of maintenance and are inherited. It also allows us to analyze sales data into relationship management as we will see later in this chapter when discussing segments.

When we create master data, a different Number Series is used. At the end of this chapter, we will look at how to change that in the code.

A contact of **Type: Person** cannot be created as the **Customer**, **Vendor**, or **Bank Account**.

Duplicates

When entering new contacts, the system can search for duplicate contacts. In the Duplicate Search String Setup table, we can enable the filtering on eight fields: **Name**, **Name2**, **Address**, **Address2**, **Post Code**, **City**, **Phone No.**, and **VAT Registration No.**

For each field, we can set up which part should be used when searching for a duplicate. We can use the option **First** and **Last** and a length, which is useful for the **Name**, **Address**, and **City** fields. Using **First** with the full length of the field will search for an exact match, which is useful for **Post Code**, **Phone No.**, and **VAT Registration No.**

In the **Marketing Setup** table, we can specify the percentage of matching criteria that should result in a warning, as shown in the following screenshot:

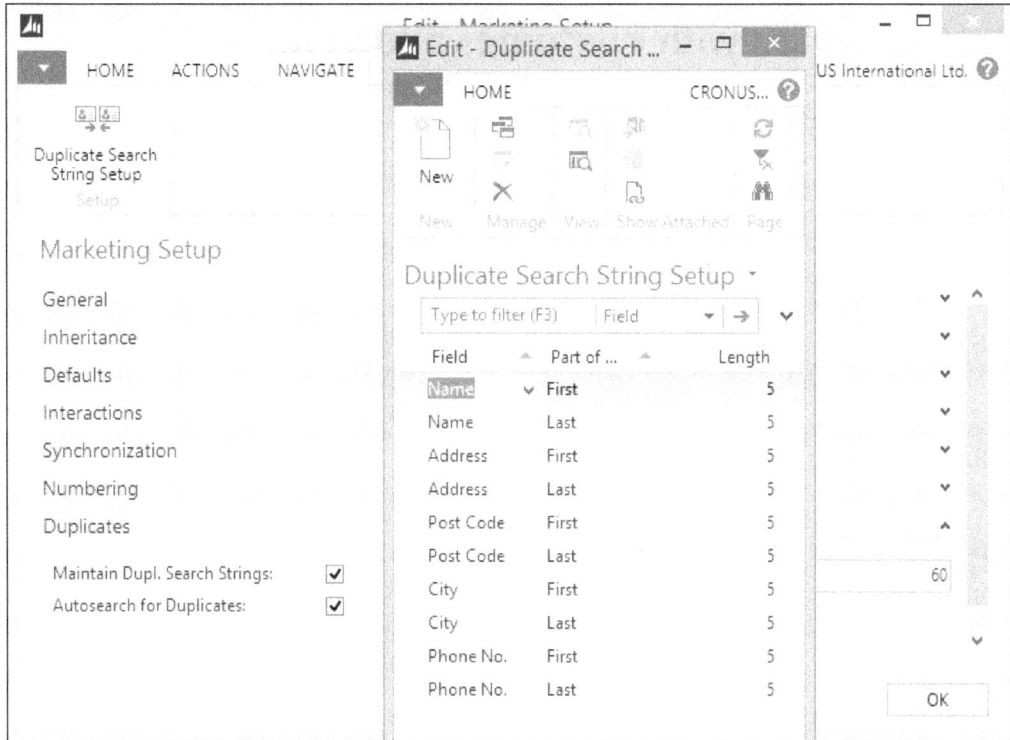

For each contact, the system will save these values in Cont. Duplicate Search String table (5086).

When we enter a new contact, the system will also generate the same strings and compare these to the ones in the database. When there is a match, the system will show a warning with the duplicate contacts.

Profiles

The contact table has a very limited number of fields and does not allow much creativity for us to add flexible information. This is where profiles are used.

Profiles allow the users to create an unlimited number of extra information sources that can be manually or automatically populated.

Let's have a look at an example profile:

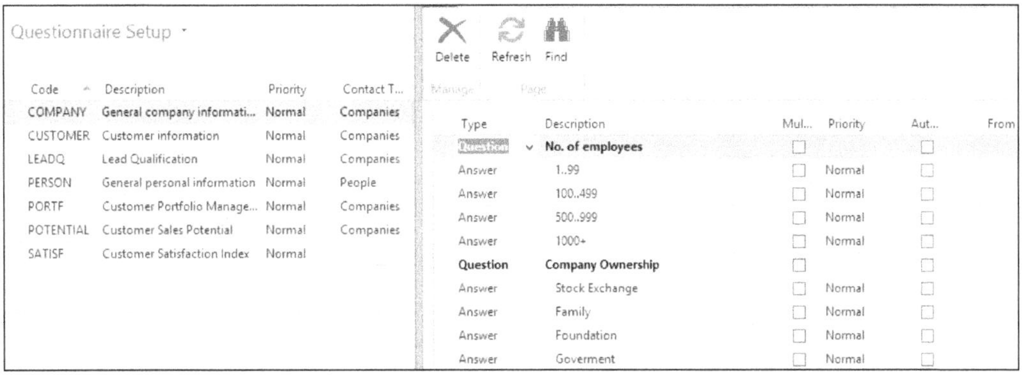

This profile is for contacts of type **Company**. It has **Question** and **Answer** lines.
A question can have one or multiple answers and we can define as many questions
and answers as we want. The last column shows how many contacts have this
profile answer.

A profile is used from the **Contact Card**.

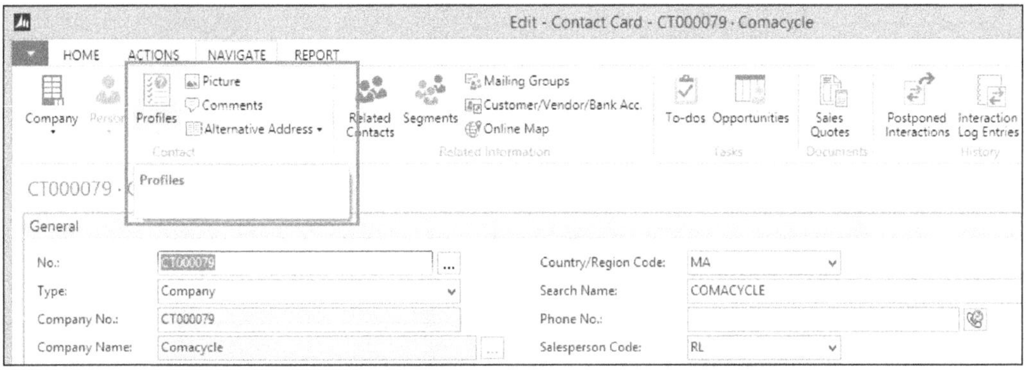

When we click on this, a new page opens where we can select the required profile and answer the questions.

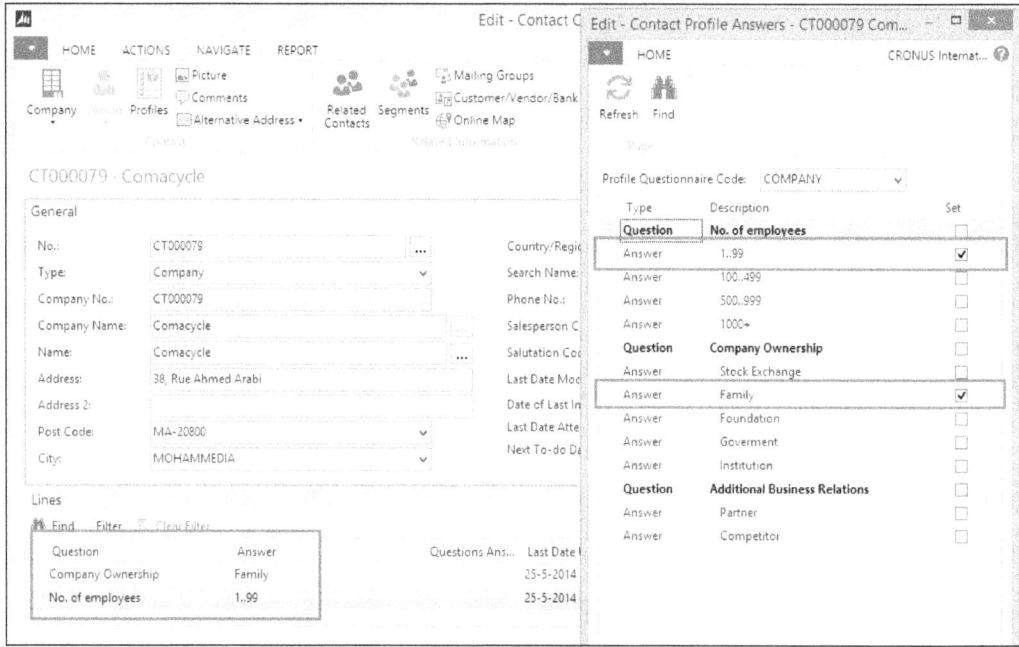

The answers are displayed in the **Lines** subpage of the **Contact Card** window.

Automatic profiles

Profiles can also be automatically answered based on formulas. This is done using the **Auto Contact Classification** option and setting up the **Question Details**.

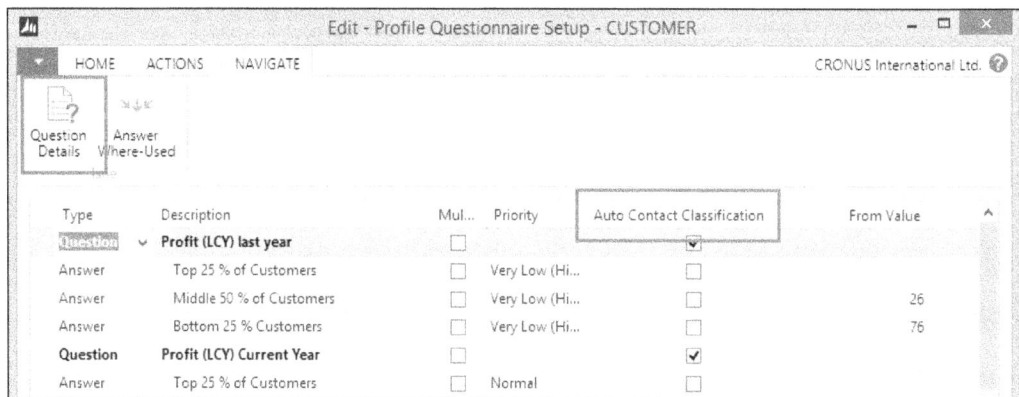

The **Profile Question Details** are fixed and hardcoded. They depend on the relationship between a contact and a customer or vendor as discussed earlier in this chapter.

We will not describe all the possibilities as this is very well covered in the online help.

When the questions are set up, the answers should have a **From Value** and **To Value** to allow the system to pick the right one.

To generate the answers, a batch job is used called **Update Contact Classification** where we can filter on a profile.

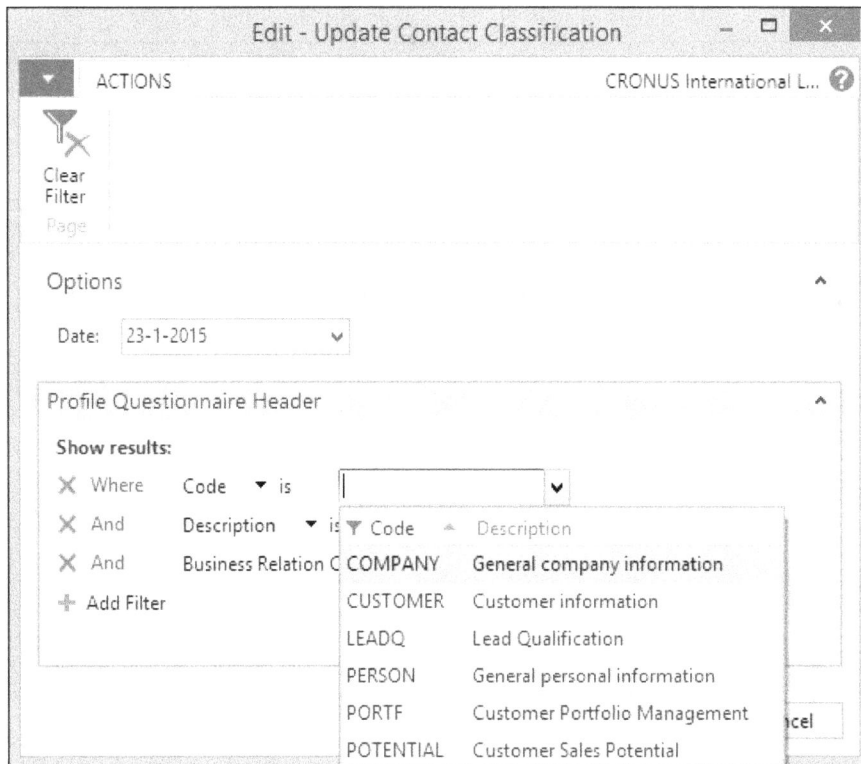

Interactions

We have all kinds of interaction moments with our contacts. Whether they are phone calls, mailings, or sending an invoice, we can register them in Microsoft Dynamics NAV.

As with profiles, there are interactions that are generated automatically and manually. Manual interactions are created using a wizard.

All interactions relate to an **Interaction Template Code**. The system allows an unlimited amount of code we can define ourselves. The interaction code will also determine how the rest of wizard will behave.

Interactions can be **Inbound** or **Outbound** and initiated by us or them. These are informative fields.

The **Wizard Action** field determines whether the wizard will generate a mail merge document, allow us to attach a previously created document, or do nothing. Mail merge allows us to create a Word document with all fields from the contact table.

Let's create an interaction and look at how that is done. To create an interaction, we choose **Create Interaction** on the contact card or list and click on the **Create Interaction** button from the **Process Actions**. This will open the following wizard:

The first page asks us what type of interaction we would like to start. Let's make a memo:

When you click Next, if your interaction template is set up to:
- Open, then the relevant attachment is opened.
- Import, then the Import File dialog box is displayed.

This is the next step as our interaction code defines that we will generate a mail merge:

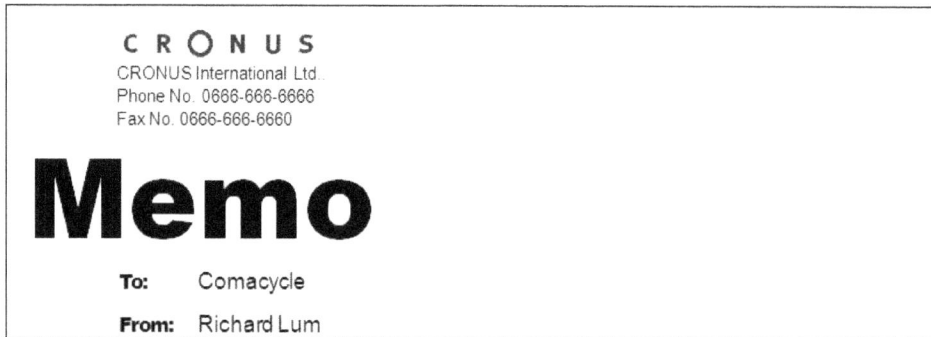

C R O N U S
CRONUS International Ltd.
Phone No. 0666-666-6666
Fax No. 0666-666-6660

Memo

To: Comacycle

From: Richard Lum

We can now create the memo in Microsoft Word with all necessary fields already filled in.

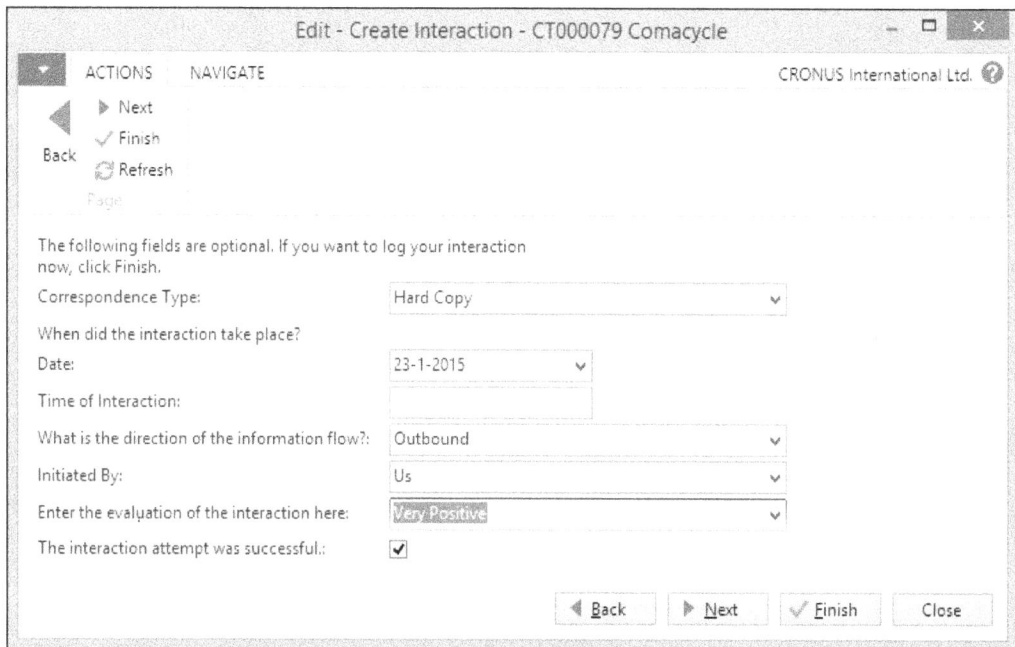

Edit - Create Interaction - CT000079 Comacycle

ACTIONS   NAVIGATE   CRONUS International Ltd.

Back
▶ Next
✓ Finish
🔁 Refresh
Page

The following fields are optional. If you want to log your interaction now, click Finish.

Correspondence Type:	Hard Copy

When did the interaction take place?

Date:	23-1-2015
Time of Interaction:	
What is the direction of the information flow?:	Outbound
Initiated By:	Us
Enter the evaluation of the interaction here:	Very Positive
The interaction attempt was successful.:	✓

◀ Back   ▶ Next   ✓ Finish   Close

After closing Microsoft Word, we move on to the next step and when we populate all fields, we can finish the wizard. This will save the interaction in the database and print the memo since we choose **Hard Copy** as **Correspondence Type**.

> It is also possible to postpone interactions and restart them later.

Automatic interactions

Some interactions can also be automatically generated, for example, each time we print an invoice or shipment.

Which interaction code is used for each transaction is defined in the **Interaction Template Setup**. For every print, we want an interaction log entry to be generated and we need to set up a code.

Edit - Interaction Template Setup	

HOME — CRONUS International Ltd.

View | Edit | OneNote | Notes | Links | Refresh | Clear Filter | Go to | Previous | Next

Manage | Show Attached | Page

Interaction Template Setup

General

E-Mails:	EMAIL	Outgoing Calls:	OUTGOING
Cover Sheets:	COVERSH	Meeting Invitation:	MEETINV

Sales

Invoices:	S_INVOICE	Statements:	S_STATM
Credit Memos:	S_C_MEMO	Reminders:	S_REMIND
Order Confirmations:	S_ORDER_CF	Return Orders:	S_RET_ORD
Quotes:	S_QUOTE	Return Receipts:	S_RET_RCP
Blanket Orders:	S_B_ORDER	Finance Charge Memos:	S_FIN_CHG
Shipment Notes:	S_SHIP		

Be careful when printing a lot of documents, as the interaction log entry table can be locked for a longer period forcing other users in the database to wait until the process is completed. To avoid this, enable auto-increment on this table as described in this blog at `https://marijebrummel.blog/2014/05/25/tip-14-autoincrement-interaction-log-entries/`.

Other automatically created interaction log entries are created by segments, which we will look at later in the chapter.

Finished interactions

When completed, the interactions are connected to a contact and can be used for analysis purposes. It is also possible to start a To-do from an interaction. We'll look at that in the next paragraph.

To-do's

The To-do's are the lowest level of activities in the relationship management model. They are best compared to Masks or Meetings in Microsoft Outlook.

To-do's can be created directly in the system or from another event. We can create a To-do from the interaction we just created. Let's do this.

The reference here is the tab, Create To-do, and hence the cut-off text at the side is fine

When we click on **Create To-do** form the **Interaction Log Entries**, the system shows us a wizard that will guide us through the process, just like the **Interaction** wizard.

There are three types of To-do's, **Standard** (blank), **Meeting**, and **Phone Call**. The steps in the wizard depend on the type we select. Let's select a **Meeting**.

The next step asks the attendees for the meeting and allows a template for the invitation, which then again will create an Interaction Log Entry.

> To perform this step, the To-do organizer should have a valid
> e-mail address. This can be set up in the sales persons.

The next step only asks for a location so we will click on **Finish**.

When we now open the To-do's from the **Sales & Marketing Department**, we can
open the **Sales Person** per day matrix, which shows us the meeting we just created.

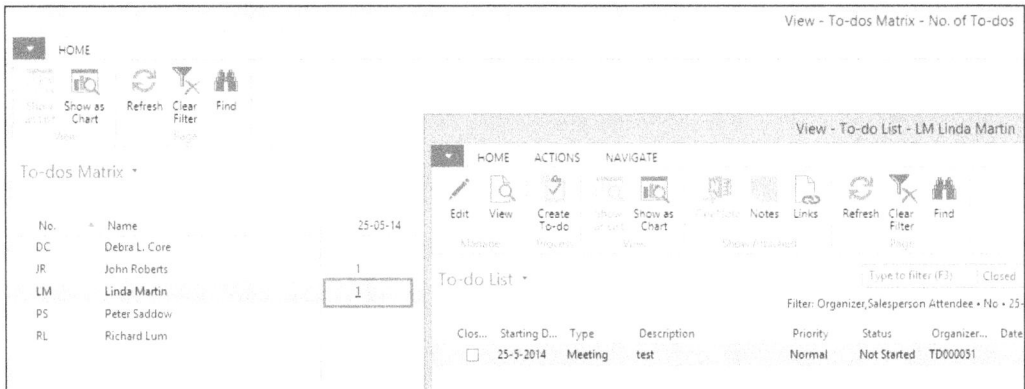

The cut-off text is not a part of the referenced section in the screenshot

We'll see more of To-do's when we discuss **Opportunities** and **Outlook Integration**.

Opportunities

When we discussed profiles, we could already see that relationship management
is tightly integrated with the ERP part of the application. This is also the case
for opportunities.

Opportunities allow us to manage all the quote requests we get from our prospects,
creating a workflow that will guide us to a deal that is won or lost. This then allows us
to analyze the win and lose deals and change our business based on this information.

We can analyze the sales pipeline and make a proper judgement of our future order
position allowing us to schedule capacity in time.

Workflow

Each opportunity we create will follow a sales cycle in the system. This will guide us
step by step though the process.

Let's have a look at the sales cycles in the CRONUS database.

There are four sales cycles defined. The most important field is the **Probability Calculation** formula. This will determine how the system calculates the current value of all opportunities with this code. We can see the **Calculated Current Value** by opening the **Statistics** window of a sales cycle, as shown in the following screenshot:

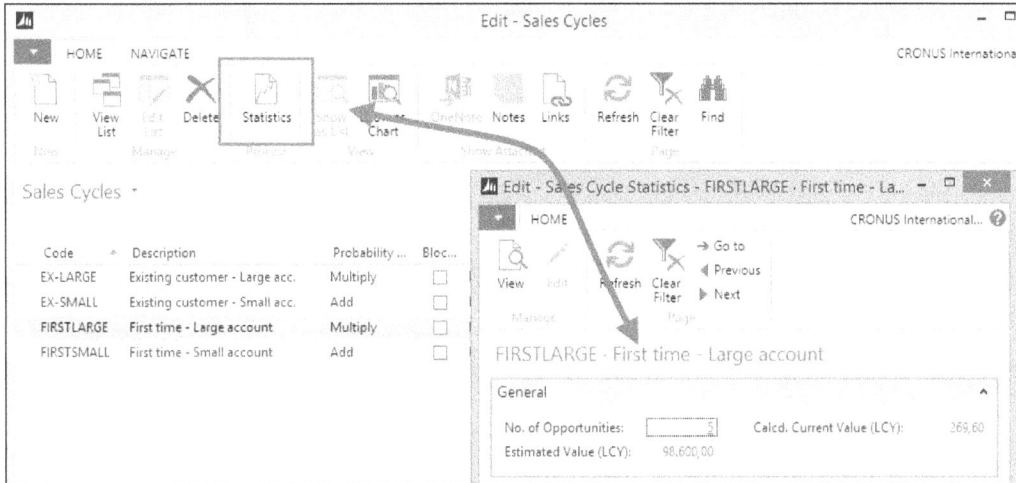

There are four options to choose from: Multiply, Add, Chances of Success %, and Completed %. The function UpdateEstimates in the Opportunity Entry (5093) table calculates this:

```
UpdateEstimates()
IF SalesCycleStage.GET("Sales Cycle Code","Sales Cycle Stage")
THEN BEGIN
  SalesCycle.GET("Sales Cycle Code");
  CASE SalesCycle."Probability Calculation" OF
    SalesCycle."Probability Calculation"::Multiply:
      BEGIN
        "Probability %" := "Chances of Success %" *
                  SalesCycleStage."Completed %" / 100;
      END;
    SalesCycle."Probability Calculation"::Add:
      BEGIN
        "Probability %" := ("Chances of Success %" +
                  SalesCycleStage."Completed %") / 2;
      END;
    SalesCycle."Probability Calculation"::"Chances of Success %":
```

```
      BEGIN
        "Probability %" := "Chances of Success %";
      END;
    SalesCycle."Probability Calculation"::"Completed %":
      BEGIN
        "Probability %" := SalesCycleStage."Completed %";
      END;
  END;
  "Completed %" := SalesCycleStage."Completed %";
  "Calcd. Current Value (LCY)" := "Estimated Value (LCY)" *
                          "Probability %" / 100;
  END;
```

The `Probability Calculation` first calculates a `Probability %` field, which will
then lead to the required `Calculated Current Value`.

Sales stages

Each sales cycle has different stages that will guide us through the sales process.

The current sales stage of an opportunity defines the `Completed %` field. We can decide with **Allow Skip** option whether a sales stage is mandatory. The quote required will force us to assign a sales quote to this opportunity as we will see later when we create an opportunity.

Activity codes

Each sales stage has an activity code. This will define which To-do's are created to support us in the sales process.

This is a very powerful tool, enabling sales people to create a workflow for each sales process.

Let's create an opportunity and see what happens in the system.

Creating an opportunity

An opportunity starts by selecting an existing contact or creating a new one. From the **Contact Card**, we can navigate to **Related Information | Contact | Opportunities | List**.

This leads us to a filtered lists of opportunities linked to this contact.

1. Here we can select **Create Opportunity**.

2. This opens the wizard that will guide us though the process. In the first window, we enter the description `Sell Chairs` and click on **Next** to take us to the second step.

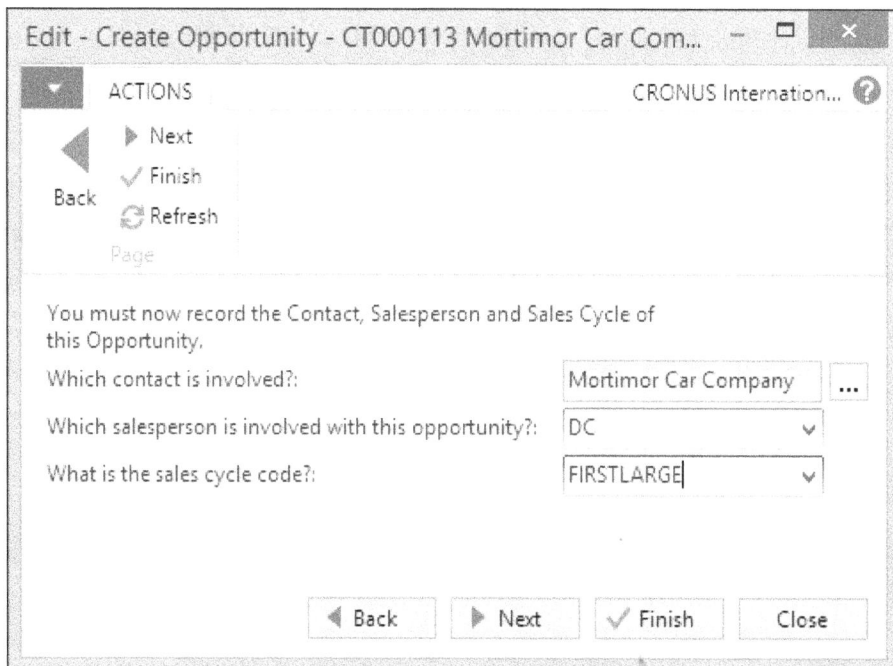

3. In this step, we choose **Sales Cycle** code **FIRSTSMALL** and select **Finish**.

4. Selecting **Next** will allow us to enter additional information, such as assigning a sales campaign, and activating the first stage. We will skip that now and discuss campaigns later in this chapter.

    When we now open the created opportunity, the information should look like the following screenshot. There are no activity lines as we have not yet activated the first stage.

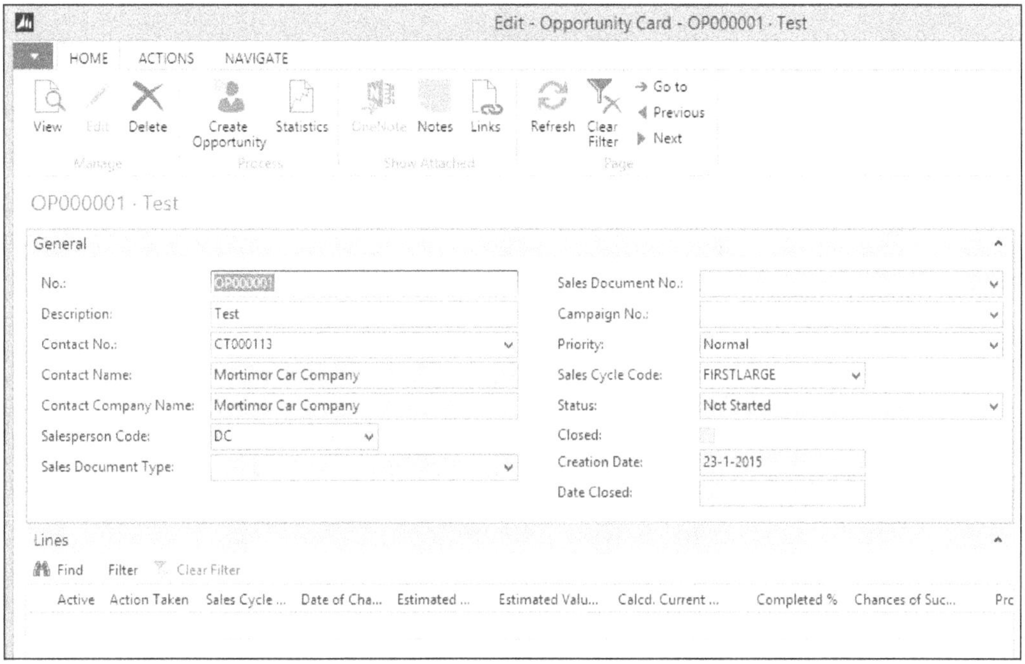

The cut-off text is not a part of the reference in this screenshot

5. Let's activate the first stage and see what happens. We do that by navigating to **Actions | Functions | Update**. We enter a wizard where we select **First**.

6. We'll click on **Next** twice and enter step three of the wizard.

7. In this step, we should enter the estimated sales value and **chance of success** (%) of getting this deal. This is important to calculate the **calculated estimated value** we discussed earlier.

8. When we click on **Finish**, we come back to the **Opportunity** page and see that the current value is **260,00**.

The cut-off text is not a part of the reference in this screenshot

Since the probability calculation of this sales cycle is **Add**, the formula is:

```
"Probability %" := ("Chances of Success %" +
    SalesCycleStage."Completed %") / 2;

"Calcd. Current Value (LCY)" := "Estimated Value (LCY)" *
    "Probability %" / 100;
```

This will lead to `(50 + 2) / 2 = 26 and 1000 * 26 / 100 = 260`.

9. Now we navigate to **Related Information | Opportunity | To-Dos** and see that the system has created two To-do's for us that we have to complete.

The cut-off text is not a part of the reference in this screenshot

10. This will help us remember our daily tasks and allow management to see nothing is forgotten. The next stages in this sales cycle are **Qualification** and **Presentation**.

Stage	Description	Completed %	Activity Code	Quo...	Allo...	Date Formula	Co...
	Initial	2	INIT	☐	☐		No
2	Qualification	5	QUAL	☐	☐		No
3	Presentation	40	P-WORK	☑	☑		No
4	Proposal	60	PROPOSAL	☑	☐		No
5	Sign Contract	95	SIGN	☑	☐		No

11. We can enter these stages by entering the wizard again and selecting **Next**.

12. After selecting the **Next** button twice, we hit step three. Since one of our To-do's was verifying the quality of the opportunity, we can now say for example that the chance of success is 80 percent.

Edit - Update Opportunity - CT000113 Mortimor Car Company CT000113 ...

ACTIONS   CRONUS International Ltd.

Back   Next   ✓ Finish   Sales Quote   🔄 Refresh

Page

You can now change the estimated values regarding the opportunity.

What is the estimated sales value (LCY)?:	1.000,00
What is the chance of success (%)?:	80
What is the estimated closing date?:	23-1-2015
Cancel existing open to-dos.:	☐

◀ Back   ▶ Next   ✓ Finish   Sales Quote   Close

13. We'll select the **Cancel existing open to-dos** Checkbox to make sure our workflow is updated. You will see that the **Calculated Current Value** has increased to **425,00**:

Active	Action Taken	Sales Cycle ...	Date of Cha...	Estimated ...	Estimated Valu...	Calcd. Current ...	Completed %	Chances of Suc...
✓	Next	2	23-1-2015	23-1-2015	1.000,00	425,00	5	80
☐		1	23-1-2015	23-1-2015	1.000,00	260,00	2	50

14. When we enter the next stage, we will get the following error message telling us that assigning a quote is mandatory to enter the next step:

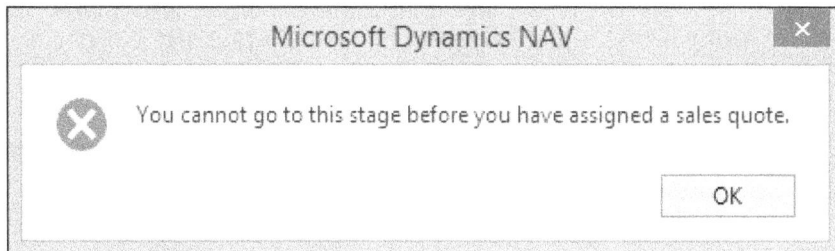

Microsoft Dynamics NAV

❌ You cannot go to this stage before you have assigned a sales quote.

OK

Sales quote

To assign a sales quote to an opportunity, we navigate to **Actions | Functions | Assign Sales Quote** from the **Opportunity Card**. This will open a new sales quote with all fields populated from the opportunity.

> To assign a quote to a contact without a **Sell-to Customer No.**, we need to use the **Sell-to Customer Template Code**. This can be used when the **Show more fields** option is activated on the **General** fast tab.

We will select two furniture items and populate the **Quantity** and **Line Discount** % fields.

When we now update the opportunity, we can use the quote amount of 796,80 which will lead to a **Calculated Current Value** of 478,08 in step three and 557,76 in step four.

> To update the opportunity to step 4, the sales person should have a valid e-mail address, which can be set up in the sales persons.

Closing the deal

Step five is the final step in the sales cycle stages we used in our example. Now we need to tell the system whether the deal is won or lost. To do this, we navigate to **Actions | Functions | Close** from the **Opportunity Card**. We will select **Won** and click on **Next**.

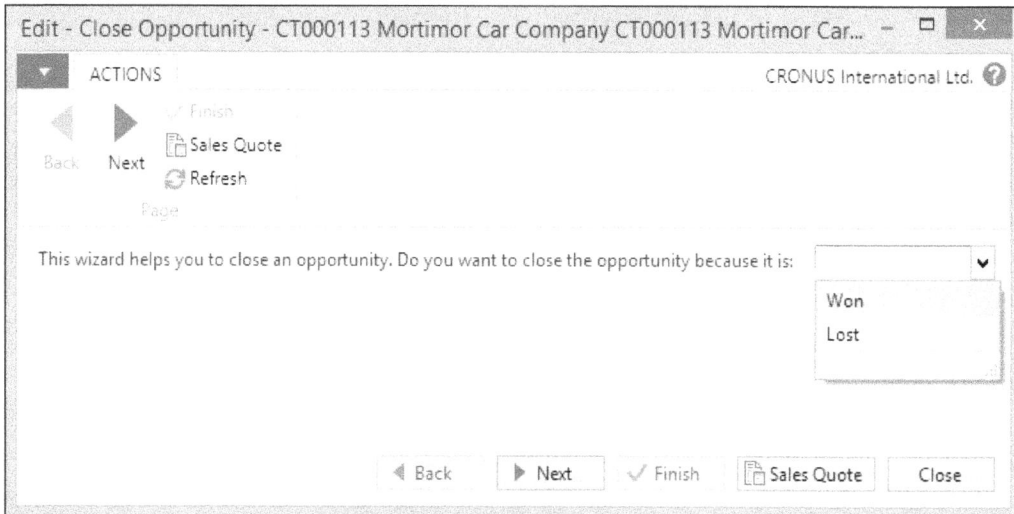

After selecting a valid reason and the sales amount, we can close the deal.

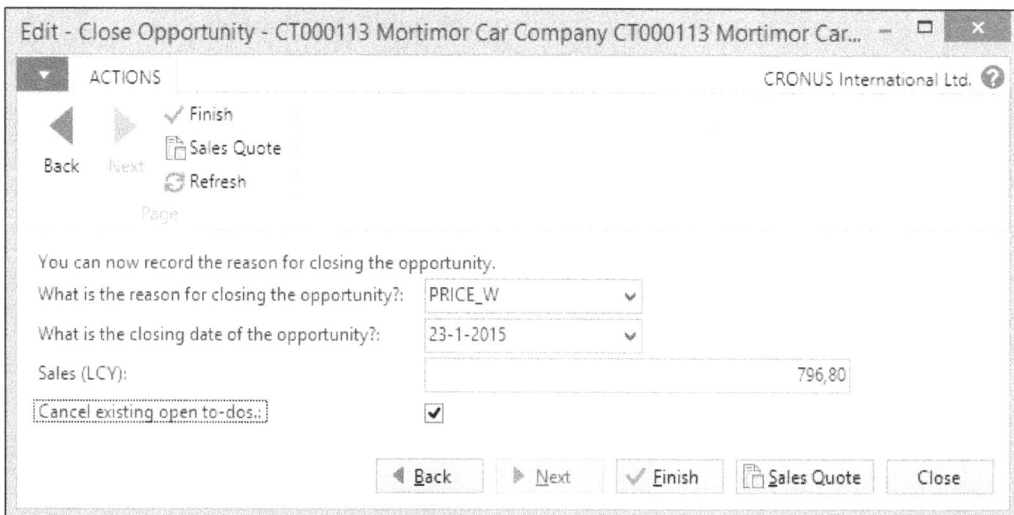

The system now creates a customer for this contact and updates the quote with this number. We need to promote the quote to an order manually.

Creating segments

Segments allow us to slice and dice the data in our system to create a filtered list of contacts. This information can then be used to create an interaction such as a mailing or start a sales campaign.

Since Microsoft Dynamics NAV relationship management is integrated with the ERP system, we can filter on both RM and ERP data.

Let's create a new segment and look at the possibilities:

The segment has a **No.** and **Description field**. The no. can be defined using the Number Series.

On the **Interaction** tab, we select **Interaction Template Code**. We will select an interaction that generates a Word document so we can use the mail merge capabilities of segments.

The **Unit Cost (LCY)** is important to determine the total cost of this segment especially when we use it with campaigns, as we will see later in the chapter.

Adding contacts

With our segment defined, we can now start filtering the system for contact information by navigating to **Actions** | **Functions** | **Contacts** | **Add Contacts**.

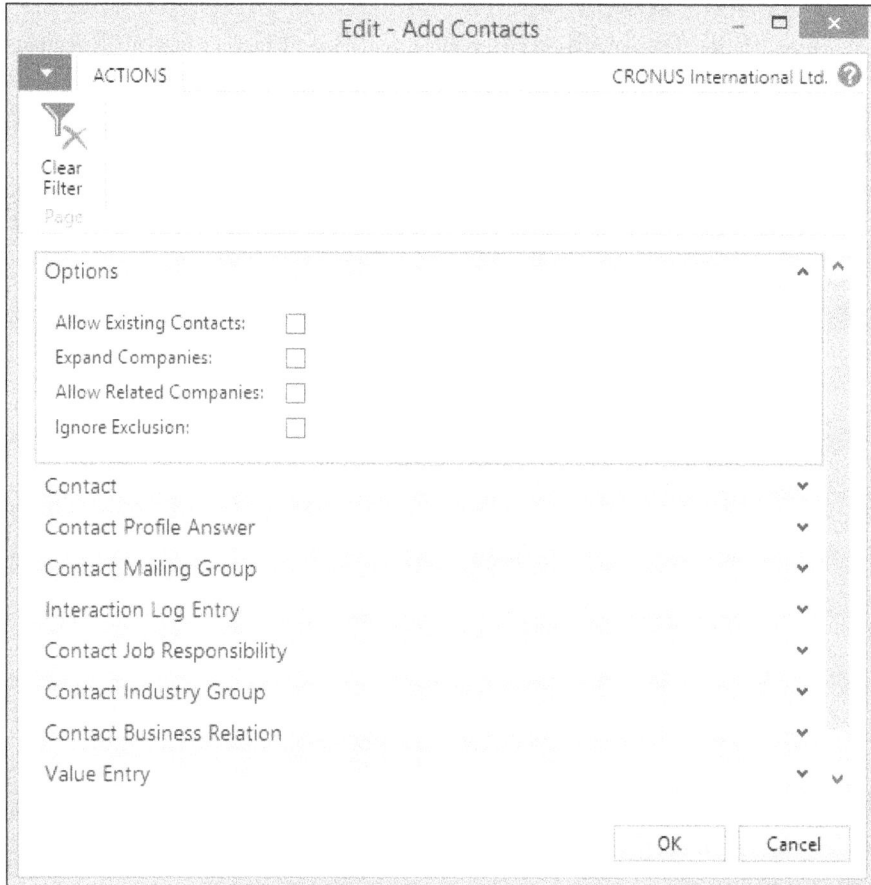

```
Edit - Add Contacts                        -  □  ×

ACTIONS                            CRONUS International Ltd. 

Clear
Filter
Page

Options                                              ^  ^

   Allow Existing Contacts:     ☐
   Expand Companies:            ☐
   Allow Related Companies:     ☐
   Ignore Exclusion:            ☐

Contact                                                 ˅
Contact Profile Answer                                  ˅
Contact Mailing Group                                   ˅
Interaction Log Entry                                   ˅
Contact Job Responsibility                              ˅
Contact Industry Group                                  ˅
Contact Business Relation                               ˅
Value Entry                                          ˅  ˅

                              OK          Cancel
```

This opens a selection window, allowing us to filter on different parts of the application:

- **Options**: This is further divided into four categories:
    - ° **Allow Existing Contacts**: If you run multiple selections and check this option, the system will create new segment lines each time a contact is within the selection.
    - ° **Expand Companies**: When you select this option, the system will add the persons related to the companies in the selection.

- ° **Allow Related Companies**: When **Expand Companies** is selected, this option will delete the company record if a company has one or more persons in the filter.
- ° **Ignore Exclusion**: A contact can be ignored on segments. Checking this flag will ignore this field.

- **Contact**: Here we can filter directly on all fields in the contact table. For example, all contacts in the country NL.
- **Profile**: This allows us to filter on any profile answer. When we use automatic profile answers, we can for example filter on customers with a specific turnover or profit value.
- **Mailing Group**: We can save any segment to a mailing group allowing easy reuse of previously generated filters.
- **Interaction Log Entry**: We can filter on contacts who have had specific interaction codes. For example, everyone who had a sales invoice in the last year.
- **Job Responsibility**: If we want to send out a mail to all managers, we select the matching job responsibility code.
- **Industry Group**: This allows us to filter out companies in specific industries.
- **Business Relation**: This is by default used to integrate with customers, vendors, and bank accounts but can also be expanded with extra information.
- **Value Entry**: This is probably the most powerful filter where we can filter on specific item numbers and posting dates from the related contact.

Refine/reduce contacts

After adding all contacts from The Netherlands, we might want to refine or reduce this, which can be done with the same filtering as adding contacts. Refining will check whether the contacts in the segments match the specific filter criteria and reducing will remove all contacts in the segment that match the criteria.

We will reduce the segment with City Waalwijk.

Segment criteria

We can now ask the system what criteria we used by navigating to **Related Information | Segments | Criteria**.

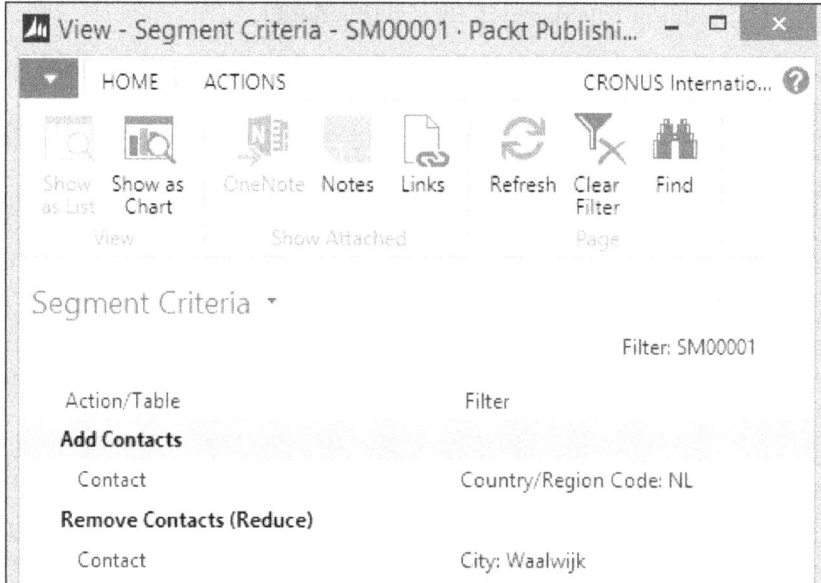

This allows us to see what we did, but also to undo the last actions or save the criteria.

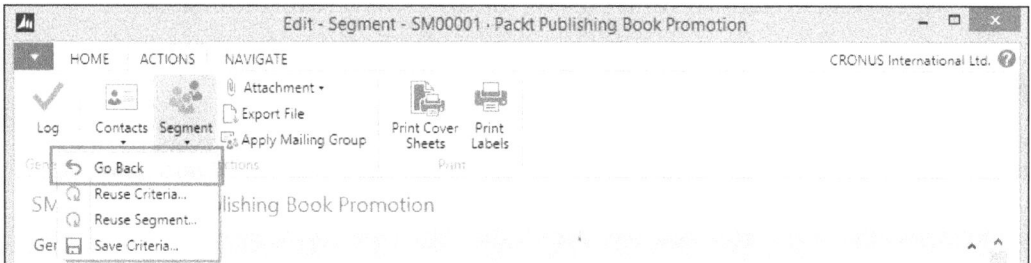

Mailing groups

Another option to reuse a segment is to apply a mailing group to all contacts in a segment. To start this, we click on **Apply Mailing Group** in the **ACTIONS** tab from the **Segment Card**.

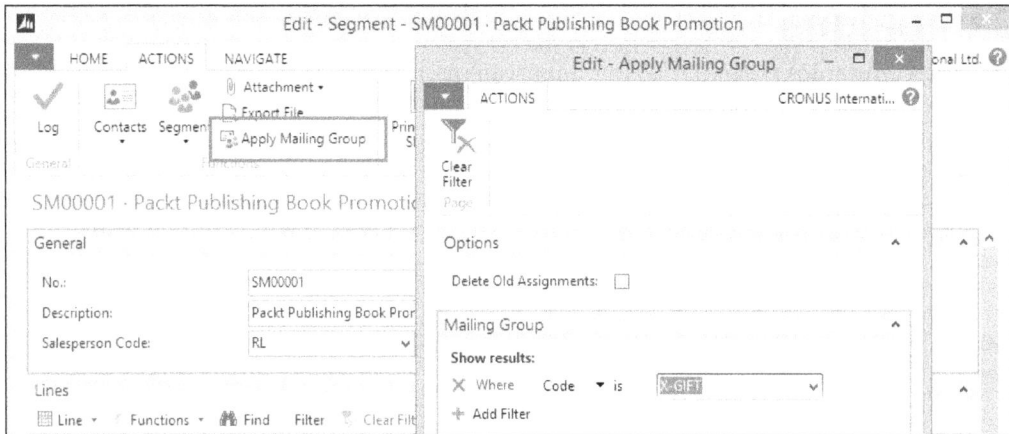

This will create a record in the Contact Mailing Group table for each contact in the segment.

Log segment

When the segment is finished, it should be logged. Logging the segment will start the mail merge process in our segment and create the.

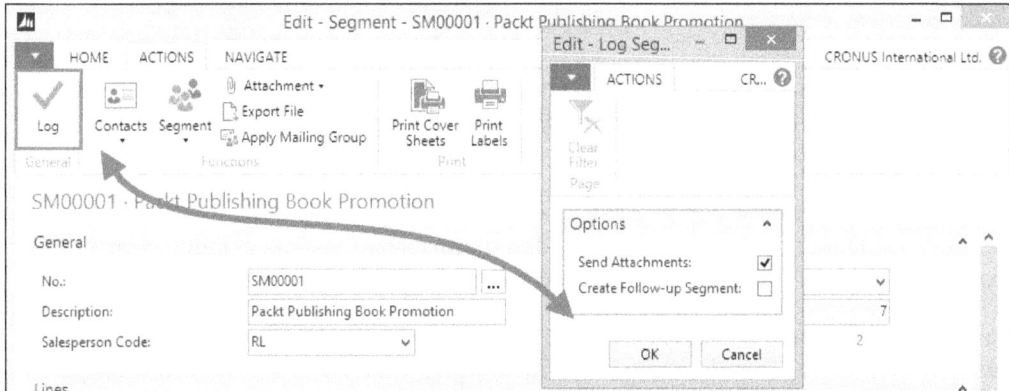

[
Using this option will also print the letters in this example.
For an exercise it might be useful to enable a PDF printer or
turn of your printer and remove the print job.
]

If required, the system can directly generate a follow up segment if we wanted to use this segment with a campaign.

Campaigns

Most big companies with marketing departments have sales campaigns to improve their sales. These are typically periods where some items are more interesting for customers to buy.

With the campaigns in Microsoft Dynamics NAV, we can manage the sales prices and see the results of a specific campaign both from a cost and profit viewpoint.

Let's open a campaign and see what information it contains:

Each campaign has a unique **No.** field that can be created using Number Series and **Description**. The **No.** field should be carefully chosen since it will be used throughout the application where this campaign is used.

The **Status Code** options can be custom defined but do not impact business logic. The **Starting Date** and **Ending Date** fields are important for the pricing information. The special price and discounts will only be valid within these periods.

Via the **Invoicing** tab, we can see that campaigns are integrated with dimensions. This gives us the powerful option to define a dimension code for each campaign and create an analysis view to analyze the results in the financial part of Microsoft Dynamics NAV, like we discussed in the previous chapter.

Pricing

Microsoft Dynamics NAV allows special item pricing for campaigns. If a sales order is generated from a campaign, the system will use the special price automatically.

By navigating to **Related Information** | **Campaign** | **Sales Prices**, we can enter the pricing information for this campaign.

This price table is filtered exactly the same way as discussed in our example application in *Chapter 2, A Sample Application*.

Segments

To select customers or prospects for a campaign, we need to create one or more segments. These segments should be connected to the campaign using the **Campaign No.** field. Everyone related to these segments will get the specific prices and discounts.

The segments are also used to create the interaction log entries and To-do's for this campaign. We need to make our target group aware that this campaign exists by sending them a letter, fax, e-mail, or even a phone call.

Activate

By activating the campaign, the system will add all contacts to the campaign group and create interaction log entries.

The interaction log entries will be used to calculate the cost of a campaign. Each interaction has a specific cost and all costs add up to the total amount on the campaign.

When an opportunity comes in, we can point this to a specific campaign. The value of this opportunity is also used in estimating the success of the campaign.

The campaign is also copied into the sales documents using the dimensions attached to the campaign. This allows us to further analyze the results.

Outlook integration

Salespeople are often on the road without online access to the ERP system, and Microsoft Dynamics NAV does not have an offline mode. To solve this problem, Microsoft Dynamics NAV is integrated with Microsoft Outlook. This allows salespeople to view contacts and tasks offline and replicate with the back office system when possible.

If salespeople use a Windows Mobile phone with Microsoft Outlook, they can even have all their Microsoft Dynamics NAV information on their device.

Using user-defined views will also enable us to synchronize other Microsoft Dynamics NAV data to Microsoft Outlook, for example, the customer table with the current value of the **Balance** field or the item table with the current inventory.

We will discuss the possibilities of interfacing with Microsoft Outlook in *Chapter 9, Interfacing*.

E-mail logging

Microsoft Dynamics NAV also has a capability to read exchange shared folders such as `info@` mailboxes. For each e-mail, the system can generate Interaction Log Entries and To-do's.

The setup

Before implementing relationship management, we should properly set up the options. This can be done in the **Marketing Setup**.

Let's take a look at all the fields:

- **Attachment Storage Type**: The attachments in the interaction log entries can either be stored in the database (embedded) or on the filesystem (disk file). It is highly recommended to store them on the filesystem.

- **Attachment Storage Location**: If we chose to store the attachments on file system, this is where we specify the path.

- **Index Mode**: When using a contact search, this should be set to **Auto**. It might have a small drawback on performance and cause the database to become bigger.

- **Inheritance**: When entering a person's profile, it can inherit the salesperson code, territory code, country/region code, language code, address details, and communication details from the company it belongs to.

- **Defaults**: A new contact can get a default salesperson code, territory code, country/region code, language code, or correspondence type. There is a different default salutation code for companies and persons.

- **Default Sales Cycle Code**: Every new opportunity will automatically get this code.

- **Mergefield Language ID**: This defines if the Word merge fields are in the local language or in English.

- **Synchronization**: Here, we enter the default business relation code for customers, vendors, and bank accounts.

- **Maintain Dupl. Search strings**: Check this field if duplicate contact functions are used.

- **Autosearch for Duplicates**: Use this option if the system should automatically search when entering new contacts.

- **Search Hit %**: This determines the percentage of matching lines from the duplicate search string setup should have to qualify as a duplicate contact.

Customizing relationship management

RM is a complete module that is not often highly customized or verticalized. However, we will describe some possible changes and how to integrate an add-on, in our case the squash application with relationship management.

All examples in this chapter are part of the objects downloaded for *Chapter 2, A Sample Application*.

Salutation formula types

By default, the system has two salutation formula types, formal and informal, allowing us to print Dear Mrs. Brown, or Dear Angela, but what if we want to print Attn. Mrs. Brown?

For this, we need to first add an option to the **Salutation Type** field in the **Salutation Formula** table.

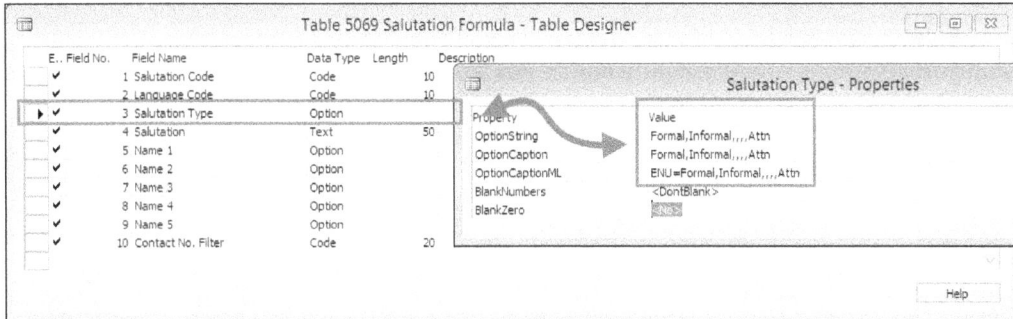

E.. Field No.	Field Name	Data Type	Length	Description
✓	1 Salutation Code	Code	10	
✓	2 Language Code	Code	10	
▶ ✓	3 Salutation Type	Option		
✓	4 Salutation	Text	50	
✓	5 Name 1	Option		
✓	6 Name 2	Option		
✓	7 Name 3	Option		
✓	8 Name 4	Option		
✓	9 Name 5	Option		
✓	10 Contact No. Filter	Code	20	

Salutation Type - Properties

Property	Value
OptionString	Formal,Informal,,,,Attn
OptionCaption	Formal,Informal,,,,Attn
OptionCaptionML	ENU=Formal,Informal,,,,Attn
BlankNumbers	<DontBlank>
BlankZero	<No>

Support the formula

Next, we want to use the formula when printing a Contact Cover Sheet. This uses the **Format Address** functionality from codeunit 365.

This codeunit is the single point in Dynamics NAV where all the address formatting is done.

The formatting of contact persons is done in the `ContactAddrAlt` function. We should make the following change:

```
ContactAddrAlt()
...
  ContIdenticalAddress:
    WITH ContAltAddr DO BEGIN
      GET(Cont."Company No.",CompanyAltAddressCode);
      FormatAddr(
        AddrArray,"Company Name","Company Name 2",
        Cont.Name,Address,"Address 2",
        City,"Post Code",County,"Country/Region Code");
    END;
  (Cont.Type=Cont.Type::Person) AND
  (Cont."Company No." <> ''):
```

```
         WITH Cont DO
           FormatAddr(
//             AddrArray,ContCompany.Name,ContCompany."Name 2",
//             Name,Address,"Address 2",
             AddrArray,ContCompany.Name,ContCompany."Name 2",
             GetSalutation(5, Cont."Language Code"),Address,
             "Address 2",City,"Post Code",County,
             "Country/Region Code")
```

> Always comment out the original line of code before you make a change. This will enable you to always go back to standard code and help when upgrading this solution to a newer version.
>
> Most NAV partners and developers have their own way of documenting and commenting. The example in here is the minimum comment requirement. We will discuss versioning objects in *Chapter 10, Application Design*.

The GetSalutation function

In our modification, we use the GetSalutation function in Contact table (5050) instead of the **Name** field. Let's have a look at that function and analyze what it does:

```
GetSalutation()
IF NOT SalutationFormula.GET("Salutation Code",LanguageCode,
  SalutationType)
THEN
  ERROR(Text021,LanguageCode,"No.");

SalutationFormula.TESTFIELD(Salutation);

CASE SalutationFormula."Name 1" OF
  SalutationFormula."Name 1"::"Job Title":
    NamePart[1] := "Job Title";
  SalutationFormula."Name 1"::"First Name":
    NamePart[1] := "First Name";
  SalutationFormula."Name 1"::"Middle Name":
    NamePart[1] := "Middle Name";
  SalutationFormula."Name 1"::Surname:
    NamePart[1] := Surname;
  SalutationFormula."Name 1"::Initials:
    NamePart[1] := Initials;
```

```
    SalutationFormula."Name 1"::"Company Name":
      NamePart[1] := "Company Name";
END;

CASE SalutationFormula."Name 2" OF
  ...
END;
...
FOR i := 1 TO 5 DO
  IF NamePart[i] = '' THEN BEGIN
    SubStr := '%' + FORMAT(i) + ' ';
    IF STRPOS(SalutationFormula.Salutation,SubStr) > 0 THEN
      SalutationFormula.Salutation :=
        DELSTR(SalutationFormula.Salutation,STRPOS(SalutationFormula.
Salutation,SubStr),3);
  END;

EXIT(STRSUBSTNO(SalutationFormula.Salutation,NamePart[1],
  NamePart[2],NamePart[3],NamePart[4],NamePart[5]))
```

The function uses two parameters: SalutationType and LanguageCode. With these values and the salutation code of the contact, it checks whether there is a valid formula. Since we only added a new option, the code still works because at database level, the **Option** field is translated to an **Integer**.

> For documentation purposes, we could also implement the new option value in this function. The downside of this would be that we do a modification that is not technically necessary but needs to be maintained and upgraded.

Depending on the order of the formula, the necessary name fields are combined and used as the return value of the function.

Setup the salutation formula

If we want to use our new salutation formula, we need to set it up first. We will do this for F-MAR to test it with CT100191 Megan Sherman from American Wood Exports.

Langua...	Salutati...	Salutation	Name 1	Name 2	Name 3	Name 4	Name 5
	Formal	Dear Ms. %1 %2 %3,	First Name	Middle Name	Surname		
	Informal	Hi %1,	First Name				
DAN	Formal	Kære Fru. %1 %2 %3,	First Name	Middle Name	Surname		
DAN	Informal	Hej %1,	First Name				
DEU	Formal	Sehr geehrte Frau %1 %2 %3,	First Name	Middle Name	Surname		
DEU	Informal	Hallo %1,	First Name				
ENU	Formal	Dear Ms. %1 %2 %3,	First Name	Middle Name	Surname		
ENU	Informal	Hi %1	First Name				
ENU	Attn	Attn. Ms. %1 %2 %3	First Name	Middle Name	Surname		
ESP	Formal	Estimada Señora %1 %2 %3,	First Name	Middle Name	Surname		
ESP	Informal	Estimada Señora %1 %2 %3,	First Name	Middle Name	Surname		
FRA	Formal	Chère Madame %1 %2 %3,	First Name	Middle Name	Surname		

Test the solution

After adding the new formula, we print a cover sheet from the contact card using the **Contact Cover Sheet** option from the **Report** actions. The result will look like this:

Contact - Cover Sheet

1 of 2? 100% Find Next

Cover Sheet

American Wood Exports
Attn. Ms. Megan Sherman
723 North Hampton Drive
New York, US-NY 11010
USA

CRONUS International Ltd.
5 The Ring
Westminster
W2 8HG London

Customer and vendor numbering

Another common requirement from end users is to maintain the same number when creating a customer or vendor from a contact.

This can be done by adding one line of code to the `CreateCustomer` function in the contact table:

```
CreateCustomer()

...

CLEAR(Cust);
Cust.SetInsertFromContact(TRUE);
//* Maintain Contact No. >>>
Cust."No." := "No.";
//* Maintain Contact No. <<<
Cust.INSERT(TRUE);
Cust.SetInsertFromContact(FALSE);
```

This works because by populating the `No.` field, the Number Series functionality in the `OnInsert` trigger does not start:

```
OnInsert()
IF "No." = '' THEN BEGIN
  SalesSetup.GET;
  SalesSetup.TESTFIELD("Customer Nos.");
  NoSeriesMgt.InitSeries(SalesSetup."Customer Nos.",
    xRec."No. Series",0D,"No.","No. Series");
END;
...
```

Disabling the direct creation of customers and vendors

When using this option, it should be disabled to directly create a customer or vendor. This can be done easily by removing the `No. Series` from the **Sales & Receivables Setup** and **Purchases & Payables Setup**. This results in a runtime error message when creating the customer or vendor.

Sharing contact information across companies

When more companies have their administration in Microsoft Dynamics NAV, they most often have the same owner or group of owners that want their contact data to span across their companies.

This can be achieved by sharing some tables across all companies and changing some business logic.

Share tables

By default, Microsoft Dynamics NAV will create a separate instance of each table for each company. This can be changed with the `DataPerCompany` property in the table designer.

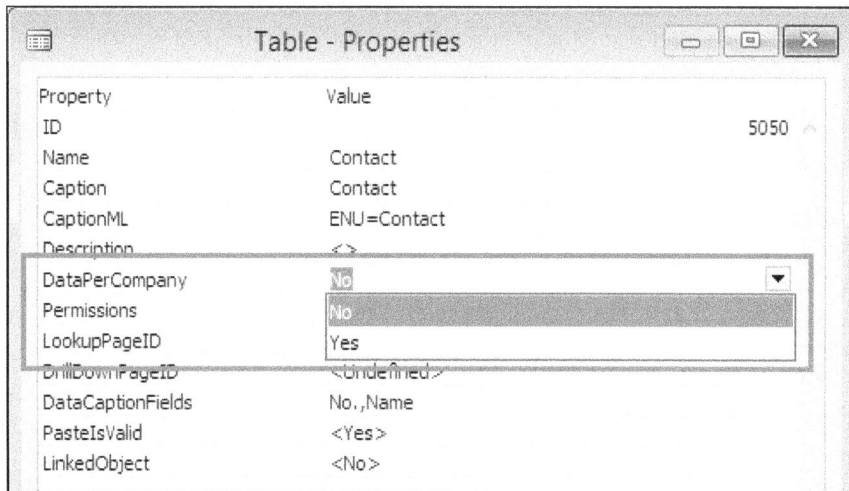

Property	Value	
	Table - Properties	
ID		5050
Name	Contact	
Caption	Contact	
CaptionML	ENU=Contact	
Description	<>	
DataPerCompany	No	▼
Permissions	No	
LookupPageID	Yes	
DrillDownPageID	<Undefined>	
DataCaptionFields	No.,Name	
PasteIsValid	<Yes>	
LinkedObject	<No>	

The following lists should be shared across the database since they contain the main contact information and the link to the customer and vendor data:

- 5050 - Contact
- 5051 - Contact Alt. Address
- 5052 - Contact Alt. Addr. Date Range
- 5053 - Business Relation
- 5054 - Contact Business Relation

This will allow us to reuse contact data in all companies. Other tables are optional to share but might be useful.

By sharing the **Contact Profile Answer** table, other companies can see how a customer is doing within the group.

The segment tables could be shared in order to slice and dice information across the company. This also requires the criteria tables to be shared.

> When you share the profile or segment tables, the reports that calculate them should be started for each company individually in the database.

Campaigns and opportunities should not be shared since that interfaces with the ERP system. Never share financial tables such as the value entry or document tables.

Interaction log entries could be shared but we should realize that most table relations to sales and purchase documents will not work when we are in the wrong company.

Business relation

When sharing the contacts across the companies, we are interested to see in which company contacts are customer and vendor. We also want to maintain those tables when the contact information changes.

This means that besides sharing the Contact Business Relation table, we should also add a field indicating the company and add this field to the primary key.

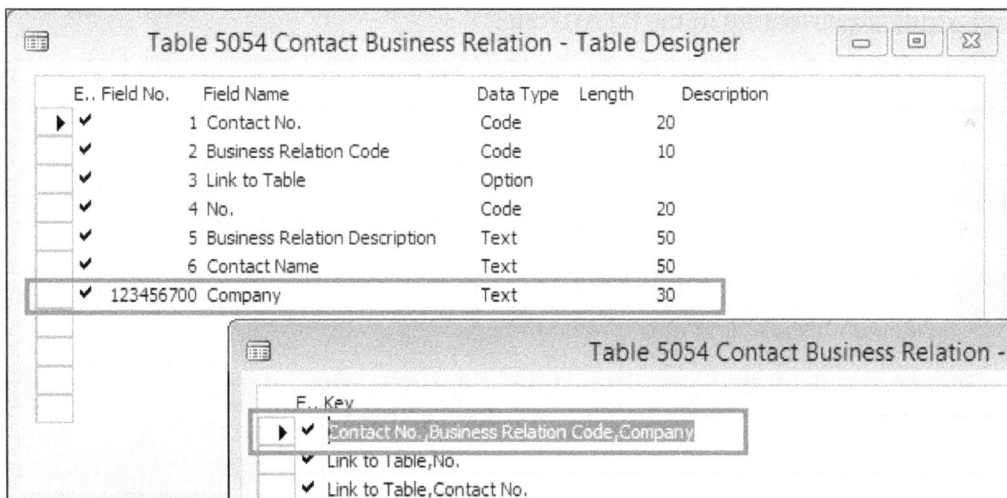

C/AL code modifications

To make this customization work, we need the C/AL code to understand what we want to do. It needs to understand that we added the company. Let's go through all the functions we need to change to make this work.

The functions that create the customer and vendor records we saw in *Chapter 2, A Sample Application*, should also be checked, for example, the function `CreateCustomer` in the contact table.

```
CreateCustomer()
...

ContBusRel.RESET;
ContBusRel.SETRANGE("Contact No.","No.");
ContBusRel.SETRANGE("Link to Table",ContBusRel."Link to
Table"::Customer);
//* Company Sharing >>>
ContBusRel.SETRANGE(Company, COMPANYNAME);
//* Company Sharing <<<
IF ContBusRel.FIND('-') THEN
  ERROR(
    Text019,

...
```

And a little bit further up in the C/AL code:

```
ContBusRel."Contact No." := ContComp."No.";
ContBusRel."Business Relation Code" := RMSetup."Bus. Rel. Code for
Customers";
ContBusRel."Link to Table" := ContBusRel."Link to Table"::Customer;
//* Company Sharing >>>
ContBusRel.Company := COMPANYNAME;
//* Company Sharing <<<
ContBusRel."No." := Cust."No.";
ContBusRel.INSERT(TRUE);
```

We should also check the code that maintains data integrity, which is the `CustVendBank-Update Codeunit (5055)` that we discussed in *Chapter 2, A Sample Application*:

```
UpdateCustomer()
WITH Cust DO BEGIN
//* Company Sharing >>>
```

```
    CHANGECOMPANY(COMPANYNAME);
//* Company Sharing <<<
    GET(ContBusRel."No.");
    ...
END;
```

Here, we use the CHANGECOMPANY C/AL command to change the company for a specific instance of a variable.

> There are more functions impacted such as the UpdateQuotes function in the contact table. Analyze your database before implementing this feature.

Number Series

The last change we should do for a properly working system is create a new instance of the Number Series functionality.

This can be achieved relatively easily since the Number Series are an isolated set of objects.

In the object designer, we should filter on this set of objects and export them to a .txt file.

- Table (308): No. Series
- Table (309): No. Series Line
- Table (310): No. Series Relationship
- Report (21): No. Series
- Report (22): No. Series Check
- Codeunit (396): NoSeriesManagement
- Page (456): No. Series
- Page (457): No. Series Lines
- Page (458): No. Series Relationships

In this file, we can renumber them and rename them so we get something like this:

- Table (123456721): No. Series (Shared)
- Table (123456722): No. Series Line (Shared)
- Table (123456723): No. Series Rel. (Shared)
- Report (123456721): No. Series (Shared)
- Report (123456722): No. Series Check (Shared)

- Codeunit (123456721): NoSeriesManagement (Shared)
- Page (123456721): No. Series (Shared)
- Page (123456722): No. Series Lines (Shared)
- Page (123456723): No. Series Rel. (Shared)

Where, the tables should be `DataPerCompany` No.

Final steps

When we have shared Number Series functionality, we can implement this in the existing objects.

1. The **Contact Nos.** field in the marketing setup table should change the table relation to the Shared No. Series table as well as the **No. Series** field in the contact table.

2. The `NoSeriesMgt` variable in the contact table should move from `NoSeriesManagement` to `SharedNoSeriesMgt`.

Alternative approaches

Sharing the contact information across companies is a change that has been implemented by many companies and can be considered safe. Other tables in Microsoft Dynamics NAV are more difficult to share because of financial or operational information.

A typical example in the standard application is `Item table (27)`. This contains a field `Cost is Adjusted (29)`, which is used when running cost adjustment. If this table will be shared across all companies, it would create a major issue with running this function. We will discuss cost adjustment in *Chapter 5, Production*.

For this issue, there are two commonly implemented solutions:

- **Shared Master Items**: We can create a new table called master item. This table is shared across all companies and contains the information we share like descriptions and pricing. When the data in this table is changed, it should enable a mechanism comparable to the `CustVendBank-Update Codeunit (5055)`, which updates the items in the other companies using the `CHANGECOMPANY` C/AL function.

- **External Synchronization**: We could implement something that will export the changes done in one company into an XML file. An Application Server can run in the background and read this xml file and implement these changes to other companies in the database or even other databases.

The first solution with master items looks a lot like the way contacts work in the standard application and is a perfect example of look, learn, and love using proven data structures in customized solutions.

Adding contacts to segments

The last change we are implementing in relationship management is adding a table to the **Add Contacts** functionality in segments.

We have seen that it is already complete but a vertical solution might want to integrate its ledger entry tables here.

For this example, we will make it possible to filter in the squash ledger entries from the example application in *Chapter 2*, *A Sample Application*.

Expanding report

The first step is to add the squash ledger entries as DataItem to the Add Contacts report (5198). We will copy the functionality from the Value Entries as this is comparable functionality.

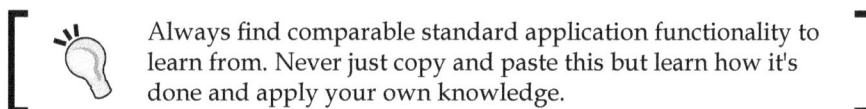

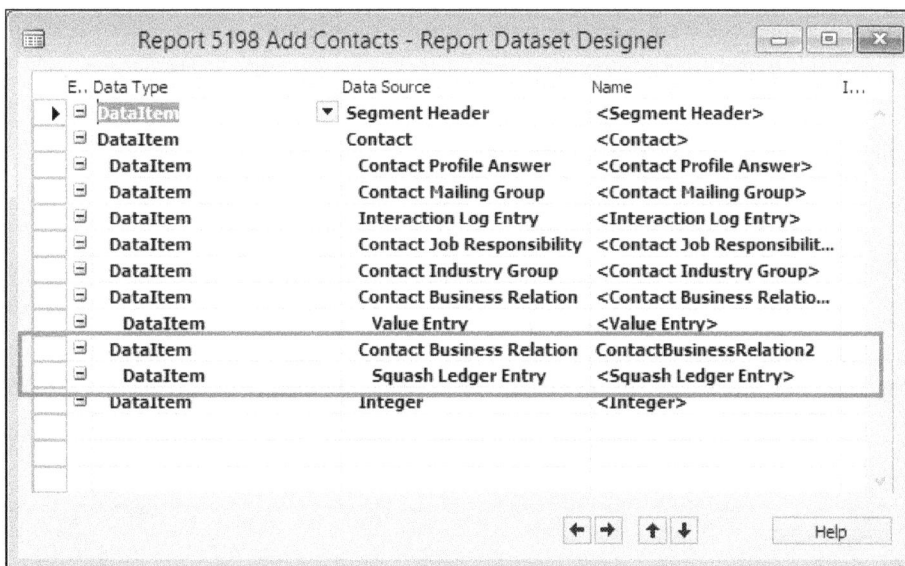

> Always find comparable standard application functionality to learn from. Never just copy and paste this but learn how it's done and apply your own knowledge.

Report 5198 Add Contacts - Report Dataset Designer			
E.. Data Type	Data Source	Name	I...
DataItem	Segment Header	<Segment Header>	
DataItem	Contact	<Contact>	
DataItem	Contact Profile Answer	<Contact Profile Answer>	
DataItem	Contact Mailing Group	<Contact Mailing Group>	
DataItem	Interaction Log Entry	<Interaction Log Entry>	
DataItem	Contact Job Responsibility	<Contact Job Responsibilit...	
DataItem	Contact Industry Group	<Contact Industry Group>	
DataItem	Contact Business Relation	<Contact Business Relatio...	
DataItem	Value Entry	<Value Entry>	
DataItem	Contact Business Relation	ContactBusinessRelation2	
DataItem	Squash Ledger Entry	<Squash Ledger Entry>	
DataItem	Integer	<Integer>	

We cannot copy and paste the table relation from the other contact business relation `DataItem` since squash players are contact persons, not companies. Our table relation should be `Contact No.=FIELD(No.)`.

The code in our Contact Business Relation table tells us that we need two new variables or the type Boolean, `SquashFilters` and `SkipSquashLedgerEntry`:

```
ContactBusinessRelation2 - OnPreDataItem()
IF ContactOK AND ((GETFILTERS<>'') OR SquashFilters) THEN
  ContactOK := FALSE
ELSE
  CurrReport.BREAK;


ContactBusinessRelation2 - OnAfterGetRecord()
SkipSquashLedgerEntry := FALSE;
IF NOT SquashFilters THEN BEGIN
  ContactOK := TRUE;
  SkipSquashLedgerEntry := TRUE;
  CurrReport.BREAK;
END;
```

The `SquashFilters` is determined in the `OnPreReport` trigger:

```
Report - OnPreReport()
ItemFilters := "Value Entry".HASFILTER;

//* Squash >>>
SquashFilters := "Squash Ledger Entry".HASFILTER;
//* Squash <<<
...
```

The code in the Squash Ledger Entry `DataItem` should look like this:

```
Squash Ledger Entry - OnPreDataItem()
IF SkipSquashLedgerEntry THEN
  CurrReport.BREAK;

CASE ContactBusinessRelation2."Link to Table" OF
  ContactBusinessRelation2."Link to Table"::"Squash Player":
  BEGIN
    SETRANGE("Squash Player No.",
      ContactBusinessRelation2."No.");
  END;
  ELSE
    CurrReport.BREAK;
END;
```

```
Squash Ledger Entry - OnAfterGetRecord()
ContactOK := TRUE;

IF ContactOK THEN
  CurrReport.BREAK;
```

Make sure we filter on our instance of Contact Business Relation and that we filter on our link to the squash player table.

The `ContactOK` indicates that all contact persons connected to this squash ledger entry will be inserted.

Implementing criteria filters

To support the criteria filter functionality, we need to make two changes, one to the **Add Contacts** report and the other to the `SegCriteriaManagement` codeunit.

In the **Add Contacts** report, we add this C/AL code to the `OnPreReport` trigger. This will make a call to the `SegCriteriaManagement Codeunit (5062)`:

```
OnPreReport()
...
SegCriteriaManagement.InsertCriteriaFilter(
  "Segment Header".GETFILTER("No."),DATABASE::"Value Entry",
  "Value Entry".GETFILTERS,"Value Entry".GETVIEW(FALSE));
//* Squash >>>
SegCriteriaManagement.InsertCriteriaFilter(
  "Segment Header".GETFILTER("No."),
    DATABASE::"Squash Ledger Entry",
    "Squash Ledger Entry".GETFILTERS,
    "Squash Ledger Entry".GETVIEW(FALSE));
//* Squash <<<
```

In the `SegCriteriaManagement` codeunit, we add this code to the `SegCriteriaFilter` function, which will require a new local variable for `Squash Ledger Entry`:

```
SegCriteriaFilter()
...

CASE TableNo OF
  ...
//* Squash Ledger Entry >>>
  DATABASE::"Squash Ledger Entry":
    BEGIN
      SquashLedgEntry.SETVIEW(View);
```

```
            EXIT(SquashLedgEntry.GETFILTERS);
        END;
//* Squash Ledger Entry <<<
END;
```

Test solution

Now, we can test the solution by trying to add all squash player of type **Member** to a **Segment**:

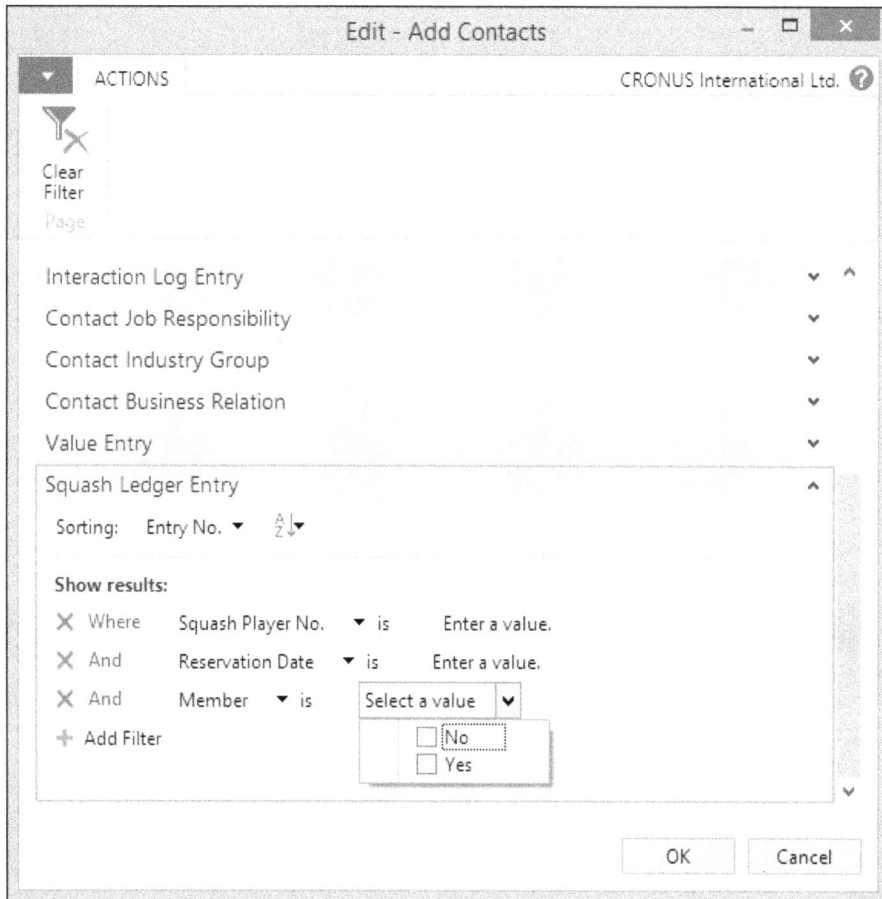

The result is a segment with the required squash players.

Segment Criteria ▾		
		Filter: SM00001
Action/Table	Filter	
Add Contacts		
Squash Ledger Entry	Member: Yes	

> This change also needs to be implemented to the reduce/refine functionality, which works similar to the add contacts report.

Summary

In this chapter, we took a deep dive into the Microsoft Dynamics NAV relationship management functionality. We learned how it is integrated with the ERP part of the system. Relationship management can be very useful to analyze sales data. With profiles, we can filter on turnover and profit figures and use them in segments.

Interaction Log Entries allow us to keep track of all the contact moments with the people we do business with. Outlook integration can be used for salespeople to work remotely and synchronize with the system.

Campaigns and opportunities help us to keep track of the quote process and make our sales working more efficient.

Lastly, we looked at some common requirements to change the relationship management system to meet our company's specific requirements.

In the next chapters, we will look at the ERP part of Microsoft Dynamics NAV starting with the process in *Chapter 5, Production*, and *Chapter 6, Trade*.

5
Production

The previous chapters introduced the key concepts of Microsoft Dynamics NAV as well as the details of the financial application and CRM. These horizontal modules can be implemented in most industries without big structural changes.

In this chapter, we will discuss three ways of implementing production in Microsoft Dynamics NAV using the standard functionality and customized features.

We'll discuss item tracking and item costing and what procedures and objects are used to get this working correctly in the application. For manufacturing, we will discuss the general concepts and data model rather than going into the details of each and every functional possibility.

We will also discuss kitting, which is only available in a limited number of countries such as North America, France, and Australia, but will most likely be moved to the worldwide version in future versions.

At the end of the chapter, we will look at the five different vertical industries and highlight two specific features of these industries that are not implemented in the standard product and discuss how the problems could be solved.

After reading this chapter, you will have a better understanding about the concepts of production in Microsoft Dynamics NAV, how this fits together with the rest of the application, and how to think out of the box if it does not immediately fit your process.

What is production?

Production is the process of creating a new product using raw materials or prefabricated items and resources.

Production as we know it today started centuries before the industrial revolution with craftsmen and assistants creating products using raw materials produced by nature and farmers. Today, this method of production still exists for many luxury items such as custom-made furniture or clothes.

The industrial revolution changed production into manufacturing, with the introduction of machines and mass production. This allowed production to grow by being less dependent on craftsmen and manual labor.

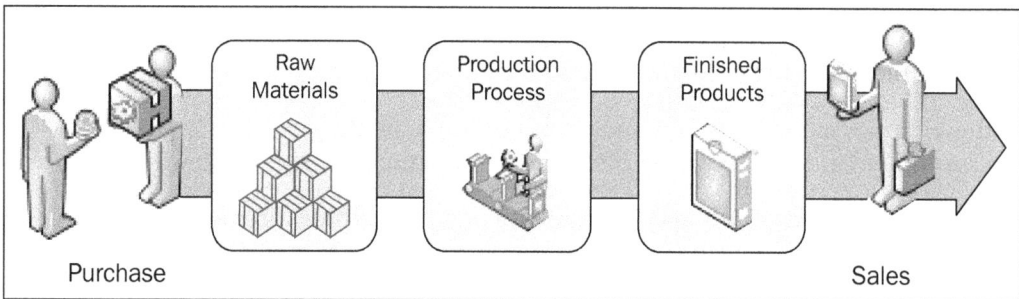

The introduction of computers in manufacturing companies allows the production of more sophisticated items and has made manufacturing more flexible.

To implement Microsoft Dynamics NAV for production companies, it is crucial to understand which level of production is being used in your company.

Production methodologies

In this chapter, we will differentiate between the following three production methodologies:

- **Assembling production**: When production is combining items into one new item without changing the items or scrap, we will refer to it as assembling.

- **Manufactured production**: This is the most complex production method to be implemented in Microsoft Dynamics NAV. Raw materials are combined into one or more products leaving scrap.

- **Specialized production**: These are often one off items or items produced in small numbers. The system should support the basics of the production process but should still be flexible enough to fit the company.

Raw materials

Each product we consume starts out as raw materials, such as cotton, iron ore, logs, and oil, which are then processed to be used in a production process. Other raw materials are water and air or fruits and vegetables. All raw materials are produced by mother nature. The production of some raw materials such as logs, cotton, fruits, and vegetables, can be influenced by humans. Other raw materials are more limited such as iron ore, oil, and water.

Basic production principles

Before going into Microsoft Dynamics NAV, we will discuss some terminology that is important to understand the concepts of production in ERP.

Bill of materials

The bill of materials defines what components are used to assemble or manufacture one item. The components in the bill of materials are also items, so before creating a new bill of materials, all component items must be created in the system.

> In Microsoft Dynamics NAV, there are two separate bill of material definitions, one for assembling and the other for manufacturing.

Material requirements planning

Material requirements planning (MRP) was introduced in the 1960s as a calculation method for production scheduling and was quickly replaced by **Manufacturing Resource Planning** (MRP II).

While ERP replaces MRP, MRP is still a crucial part of ERP applications.

Microsoft Dynamics NAV has a built-in MRP algorithm but also allows developers to create their own algorithms using the built-in data model. MRP analyzes dependent demand, which is demand that comes from production orders for components.

Garbage In Garbage Out

The biggest risk in running MRP algorithms is the **Garbage In Garbage Out** (**GIGO**) principle. To plan well, the data in the system must be absolutely correct or the planning will contain errors.

If, for example, the shipment dates in the sales orders are not entered correctly, the planning algorithm has no chance of giving correct results. The garbage in (wrong dates) will result in garbage out (wrong planning).

Master Production Schedule

Master Production Schedule (**MPS**) is the term used for production planning and scheduling. An MPS is used for decision making, linking supply and demand. It analyzes independent demand, that is, demand that comes from sales orders, service orders, and the production forecast.

Item costing

For manufacturing companies, it is crucial to be able to calculate real item costing and profitability. The cost of an item consists of the costs of all the components it was created from, as well as the production time and cost of any machinery used.

In production companies, high costs are incurred before an item can be even manufactured and sold. Machines need to be purchased and installed and new manufacturing plants may need to be built.

Item tracking

Item tracking is a relatively new concept that was introduced due to the need to be able to trace back an item to its original production batch in the supply chain. Whenever something is wrong with a specific item, it is interesting to see whether other items that were produced in the same batch have the same issue and maybe even require a recall of all items.

Quality control

During the production process and especially at the end, quality control is a crucial stage. Items can be rejected completely or may require extra handling.

In quality control, items are checked for mistakes. The way this is done depends on the production process. In the automobile industry, all cars are checked individually, while in the chemical industry, parts of batches are taken out and checked, assuming that the rest of the batch has the same quality.

Quality control is always at the end of the production process but can also be in between each of the main production processes. Sometimes, the item that is manufactured depends on the result of quality control. In this case, each level of quality is represented by a special item number.

Energy and waste

When manufacturing an item, the obvious components are the items in the bill of materials. It is becoming exceedingly crucial to use less energy and leave less waste materials in this process as our environment is becoming more and more vulnerable. As recycling is becoming increasingly important, these components have a bigger pressure on production cost and planning.

Association for Operations Management

To learn more about production, it is interesting to study the materials provided by the **Association for Operations Management (APICS)**. APICS is the organization that is recognized worldwide as the leading authority on manufacturing standards, similar to how the W3C is considered the authority on XML standards.

> More information about APICS can be found at
> http://www.apics.org/.

Getting started

Let's walk through two scripts to generate a new item with a bill of materials: one for an assembling process and the other for manufacturing.

We will set up both, item costing and item tracking for these products.

> The examples are created using a CRONUS W1 Microsoft
> Dynamics NAV 2013 Release 2 database without changes.

Assembling

In our company, we want to start producing office chairs. These chairs consist of five wheels, a pedestal, a seat, and two arm rests. We will create these four components as a new item and one new item for the end product.

All the items will have a different costing method to demonstrate the effect of cost changes. The end product will support serial number item tracking with a one year warranty period.

Design patterns

Before going into the application, we will have a look at how this process is solved in Microsoft Dynamics NAV. The following diagram illustrates the process:

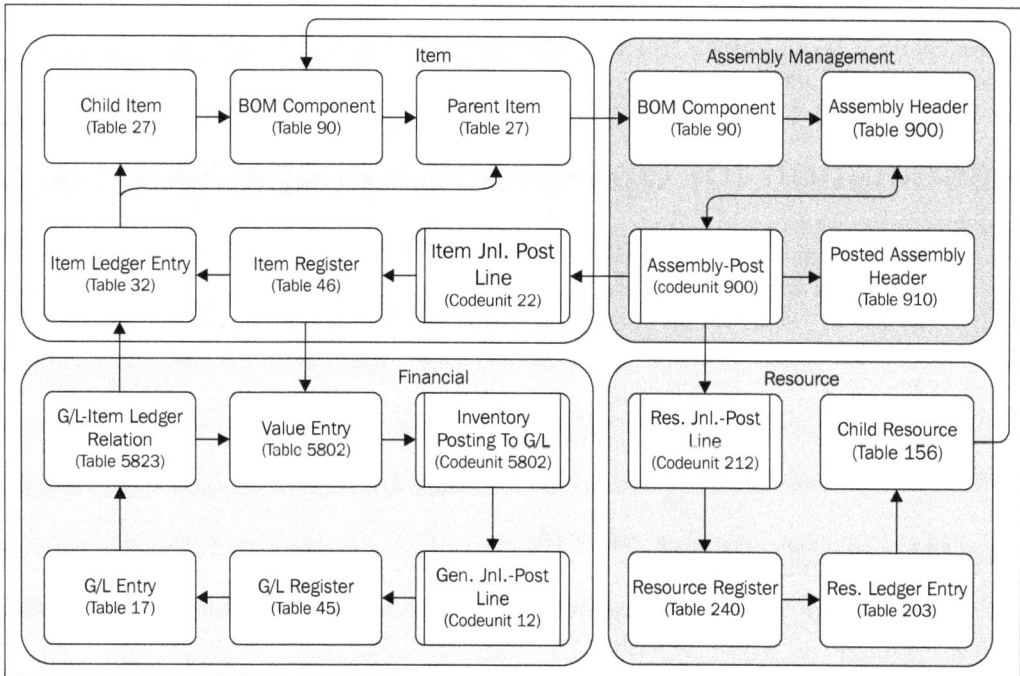

It starts with creating the components and end products as items in the database and connecting them using the **BOM Component** table. A **BOM Component** can also contain **Resources**.

If the components are in stock, we can use the assembly documents to create the products. When posting the assembly document, the components are consumed and the product is created. During this process, the system will create **Resource Ledger Entries**, **Item Ledger Entries**, and **Value Entries**.

The **Value Entries** can be posted in the general ledger using the **Inventory Posting to G/L** routine, either manual or in real time. This completes the process.

The items

For this example, we will need to create five items, four components, and one end product. We will assign an estimated unit cost to the components and a unit price to the end product, as shown in the following table:

No.	Description	Base UOM	Unit cost	Unit price	Costing
CHAPTER5-C1	Chapter 5 | Wheel	PCS	5		FIFO
CHAPTER5-C2	Chapter 5 | Pedestal	PCS	60		LIFO
CHAPTER5-C3	Chapter 5 | Seat	PCS	120		Average
CHAPTER5-C4	Chapter 5 | Arm Rest	PCS	35		Standard
CHAPTER5-P1	Chapter 5 | Office Chair	PCS		500	Specific

> In a real implementation, we would never set up a bill of materials with so many different costing methods for each item. This is strictly for the purpose of explaining what each costing method does and that Microsoft Dynamics NAV is technically capable of dealing with this.

Item costing

Item costing determines the calculation method of the item costs. We will assign a different costing method to each Item. Let's briefly discuss the available costing methods in Microsoft Dynamics NAV:

- **FIFO**: First in First out. The cost of the oldest item ledger entry is used.

- **LIFO**: Last in First out. The cost of the newest item ledger entry is used.

> When using FIFO or LIFO, the cost is applied within **Lot No.** if item tracking is used with Lot numbering. That is, the cost associated with the specific **Lot No.** is used.

- **Average**: Each time we purchase items, the total costs are divided by the total quantity. The result is used as unit cost.

- **Standard**: The user will define the unit cost manually. All deviations in purchase pricing are posted as profit or loss when invoicing.

- **Specific**: This is always combined with item tracking and serial numbers. Each serial number uses its own unique unit cost.

> The costing methods are not related to the warehouse picking method but only apply to financial costing calculations.

Item tracking

All our chairs will get a serial number with a one year warranty period. This enables us to track all individual chairs when they come back to the factory with issues.

Item tracking in Microsoft Dynamics NAV can be done both on individual Serial numbers and Lot numbers for a group of items.

Serial Numbers and **Lot Numbers** are fields in the Item Ledger Entry table (32). The consequence of this will be that for each serial number or Lot number, an individual record will be created in the table. When using serial numbers, this can lead to a massive increase in the table size.

The Lot numbers and item numbers are saved in the Reservation Entry table (337) during the document entry process. A reservation entry can be assigned to any table in Microsoft Dynamics NAV, for example, sales lines, item journal lines, or production order.

When a document is posted and the item ledger entry is created, the reservation entry is removed and replaced by a tracking specification record that has the same value in the **Entry No.** field as the corresponding item ledger entry.

> A reservation entry used for item tracking should not be confused with normal reservation entries in the sales and purchase process.

The process of item tracking in Microsoft Dynamics NAV works as drawn in the following schema:

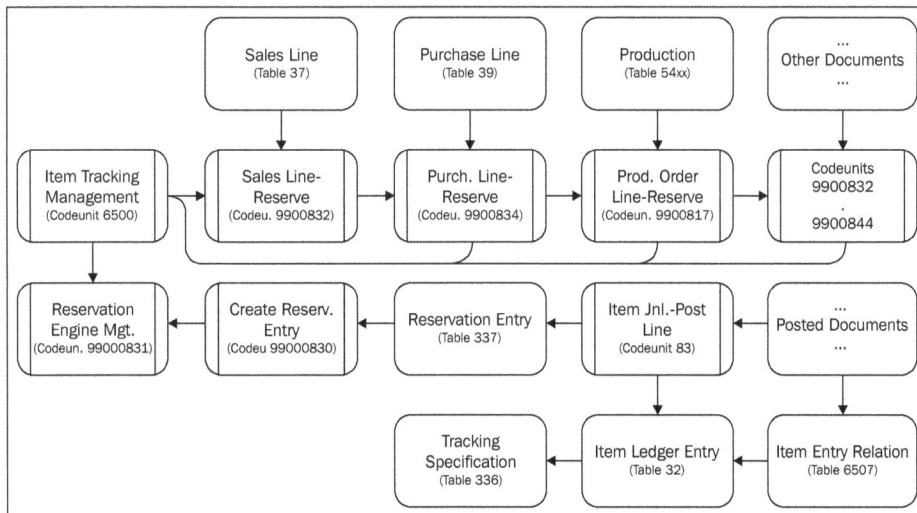

Technically, item tracking in Microsoft Dynamics NAV is very complex and should only be changed by experienced developers after careful analysis.

We will discuss the reservation process in more detail in *Chapter 6, Trade*.

The bill of materials

When the items are created, the costing method is defined and item tracking is set up. The next step is to create the bill of materials for the office chair. This can be done using the **Bill of Materials** option in the **Assembly List** in the **Item List** or **Card** page.

The bill of materials defines the component items and resources that will be used to create one new end product.

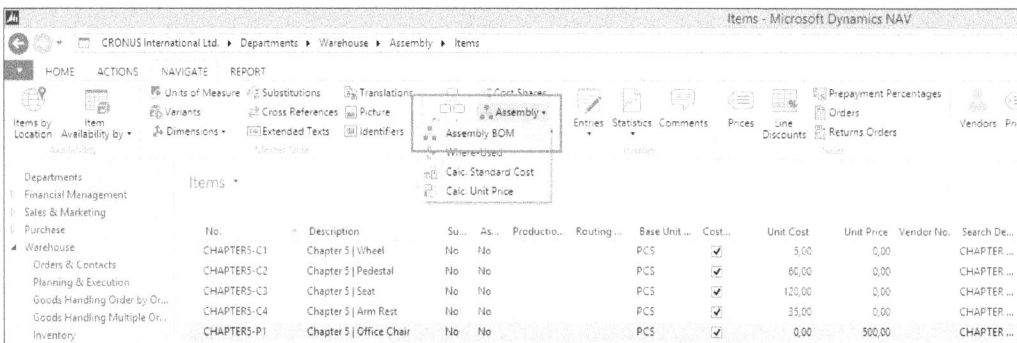

We set up the components as discussed earlier using five wheels, one pedestal, and seat and two arm rests.

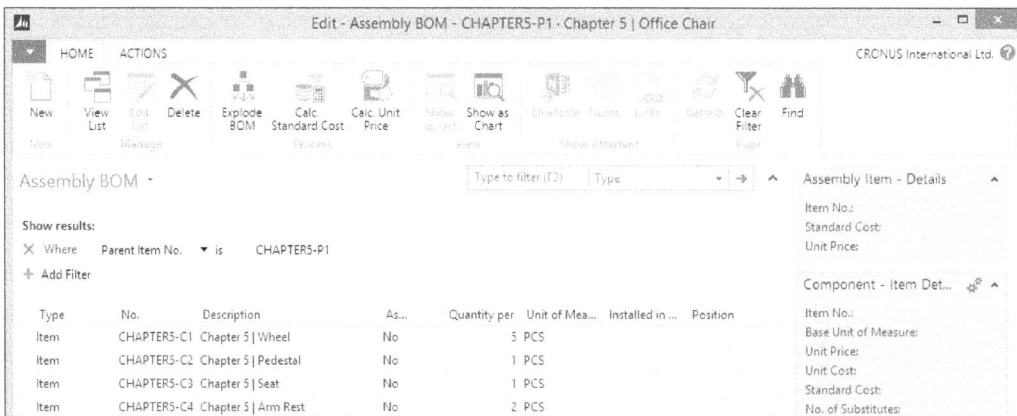

Calculating the standard cost

The components we selected for the bill of materials have a unit cost. Together these items can determine the unit cost of our end product.

We can calculate the standard cost of the office chair by selecting **Calc. Standard Cost** in the same **Assembly** menu we used for the bill of materials.

> The name **Calc. Standard Cost** in the calculation option is not to be confused with the costing method. This function should be executed for all costing methods.

The standard cost is now calculated using the unit cost of the components and the overhead rate and indirect cost percent. We will not use the latter in our example.

```
((5*5) + (1*60) + (1*120) + (2*35)) = 275
```

Creating the inventory

Before we can assemble the chairs, we need to purchase the components. For this, we will create a purchase order with eight purchase lines. We will purchase the components for other prices than the unit cost in the system, allowing us to show what the impact of the costing methods is.

The purchase order will be received and invoiced.

> If the purchase order is only received and not invoiced, the example might not work because expected cost posting to G/L is not activated in the CRONUS database.

Adjusting cost item entries

The purchase order we just created, received, and invoiced has a different unit cost compared to the unit cost we initially set up in our items.

Depending on the costing method of the items, this will have an impact on the unit cost. When we take a look at the new unit cost of the items we created, we can see that this was impacted by the purchase order. However, the values are not correct. The system only adopts the first change of unit cost.

No.	Description	Su...	As...	Base Unit ...	Cost...	Unit Cost	Unit Price
CHAPTER5-C1	Chapter 5 | Wheel	No	No	PCS	☐	4,00	0,00
CHAPTER5-C2	Chapter 5 | Pedestal	No	No	PCS	☐	70,00	0,00
CHAPTER5-C3	Chapter 5 | Seat	No	No	PCS	☐	115,00	0,00
CHAPTER5-C4	Chapter 5 | Arm Rest	No	No	PCS	☐	35,00	0,00

To correct this, we need to run the Adjust Cost Item Entries (Report 795) batch. This will determine the new unit cost based on the costing method.

No.	Description	Su...	As...	Base Unit ...	Cost...	Unit Cost	Unit Price
CHAPTER5-C1	Chapter 5 | Wheel	No	No	PCS	☑	4,50	0,00
CHAPTER5-C2	Chapter 5 | Pedestal	No	No	PCS	☑	65,00	0,00
CHAPTER5-C3	Chapter 5 | Seat	No	No	PCS	☑	117,50	0,00
CHAPTER5-C4	Chapter 5 | Arm Rest	No	No	PCS	☑	35,00	0,00

The unit cost for FIFO, LIFO, and average have been recalculated while the standard cost has not been impacted by the transactions.

> The **Adjust Cost Item Entries** report should be scheduled to run periodically in your database. Even if the database is set to use Expected Cost Posting and Auto Cost Posting.

Posting inventory cost to G/L

Microsoft Dynamics NAV supports posting the inventory cost to the general ledger. This enables accountants to have a single point for data analysis rather than printing an inventory report and using the figures manually for reports to the management.

This can be done using the **Post Inventory Cost to G/L** function (report 1002), as shown in the following screenshot:

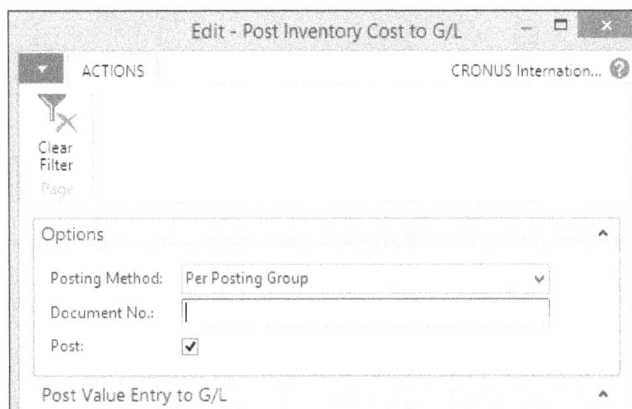

Check, check, and double check

To check whether the value entries and the general ledger are synchronized, we can run Inventory Valuation (Report 1001). This will show us the inventory value versus the amount posted to the general ledger.

Inventory Valuation
CRONUS International Ltd.

Item No: CH*

| Inventory Posting Group Name | | Base | As of | | Increases (LCY) | | Decreases (LCY) | | As of 23-01-15 | | Cost Posted to |
Item No.	Description	UoM	Quantity	Value	Quantity	Value	Quantity	Value	Quantity	Value	G/L
RAW MAT											
CHAPTER5-C1	Chapter 5 | Wheel	PCS	0	0,00	10	45,00			10	45,00	45,00
CHAPTER5-C2	Chapter 5 | Pedestal	PCS	0	0,00	2	130,00			2	130,00	130,00
CHAPTER5-C3	Chapter 5 | Seat	PCS	0	0,00	2	235,00			2	235,00	235,00
CHAPTER5-C4	Chapter 5 | Arm Rest	PCS	0	0,00	4	140,00			4	140,00	140,00
RAW MAT				0,00		550,00		0,00		550,00	550,00
Total				0,00		550,00		0,00		550,00	550,00

Recalculating the standard unit cost

The standard unit cost we calculated for our office chair was 275. This was based on our assumption of purchase prices. Now that we have really purchased and received the components, we can calculate a new unit cost based on the real prices.

In this example, the price will still be 275 since the total price of all purchased items is 550. The inventory allows us to make two chairs with these materials:

```
(550 / 2) = 275
```

> With this calculation method, it is possible to check the results of the Calculate Unit Cost algorithm.

Assembly orders

Now that we have the components in stock and the unit cost correct, we can create a chair. We will do this using an assembly order.

In the assembly order, we need to create one line for each item we want to assemble. The components are automatically used when posting the order. We will use the Purchasing Agent Role Center (9007) for this.

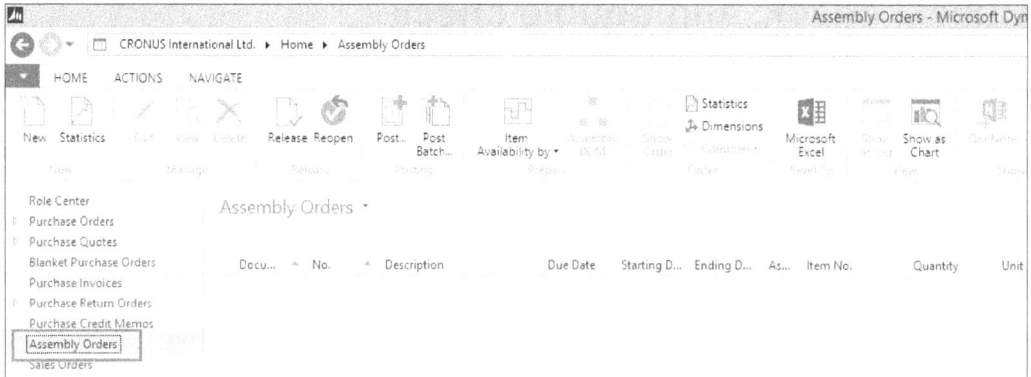

Assembly orders

After creating a document for the office chair, while trying to post the document, we will receive an error message because we first need to specify the serial numbers.

Specifying Serial Number

Serial numbers and Lot numbers can be set up using the **Item Tracking Lines** option. This opens the **Item Tracking Line** page (6510). This page is able to show both the reservation entries during the registration process as well as the tracking specification if the item ledger entry is already created.

We will manually create a new serial number. Microsoft Dynamics NAV also supports system generated serial numbers.

We can now post this assembly order and will have one office chair in stock with a serial number.

Check costing (again)

Creating the office chair changed the inventory of the component items and therefore might have affected the costing of our items. However, when we now check our items, the unit cost has not changed.

No.	Description	As...	Base Unit ...	Cost...	Unit Cost	Unit Price
CHAPTER5...	Chapter 5 | Wheel	No	PCS	☐	4,50	0,00
CHAPTER5...	Chapter 5 | Pedestal	No	PCS	☐	65,00	0,00
CHAPTER5...	Chapter 5 | Seat	No	PCS	☐	117,50	0,00
CHAPTER5...	Chapter 5 | Arm Rest	No	PCS	☐	35,00	0,00
CHAPTER5...	Chapter 5 | Office Chair	Yes	PCS	☐	275,00	500,00

Even so, with the current inventory, the unit cost might be different. Remember we used 5 wheels using FIFO costing 4 and one seat using LIFO costing 70.

Let's run **Adjust Cost Entries** using the **Posting to G/L** option:

No.	Description	As...	Base Unit ...	Cost...	Unit Cost	Unit Price
CHAPTER5...	Chapter 5 | Wheel	No	PCS	☑	5,00	0,00
CHAPTER5...	Chapter 5 | Pedestal	No	PCS	☑	70,00	0,00
CHAPTER5...	Chapter 5 | Seat	No	PCS	☑	117,50	0,00
CHAPTER5...	Chapter 5 | Arm Rest	No	PCS	☑	35,00	0,00
CHAPTER5...	Chapter 5 | Office Chair	Yes	PCS	☑	267,50	0,00

The unit cost has changed and now shows us that we have used the first five wheels using FIFO, leaving the other five wheels in the inventory for a value of **5**. We used the last seat using LIFO, leaving the first seat in the inventory for a value of **70**.

When we run the **Inventory Valuation,** we can see that producing the first chair actually costs **267,50** but we posted **275**.

Inventory Valuation

CRONUS International Ltd.

zondag 1 juni 2014
Page   1
MARK-PC1\MARK

Item No. CH*

Inventory Posting Group Name		Base UoM	As of		Increases (LCY)		Decreases (LCY)		As of 23-01-16		Cost Posted to G/L
Item No.	Description		Quantity	Value	Quantity	Value	Quantity	Value	Quantity	Value	
FINISHED											
CHAPTER5-P1	Chapter 5 | Office Chair	PCS	0	0,00	1	275,00			1	275,00	275,00
FINISHED				0.00		275.00		0.00		275,00	275,00
RAW MAT											
CHAPTER5-C1	Chapter 5 | Wheel	PCS	0	0,00	10	45,00	5	22,50	5	22,50	22,50
CHAPTER5-C2	Chapter 5 | Pedestal	PCS	0	0,00	2	130,00	1	65,00	1	65,00	65,00
CHAPTER5-C3	Chapter 5 | Seat	PCS	0	0,00	2	235,00	1	117,50	1	117,50	117,50
CHAPTER5-C4	Chapter 5 | Arm Rest	PCS	0	0,00	4	140,00	2	70,00	2	70,00	70,00
RAW MAT				0.00		550,00		275,00		275,00	275,00
Total				0.00		825,00		275,00		550,00	550,00

Recalculating the unit cost (again)

When we run **Calculate Unit Cost** for our office chair, we can see that the new cost will be 282,50.

```
(5*5) + (1*70) + (1* 117,50) + (2*35) = 282,50
```

Together with the first chair worth 267,50, we match our purchase invoice worth 550.

Standard cost worksheet

We need to correct the cost of the first chair, which is currently on inventory to have a correct inventory value. We can do this using the **Standard Cost Worksheets**, as shown in the following screenshot:

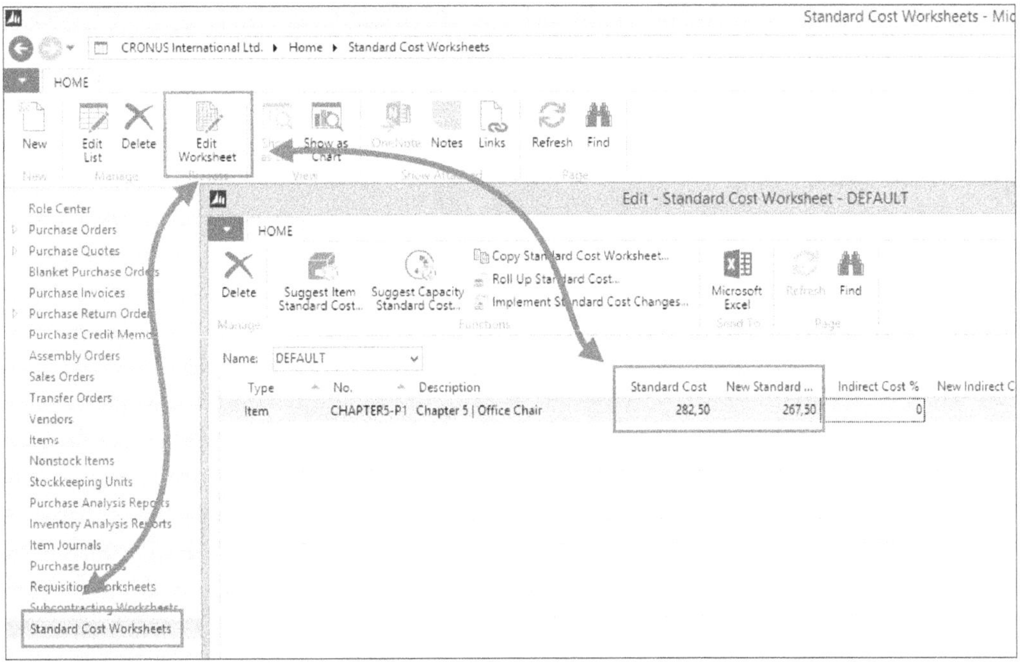

This worksheet allows us to correct old value entries by creating an entry in the Item Revaluation Journal when we select the **Implement Standard Cost Change** option. This will create a new value entry with the delta values to keep track of changes.

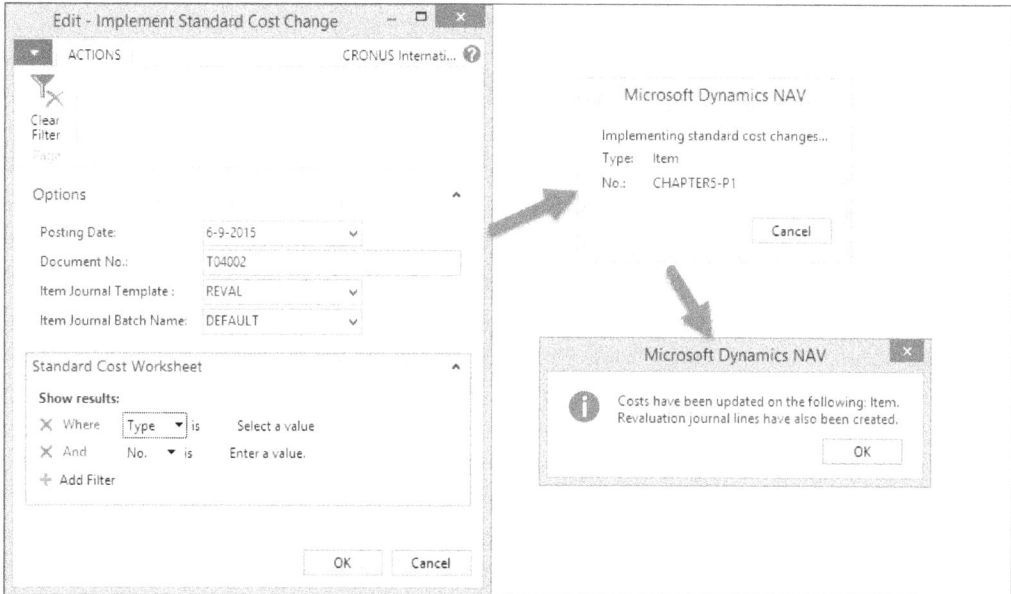

Item Revaluation Journal

The last step is to post the **Item Revaluation Journal** and run the **Post Inventory Cost to G/L** routine.

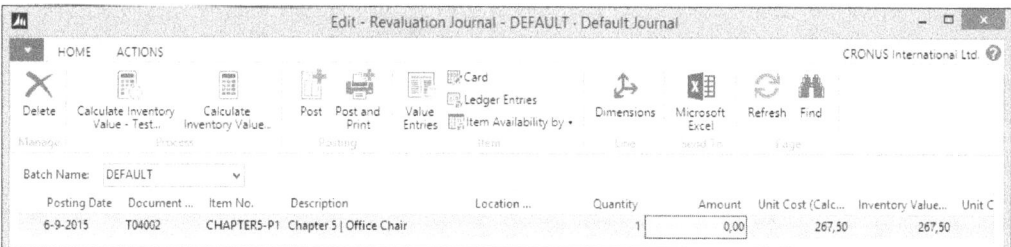

> We also need to run the **Calculate Standard Cost** for the office chair since this batch will reset the unit cost to **267,50**.

The result

When we now run the **Inventory Valuation Report,** we can see that the **Office Chair** on stock is worth **267,50** and the remaining inventory is **282,50**:

Inventory Valuation

CRONUS International Ltd.

zondag 1 juni 2014
Page   1
MARK-PC1\MARK

Item No. CH*

Inventory Posting Group Name		Base UoM	As of		Increases (LCY)		Decreases (LCY)		As of 23-01-16		Cost Posted to G/L
Item No.	Description		Quantity	Value	Quantity	Value	Quantity	Value	Quantity	Value	
FINISHED											
CHAPTERS-P1	Chapter 5 | Office Chair	PCS	0	0,00	1	267,50			1	267,50	267,50
FINISHED				0,00		267,50		0.00		267,50	267,50
RAW MAT											
CHAPTERS-C1	Chapter 5 | Wheel	PCS	0	0,00	10	45,00	5	20,00	5	25,00	25,00
CHAPTERS-C2	Chapter 5 | Pedestal	PCS	0	0,00	2	130,00	1	60,00	1	70,00	70,00
CHAPTERS-C3	Chapter 5 | Seat	PCS	0	0,00	2	235,00	1	117,50	1	117,50	117,50
CHAPTERS-C4	Chapter 5 | Arm Rest	PCS	0	0,00	4	140,00	2	70,00	2	70,00	70,00
RAW MAT				0,00		550,00		267,50		282,50	282,50
Total				0,00		817,50		267,50		550,00	550,00

Summarizing item costing in 10 steps

All the steps we performed in the example can be summarized in this 10 step process diagram:

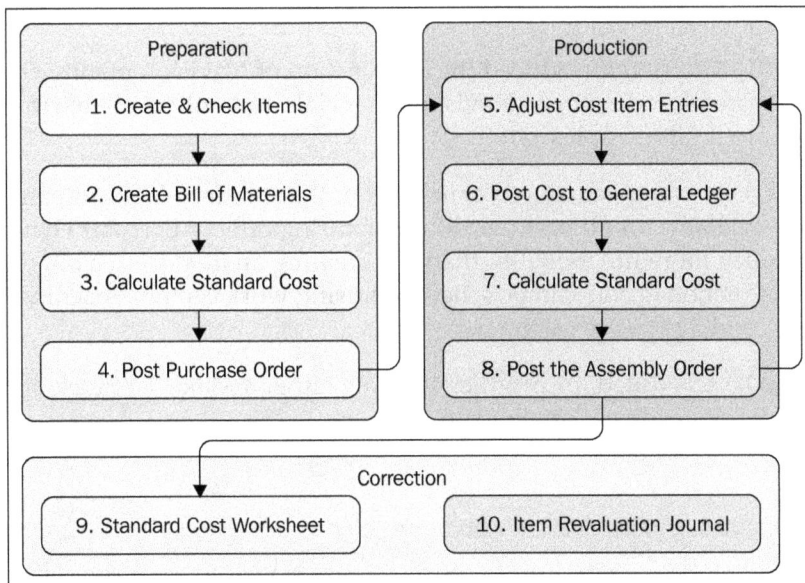

Let's have a look at the steps briefly:

1. We start by creating new items and setting up the costing method.
2. Then we create the bill of materials for the production item.
3. Run the **Calculate Standard Cost** routine to get a unit cost for the production item.
4. Purchase the necessary items for production.
5. Run the **Adjust Cost Item Entries** routine.
6. Synchronize the value entries with the G/L Entries using the **Post Inventory Cost to G/L** routine.
7. Recalculate the standard cost if desired.
8. Create an assembly order and post the document.
9. Run **Standard Cost Worksheet** to change the standard cost.
10. Run the **Item Revaluation Journal** to implement the standard cost for old value entries.

Manufacturing

The assembly management module was added to the Microsoft Dynamics NAV product in Version 2013 and replaced the BOM Journal that existed since the introduction of the Windows version in 1995. Both enable us to create a new item out of other items.

In Version 2.01, Navision introduced the first version of Navision manufacturing. This was a separate product from Navision financials and only available for certified partners because of its complexity.

With Version 3.00, manufacturing became part of the standard Navision attain package and available for all partners. Manufacturing offers Microsoft Dynamics NAV users much more functionality than just creating an item from a bill of materials. Production orders can be scheduled using work centers, machine centers, tools, and a capacity calendar.

The items can be scheduled for production using either a Make-To-Stock or a Make-To-Order policy in a planning run.

The system calculates the required BOM components and can create purchase orders if the inventory is insufficient using a complex demand and supply process. If we put this into a design pattern, it looks like this:

The **Production Order** is the center of the process, which is created by items having a **Production BOM** that are either on sales order or low on inventory.

The **Planning Run** populates the **Planning Worksheet**, which is based on the **Requisition Line** table (246). The planning worksheet can be used to create the production orders and purchase orders.

During the production process, the **Consumption Journal** is used to record the use of the child items from **Production BOM** and the **Output Journal** creates the new item once it is finished. Alternatively, these steps can be combined in the **Production Journal**.

Let's demonstrate this with the next example using the **Production Planner** role center (9010).

We will create mahogany English desks using raw materials, machines, and resources.

The items, machines, and work centers

For the desks, we need mahogany wood, green leather, glue, lacquer, and handles. To create one desk, the carpenter needs four days and one carpentry unit with tools. The painter needs one day to varnish the desk in the paint booth and the assembly department wraps up the components in boxes and needs four hours.

We need the following items for this example:

No.	Description	Base UOM	Replenishment System	Unit Cost	Unit Price	Manufacturing Policy
CHAPTER5-P1	Mahogany English Desk	PCS	Prod. Order	286,25	999	Make-to-Order
CHAPTER5-C1	Mahogany Log	PCS	Purchase	100		-
CHAPTER5-C2	Green Leather	PCS	Purchase	60		-
CHAPTER5-C3	Glue	CAN	Purchase	15		-
CHAPTER5-C4	Mahogany Lacquer	CAN	Purchase	25		-
CHAPTER5-C5	English Desk Handles	PCS	Purchase	10		-

The following list is for machine centers:

No.	Name	Work Center No.	Capacity	Efficiency
01-CARP	Std. Carpentry Unit w. Tools	400	1	100
02-PAINT	Paint Booth	300	1	100
03-PACK	Packaging Department	200	1	100

Capacity

The planning run and the requisition worksheets will use capacity if it is defined. The capacity is defined for each **Work Center** and **Machine Center**.

The capacity is stored in the **Calendar Entries**, which are created using codeunit **CalendarManagement (99000755)** and reports **Calculate Work Center Calendar (99001046)** and Calc. Machine **Center Calendar (99001045)**. Capacity is based on the concurrent capacity, from either the machine or work center, and the assigned shop calendar.

Just like the interaction log entries, the calendar entries are directly inserted instead of going through a journal first.

Calendar entries

When properly configured, the **Planning Worksheet** will calculate the starting and ending dates for the production order and each operation in order to meet the shipment date on the sales order line.

Production bill of materials

Setting up the Production bill of materials for manufacturing is not much different from the assembly functionality but it contains extra functionality.

Production

The Production BOM uses its own header record with a number series, description, and search description. The **Status** field is used to determine whether the product is new, certified, under development, or closed. Together with the versioning, it enables us to maintain multiple BOMs during the product's life cycle.

The components of the bill of materials are saved as lines and support using scrap. The **Scrap** % is calculated when running the MRP and calculating the unit cost.

Routing

The **Routing Setup** determines how long it will take to produce one item and which work centers and machine centers are used in the process.

The **Routing Setup** gives you advanced features such as parallel and serial planning, and setup time. For our example, we will keep it simple and only use the **Run Time**.

Testing and low-level code

We are now almost set to start testing our manufacturing item. We have set up the items and machine centers, calculated the calendar entries, and set up a routing.

The last step in the process is to calculate the low-level code. This field, which is stored both in the item and production BOM table, determines how low the item is in the BOM ranking. Low-level code zero means this is a parent item and one or higher is a child item or a child of a child item.

> The maximum value of the low-level code can be 50, but in reality this will be very difficult to work with and bad for system performance.

> If you received an error that you have exceeded 50 levels, check the production BOMs to ensure that there is no circular reference. It is possible to have a parent item consume a child item that consumes the parent.

The low-level codes can be calculated automatically or manually. For automatic calculation, the **Dynamic Low Level Code** feature should be activated.

Due to NAV ability to create a production BOM before it is attached to an item, the dynamic low-level code is not always accurate. Prior to a planning run, it is good practice to run the **Calculate Low Level Code (Codeunit 99000793)**.

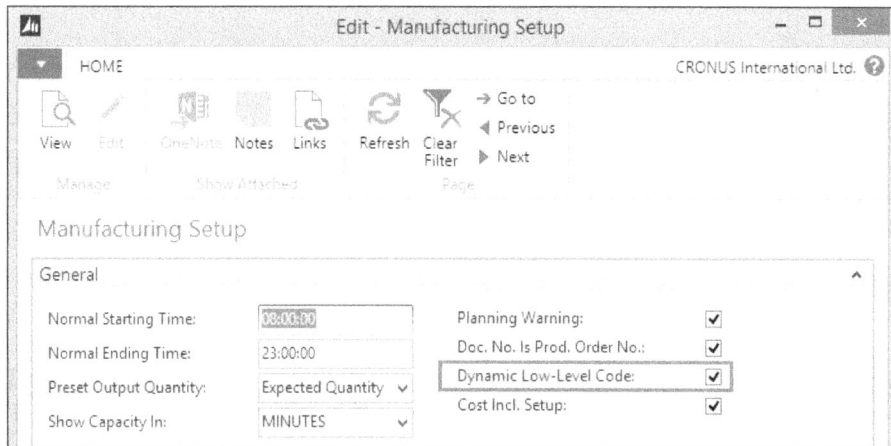

Activating **Dynamic Low Level Code** can however impact the performance of your system, so for most installations, it is preferable to periodically calculate this using **Codeunit Calc. Low-level code (99000853)**.

Simulation, sales orders, or inventory

There are three ways in Microsoft Dynamics NAV to create a production order. The easiest way is to manually enter them one by one. This can even be a simulation production order to test whether everything is set up as required.

Manual order entry is very time-consuming and is not often used by manufacturing companies. Most of them use MRP programs to plan the orders. When this is done using an external application, the interface will then create the production orders.

The MRP algorithm in Microsoft Dynamics NAV supports two policies, Make-To-Stock and Make-To-Order.

Make-To-Stock

Make-To-Stock, also called Build-To-Stock is often used for high volume items, which are sold to trading companies. When this manufacturing policy is used, the reordering policy should be used. Reordering policies will be discussed in *Chapter 6, Trade*.

Make-To-Order

Make-To-Order is often used in demand-driven items such as automobiles. Keeping these items in the inventory is very expensive. The manufacturing process is started after the item is sold.

However, most companies that use Make-To-Order have reserved time slots where these items can be scheduled, so the production capacity is already reserved but the item is not yet determined.

When using Make-To-Order, the MRP run will create production orders for all sales orders. We will use this manufacturing policy in our example.

The sales order

For our example, we need a sales order for one or more English desks.

> Be careful when picking a location since this will be the location where the desk will be manufactured.

1001 · The Cannon Group PLC

General

No.:	1001 ...	Document Date:	22-1-2015
Sell-to Customer No.:	10000	Requested Delivery Date:	
Sell-to Customer Name:	The Cannon Group PLC	External Document No.:	
Sell-to City:	Birmingham	Salesperson Code:	PS
Posting Date:	22-1-2015	Status:	Open
Order Date:	22-1-2015		

⌄ Show more fields

Lines

Line ▾   Functions ▾   Order ▾   Find   Filter   Clear Filter

Type	No.	Description	Location C...	Quantity	Qty. to Assemb...	Reserved Qu...	Unit of Mea...	Unit Price Ex
Item	CHAPTER5-P1	Mahogany English Desk	BLUE	10	...		PCS	9

Calculating MPS and MRP

The planning run in Microsoft Dynamics NAV creates lines in the requisition or planning worksheets. This worksheet structure is very important in the sales/purchase/production process. This worksheet can create purchase orders and production orders for sales orders.

Requisition versus planning versus subcontracting worksheets

The **Requisition Worksheet** can show different user interfaces (pages) allowing users to do different tasks.

Req. Worksheet Templates ▾

Type to filter (F3)   Name   ▾ →

Show results:

✕ Where   Name   ▾ is   Enter a value.

✛ Add Filter

Name	Description	Recurring	Page ID	Page Caption
PLANNING	Planning Worksheet	☐	99000852	Planning Worksheet
REQ	Req. Worksheet	☐	291	Req. Worksheet

The **Requisition Worksheet** does not have a general post line routine like the other journals. Each worksheet type uses a different process. The following schema shows how the requisition process ties together:

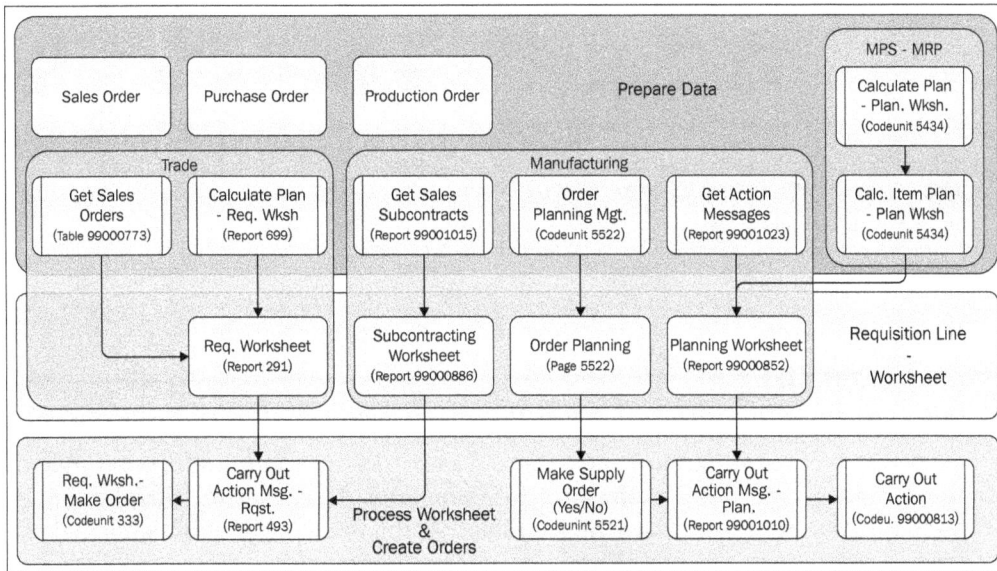

The **Trade** section will be discussed in *Chapter 6, Trade*. In this chapter, we will focus on the planning (MPS and MRP) process and the manufacturing part.

> The requisition worksheet process allows us to create our own process to prepare data using custom settings to generate the worksheet lines and even to build our own planning algorithm in a new C/AL object that will create requisition lines.

Inventory profile offsetting

The actual heart of the MRP calculation in Microsoft Dynamics NAV is codeunit Inventory Profile Offsetting (99000854), which is called from codeunit Calc. Item Plan - Plan Wksh. (5431) in our schema.

This codeunit is not easy to understand and should only be changed by specialized developers after careful analysis. The process uses the inventory profile buffer table during the calculation to build up information and starts with the function `CalculatePlanFromWorksheet`:

```
                        Codeunit 99000854 Inventory Profile Offsetting - C/AL Editor
 CalculatePlanFromWorksheet(VAR Item : Record Item;ManufacturingSetup2 : Record "Manufacturing Setup"
    PlanToDate := ToDate;
    InitVariables(InventoryProfile[1],ManufacturingSetup2,Item,TemplateName,WorksheetName,MRPPlanning);
    DemandtoInvProfile(InventoryProfile[1],Item,ToDate);
    ForecastConsumption(InventoryProfile[1],Item,OrderDate,ToDate);
    BlanketOrderConsump(InventoryProfile[1],Item,ToDate);
    SupplytoInvProfile(InventoryProfile[1],Item,ToDate);
    UnfoldItemTracking(InventoryProfile[1],InventoryProfile[2]);
    FindCombination(InventoryProfile[1],InventoryProfile[2],Item);
    PlanItem(InventoryProfile[1],InventoryProfile[2],OrderDate,ToDate,RespectPlanningParm);
    CommitTracking;
```

Atomic coding

The code unit in this image in the standard Microsoft Dynamics NAV application is a perfect example of atomic coding, also known as workflow coding. With this style of programming, you break down the code into functions that have functional naming and leave out any programming while calling the functions one by one. This makes your code easier to read for others and cheaper to maintain.

Let's look at the functions in this code unit:

- `InitVariables`: This function is used to clear and initialize variables used in this codeunit.

- `DemandtoInvProfile`: Here, the system creates records in the Inventory Profile table for Sales Orders, Service Orders, and Production Orders that may require items.

- `ForecastConsumption`: If **Use Forecast on Locations** is used in the manufacturing setup, additional demand lines are created in the inventory profile buffer based on the production forecast.

- `BlanketOrderConsump`: Additional demand is inserted for all blanket sales orders with a **Shipment Date** and **Outstanding Qty.** within the calculation period.

- `SupplytoInvProfile`: The current inventory, purchase orders, and production orders are added to the **Inventory Profile** as possible supply.

- `UnfoldItemTracking`: If the item uses **Item Tracking**, this function makes sure that Lot numbers and serial numbers match.

> In this function, Microsoft developers use a trick that when a temporary table with more dimensions, the values in both tables are identical. This blog entry at `https://marijebrummel.blog/2014/06/01/tip-27-using-temp-tables-in-arrays/`.

- `FindCombination`: This function creates temporary **Stock Keeping Unit** records for each SKU that requires replenishment. If the item does not have any SKU, the system will create a temporary SKU record.

- `PlanItem`: This is where the actual requisition lines are created for the item, based on the information in the **Inventory Profile** table and the setup.

- `CommitTracking`: This function saves information stored in temporary record variables to actual data in the database for reservation entries and action messages.

Calculating a plan

Let's run the **Planning Worksheet** for our English desk and see what planning lines we get.

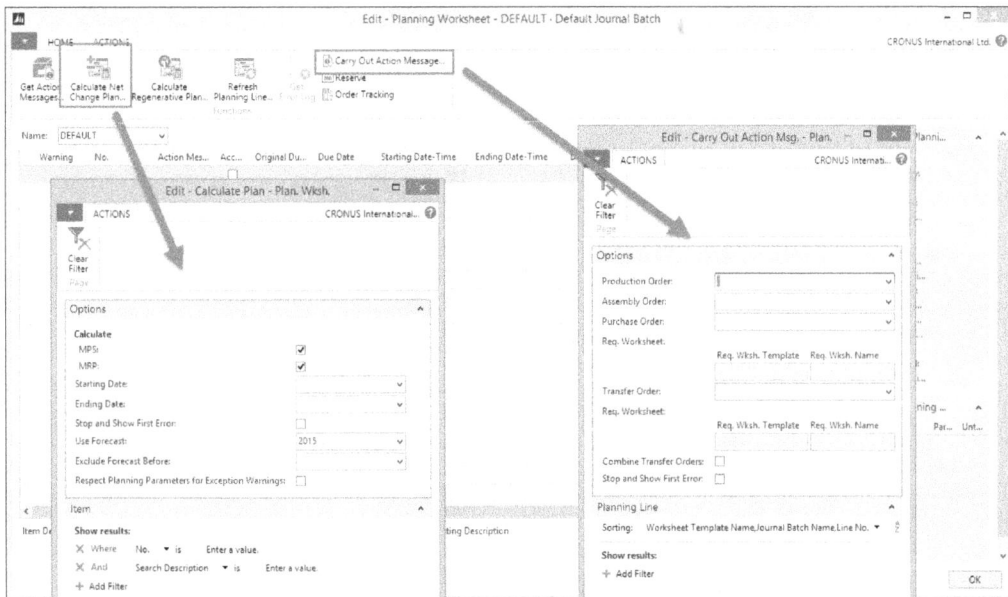

The MPS and MRP run is started from the **Planning Worksheet**. We need to enter a starting date and an ending date. In the CRONUS database using our example, we can use the current workdate.

When the MPS and MRP run is finished, we can start the process to **Carry Out Action Message** to create the **Production Order**.

Production order workflow

The production order is now created and ready to be started. The first status is **Planned** or **Firm Planned**. During the planned status, Microsoft Dynamics NAV can automatically change the production order.

Once the production order is released, it can no longer be automatically changed.

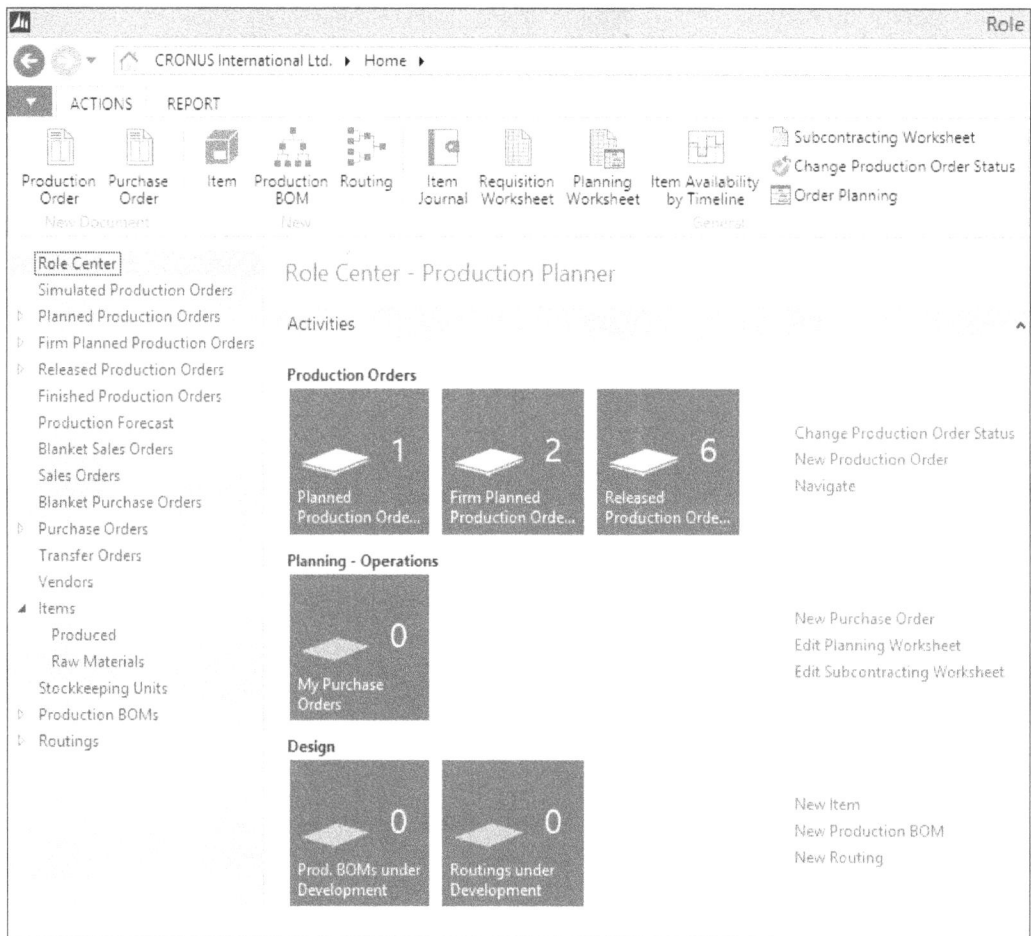

To release a production order, the components need to be available. In our test scenario, this is not yet true since we created new items, which have not been purchased.

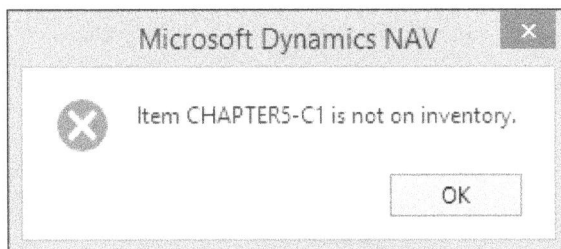

Let's see how we can do this.

Purchase orders

To create the purchase orders, we'll use the **Order Planning** worksheet to illustrate another method of planning. This will create requisition lines for the production order we just released.

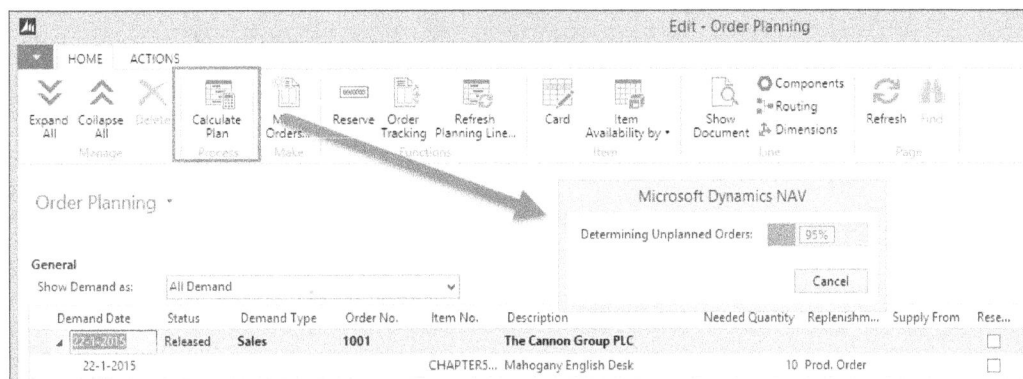

Once the requisition lines are created, we need to specify a vendor number in the **Supply From** field and then start the **Make Orders** process to generate the **Purchase Orders**.

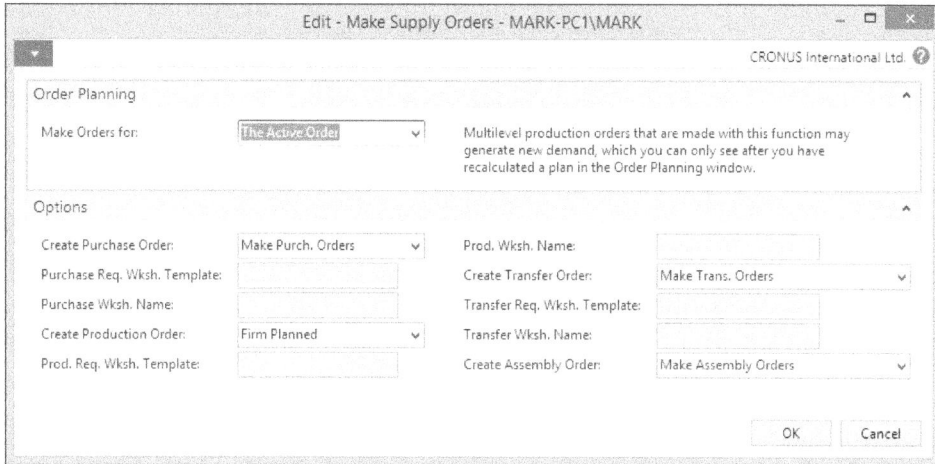

The **Purchase Order** can be received. This allows us to release the **Production Order**.

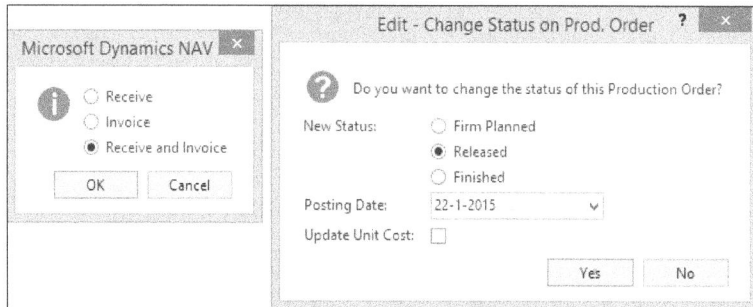

Finishing production

When the production order is finished, the end product should be in the inventory and the components should be consumed. This consumption process is called flushing.

This is done using the **Consumption Journal** and **Output Journal** and can be done automatically and manually.

> An alternative to the Consumption and Output Journal is the Production Journal that combines the functionality into one journal.

The Consumption Journal is automatically posted when the flushing method in the item card is set to Forward, Backward or Pick + Forward, Pick + Backward.

When using Forward, the Consumption Journal is posted when the production order is released, Backward will post when the production order is set to finished. Pick + Forward and Pick + Backward can be used in combination with **Warehouse Management Locations**.

Specialized production

The last production methodology we discussed at the beginning of the chapter is specialized production.

These are items produced in small numbers or items that have very different specifications each time they go into production. For these companies, creating a bill of materials each time an item changes is just too much work compared to the extra information they would get.

Jobs

Still, these companies want to register their production orders and get a clear view of their inventory. Most companies doing this kind of production are using the jobs functionality of Microsoft Dynamics NAV.

We will discuss this in *Chapter 8, Consulting*, where we will assemble custom-made computer systems with different components as an example.

Vertical industry implementation

Microsoft Dynamics NAV is used in many different vertical industries. Vertical industries often require specific features. Rather than trying to implement all these features in the standard product, Microsoft Dynamics NAV supports the framework and allows developers to design and create vertical features.

For these features, the 80/20 rule applies; Microsoft delivers 80 percent of the framework, which costs 20 percent of our time to implement. The missing 20 percent of the functionality is developed costing 80 percent of the budgeted time.

In this chapter, we will discuss how Microsoft Dynamics NAV is used for production in five different vertical industries. For each industry, we will discuss two specific vertical features and how they could be solved.

> Most industries have solid add-on solutions available designed by certified Microsoft Dynamics NAV partners that have been implemented at multiple sites. It is highly recommended to look at those add-on solutions instead of reinventing the wheel and rewriting an add-on that already exists.

Fashion

The general challenge in the fashion industry is sizes and colors. Each item can be produced and sold from XXS to XXXL and from pink to orange to green while remaining the same item.

This calls for the creative use of variants, which are heavily used by the available vertical solutions on the market.

Bill of materials

To use manufacturing with variants, the bill of material structure should be changed since this exists by default on the item level. However, each size uses different quantities of fabric and the different colors of fabric are often represented by another item number in the raw materials.

A solution for this might be to move the bill of materials from **Item level** to **Stock Keeping Unit level**. An SKU supports variants for costing and the inventory.

Shipping worksheet

Fashion companies produce items for a collection. Customers have the possibility to reserve on a collection in order for the production manager to determine how many to produce. Based on these numbers and an extra safety inventory, the production orders are created. Once the production orders are finished, the company needs to decide who gets the first items. This can be best described as a reversed make-to-order mechanism.

To enable this in Microsoft Dynamics NAV, we could create a worksheet that will create lines for each combination of production orders and sales orders. For each sales order that will be shipped, we could create a **Warehouse Pick** and **Shipment** from the **Shipping Worksheet**.

We will discuss stock keeping units, warehouse picks, and shipments in *Chapter 6, Trade*.

Automotive

In the automotive industry, Microsoft Dynamics NAV is mostly used by car manufacturing suppliers, the companies that make prefabricated parts out of raw materials.

Tooling and amortization

In these companies, the **Production Part Approval Process (PPAP)** is very important as well as the tooling amortization since the initial investments in tooling before the production process starts is high.

To support this, extra functionality needs to be developed for the tooling and BOM process. For example, the table Routing Tool (table 99000802) can be connected to a Fixed Asset (table 5600).

Item tracking

When something is wrong with a component of a car, it is important to be able to see what other cars have, the same components built by the same factory and tools using the same base materials.

In Microsoft Dynamics NAV, it is possible to use a single Lot no. for a component or an end product and to trace this back. It is not possible to simply move the Lot no. of the component to the end product or copy information from the component's Lot no. such as a container no. or a quality code to the end product.

To support this, we need to change the item tracking process. A good place to start would be the item journal where the reservation entry is moved to the item ledger entry.

Medicines

When used by companies that manufacture medicines, using the expiration date for Lot numbers correctly is highly important.

Lot numbers and expiration dates

In Microsoft Dynamics NAV, expiration dates are defined in the **Item Ledger Entries** and the **Warehouse Entries**.

It is not possible to define a single expiration date for a Lot. This can be changed by adding this field to the Lot No. Information table (6505). This table allows companies to predefine Lot numbers to be used in the production process.

By default, the expiration date is calculated based on the document date multiplied with the **Expiration Calculation** field in the Item table (27).

The Lot No. Information table can be used to save additional information about the specific production batch.

Quality control

Quality control is important in most production processes but maybe extra important when dealing with medicines. Usually a small part of a Lot is taken for quality control.

In Microsoft Dynamics NAV, we can define quality measures in the Prod. Order Rtng Qlty Meas. Table (5413). However, these values are only saved as information for the production order.

To enhance quality control, we could add a document structure where a quality check document is created from a production order. The information should be saved in the Lot No. Information table.

When a Lot does not have the required quality, a workflow should be started. This workflow will lead the user through a process where decisions can be made. Sometimes, the quality can be improved and the items can still be used. Sometimes the item number even depends on the quality of the product.

Quality control is in between the Consumption Journal and the Output Journal. During the final quality check, the BOM items are used, but the final item is not yet available.

Food

In the food industry, everything is about expiration dates and fresh products. Inventory is never very high and the rate of circulation is very high.

Zero inventory

For this reason, it should be possible for fresh food companies to zero the inventory of certain Lot numbers once the expiration date is closing or has expired.

This could normally be done using the Physical Inventory Journal. Doing this manually with Lot numbers can be quite a job for someone to do this every day so for this vertical solution, we could create a function to do this. This function would create an Item Journal Line (83) with the field Phys. Inventory (56) activated and also create the Reservation entry for tracking and post the line automatically.

Ordering schedules

Fresh food companies use daily production processes that start on scheduled times. Each day, the factory starts the production process but the production numbers can be different based on the orders.

This can be done using the Make-To-Order policy but we need to make sure that there will be no new sales orders when the calculation process starts.

This can be achieved by creating an order schedule policy. New sales lines can be created for each item until a certain time. When the time has elapsed, the salespeople will get an error message. This allows the production planner to start the calculation process at a fixed time each day, knowing the sales orders quantities can be trusted.

Furniture

The furniture industry is a large and very old industry that existed long before the industrial revolution and the introduction of computers.

We can roughly split the furniture industry into two parts. The first part has moved production to be standardized using size and color matrixes, which we can compare to the fashion industry. When buying a table or kitchen, the customer can choose from different sizes and colors. Depending on the number of choices, the products are either Made-To-Stock (IKEA) or Made-To-Order.

The second part is furniture manufacturers who still produce custom-made items. A desk or kitchen at these manufacturers can have any size or color. For these companies, it is next to impossible to create a bill of material for each custom item so they use predefined calculations with item categories.

For the examples in this book, we will discuss the second category.

Calculations

Companies building custom-made furniture need the possibility to calculate the use of materials and resources, both at the item category and real item level. For this, we can create a calculation module with this data and posting model.

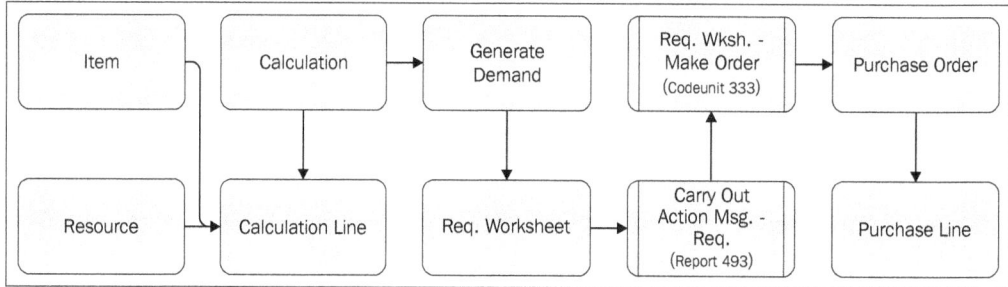

The basic structure of this calculation module is explained in *Chapter 8, Consulting*, where we have combined this into the jobs functionality of Microsoft Dynamics NAV.

Inventory

Our furniture company uses a combination of product-specific items that are one of a kind and inventory items that are used in most of the products.

These items are combined into the end product and should be consumed when the product is finished. When the calculation module is integrated with jobs, for example, it would be possible to flush the components when the job is completed. This functionality can be compared to the posting of the Consumption Journal when a production order is finished.

The inventory items can be updated weekly using the Physical Inventory Journal and inventory counting. This enables us to use the requisition worksheet and reordering policy we will discuss in *Chapter 6, Trade*.

Summary

In this chapter, we discussed how three production methodologies can be implemented in the Microsoft Dynamics NAV product. We introduced the concepts of item tracking and item costing. We took a tour through the manufacturing process using different requisition worksheets and talked about the solution for MRP.

Lastly, we looked at how production can be implemented for different vertical industries. In the next chapter, we will have a closer look at the trade process in Microsoft Dynamics NAV.

6
Trade

In the previous chapter, we discussed how Microsoft Dynamics NAV can help us to streamline our production process using both the standard application as well as customized solutions. We talked about five vertical industries and how to fit the application for them.

In this chapter, we will discuss how to use Microsoft Dynamics NAV for these companies using sales and purchase documents and how to integrate this with the built-in Warehouse Management and Reservation processes.

The primary focus of this chapter is on how the application is designed, and where to go to change or enhance the design. Basic knowledge of how to create and process sales and purchase documents in Microsoft Dynamics NAV is a prerequisite.

We will use examples from the same vertical industries—automotive, fashion, medicines, food, and furniture—which we discussed in the previous chapters. After reading this chapter, you will have a good understanding of how to implement Microsoft Dynamics NAV in trading companies.

The process

A trading company purchases and sells items without changing them. The main activities are purchase, storage, packaging, sales, and shipping, as shown in the following screenshot:

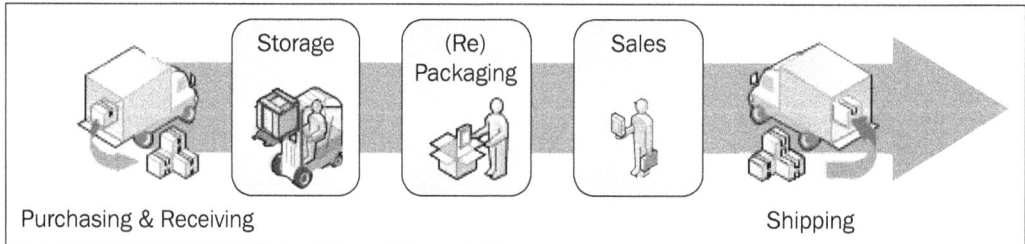

Managing the inventory is very important in these companies. Having inventory is crucial for delivering on time and not having to say "no" to customers.

Wholesale versus retail

Traditionally, trading companies are divided into wholesale and retail companies. Wholesale companies sell to business and retail companies sell to consumers. Microsoft Dynamics NAV supports both and from the perspective of design (table and posting structure), there is not much difference.

The biggest difference between wholesale and retail for the application is the transaction volume. While the total turnover of a wholesale company can be much higher compared to a retailer, the retailer often has more, smaller transactions. It can be a challenge from an application design perspective to retain a solution that performs well.

Another issue with high volume transaction systems is traceability of the data. Whenever something goes wrong, it is very important to see where this has started and how much data was impacted by the mistake. In low transaction systems, it is easier to find this manually.

Sales and purchasing

Traditionally, salespersons used to work with paper order forms. They would write down the customer name and address and the items or services required.

Paper order form

In Microsoft Dynamics NAV, the paper document is replaced by a sales and purchase document using a header for the general order information and lines to register the items and services.

The posting process breaks down the information in the document into the journals and posts them, so the end user does not have to worry about this. The application reuses the same posting routines as we discussed in earlier chapters.

Let's look at how the documents and journals tie together by drawing the table and transaction scheme for this:

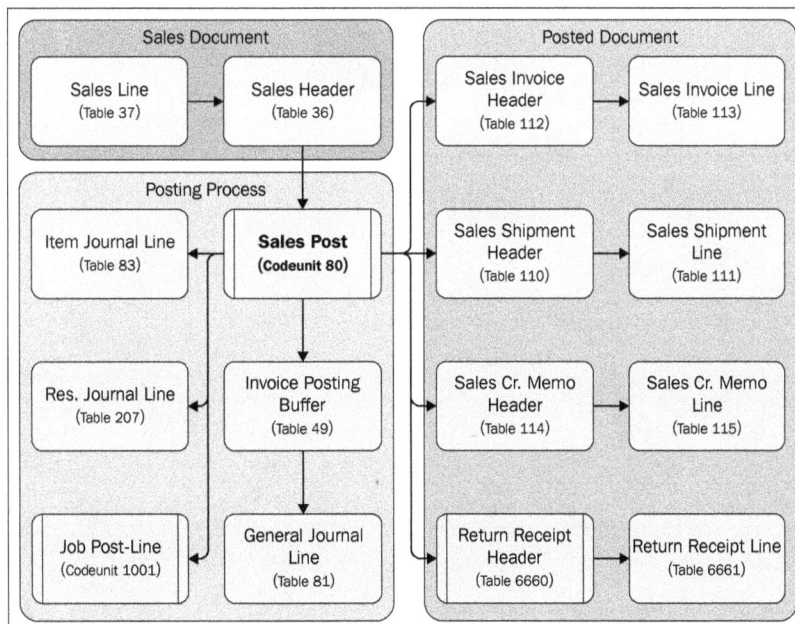

The first step is creating the document. When we create this **Sales Document** (**Sales Header** and **Sales Line**), nothing is posted. We are only entering the information into the system that can be changed at any time.

When we start the **Codeunit Sales-Post (80)**, the system will create all the journals for us and post them. When we sell an item, the system will create an **Item Journal Line**, and when we sell a resource, the system creates a **Resource Journal Line**, and so on.

The **Invoice Posting buffer** is used to create the entries in the **General Journal Line**. We already discussed this feature in *Chapter 3, Financial Management*.

Microsoft Dynamics NAV allows us to create four different kinds of posted sales documents: invoices, shipments, credit memos, and return receipts. We will discuss all these types later in this chapter.

Transaction mirroring

The unique concept of sales and purchase in Microsoft Dynamics NAV is the mirroring of the transaction structure. Once we understand how the sales transactions fit together, it will be easy to understand the structure of a purchase.

Let's demonstrate this by comparing the first fields in **Table 37 Sales Line** and **Table 39 Purchase Line**, as shown in the following screenshot:

E.. Field No.	Field Name	Data Type	Length
✓	1 Document Type	Option	
✓	2 Sell-to Customer No.	Code	20
✓	3 Document No.	Code	20
✓	4 Line No.	Integer	
✓	5 Type	Option	
✓	6 No.	Code	20
✓	7 Location Code	Code	10
✓	8 Posting Group	Code	10
✓	10 Shipment Date	Date	
✓	11 Description	Text	50
✓	12 Description 2	Text	50
✓	13 Unit of Measure	Text	10
✓	15 Quantity	Decimal	
✓	16 Outstanding Quantity	Decimal	
✓	17 Qty. to Invoice	Decimal	
✓	18 Qty. to Ship	Decimal	
✓	22 Unit Price	Decimal	
✓	23 Unit Cost (LCY)	Decimal	
✓	25 VAT %	Decimal	
✓	27 Line Discount %	Decimal	
✓	28 Line Discount Amount	Decimal	
✓	29 Amount	Decimal	
✓	30 Amount Including VAT	Decimal	
✓	32 Allow Invoice Disc.	Boolean	
✓	34 Gross Weight	Decimal	
✓	35 Net Weight	Decimal	
✓	36 Units per Parcel	Decimal	
✓	37 Unit Volume	Decimal	
✓	38 Appl.-to Item Entry	Integer	
✓	40 Shortcut Dimension 1 Code	Code	20
✓	41 Shortcut Dimension 2 Code	Code	20
✓	42 Customer Price Group	Code	10
✓	45 Job No.	Code	20

Table 37 Sales Line - Table Designer

E.. Field No.	Field Name	Data Type	Length
✓	1 Document Type	Option	
✓	2 Buy-from Vendor No.	Code	20
✓	3 Document No.	Code	20
✓	4 Line No.	Integer	
✓	5 Type	Option	
✓	6 No.	Code	20
✓	7 Location Code	Code	10
✓	8 Posting Group	Code	10
✓	10 Expected Receipt Date	Date	
✓	11 Description	Text	50
✓	12 Description 2	Text	50
✓	13 Unit of Measure	Text	10
✓	15 Quantity	Decimal	
✓	16 Outstanding Quantity	Decimal	
✓	17 Qty. to Invoice	Decimal	
✓	18 Qty. to Receive	Decimal	
✓	22 Direct Unit Cost	Decimal	
✓	23 Unit Cost (LCY)	Decimal	
✓	25 VAT %	Decimal	
✓	27 Line Discount %	Decimal	
✓	28 Line Discount Amount	Decimal	
✓	29 Amount	Decimal	
✓	30 Amount Including VAT	Decimal	
✓	31 Unit Price (LCY)	Decimal	
✓	32 Allow Invoice Disc.	Boolean	
✓	34 Gross Weight	Decimal	
✓	35 Net Weight	Decimal	
✓	36 Units per Parcel	Decimal	
✓	37 Unit Volume	Decimal	
✓	38 Appl.-to Item Entry	Integer	
✓	40 Shortcut Dimension 1 Code	Code	20
✓	41 Shortcut Dimension 2 Code	Code	20
✓	45 Job No.	Code	20

Table 39 Purchase Line - Table Designer

Help

The fields in both tables are equally numbered and serve the same process even though they use different terminology, for example, field 18, **Qty. to Ship** (sale) and **Qty. To Receive** (purchase).

Some fields are different because they don't make sense to be in both processes, for example, **Unit Price (LCY)** (field 31) in purchase and **Customer Price Group** (field 42) in sales.

The purchase process also uses the same posting methodology. The purchase header (38) and purchase line (39) tables are posted using the codeunit Purch.-Post (90) in the purchase receipt, invoice, credit memo, and return shipment documents.

Let's have a closer look at the sales process.

Sales

The sales process supports six document types that are normalized into two tables, sales header (36) and sales line (37).

Each process can have its own Number Series and has a special card and list page, but they all share the same business logic. Let's discuss the document types:

- **Quote**: When a customer would like to know the terms and conditions of making a purchase, we can make a quote. This will show all the calculations such as pricing and VAT.

- **Blanket Order**: This is a pre-order status. When used, we have an agreement with the customer without knowing the exact shipment date.

- **Order**: This is used for the actual order document.

- **Invoice**: This can be used in two ways; directly, without a sales order if the company only invoices directly on G/L Accounts, or we can use the invoices to invoice one or more shipments.

- **Credit Memo**: We can use a credit memo when we credit on a G/L Account.

- **Return Order**: If a customer returns an item, we can use a return order to reverse the inventory process.

Orders

The main process is the order. The other document types are designed to support this. Sales orders can be created directly or via a quote or blanket order. There are two differences between a quote and a blanket order:

- Quotes can only be fully transferred into a sales order, not in parts.
  For example, a blanket order of 100 items can be split into 10 deliveries of 10 items with different shipping dates.

- A customer with a quote has the possibility to say yes or no. When the answer is no, there will be no transaction. Therefore, quotes are not used in the supply and demand calculation, as we discussed in the previous chapter. A blanket order is a real order. The customer should eventually purchase the complete quantity that was agreed. Therefore, the blanket orders are used in the supply and demand calculation.

Quote to order and blanket order to order

Although the quotes and blanket to orders are stored in the same table, the records are physically deleted from the table and inserted using another document type. This is done in codeunits sales-quote to order (86) and blanket sales order to order (87).

When comparing these codeunits in compare tools, such as Beyond Compare or Araxis, we can see that there is a lot of similarity. They both create a new sales order.

Quote to order

When moving a quote to an order, the complete quote is copied and then deleted. A quote can be created from an opportunity in CRM as we discussed in *Chapter 4, Relationship Management*. Therefore, the opportunity is updated when this happens.

Blanket order to order

A blanket order can be moved in parts. Therefore, business logic is implemented to calculate the remaining quantity. There is no link between blanket orders and CRM and it is also not possible to create a blanket order from a quote.

Creating a new sales order

In order to understand the examples in this chapter, we will discuss the most important fields of the sales order. A sales document contains one header and multiple lines.

While the sales header table contains more static registration of information, the sales line has more real business logic, such as price calculation, inventory availability, and VAT. We will discuss how this business logic is normalized.

1002 · The Cannon Group PLC

General

No.:	1002		Document Date:	22-1-2015
Sell-to Customer No.:	10000		Requested Delivery Date:	
Sell-to Customer Name:	The Cannon Group PLC		External Document No.:	
Sell-to City:	Birmingham		Salesperson Code:	PS
Posting Date:	22-1-2015		Status:	Open
Order Date:	22-1-2015			

Lines

Line ▾ | Functions ▾ | Order ▾ | Find | Filter | Clear Filter

Type	No.	Description	Quantity	Unit of Mea...	Unit Price Excl. ...	Line Amount Ex...	Line Discount %	Qty. to Ship	Quantity Shipped
G/L Account	6120	Sales, Retail - EU	1					1	
Item	70000	Side Panel	1	PCS	30,70	30,70		1	
Resource	LIFT	Lift for Furniture	1	HOUR	292,00	292,00		1	
Fixed Asset	FA000060	Conveyor Lift	1					1	
Charge (Item)	S-FREIGHT	Misc. Freight Charges (Sales)	1					1	

Sales header

All document types are uniquely numbered. The primary key fields of the sales header table are **Document Type** and **No.**.

[
It is very useful to use Number Series code that makes sense to the end users, for example, SO13-0012 for sales order 12 in the year 2013 and SQ14-0312 for sales quote 312 for 2014.
]

The sales document contains the following two different customer no. fields:

- **Sell-to Customer No.**: This is the primary customer no. field, which defines the customer who requested the order to be created. This customer number is used to calculate the discounts.

- **Bill-to Customer No.**: By default, the **Sell-to Customer No.** will also receive the invoice. By changing this field to another customer, this will make the invoice print out containing other customer details.

A sales document contains some dates that are used for different purposes:

- **Posting Date**: This date is used for posting to the various ledgers

- **Document Date**: This date is used for the accounts receivable

- **Shipment Date**: This date is for the calculation or the inventory availability

- **Due Date**: This date is the last date at which the bill-to customer is expected to pay the invoice

Sales lines

Each sales document can contain an almost unlimited number of sales lines. By default, the sales lines are numbered 10000, 20000, 30000, and so on.

The numbering is done using the `AutoSplitKey` property on the sales line page and the increment cannot be changed. When a user inserts new records between two existing lines, the program will calculate the new number to be exactly between the old values, for example, 10000, 15000, 17500, 18750, 19375, 19687, 19843, 19921, 19960, 19980, 19990, 19995, 19997, 19998, 19999, and 20000. If there is no more room, the system will generate a runtime error message, as shown in the following screenshot:

Microsoft Dynamics NAV ☒

❌ The line cannot be split.

OK

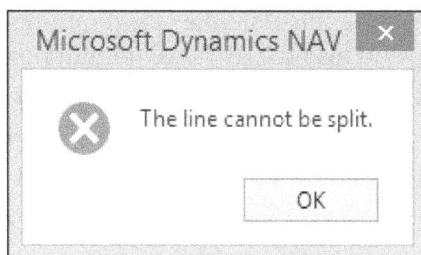

Master data options

A sales line can contain a reference to six types of master data defined by the **Type** field. These types are: **Text** (blank option), **G/L Account**, **Item**, **Resource**, **Fixed Asset**, and **Charge** (item).

The type that we specify here determines which journal will be used later when we post this sales document. However, each line can contain financial information, which will be processed to the general ledger via the posting buffer table.

In the next chapter, we will discuss how to add a new type to this process.

Sales line fields

To create a new sales line and start the important business logic in Microsoft Dynamics NAV, we need to know about the following fields:

- **Type**: This defines the master data type the sales line uses and eventually the journal that will be used during posting

> When the **Type** field changes after the sales line was created, the record is cleared and the fields get their default values.

- **No.**: This is the actual reference to the unique number of the master data type that is used

> When the **No.** field is changed, the previous quantity is used to recreate the sales line with the new master data.

- **Quantity**: This is used to calculate the sales amounts for the invoicing and in the case of an item, and also the physical quantity of the changes in inventory

- **Outstanding Quantity**, **Qty. to Invoice**, and **Qty. to Ship**: These fields are designed to use for partial shipping and invoicing of an order

- **Unit Price** and **Unit Cost (LCY)**: The fields are used to calculate the sales amount and profit

- **Line Discount %** and **Line Discount Amount**: These fields are used to determine the discounts

Validation flow

The sales line table has a specific validation flow of functions that is important to understand before making changes to the table. This flow is based on the normal way an end user creates a sales line.

To create a sales line, only four fields are populated and the line is ready to use. After setting the type and choosing a no., the end user types in the **Quantity** field and if necessary, the **Unit Price** field.

Let's analyze the C/AL code in the OnValidate trigger of the three fields that can calculate the sales line.

> When changing these C/AL routines, make sure to use the *Test near*, *Test far*, *Do it*, and *Clean up* methods that we discussed in *Chapter 1*, *Introduction to Microsoft Dynamics NAV*.

No. | field 6

The C/AL code in the OnValidate trigger starts by doing the initial testing, if the change is allowed. After this, the record is cleared and the old values for the **No.** field and **Quantity** fields are applied, as follows:

```
TempSalesLine := Rec;
INIT;
Type := TempSalesLine.Type;
"No." := TempSalesLine."No.";
IF "No." = '' THEN
  EXIT;
IF Type <> Type::" " THEN
  Quantity := TempSalesLine.Quantity;
```

Then, the sales line inherits the values from the sales header, if required, and the date fields are calculated, as follows:

```
"Sell-to Customer No." := SalesHeader."Sell-to Customer No.";
"Currency Code" := SalesHeader."Currency Code";
...


"Promised Delivery Date" := SalesHeader."Promised Delivery Date";
...


UpdateDates;
```

> The sales header information is not present in the sales line when an end user picks a value for the **No.** field. We cannot use the customer information for table relations.

When this is done, we see a CASE statement where the master data is acquired. This would be the place where we would move newly added fields from master data to the sales line table.

```
CASE Type OF
  Type::" ":
    ...
  Type::"G/L Account":
    ...
  Type::Item:
    ...
 Type::Resource:
    ...
  Type::"Fixed Asset":
    ...
  Type::"Charge (Item)":
    ...
END;
```

When this is done, the quantities are calculated and the unit price is calculated.

```
IF Type <> Type::" " THEN BEGIN
  IF Type <> Type::"Fixed Asset" THEN
    VALIDATE("VAT Prod. Posting Group");
  VALIDATE("Unit of Measure Code");
  IF Quantity <> 0 THEN BEGIN
    InitOutstanding;
```

```
    IF "Document Type" IN ["Document Type"::"Return Order","Document
Type"::"Credit Memo"] THEN
        InitQtyToReceive
    ELSE
      InitQtyToShip;
    UpdateWithWarehouseShip;
  END;
  UpdateUnitPrice(FIELDNO("No."));
END;
```

The latter is very important for our analysis. After this function, other code is executed but this is not important for this example.

Quantity | field 15

Just like the **No.** field, the **Quantity** field also first checks whether the change is allowed. When this is done, the following section of C/AL code is important:

```
IF Type = Type::Item THEN BEGIN
  UpdateUnitPrice(FIELDNO(Quantity));

  ...

  CheckApplFromItemLedgEntry(ItemLedgEntry);
END ELSE
  VALIDATE("Line Discount %");
```

In the preceding C/AL code, we should notice again the `UpdateUnitPrice` function and also the validation of the `Line Discount %` field.

Unit price | field 22

This field has little C/AL code. When changing the unit price manually, the C/AL code will trigger the `Line Discount %` field:

```
TestStatusOpen;
VALIDATE("Line Discount %");
```

Before going to this field, let's first have a look at the `UpdateUnitPrice` function we noticed earlier in the **Quantity** and **No.** field.

UpdateUnitPrice

The `UpdateUnitPrice` function executes the following C/AL code:

```
IF (CalledByFieldNo <> CurrFieldNo) AND (CurrFieldNo <> 0) THEN
  EXIT;

GetSalesHeader;
```

```
      TESTFIELD("Qty. per Unit of Measure");

      CASE Type OF
        Type::Item,Type::Resource:
          BEGIN
            PriceCalcMgt.FindSalesLineLineDisc(SalesHeader,Rec);
            PriceCalcMgt.FindSalesLinePrice(SalesHeader,Rec,
              CalledByFieldNo);
          END;
      END;
      VALIDATE("Unit Price");
```

After doing the checks, the sales price calculation routines we discussed in *Chapter 2, A Sample Application*, are executed. This is codeunit Sales Price Calc. Mgt. 7000.

When this is done, it validates the field Unit Price that we already analyzed. This leads us to one single point; the OnValidate trigger of Line Discount %.

Line Discount % | field 27

The C/AL code in this OnValidate trigger first calculates the line discount amount based on the unit price and then starts the UpdateAmounts function, as follows:

```
      TestJobPlanningLine;
      TestStatusOpen;
      "Line Discount Amount" :=
        ROUND(
          ROUND(Quantity * "Unit Price",Currency."Amount Rounding
      Precision") *
          "Line Discount %" / 100,Currency."Amount Rounding Precision");
      "Inv. Discount Amount" := 0;
      "Inv. Disc. Amount to Invoice" := 0;
      UpdateAmounts;
```

UpdateAmounts

The UpdateAmounts function completes the creation of the sales line and this is where our quest ends.

The two most important other functions that are executed in this function are the UpdateVATAmounts for VAT calculation and the credit limit check for the customer in CustCheckCreditLimit.SalesLineCheck(Rec).

VAT calculation

The VAT calculation in Microsoft Dynamics NAV is not normalized in one application area but redeveloped everywhere. This makes VAT calculation one of the most complex application areas to make changes to.

Code cloning

The VAT calculation is not only done in the sales line, purchase line, and general journal line table, but also in more specific function tables such as the service line. This is done by making a full copy of the C/AL code.

This phenomenon is known as code cloning in computer science. Although code cloning simplifies application design, it is considered bad practice and should be avoided at all times. In this case, it would have been better if VAT would have been calculated in a generic engine.

It is therefore highly recommended not to change VAT calculation in Microsoft Dynamics NAV.

> If VAT calculation is required in a customized solution, it can be done using the general journal line as a temporary table. By populating the necessary fields and starting the calculation, we can use the results without copying the VAT calculation to our own solution.

Invoicing

In Microsoft Dynamics NAV, a sales order can be shipped and invoiced directly from the document.

However, not all companies have a combined shipping and invoicing process. Some companies ship the goods first and send the invoice later, most of the time using combined invoicing.

Prepayments

Besides separating the invoice moment from the shipping moment, Microsoft Dynamics NAV also allows a prepayment process. This prepayment process is designed to work on top of the normal invoicing process. This means it does not replace the invoice but instead creates an extra invoice.

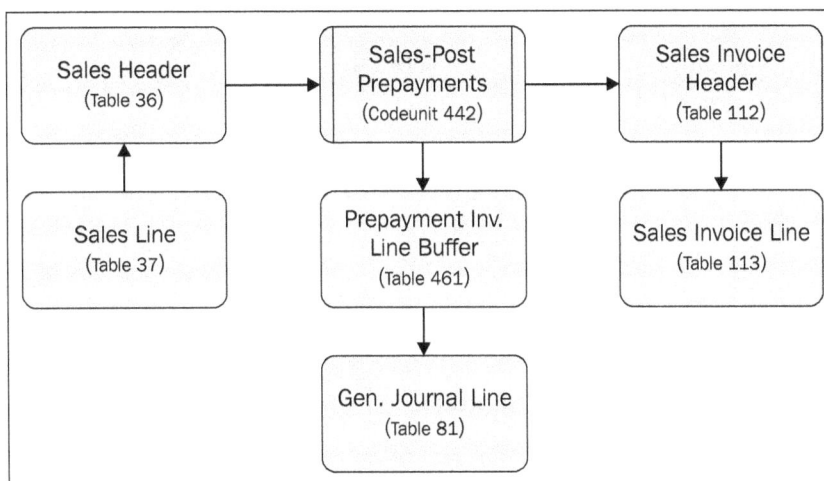

This invoice is not created in codeunit sales-post (80) but in codeunit sales-post prepayments (461).

> Using prepayments in Microsoft Dynamics NAV will always generate a minimum of two invoices per sales order.

When the order is eventually invoiced, the prepayment invoice is deducted from the invoice amount.

> The design of this solution by Microsoft teaches us and demonstrates that to generate a posted sales invoice, it is not specifically necessary to start codeunit sales-post 80.

Combined invoicing

Combined invoicing of shipments can be done manually or using a batch report.

Manual

To manually combine shipments on a sales invoice, we can use the **Sales-Get Shipment Codeunit (64)**.

This codeunit can be started from the actions on a sales invoice subpage (47) and displays the sales shipment lines that are not yet completely invoiced.

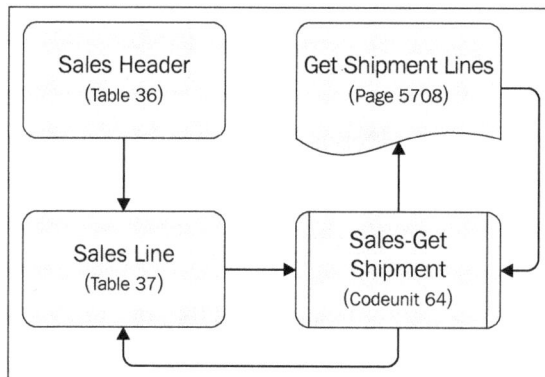

The C/AL code, however, is not completely within the codeunit; the process starts in the codeunit and runs the page. The page then again starts a function in the codeunit.

Docum...	Bill-to Cu...	Type	No.	Description	Unit of Mea...	Quantity	Quantity Invoic...	Qty. Shipped N...
102028	10000	Item	1920-S	ANTWERP Conference Table	PCS	1	0	1
102034	10000	Item	70000	Side Panel	PCS	1	0	1
	10000	Item	70001	Base	PCS	1	0	1
	10000	Item	70002	Top Panel	PCS	1	0	1

Batch

The Combine Shipments report (295) can be used to create one invoice for multiple shipments in batch. It works in a similar way as the Combine Invoice report we created in *Chapter 2, A Sample Application*.

The C/AL code that creates the sales line for the invoice is normalized and used in both codeunit sales-get shipment (64) and combine shipments report (295). The function is located in the sales shipment line table (111) and is called `InsertInvLineFromShptLine`.

> To enable combined shipments, the Boolean field Combine Shipments (87) should be set to **Yes** in the customer table. This value is inherited into the sales header for the sales order document.

Credit memo and return orders

The credit memo and return order document types are used to reverse the order process.

Purchasing

Before we can ship the items we sold, we first need to purchase or produce them. We discussed the production process in the previous chapter, so let's focus on the purchasing process.

Technically, the sales and purchase process are mirrored transactions and the application design is similar. The purchase header table has the same document types: quote, order, invoice, credit memo, blanket order, and return order, and the same posting process.

So instead of going into the similarities, we will discuss the differences.

Resources

In Microsoft Dynamics NAV, it is not possible to purchase resources. When we take a closer look at the **Type** field (5), we can see that the option is left blank:

Table 37 Sales Line - Table Designer

E..	Field No.	Field Name	Data Type	Length	Option String
✔	1	Document Type	Option		Quote,Order,Invoice,Credit Memo,Blanket Order,Return Order
✔	2	Sell-to Customer No.	Code	20	
✔	3	Document No.	Code	20	
✔	4	Line No.	Integer		
✔	5	Type	Option		,G/L Account,Item,Resource,Fixed Asset,Charge (Item)
✔	6	No.	Code	20	

Table 39 Purchase Line - Table Designer

E..	Field No.	Field Name	Data Type	Length	Option String
✔	1	Document Type	Option		Quote,Order,Invoice,Credit Memo,Blanket Order,Return Order
✔	2	Buy-from Vendor No.	Code	20	
✔	3	Document No.	Code	20	
✔	4	Line No.	Integer		
✔	5	Type	Option		,G/L Account,Item,,Fixed Asset,Charge (Item)
✔	6	No.	Code	20	
✔	7	Location Code	Code	10	

Drop shipments

When selling items that are not in the inventory, it is possible to purchase the items from a vendor and have them directly shipped to the customer. This process is called drop shipments.

This process can be handled manually and using the requisition worksheet.

Manual

To create a drop shipment manually, the purchase order should first be created using the **Sell-to Customer No.** from the corresponding sales order as the shipping address:

When this is done, we can start the codeunit Purch.-Get Drop Shpt. (76) from **ACTIONS** on the purchase order. This function will show a list of all sales orders for this **Sell-to Customer No.** regardless of whether drop shipment is possible.

If we select a sales order without sales lines that are marked for drop shipment, we get the following error message:

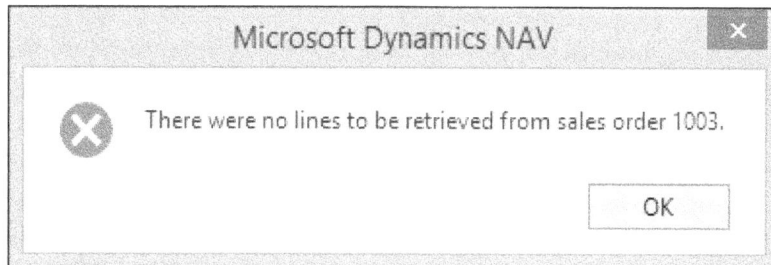

After retrieving the sales information, the sales line and purchase line table are connected to each other by populating the **Purchase Order No.**, **Purch. Order Line No.**, **Sales Order No.**, and **Sales Order Line No.** fields.

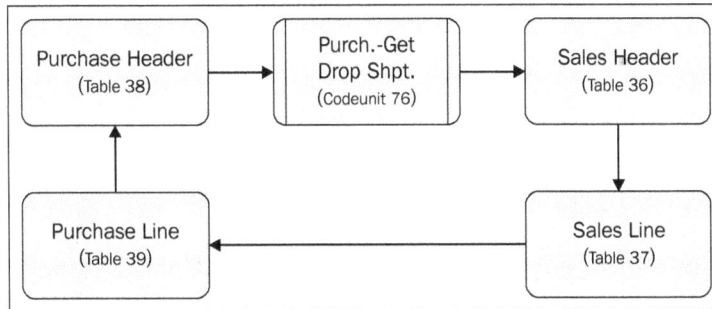

These fields are numbered 71 and 72 in the sales line and purchase line table.

Requisition worksheet

We introduced the requisition worksheet in the previous chapter when we discussed the planning process. The requisition worksheet can also be used for the **Drop Shipment** functionality:

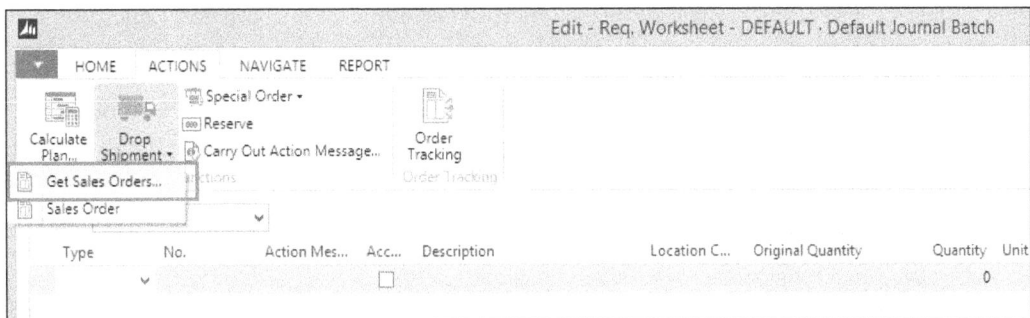

This will start the Get Sales Orders report (698), which will filter on all sales lines marked for drop shipment and creates a line in the requisition worksheet table.

This line can be processed by carrying out the action messages. This function will also connect the sales order to the purchase order using fields 71 and 72.

> The C/AL code for manual drop shipment and using the requisition worksheet is not normalized (code cloning). This means that changes done in one method should also be done in the other method and maintained twice.

Document releasing and approval process

Within the sales and purchase document process, there is a workflow available for releasing and approving a document. This is taken care of by a single status field and two processes.

Status

The **Status** field (120) in the sales header and purchase header table indicates the status of the process. There are four options: **Open**, **Released**, **Pending Approval**, and **Pending Prepayment**.

Two of these status fields, **Open** and **Released**, are mandatory to use. **Pending Approval** and **Pending Prepayment** are optional.

We have already discussed prepayments earlier in this chapter.

Releasing a document

Before a document can be posted, it is mandatory to release it. This is done by the codeunits Release Sales Document (414) and Release Purchase Document (415). These codeunits are, as you may have guessed, almost identical.

The codeunit performs a number of tests before setting the status to **Released**. Let's discuss some of these checks:

- A typical example of Test Near, the customer number should not be blank:

```
TESTFIELD("Sell-to Customer No.");
```

- There should be at least one sales line with a Quantity:

```
SalesLine.SETRANGE("Document Type","Document Type");
SalesLine.SETRANGE("Document No.","No.");
SalesLine.SETFILTER(Type,'>0');
SalesLine.SETFILTER(Quantity,'<>0');
IF NOT SalesLine.FIND('-') THEN
  ERROR(Text001,"Document Type","No.");
```

- When the testing is done, some final calculations are implemented. These calculations are document calculations that span over the individual sales lines:

```
SalesSetup.GET;
IF SalesSetup."Calc. Inv. Discount" THEN BEGIN
  CODEUNIT.RUN(CODEUNIT::"Sales-Calc. Discount",SalesLine);
  GET("Document Type","No.");
END;
```

- The following codeunit calculates the invoice discount:

```
SalesLine.SetSalesHeader(Rec);
SalesLine.CalcVATAmountLines(0,Rec,SalesLine,TempVATAmountLine0);
SalesLine.CalcVATAmountLines(1,Rec,SalesLine,TempVATAmountLine1);
SalesLine.UpdateVATOnLines(0,Rec,SalesLine,TempVATAmountLine0);
SalesLine.UpdateVATOnLines(1,Rec,SalesLine,TempVATAmountLine1);
```

- At the end of the releasing process, the VAT calculation is completed.

- Releasing a document also calculates the **Amount** and **Amount Including VAT** fields on the sales line.

Manual versus automatic releasing

By default, Microsoft Dynamics NAV releases the document automatically. The posting codeunits sales-post (80) and purchase-post (90) contain the following C/AL code:

```
IF (Status = Status::Open) OR (Status = Status::"Pending Prepayment")
THEN BEGIN
  TempInvoice := Invoice;
  TempShpt := Ship;
  TempReturn := Receive;
  GetOpenLinkedATOs(TempAsmHeader);
  CODEUNIT.RUN(CODEUNIT::"Release Sales Document",SalesHeader);
  TESTFIELD(Status,Status::Released);
  Status := Status::Open;
  Invoice := TempInvoice;
  Ship := TempShpt;
  Receive := TempReturn;
  ReopenAsmOrders(TempAsmHeader);
  MODIFY;
  COMMIT;
  Status := Status::Released;
END;
```

This code temporarily releases the document by starting the release codeunit but then sets the status back to **Open**, modifies the records, and commits the transaction. Then, the status is set to **Released**.

Whenever there is an error afterwards, the status will still be **Open** since that was the status before the COMMIT.

Document approval

On top of the release process is a document approval workflow. This feature is designed to work on top of the functionality we already discussed and is optional.

Deleting sales and purchase documents

During the life cycle of our application, many documents will be created. There might come a day when this exceeds the point where some maintenance is required.

Data deletion

In the **IT Administration** section of the **Departments Role Center**, we can find a **Data Deletion** section, which is designed for IT administrators to clean up data, as shown in the following screenshot:

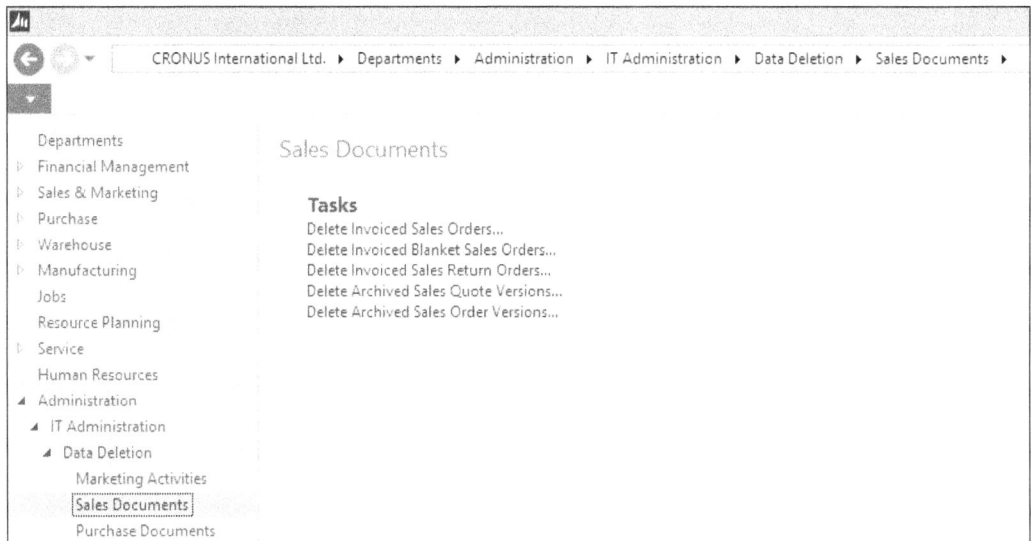

When a sales order is invoiced using **Get Shipment Lines** or **Combined Invoicing**, the sales order is not automatically deleted, nor are completely handled blanket orders.

Leaving old orders in the database may lead to large tables. Since these document tables are heavily inserted and modified throughout the working day by many people, this may lead to unnecessary overhead in the database.

Deletion of shipments and invoices

Microsoft Dynamics NAV allows users to delete posted shipments and invoices when they are printed.

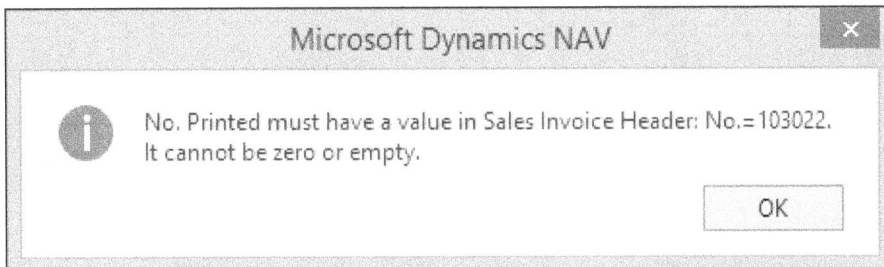

Although it should be considered carefully, it might be necessary for some companies to periodically clean up this data. Most companies never look at the shipments once the items are delivered to their customers.

Cleaning up these tables will have a positive impact on the performance and maintainability of your system if it reaches the size of roughly 50-100 GB.

> When designing business analysis reports, never use data from the sales shipment header or line table since they might get deleted. Always use the ledger entry tables instead.

Inventory management

In Microsoft Dynamics NAV, inventory is kept for items in locations using **Item Ledger Entries** and **Value Entries**. On top of this, we can use **Stock Keeping Units** to have different inventory settings per item, location, and variant.

Let's start by looking at the design patterns of the inventory in Microsoft Dynamics NAV:

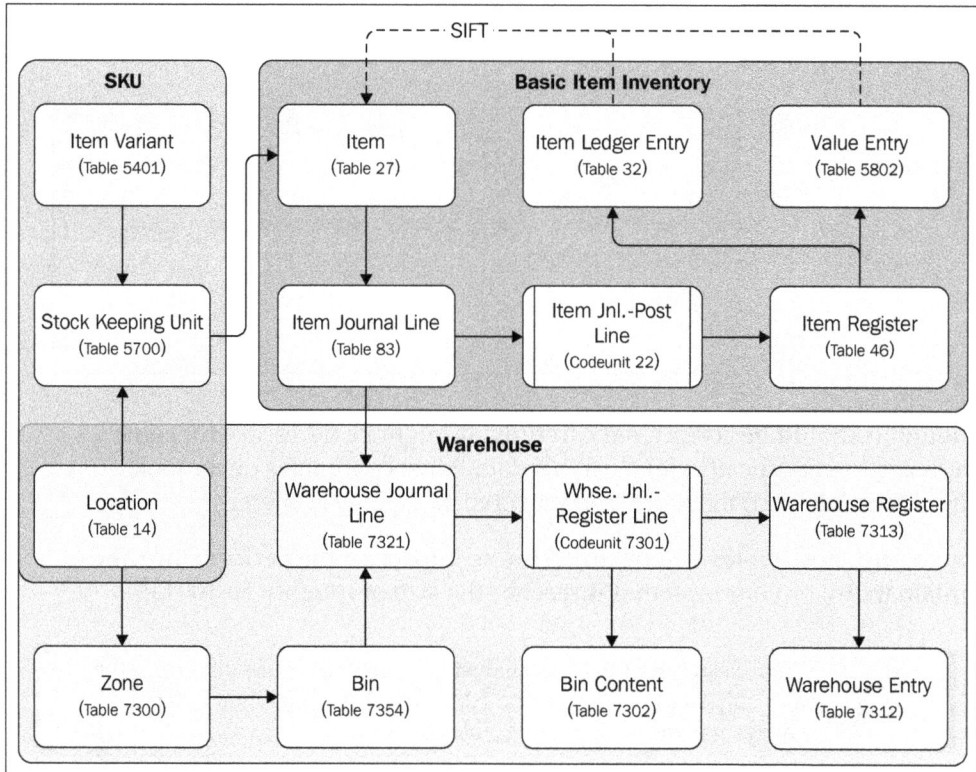

Keeping inventory can be extended with the use of warehouse management. This is designed to run on top of the **Basic Item Inventory** functionality.

Items

The item table hosts the master data for inventory management like a G/L Account does for financial management.

```
70000 · Side Panel

General                                                                    ✿ ^

No.:                    70000          ...   Search Description:  SIDE PANEL

Description:            Side Panel           Inventory:                4.201

Base Unit of Measure:   PCS        v         Qty. on Purch. Order:         0

Assembly BOM:           No                   Qty. on Prod. Order:          0

Shelf No.:              A1                    Qty. on Component Lines:      0

Automatic Ext. Texts:   ☐                     Qty. on Sales Order:          1

Created From Nonstock Item: ☐                Qty. on Service Order:        0

Item Category Code:                v         Qty. on Job Order:            0

Product Group Code:                v         Blocked:              ☐

Service Item Group:                v         Last Date Modified:   23-9-2013

                                             Stockout Warning:     Default (Yes)   v

                                                          v  Show more fields

Invoicing                                                                       ^
```

In this table, we can do the set up for each individual item such as pricing, inventory and production strategies, and tracking options.

Locations

The location table defines which level of inventory management is done. A location can either be a physical warehouse somewhere or a part of a warehouse, if one warehouse uses different warehouse strategies.

If we look at the **Location Card**, we see what we can set up:

Let's see these settings in detail:

- **General**: Here, we can specify the physical location of the warehouse. We can also specify **Use As In-Transit**. When this is specified, we can only use transfer orders to move inventory to this location.

- **Warehouse**: On this tab, we specify which level of warehouse management functionality we want to use. If everything is left blank, no warehouse entries are created when this location is used.

- **Bins**: This tab contains the default bins for most inventory activities, such as **Receipt** and **Shipment**. These values can be changed when creating the warehouse documents.

- **Bin Policies**: This tab contains some more advanced options for warehouse management.

Variants

Item variants is a powerful feature in Microsoft Dynamics NAV. It enables us to split an item into different categories without having to create a new item.

The variant code is maintained in the item ledger entries and used when applying them. Let's see an example of how this can be used.

Our company sells t-shirts. We have three sizes; small, medium, and large, and four colors; white, black, red, and blue. This enables us to create the following twelve unique variant codes:

Size and color			
S-WHITE	S-BLACK	S-RED	S-BLUE
M-WHITE	M-BLACK	M-RED	M-BLUE
L-WHITE	L-BLACK	L-RED	L-BLUE

When we purchase or produce these t-shirts, we need to specify the variant code, which is inherited into the item ledger entry.

If we sell or transfer one of these items, we can specify the same variant code. Microsoft Dynamics NAV will then use this variant code when searching for inventory.

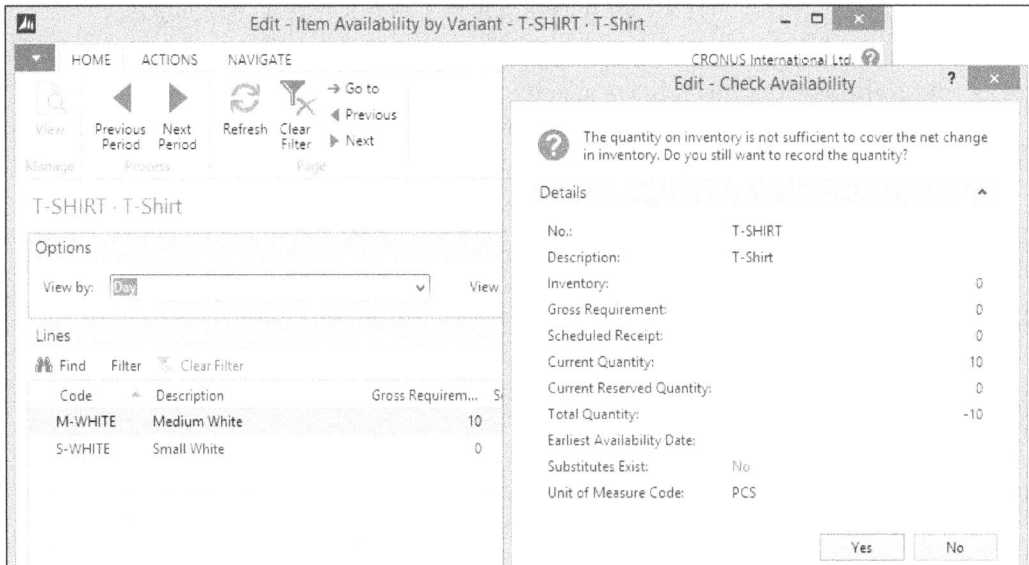

Stock keeping units

Sometimes, the same item can have more than one unit cost, replenishment system, or production method. To support this, we can use stock keeping units.

A stock keeping unit refers to an existing item, location, and variant. These three fields are the unique primary key. Let's see an example of how this can be used. Our t-shirts need to have different unit costs. In order to do this, we need to create a SKU for each variant we just created:

Item No.	Variant Code	Locat...	Replenish...	Description	Inventory	Last Direct Cost
T-SHIRT	M-WHITE		Purchase	T-Shirt	2	7,00
T-SHIRT	S-WHITE		Purchase	T-Shirt	12	6,00

When we now create two purchase order lines for the same item with a different variant code, we can see that the **Last Direct Cost** is different for each variant.

> **Stockkeeping Units** is a very powerful feature of Microsoft Dynamics. It enables you to change the settings for an item after it is created, using variant codes for each setting. Make sure the code of the variant is self-explanatory.

Creating a SKU function

When an item has many variants and locations, creating the SKU for each combination can be quite a challenge. To help in this process, we can use the **Create Stockkeeping Unit** report (5706).

The newly created SKU will inherit all the necessary fields from the item. After this, we can go in and make necessary changes to the individual SKU records:

Sales pricing

The basic unit price of an item can be set in the **Item** table. This is a static field, which is used when a new sales document is created. To use more flexible unit prices, we can use the **Sales Prices** and **Sales Discounts** functionality:

More information about pricing can be found in *Chapter 1, Introduction to Microsoft Dynamics NAV*, and *Chapter 2, A Sample Application*.

Item ledger entry application

When the inventory is created and used, the system will apply and close positive and negative item ledger entries with each other. This enables us to trace inventory.

The application is saved in **Item Application Entry** table (339). Let's have a look at the C/AL code that handles the item application.

Item application C/AL routine

Item application is done in codeunit Item Jnl.-Post Line (22) in the ApplyItemLedgEntry function. The function starts with checking whether reservations are used. Using reservations changes the way inventory application is used. We'll discuss reservations later in this chapter.

```
ApplyItemLedgEntry

. . .

CLEAR(OldItemLedgEntry);
```

```
...
REPEAT
  ItemJnlLine.CALCFIELDS("Reserved Qty. (Base)");
  IF ItemJnlLine."Assemble to Order" THEN BEGIN
    ItemJnlLine.TESTFIELD("Reserved Qty. (Base)");
    ItemJnlLine.TESTFIELD("Applies-to Entry");
  END ELSE
    IF ItemJnlLine."Reserved Qty. (Base)" <> 0 THEN BEGIN
      IF ItemLedgEntry."Applies-to Entry" <> 0 THEN
        ItemLedgEntry.FIELDERROR(
          "Applies-to Entry",Text99000000);
    END;
    ...
  END ELSE
    StartApplication := TRUE;
```

If there are no reservations made, the system will start the application code. This allows two possibilities: manual application and automatic application.

Manual application is done when the user populates the **Applies-to Entry** field in the item journal line. This is also used when users change the application.

```
IF StartApplication THEN BEGIN
  ItemLedgEntry.CALCFIELDS("Reserved Quantity");
  IF ItemLedgEntry."Applies-to Entry" <> 0 THEN BEGIN
    IF FirstApplication THEN BEGIN
      FirstApplication := FALSE;
      OldItemLedgEntry.GET(ItemLedgEntry."Applies-to Entry");
      OldItemLedgEntry.TESTFIELD("Item No.",ItemLedgEntry."Item No.");
      OldItemLedgEntry.TESTFIELD("Variant Code",ItemLedgEntry."Variant
Code");

      OldItemLedgEntry.TESTFIELD(Positive,NOT ItemLedgEntry.Positive);
      OldItemLedgEntry.TESTFIELD("Location
Code",ItemLedgEntry."Location Code");
```

In this case, the system checks whether the **Item Ledger Entry** we have specified matches the requirements. When the application is done automatically, the system will search for the best item ledger entry based on the same requirements.

```
END ELSE BEGIN
  IF FirstApplication THEN BEGIN
    FirstApplication := FALSE;
    ItemLedgEntry2.SETCURRENTKEY("Item No.",Open,"Variant Code",
      Positive,"Location Code","Posting Date");
```

```
ItemLedgEntry2.SETRANGE("Item No.",ItemLedgEntry."Item No.");
ItemLedgEntry2.SETRANGE(Open,TRUE);
ItemLedgEntry2.SETRANGE("Variant Code",ItemLedgEntry.
  "Variant Code");
ItemLedgEntry2.SETRANGE(Positive,NOT ItemLedgEntry.Positive);
ItemLedgEntry2.SETRANGE("Location Code",
  ItemLedgEntry."Location Code");

IF ItemLedgEntry."Job Purchase" = TRUE THEN BEGIN
  ItemLedgEntry2.SETRANGE("Job No.",ItemLedgEntry."Job No.");
  ItemLedgEntry2.SETRANGE("Job Task No.",
    ItemLedgEntry."Job Task No.");
  ...
END;
IF ItemTrackingCode."SN Specific Tracking" THEN
  ItemLedgEntry2.SETRANGE("Serial No.",
    ItemLedgEntry."Serial No.");
IF ItemTrackingCode."Lot Specific Tracking" THEN
  ItemLedgEntry2.SETRANGE("Lot No.",ItemLedgEntry."Lot No.");

IF Location.GET(ItemLedgEntry."Location Code") THEN
  IF Location."Use As In-Transit" THEN
    ItemLedgEntry2.SETRANGE("Transfer Order No.",
      ItemLedgEntry."Transfer Order No.");

IF Item."Costing Method" = Item."Costing Method"::LIFO THEN
  EntryFindMethod := '+'
ELSE
  EntryFindMethod := '-';
IF NOT ItemLedgEntry2.FIND(EntryFindMethod) THEN
  EXIT;
```

The actual application entry is created in the `InsertApplEntry` function.

Requirements to apply an item ledger

In order to apply an item ledger entry to another item ledger entry, certain requirements should be taken into account. We can read these requirements from the C/AL code:

* The **Item No.** should be the same for both the entries.

* The old item ledger entry should be **Open**. When an item ledger entry is fully applied, the Boolean field **Open** is set to **False**.

- The variant code and location code should be the same.

- The Boolean field **Positive** should have a reverse sign. This results in the limitation of not being able to apply one negative entry to another negative entry.

Other requirements are conditional based on system setup. For example, if the item uses a **Lot No.** or **Serial No.**, this should also match.

When the system has defined the filter, it tries to find the first record. The search method depends on the costing method. If the cost method is LIFO, the system will try to find the last record in the filter. For all other costing methods, it will find the first.

We can also see that when using Lot numbers, the application and the costing is done within the Lot number.

Value entries

In Microsoft Dynamics NAV, the physical information for Inventory is stored separately from the financial information. This information is stored in a one-to-many relation, meaning one Item Ledger Entry can have multiple Value Entries.

This enables us to specify the value information in detail in a time dimension and cost type dimension.

Direct cost

Each item ledger entry starts with at least one value entry of the type direct cost. This defines the initial value of the inventory. During the inventory lifetime, the item ledger entry can get the following four other types of value entries:

- **Revaluation**: This entry type is used when the item revaluation batch is started and the value of the item is different compared to the direct cost.

- **Rounding**: Sometimes, the inventory adjustment leads into rounding issues. The rounding is stored as a special entry type for traceability.

- **Indirect Cost**: When **Indirect Cost** % is used on the item card the system will create additional value entries for the indirect cost amount.

- **Variance**: When the item uses standard cost, the difference between the invoiced amount and the standard cost is saved as an entry type variance.

Value entries and general ledger entries

The value entries and general ledger entries are linked through the G/L - Item Ledger Relation table (5823). Each general ledger entry is linked to one or more value entries. This enables traceability and helps auditors to analyze the system.

Transfer orders

To move inventory from one location to another location, it is possible to do a negative and a positive adjustment in the **Item Journal Line**, but we can also use a **Transfer Order**, as shown in the following screenshot:

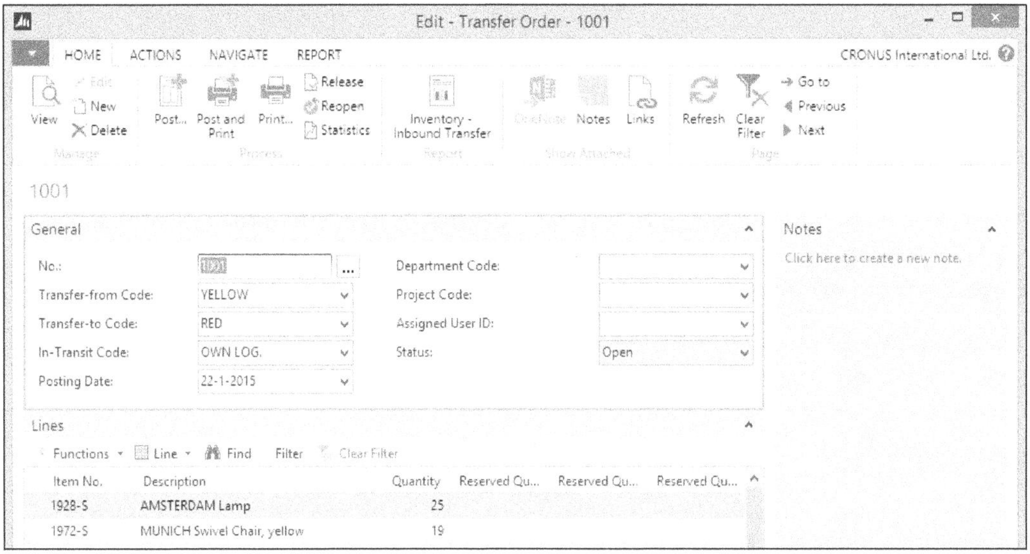

The **Transfer Order** creates the item ledger entries for each location and maintains the link for the value entries.

This means that if we move 100 items from location blue to green without having received the purchase invoice yet, the system will create value entries for the moved inventory when the invoice is posted. Let's try this for a new item.

Example

The item we will use is **Jeans**. The first step is to create the item as follows:

1. We only define the **No.**, **Description**, **Base UOM**, and the **Posting Groups**.

2. Now, we create a new purchase order with quantity 10 in location **BLUE**.

3. We receive the purchase order.

4. Using a new transfer order, we move the inventory from **BLUE** to **RED**.

   This will result in five **Item Ledger Entries** with five **Value Entries** but the total cost is zero since we have not yet received the purchase invoice.

5. Now, we create a new purchase invoice and get the receipt lines. We use a **Unit Cost** of **10**.

This results in a value entry for the original item ledger entry.

6. To create the value entries for the transfers, we need to run the Adjust Cost - Item Entries report (795). This results in all item ledger entries having the same value entries:

Posti...	Item ...	Entry No.	Entry...	Adj...	Document Type	Documen...	Item Ledger Entry No.	D...	Sa...	Cost Amount (Expec...	Cost Amount (Actual)
22-1-2015	Purchase	387	Direct Cost	☐	Purchase Receipt	107031	328		0,00	0,00	0,00
22-1-2015	Purchase	392	Direct Cost	☐	Purchase Invoice	108029	328		0,00	0,00	100,00
22-1-2015	Transfer	388	Direct Cost	☐	Transfer Shipment	108007	329		0,00	0,00	0,00
22-1-2015	Transfer	393	Direct Cost	☑	Transfer Shipment	108007	329		0,00	0,00	-100,00
22-1-2015	Transfer	389	Direct Cost	☐	Transfer Shipment	108007	330		0,00	0,00	0,00
22-1-2015	Transfer	390	Direct Cost	☐	Transfer Receipt	109004	331		0,00	0,00	0,00
22-1-2015	Transfer	394	Direct Cost	☑	Transfer Shipment	108007	330		0,00	0,00	100,00
22-1-2015	Transfer	395	Direct Cost	☑	Transfer Receipt	109004	331		0,00	0,00	-100,00
22-1-2015	Transfer	391	Direct Cost	☐	Transfer Receipt	109004	332		0,00	0,00	0,00
22-1-2015	Transfer	396	Direct Cost	☑	Transfer Receipt	109004	332		0,00	0,00	100,00

Requisition worksheets

For trading companies, it is very important to have just enough inventories; not too many, not too few. In order to do this, we can use the requisition journals together with the reordering policy on the item.

Reordering policy

The reordering policy tells the system how to calculate the moment and the quantity for item ordering. Microsoft Dynamics NAV uses the following four different reordering policies:

- **Fixed Reorder Qty.**: Each time we run the requisition journal, the system will purchase the same, fixed quantity of items. This quantity is specified in the **Reorder Quantity** field.

- **Maximum Qty.**: The system will purchase as many items to meet the value of the **Maximum Inventory** field.

- **Order**: For each sales order, a purchase order will be created. This automatically enables the reservation process for this item.

- **Lot-for-Lot**: This option will calculate the required inventory necessary to deliver the outstanding sales orders.

The quantity is calculated in the codeunit Inventory Profile Offsetting (99000854) in the `CalcReorderQty` function.

Extending the reordering policy

The ordering policy algorithms in Microsoft Dynamics NAV are very static and some trading companies need more flexibility.

One example is seasonal and depends on the weather. Toy stores need extra inventory during Christmas and garden tool stores have their peak in spring. During these peaks, the delivery times and availability is also different compared to the other times of the year.

Virtual inventory

An upcoming trend in trading companies is virtual inventory. This is the inventory that we do not control but is available to sell to our customers. The computer industry uses this frequently. Everyone can start a website for computer equipment and use the inventory of large wholesale companies.

> In order for this to work, the information should always be real time and reliable. In Microsoft Dynamics NAV, we could solve this using web services.

Warehouse management

With inventory management, we can use the locations to see where the inventory is. For some trading companies, this is good enough but some would like to be more specific in where the items are in the warehouse.

For this, we can use the **Warehouse Management Systems (WMS)** functionality in Microsoft Dynamics NAV. WMS enables us to specify zones and bins within each location.

Another feature in warehouse management is the possibility of combining sales shipments and purchase receipts in warehouse documents. Using these documents, warehouse employees can pick or put away for more than one order at the same time resulting in a more efficient way of doing logistics.

Warehouse strategy levels

Warehouse management can be used and implemented from very simple to highly advanced. To demonstrate the application design of WMS in Microsoft Dynamics NAV, we will discuss the following five possible levels of implementation. For each level, we will show the table and posting models.

- **Bin Code**: Using this field in the sales and purchase document enables the system to start creating warehouse entries.

- **Warehouse Receipt and Shipment**: This allows us to combine sales shipments and purchase receipts in one warehouse document. We cannot use the **Pick and Put-Away** activities.

- **Warehouse Put-Away and Pick**: For each purchase receipt or sales shipment, we can create a **Put-Away or Pick** journal.

- **Warehouse Receipt and Shipment + Use Put-away Worksheet**: This allows us to implement a real two-step warehouse process and receive the items on a staging location and creating put-away documents to move the items to their storage location in the warehouse.

- **Directed Put-Away and Pick**: This is the full option of WMS functionality in Microsoft Dynamics NAV. We use **Receipts**, **Shipments**, **Put-aways**, and **Picks**. Microsoft Dynamics NAV will suggest the **Bin Codes**. We can also use **Zones**, **Cross Docking**, and so on.

Location setup

The setup options in the Location table (14) enable or disable the WMS options in Microsoft Dynamics NAV. This is done on the **Warehouse** tab, as shown in the following screenshot. Each level requires a special combination of settings.

Let's have a look at the different levels:

- **Level 1**: Enable Bin Mandatory
- **Level 2**: Enable Require Receive, Require Shipment, and Bin Mandatory
- **Level 3**: Enable Require Put-away, Require Pick, and Bin Mandatory
- **Level 4**: Enable Require Receive, Shipment, Require Put-away, Require Pick, Bin Mandatory, and Use Put-away Worksheet
- **Level 5**: Enable Require Receive, Require Shipment, Require Put-away, Require Pick, Bin Mandatory, and Directed Put-away and Pick

Warehouse employees

Before we can start, the current user should be set up as a warehouse employee.

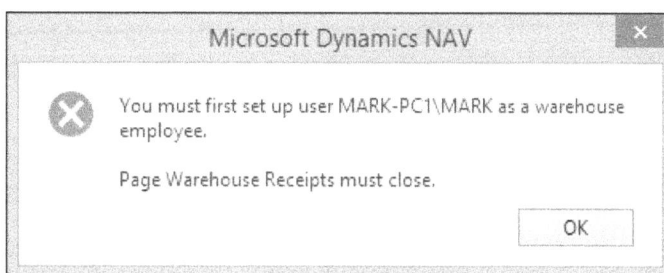

This can be done by creating a new record in the Warehouse Employee table (7301).

> Each user can be a warehouse employee in each location and can only do warehouse actions in the locations that they are assigned to.

Bin code | level 1

The starting level of implementing WMS is using the Bin table. This is done by enabling the **Bin Mandatory** field on the location. The **Bin Code** field is available in all the necessary tables, such as Purchase Line, Sales Line, and Item Journal Line.

When the **Bin Code** is used, codeunit Item Jnl.-Post Line (22) will create a Warehouse Journal Line and start the Whse. Jnl.-Register Line Codeunit (7301). This will result in the creation of Warehouse Entries (7312) and a Bin Content (7302).

Example

We will create a new location, **ORANGE**, with a bin of **BIN1**. The location uses the **Bin Mandatory** option, as shown in the following screenshot:

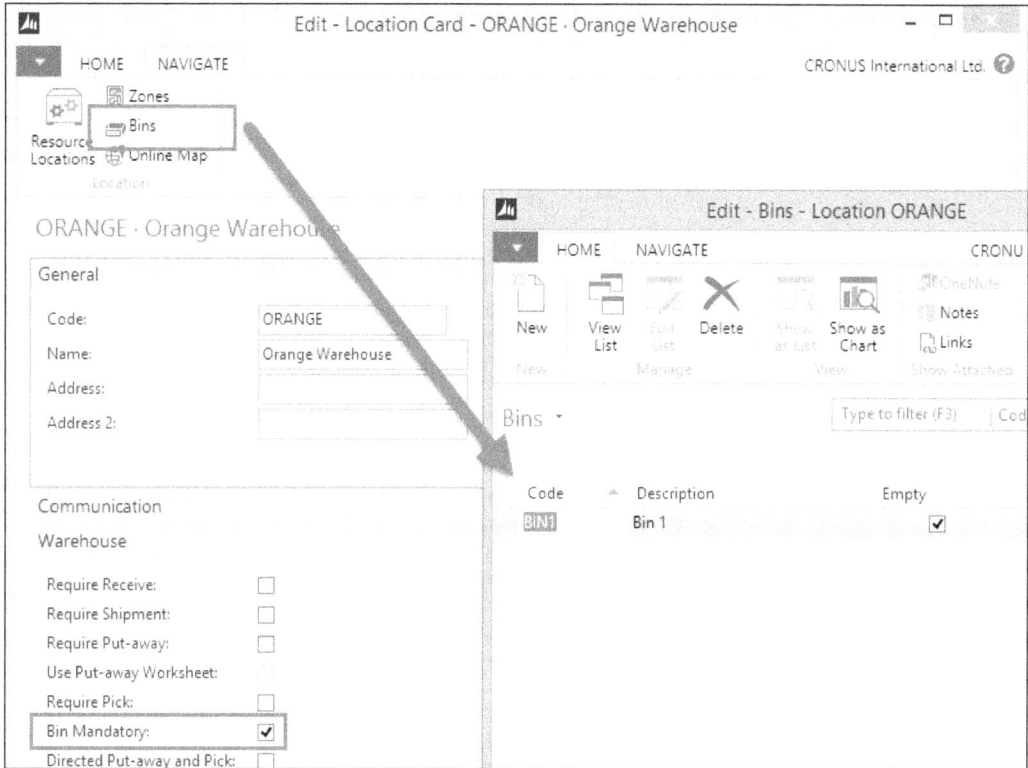

Bin Mandatory

In a new purchase order, we can now select this new Bin Code and post a receipt. The system now creates a new record in the **Bin Content** table, which enables us to see the created **Warehouse Entries**.

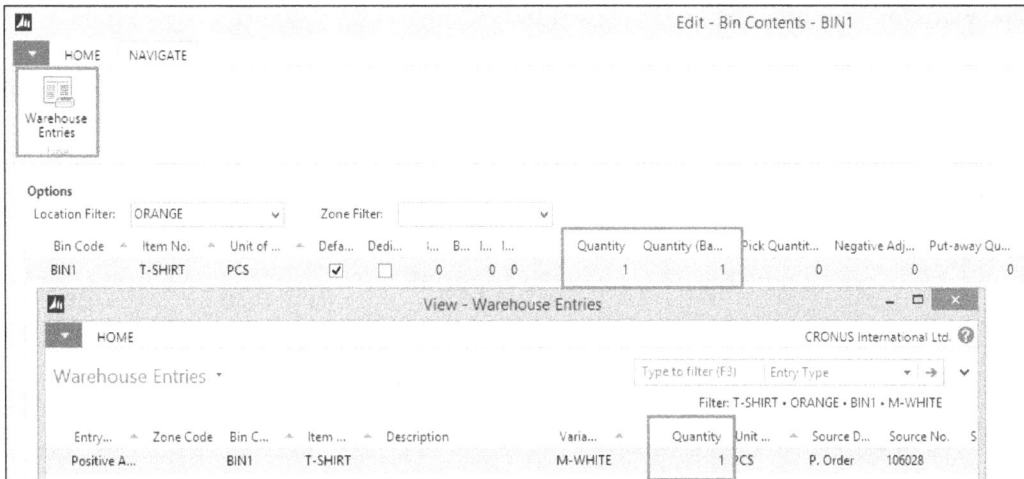

Bin content

Whenever a Bin is used for the first time, Microsoft Dynamics NAV will create a **Bin Content** record. A **Bin Content** record is neither master data nor a ledger entry or document. It is a special kind of table in the philosophy of Microsoft Dynamics NAV.

The C/AL code for the **Bin Content** handling can be found in codeunit Whse. Jnl.-Register Line (7301). To see which Bins are used for an item at any moment, we can open the **Bin Content** from the **Item Card**, as shown in the following screenshot:

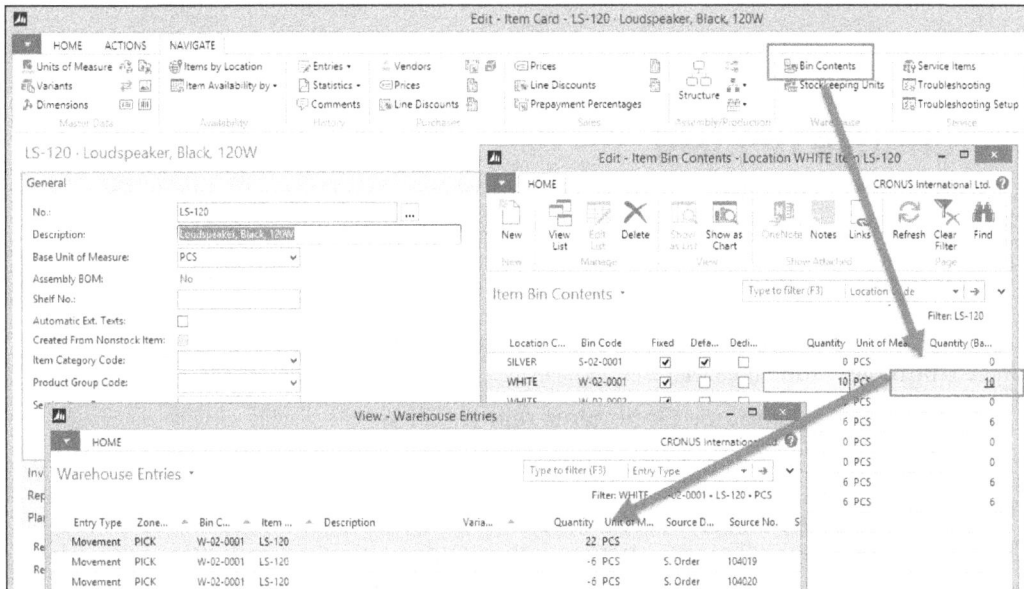

The warehouse entries can be displayed by clicking on the **Quantity (Base)** field.

Receipt and shipment | level 2

When we enable **Require Receive** and **Require Shipment** in the location, we can start using the warehouse receipt and shipment documents. These documents allow us to receive or ship multiple purchase or sales orders in one document.

Let's have a look at how this is done in the application:

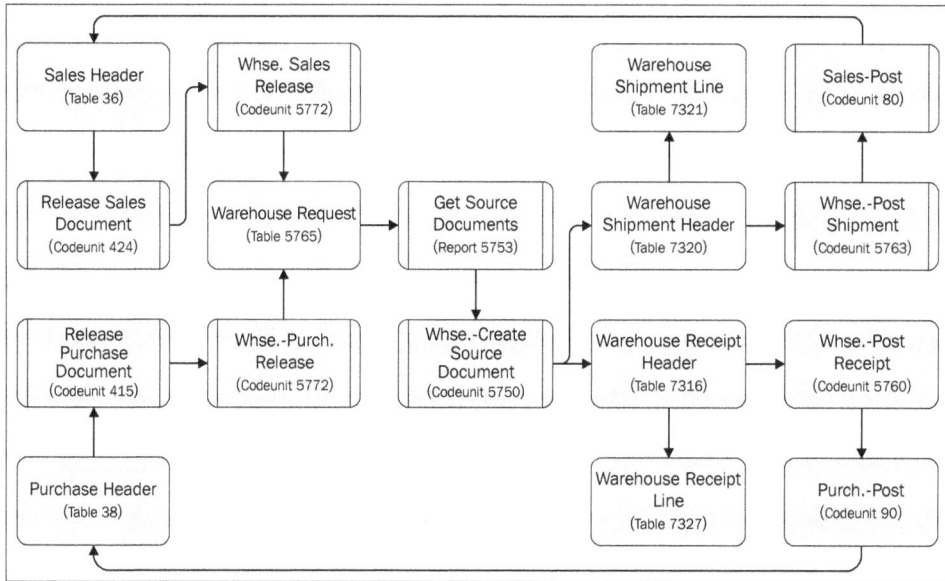

Warehouse request

All warehouse documents start with a record Warehouse Request table (5765). These records are created when a sales or purchase document is released.

The warehouse receipt or shipment can be created in the following three ways:

- Using the **Create Whse. Receipt** or **Create Whse. Shipment** option from the purchase and sales order
- Using the Get Source Documents report (5723)
- Using the **Get Source Documents** option on the **Warehouse Receipt** or **Shipment Card**

The first two options will create a new warehouse document for each sales or purchase document. The latter allows us to combine orders in one warehouse document.

Limitations

Using only the warehouse receipt and shipment document is basically just adding one layer on top of the sales and purchase document. The posting routines **Whse. Post Shipment (5763)** and **Whse. Post Receipt (5760)**, do not actually post something to the warehouse; they just write back the Bin code to the Sales Line and Purchase Line table. Technically, this uses the same C/AL code as level 1.

We can see how this is done by looking at the `InitSourceDocumentLines` function of, for example, Codeunit Whse. Post Receipt (5760):

```
InitSourceDocumentLines
WhseRcptLine2.COPY(WhseRcptLine);
WITH WhseRcptLine2 DO BEGIN
  CASE "Source Type" OF
    DATABASE::"Purchase Line":
      BEGIN
        PurchLine.SETRANGE("Document Type","Source Subtype");
        PurchLine.SETRANGE("Document No.","Source No.");
        IF PurchLine.FIND('-') THEN
          REPEAT
            . . .
            IF PurchLine."Bin Code" <> "Bin Code" THEN BEGIN
              PurchLine."Bin Code" := "Bin Code";
              ModifyLine := TRUE;
            END;
            . . .
          IF ModifyLine THEN
            PurchLine.MODIFY;
```

When the source tables are updated, the system creates a normal purchase receipt or sales shipment using codeunits sales-post (80) and Purch. Post (90).

Put-away and Pick | level 3

Instead of creating a warehouse receipt or shipment, we can also directly create a Put-away or Pick from the sales or purchase order.

To enable this, we need to activate the **Require Put-away** and **Require Pick** options on the **Location Card**.

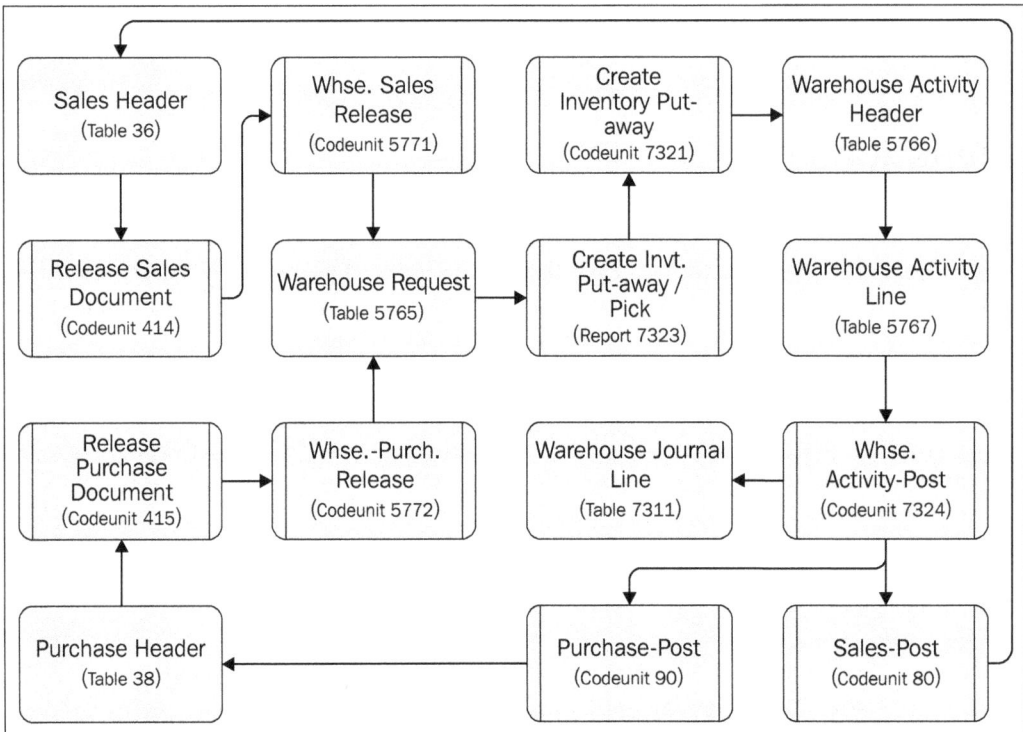

```
┌──────────────────────────────────────────────────────────────────────────────┐
│                                                                                │
│  Sales Header      Whse. Sales       Create            Warehouse Activity      │
│  (Table 36)        Release           Inventory Put-    Header                  │
│                    (Codeunit 5771)   away              (Table 5766)            │
│                                      (Codeunit 7321)                           │
│                                                                                │
│  Release Sales     Warehouse Request Create Invt.      Warehouse Activity      │
│  Document          (Table 5765)      Put-away /        Line                    │
│  (Codeunit 414)                      Pick              (Table 5767)            │
│                                      (Report 7323)                             │
│                                                                                │
│  Release           Whse.-Purch.      Warehouse Journal Whse.                   │
│  Purchase          Release           Line              Activity-Post           │
│  Document          (Codeunit 5772)   (Table 7311)      (Codeunit 7324)        │
│  (Codeunit 415)                                                                │
│                                                                                │
│  Purchase Header                     Purchase-Post     Sales-Post              │
│  (Table 38)                          (Codeunit 90)     (Codeunit 80)          │
│                                                                                │
└──────────────────────────────────────────────────────────────────────────────┘
```

Warehouse request

The warehouse request record is exactly the same as in level 2, but instead of creating a warehouse receipt or shipment, the system directly creates a warehouse activity header and line.

Warehouse activities

The warehouse activity header and line table are the internal Microsoft Dynamics NAV warehouse documents. There are five types of warehouse activity documents, they are as follows:

- **Put-away**: This document is used to move items from the receipt bin to a put-away bin. The document is generated from a warehouse receipt.

- **Pick**: This document is used to move items from a storage bin to a shipment bin. The document is generated from a warehouse shipment.

- **Movement**: This is an internal document that is used to move items internally in the warehouse.

- **Invt. Put-away**: This document is used to receive items and put them directly into the warehouse on their permanent bin. The document is created from a warehouse request.

- **Invt. Pick**: This document is used to ship items directly from the warehouse in one step. The document is created from a warehouse request.

When only using the **Require Put-away** and **Require Pick** option on a location, document types **Invt. Put-Away** and **Invt. Pick** are used. This will also make sure that the purchase order and sales order will be processed by starting codeunit sales-post (80) and Purch. Post (90).

Level 2 and level 3 comparison

Both level 2 and level 3 setup options are one-step warehouse implementations. When receiving an item, we must provide the storage bin where the item will be stored until it is sold. There is no additional step.

Using the warehouse receipt and shipment documents allows us to combine sales and purchase documents on one warehouse document. This cannot be done using direct Put-away and Pick. Using direct Put-away and Pick, we can split one sales line or purchase line into multiple bins. This cannot be done using warehouse receipt and shipment documents.

The reason for this is the way the warehouse entries are created. Level 2 uses the **Bin** field in the **Item Journal Line** to create the warehouse entries.

Using level 3, the warehouse entries are created using codeunit Whse.-Activity-Post (7324). The Bin code is not written back into the sales line or purchase line. This means we also cannot use the **Bin** code field in the purchase receipt and sales shipment documents.

Level 4 – receipt with Put-away worksheet

Most warehouses use a two-step receipt and shipment process. The first step is receiving the items on a receipt location, which is often close to the unloading docks. Then, the items are stored in their warehouse location until they are required for the production or sales process. This is step 2.

To enable this two-step process, we can combine level 2 and 3 by using the options **Require Receive**, **Shipment**, **Put-away and Pick** + **Bin Mandatory** + **Use Put-away worksheet** in the **Location Card**.

This allows us to first perform the warehouse receipt and shipment as discussed in level 2. When we process this document, it will not only post the sales order and purchase order but it will also generate a record in the Whse. Put-away Request table (7324).

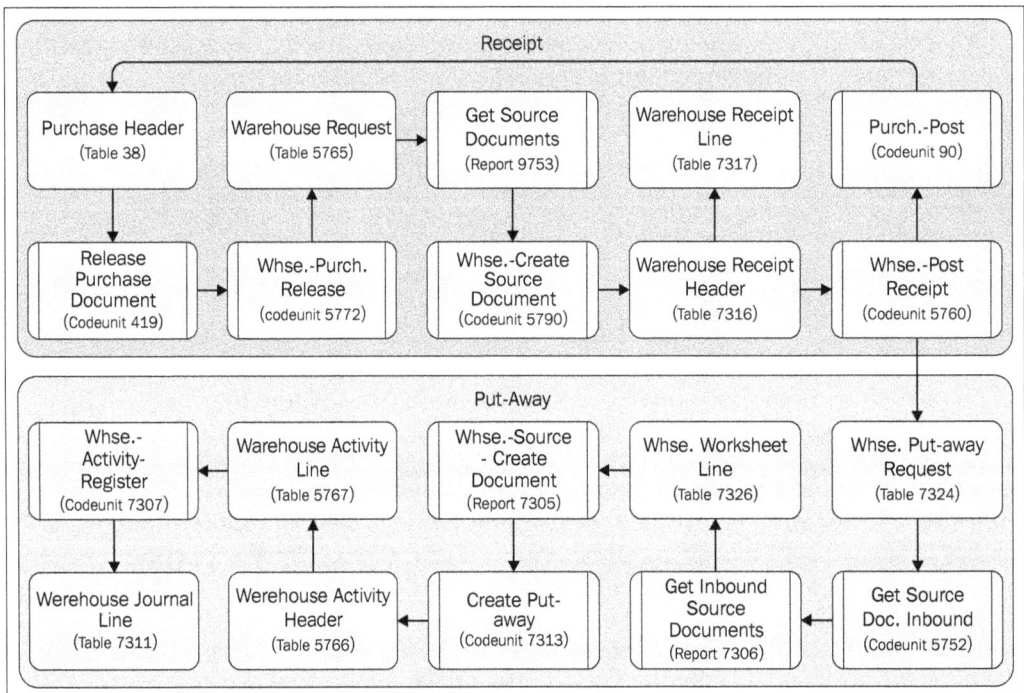

Whse.- activity register versus whse.-activity-post

When the whse. put-away request is processed using the warehouse worksheet, it will result in a warehouse activity header and line. In this context, the system will use the Put-away and pick document type that we discussed in the previous section about level 3.

Technically, the documents for level 3 and level 4 are equal, but there are the following two differences:

- In a two-step warehouse setup, the items are already in a warehouse entry. This means we have to move them. This results in two new warehouse entries but also two lines in the warehouse document.

- The two-step warehouse documents are not posted but registered. This means that the system will only create warehouse entries and no longer updates the sales and purchase documents.

Level 5 – directed put-away and pick

Combining warehouse receipts and shipments with put-aways and picks completes the table and posting diagram of WMS in Microsoft Dynamics NAV. But there are additional options to enrich the functionality.

One of these options is directed put-away and pick. When this option is activated, the system can and will help us in finding the correct bins for each warehouse activity.

Zones and default bins

Let's start with defining zones and default bins. A zone is a group of bins. Usually, they are located near each other physically but more importantly, they share some properties.

For each zone, we need to specify if it is allowed to receive, ship, put-away, and pick. This is done in the **Bin Type** list.

When defining the bins, it is recommended to use a logical name such as R-01-001 for **Receipt** row one shelf one:

Bins				^
Receipt		**Adjustment**		
Receipt Bin Code:	W-08-0001 ∨	Adjustment Bin Code:	W-11-0001 ∨	
Shipment		**Cross-Dock**		
Shipment Bin Code:	W-09-0001 ∨	Cross-Dock Bin Code:	W-14-0001 ∨	
Production		**Assembly**		
Open Shop Floor Bin Code:	W-07-0001 ∨	To-Assembly Bin Code:	∨	
To-Production Bin Code:	W-07-0002 ∨	From-Assembly Bin Code:	∨	
From-Production Bin Code:	W-07-0003 ∨	Asm.-to-Order Shpt. Bin Code:		

The default bins are set up in the **Location Card** on the **Bin** tab. These bins can always be changed on each document.

Bin calculation

The bin calculation is done for the put-away documents using templates. This template defines the rules for finding the correct bin to store the items:

Edit - Put-away Template - STD

HOME

STD

General

Code: STD   Description: Standard Template

Lines

Find   Filter   Clear Filter

Find Fixed Bin	Find Floating Bin	Find Same Item	Find Unit of Measure Match	Find Bin w. Less than Min. Qty	Find Empty Bin	Description
✔	☐	✔	✔	✔	☐	
✔	☐	✔	✔	☐	☐	
☐	✔	✔	✔	☐	☐	
☐	✔	✔	☐	☐	☐	
☐	✔	☐	☐	☐	✔	
☐	✔	☐	☐	☐	☐	

The find options are stored in the put-away template line table (7308); they are as follows:

- **Find Fixed Bin**: The system will try to find a bin, which is fixed. A fixed bin is usually reserved for a specific item.

- **Find Floating Bin**: This will try to find the first available bin.

- **Find Same Item**: This will filter on an available bin that already contains this item.

- **Find Unit of Measure Match**: This option can be used if parts of the warehouse are designed to handle a specific kind of carrier such as Euro or US pallet.

- **Find Bin w. Less than Min. Qty**: Use this option to find bins that are not fully used. If this option is not used with the **Find Same Item**, it might result in two items in the same bin.

- **Find Empty Bin**: This option will make sure we find an empty bin.

The C/AL code that handles the bin calculation is located in codeunit create put-away (7313). Let's have a look:

```
Code()
IF Location."Directed Put-away and Pick" THEN BEGIN
  BinType.CreateBinTypeFilter(BinTypeFilter,2);
  REPEAT
    QtyToPutAwayBase := RemQtyToPutAwayBase;
    IF NOT (PutAwayTemplLine."Find Empty Bin" OR
      PutAwayTemplLine."Find Floating Bin") OR
      PutAwayTemplLine."Find Fixed Bin" OR
      PutAwayTemplLine."Find Same Item" OR
      PutAwayTemplLine."Find Unit of Measure Match" OR
      PutAwayTemplLine."Find Bin w. Less than Min. Qty"
    THEN BEGIN
        //Calc Availability per Bin Content
        IF FindBinContent("Location Code","Item No.",
          "Variant Code",WarehouseClassCode)
        THEN
          REPEAT
            ...
          UNTIL (BinContent.NEXT(-1) = 0) OR EverythingHandled
    END ELSE BEGIN

        //Calc Availability per Bin
```

```
IF FindBin("Location Code",WarehouseClassCode) THEN
  REPEAT
    IF Bin.Code <> "Bin Code" THEN BEGIN
      ...
    END;
  UNTIL (Bin.NEXT(-1) = 0) OR EverythingHandled
END
UNTIL (PutAwayTemplLine.NEXT = 0) OR EverythingHandled;
```

For each record in the put-away template line table, the system will try to find a bin. This means that if the rules of the first template line fail, it will use the second template line and so forth.

The two options `Find Empty Bin` and `Find Floating Bin` eliminate using the others. If these are `true`, the system will call the `FindBin` function. For the other options, it will use the `FindBinContent` function.

Implementing and customizing warehouse management

Since there are many ways to set up WMS in Microsoft Dynamics NAV, it is very important to make the correct decisions at the start of the implementation. Moving the system from one strategy to another is quite a challenge.

It is therefore very important to discuss all possibilities and compare them to the way your company works.

> A common mistake when implementing WMS software is trying to solve procedural issues with a computer system. The simple rule is: "If it does not work without a computer system, it will most certainly not work with a computer system".

Customizing and changing WMS should be done very carefully since the data flow is very complex, especially for Microsoft Dynamics NAV standards.

Reservations

In Microsoft Dynamics NAV, it is possible to do reservations on inventory. This can help us manage our inventory more effectively. Let's discuss the reservation process with a customer scenario.

One of our customer orders 100 black t-shirts size M on January 22, 2015. Currently, we have 120 in our inventory so we can ship them without any problems. The customer wants to have them delivered on November 18. We enter a sales order with the shipping date and release the order.

The next day, another customer calls for 40 black t-shirts size M. Our inventory is still 120. This customer wants to have them delivered on May 31. We enter the sales order without a warning. Lastly, we will create a new sales order for 90 of the same t-shirts with a delivery date on July 25. Now, we get the following error message:

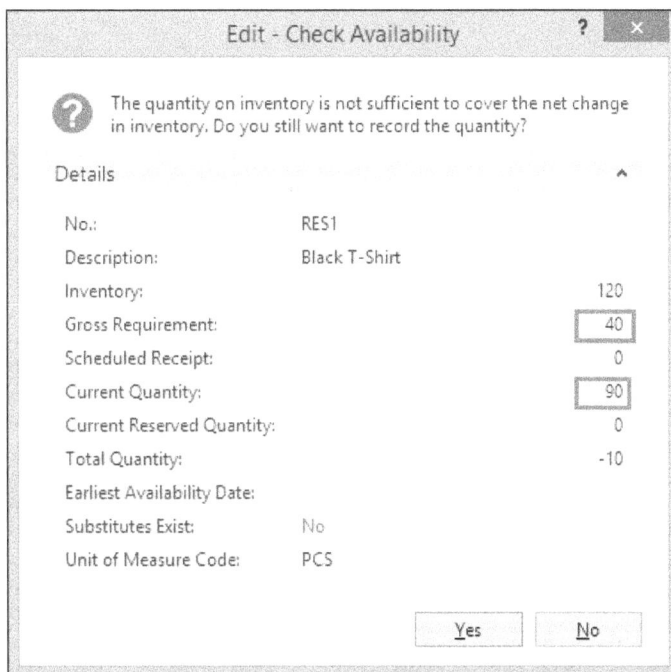

And if we now go back to the second sales order and re-enter the quantity, we get a similar message.

Check-avail. period calc.

The reason this happens lies in the way Microsoft Dynamics NAV calculates the gross requirement:

This is a two-step method where first, the requirement is calculated until the shipment date of the sales line and secondly, a Lookahead function is called using a date formula that is defined in the company information table.

The C/AL code that is used to calculate the Lookahead can be found in the QtyAvailabletoPromise function in codeunit Available to Promise (5790).

```
QtyAvailabletoPromise
Item.CALCFIELDS(Inventory,"Reserved Qty. on Inventory");
ScheduledReceipt := CalcScheduledReceipt(Item);
GrossRequirement := CalcGrossRequirement(Item);

IF FORMAT(LookaheadDateFormula) <> '' THEN BEGIN
  GrossRequirement :=
    GrossRequirement +
    CalculateLookahead(
      Item,PeriodType,
      AvailabilityDate + 1,
```

If this Lookahead functionality is not detailed enough, we can start using the reservation process.

Always versus optional reservation

The **Reservation** option can be activated on the item level and customer level and can be set to **Never**, **Optional**, and **Always**, as shown in the following screenshot:

Let's see what these options signify:

- **Never**: Reservations on this item or customer are impossible. If the item is **Reserve** as **Always** and the **Customer** as **Never**, the item wins.

- **Optional**: It is possible to reserve items for this customer; however, salespersons and warehouse employees can decide to overrule the reservation.

- **Always**: Shipping is not possible without a proper reservation. If the demand is larger than the supply, the salespersons and warehouse employees must make manual decisions of who gets what.

Reservation entries

Microsoft Dynamics NAV uses the Reservation Entry (337) table to store the reservation entries. Reservation entries can be connected to all outstanding documents and journals and posted entries. This is done using the following source fields:

- **Source Type**: This is an integer field representing the table the record is linked to, for example, 37 means sales line and 5406, prod. order line.

- **Source Subtype**: This is an option field, which is linked to the **Document Type** field when the record is linked to a sales line, purchase line record, or the status of a production order.

- **Source ID**: This is the link to the document no. of the record this line is linked to.

- **Source Batch Name**: If the record is linked to a journal, this field represents the journal batch name. If this field is used, the source ID is empty and vice versa.

- **Source Prod. Order Line**: When the record is used for a production order line or component, this field represents the production order line number.

- **Source Ref. No.:** This is an integer field, which is used to link the record to a line no. in a document, journal, or the production component. If the line is linked to a ledger entry, this field represents the entry no. field.

There are four types of Reservation Entries in Microsoft Dynamics NAV represented by the **Reservation Status** field:

- **Reservation**: These are real reservation entries, which means that a part of the current or future inventory is reserved for a production order or sales order. If the item uses the **Always** reservation option, it is not possible to work around this. If the reservation is optional, it is possible that someone else might still use these items in another process.

- **Tracking**: This option is used by the **Order Tracking Policy** option in Microsoft Dynamics NAV. This is an "underwater" process that can link supply and demand automatically. The status **Tracking** means that there is a supply as well as a demand.

- **Surplus**: This option is used for both item tracking as discussed in *Chapter 5*, *Production*, and the Order Tracking policy. The records can be identified by using the value of the item tracking field. This is set to **None** for Order Tracking policy records and **Serial No.**, **Lot No.**, and **Lot** and **Serial No.** for item tracking.

- **Prospect**: When item tracking is used, a prospect reservation record indicates an internal journal action, for example, assigning a serial number to an item journal line.

Creating a reservation

Let's go into the application and create a reservation to see what entries we get in the database.

We will do this using a new item. The item should have a Description, Base Unit of Measure, and a Gen. Prod., VAT Prod., and an Inventory Posting Group. The default value for **Reserve** is **Optional**, which we will use for this example. The default costing method is FIFO, which we will also use.

1. To demonstrate the real value of reservations, we should create two purchase orders with different dates and unit costs. With FIFO, the system would normally apply the sales order to the first item ledger entry. We will reserve on the second item ledger entry to demonstrate the impact on item costing and application.

2. When this is done, we can create a new sales order with one sales line containing the item and half the inventory and select **Reserve** from the **Functions** tab.

3. In this screen, we can take a look at the available inventory by clicking on **Available to Reserve**:

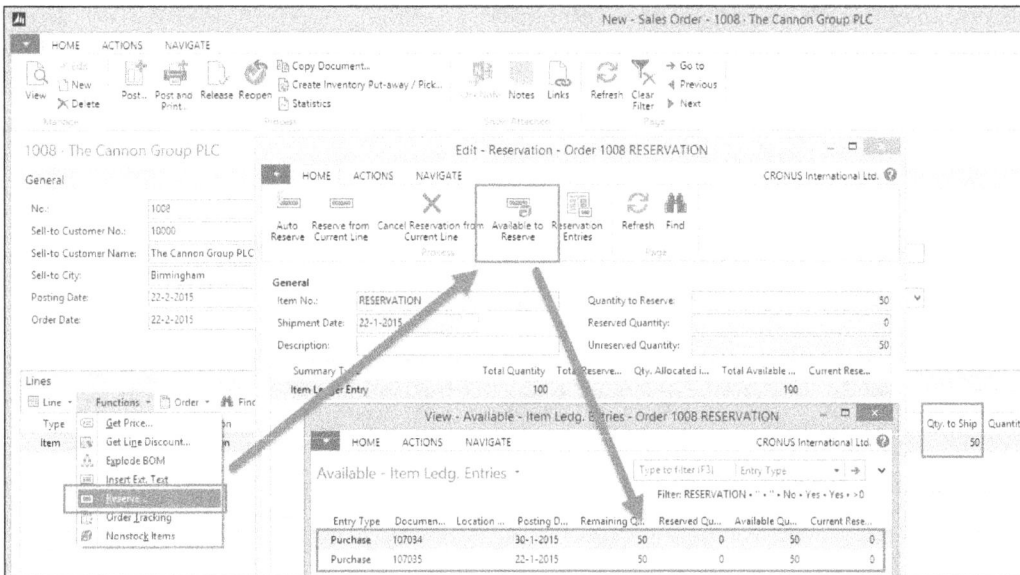

4. Here, we select the second receipt and navigate to **Actions | Functions | Reserve**. Then, we close the screen.

5. In **Sales Order Lines**, we can now see the **Reserved Quantity** as **50**:

Let's have a look at the **Reservation Entries** created in the database by running the table from the **Object Designer**:

A reservation entry of the type **Reservation** always uses to lines with the same entry no. The **Source Type** for the first entry links to the Sales Line table (37) and the second uses the Item Ledger Entry Table (32).

We ship and invoice the sales order and look at the **Item Ledger Entries** for our item:

We see that Microsoft Dynamics NAV has used the second item ledger entry, but the cost is **500**, not the **600** from the second entry.

To correct this, we run the report Adjust Cost - Item Entries (795) and have another look at the **Item Ledger Entries** and the **Value Entries** to see that it is corrected.

Order tracking policy

We have seen that reservation entries are not only used for the reservation process of inventory and item tracking but also for balancing supply and demand. This is an internal option within Microsoft Dynamics NAV that allows us to link inventory internally.

The entries are used in the supply and demand calculation to create the requisition worksheets.

Example

Let's create a copy of our reservation test item to see the differences between reservations and item tracking. This new item should have the Order Tracking Policy Tracking and Action Msg.

We will create two purchase orders with both a quantity of **50** without receiving them and create a sales order for the same item with a quantity of **80**.

If we now select **Order Tracking** from the **Sales Line Functions**, we see that the system matches supply and demand.

Let's have a look at the **Reservation Entries**:

Entry N...	Item No.	L...	Quantity (Base)	Positive	Reservation...	Description	Creation Da...	Transferred...	Source Type	Source Sub...	Source ID
4	TRACKTEST		20	☑	Surplus	Item Trackin...	22-1-2015	0	39	1	106034
6	TRACKTEST		-50	☐	Tracking	Item Trackin...	22-1-2015	0	37	1	1010
6	TRACKTEST		50	☑	Tracking	Item Trackin...	22-1-2015	0	39	1	106035
7	TRACKTEST		-30	☐	Tracking	Item Trackin...	22-1-2015	0	37	1	1010
7	TRACKTEST		30	☑	Tracking	Item Trackin...	22-1-2015	0	39	1	106034

We can see that Microsoft Dynamics NAV is now using the **Surplus** and **Tracking** types. The 20 items we have left are not linked to a demand.

Let's start the **Requisition Worksheet** for this item and see what Microsoft Dynamics NAV can do with this information.

Replenishment

Let's change the reordering policy of the item to **Lot-for-Lot** and run the **Requisition Worksheet** for this item:

Planning			
Reordering Policy:	Lot-for-Lot	**Lot-for-Lot Parameters**	
Reserve:	Optional	Include Inventory:	☑
Order Tracking Policy:	Tracking & Action Msg.	Lot Accumulation Period:	
Stockkeeping Unit Exists:	No	Rescheduling Period:	
Dampener Period:		**Reorder-Point Parameters**	

This will result in the suggestion to combine both purchase orders into one document with a different quantity.

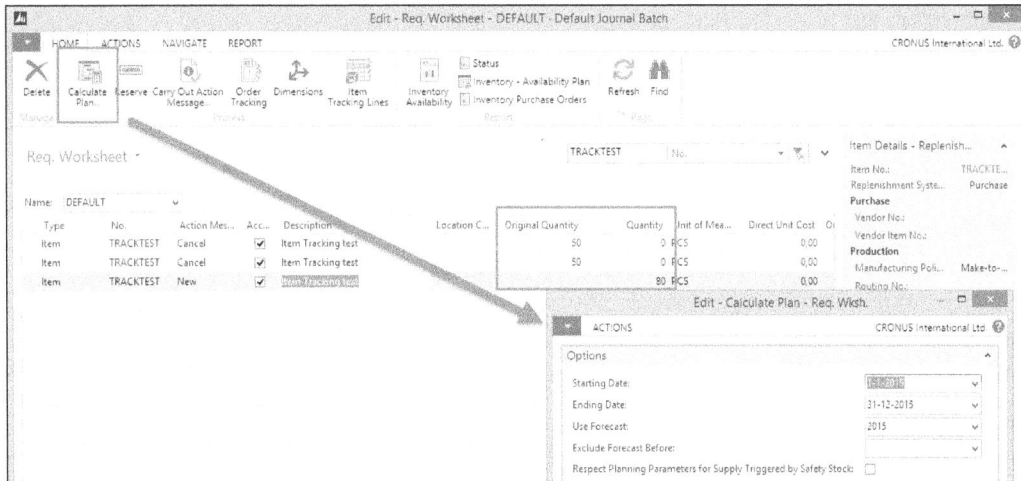

Auto increment

In Microsoft Dynamics NAV 2013, the Reservation Entry table was redesigned to use the Auto increment feature to determine unique numbering. This improves application performance and reduces locking.

Trade in vertical industries

Microsoft Dynamics NAV is used in many different vertical industries that often require specific features. Rather than trying to implement all these features in the standard product, Microsoft Dynamics NAV supports the framework and allows developers to design and create the vertical features.

For these features, the 80/20 rule applies. Microsoft delivers 80 percent of the framework which costs 20 percent of our time to implement. The missing 20 percent of the functionality is developed costing 80 percent of the budgeted time.

In this section, we will discuss how Microsoft Dynamics NAV is used for trade in five different vertical industries. For each industry, we will discuss two specific vertical features and how they could be solved.

> Most industries have solid add-on solutions available designed by certified Microsoft Dynamics NAV partners that have been implemented at multiple sites. It is highly recommended to look at those add-on solutions instead of reinventing the wheel and rewriting an add-on that already exists.

Fashion

The fashion industry has trade periods within the seasons. During spring, shops need to order the collection for the next winter and during autumn they buy summer clothes.

Sales orders

The sales orders for each collection are created as normal sales orders but with a shipment date in the future, sometimes six months or more ahead. When using variants, there should be a separate sales line for each variant, meaning, size, and color.

This can be quite a hassle to enter for sales people, so we could speed this up using a template sales line for the main item and hide the individual sizes.

Using a matrix where the x axis represents the size and y axis the color, sales people can quickly enter the quantities. When the matrix is closed, we can update the hidden sales lines. These hidden sales lines are used to calculate the production orders as discussed in *Chapter 5, Production*.

Reservations

When the production orders return from the factory, the warehouse and sales people need to decide which customer gets the items first. This can be done using the shipment date but that might not be completely fair if one customer orders in time, meaning six months ahead, and another customer orders too late with an earlier or the same shipment date.

This is where we can start using reservations. The reservations already support variants but the auto reserve functionality of Microsoft Dynamics NAV might not just do what we like.

Changing this functionality is a complex task. The C/AL code for AutoReserve can be found in codeunit Reservation Management (99000845) but should only be changed by experienced developers.

Fortunately, reservations are layered on top of the normal inventory, production, purchase, and sales process. If we change the algorithm, we can remove the current reservations and retest the code to see if the newly created reservation entries are good. This testing process should be done very carefully, on a dataset that is small enough to analyze using Microsoft Excel.

Automotive

Microsoft Dynamics NAV is used by many car dealer companies and garages because there are some strong add-on products available for this vertical industry.

On top of the normal trade process supported by Microsoft Dynamics NAV, these companies have additional business requirements. Let's discuss two of them.

Vehicle information

Each vehicle that is sold needs to be configured and ordered. The configuration should be stored in the database for future maintenance and warranty.

We can compare this to serial numbers or the lot number information table in the standard product. We could create a new master data table called **Vehicle** and create a record in this table for each car we configure or sell. The number we create for the **Vehicle** can be used as a serial number in the **Item Ledger Entry**.

For maintenance, we could have a vehicle journal that creates vehicle ledger entries each time the car comes back for servicing. This helps us keep track of the history and should include information such as mileage. The technical design of this solution can be compared to the squash application we created in *Chapter 2, A Sample Application*.

Parts management

In the automotive industry, using the right part is crucial. Different parts can be used on different types of cars and are often even brand independent.

Many vendors offer their assortment in digital formats allowing us to create interfaces with them. Parts should be defined as items, using standard features such as substitutions. As many parts can be expensive and have a low turnover speed, keeping them in the inventory can be very expensive, thus a minimum inventory should be maintained.

Parts can be connected to vehicle types. For example, a car interior mirror could be used for five types of cars. When a service engineer wants to replace such a mirror, he/she can use a filtered item list of all available parts.

Pharmaceuticals/medicines

In a pharmacy or at another medicine supplier, it is normal that not just every customer is allowed to purchase any item. They cannot sell medicines against cardiac arrhythmia to a healthy person.

Even when someone is allowed to use a certain medication, it is often limited to certain doses. People are often insured for the cost of these medicines but most insurance companies require a contribution.

Medication card

Microsoft Dynamics NAV does not support item regulation. To support this, we should create new functionality that links items to customers but also allows us to enter the doses and frequency.

From this template, we could periodically create sales orders and shipments. Whenever we ship the medicines, we need to update the template.

Contribution invoicing

When customers need to pay a part of the medication as an own contribution, we require the system to create two sales invoices for one sales order.

This is possible using the standard pre-payment functionality in Microsoft Dynamics NAV. We could send a pre-payment invoice to the customer and handle the other invoices to the insurance companies using combined invoicing. The pre-payments will be automatically deducted from the invoice amount but the value entries on the items will remain intact.

However, the standard system does not allow us to create a pre-payment invoice to another Bill-to Customer No. This would have to be designed and developed.

Food

Where fashion companies have two or three large ordering moments per year where customers carefully consider what to order, most food companies have a daily ordering process of high volume items.

This ordering process is often done by phone or fax where the retailer calls and tells the call center employees what to ship the next day.

Assortment

Most food companies use an assortment of products. This assortment can change from season to season or contain special action items but is usually stable since that is what most consumers want; meatballs on Monday, pork chops on Tuesday, and so on.

To save valuable time creating a new sales order with the same items each day, we could have the system do this at night.

This could be done using Standard Customer Sales Codes. This standard function in Microsoft Dynamics NAV allows us to create template sales orders with multiple items or other master data supported by the sales process. It also supports fixed quantities that can be adjusted when the sales orders are created.

The sales order can be created from the Customer Sales Codes using the **Get. Std. Cust Sales Codes** function, as shown in the following screenshot:

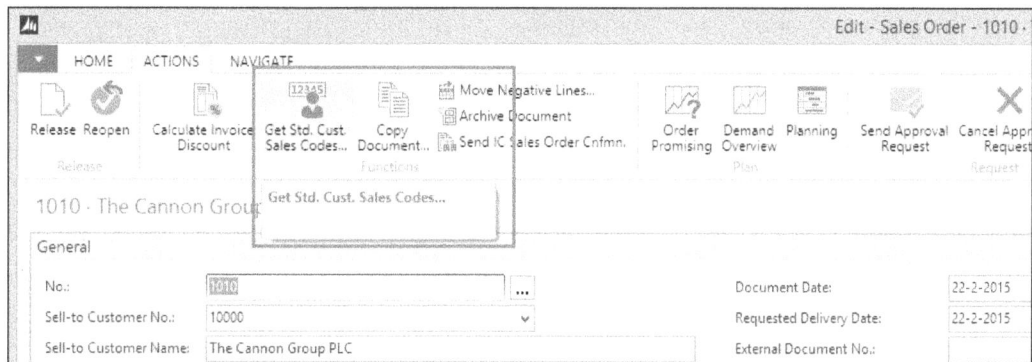

Sales order creation

This function could be scheduled in the **Job Scheduler** to create new sales order each night for the next day. We will discuss the job scheduler in *Chapter 9, Interfacing*.

Fast order entry

When the retailer contacts the call center to complete the sales order, the order entry person should be able to quickly find the correct sales line. If the assortment contains 150 items, this can be quite challenging.

This can be solved by implementing a fast order entry functionality that enables users to key in an item number and quantity on the sales header. The values will be updated in the correct sales line and blanked for the next entry.

With this functionality, the end user can always work from the same place without searching for the correct sales line.

Furniture

The furniture trading companies have similar issues with variants like fashion companies, with some key differences.

Items like office chairs and desks have far more options compared to clothes and when sold, most consumers buy few with the same specifications rather than a collection of different sizes.

Variant configuration

The price of furniture is dependent of the configuration, which fabric we want for the seat, the type of armrest, or even the type of wheel. This configuration also determines the item number.

An office chair or desk can have as much as 1200 possible combinations. We do not want to register all these combinations as items or even as variants.

Most furniture suppliers offer online systems or small external software packages to determine the combination. Once the combination is identified, we can create a new variant code or see if the variant already exists and create the sales order.

One-off items

Furniture retailers often have many collections they can sell with thousands of items. Most of the items in these collections will never be sold, or get sold as one-off items that are only sold once to one customer.

In this case, it does not make sense to create an item with an item cost and inventory value, but we still want to have some traceability of the item.
This calls for two solutions:

- We could create a collection item, which we can reuse each time we sell an item that is similar to another item but not exactly the same, for example, a lamp with a different foot color. On the sales line, we create the possibility for sales people to enter the vendor/collection and an item category. The system should then search for the template item.

- Another solution is to create a new item runtime from the sales order. The sales person will also select the vendor/collection and item category and the system should show a list with items already in the database. If the item is not created, the system should create the item using a template for the posting groups. The sales person can immediately use it and we then have traceability of the items we sold.

Summary

With this chapter, we end our quest exploring the production and trade functionality around the items in Microsoft Dynamics NAV. We discussed the application design of sales and purchase documents in Microsoft Dynamics NAV and how they are mirrored. We talked about the different document types and how they work together from quote or blanket order to order, and invoice or return order, and credit memo.

The sales and purchase line validation methodology helps us to calculate the pricing, inventory and VAT using a special structure of functions that is linked to the way end users create these lines.

Sales and purchase orders have a mandatory release process that can be extended with document approval and prepayments. The items have a two-layer inventory process using item ledger entries on locations and warehouse entries on bins and zones. We can use transfer orders to move items from one location to another and warehouse documents to move items from bin to bin and zone to zone. A warehouse is set up in the location and can have different levels. The setup level should match the physical process in the warehouse.

Item application and costing is tied together with the reservation process in Microsoft Dynamics NAV. The Reservation Entry table adds a new level to the inventory process linking documents, journals, and entries together to level supply and demand. When used, the reservation process can overrule the costing method.

At the end of the chapter, we talked about different ways to implement this in vertical solutions and what gaps would have to be solved and how. This demonstrates the flexibility and the power of the standard transaction structure in Microsoft Dynamics NAV.

In the next chapter, we will take this to a new level where we will design and build a real-world vertical solution for Microsoft Dynamics NAV that will enable us to create combine sales shipment in routes for trucks. We will also create a new solution on top of Microsoft Dynamics NAV using the application as a development environment to build something new with respect to the methodology of the application.

7
Storage and Logistics

In the previous chapters, we looked at how companies work with ERP in production and trade businesses. All these companies work together to bring finished products to the stores where end consumers can buy them.

During this process, the products move around between the companies. This is done using different kinds of transportation, such as trucks, ships, trains, and airplanes. It may also be necessary to store the products in a warehouse until they are sold or moved to the shops.

More and more companies make a decision to outsource logistics rather than having their own transportation. When this is the case, logistics can be a separate part of the supply chain. This chapter discusses the process and the effects on the ERP system.

One of the specific aspects of logistics companies is that the products they handle are not their property. Although they are a part of the total cost of the consumer product, they don't care about the detailed value of their inventory. Logistics companies sell warehouse handling, storage, and transportation as services.

Microsoft Dynamics NAV does not have built-in functionality to handle this so, in this chapter, we will discuss how to design an application to do this.

There are several add-on solutions for this business and in a real-world situation those add-ons should be evaluated as potential solutions. In this chapter, we will discuss how to design and create a basic framework for such an add-on application that can be easily extended without adding too much complexity.

[The objects provided with this chapter should never be implemented at a real-customer scenario. They are for the purpose of this chapter's examples only.]

After reading this chapter, you will have a better understanding of how to design a solid add-on solution and how to integrate it into the standard Microsoft Dynamics NAV product.

How to read this chapter

In this chapter, we will demonstrate how an add-on for Microsoft Dynamics NAV should be designed. In this example, we create a solution for a Storage & Logistics company. This is chosen because the functionality is similar to the existing functionality in Microsoft Dynamics NAV (warehousing) and is a good example of building on top of standard application features.

We will start by analyzing the business process and then discuss the reasons why we won't use standard application features and explain the modules our new application will have.

The next step is to go deeper into these modules and define the design patterns for each of them. We will then walk through the application like we did in the previous chapters and reverse engineer it to explain how all the pieces were designed.

To do this, we need to download and install the application. As we progress in the chapter, we will discuss most of the objects that can be opened and analyzed in the Microsoft Dynamics NAV development environment.

[Open the objects as we move along in the chapter to learn more. The objects are rich in functionality, which cannot all be discussed in detail in this book.]

Chapter objects

With this chapter, some objects and **Dynamic-link library** (DLL) files are required. The *Appendix*, *Installation Guide*, describes how to import and activate them.

After the import process is complete, make sure that your current database is the default database for the Role Tailored Client and run **Page 123456701**, **Storage & Logistics Setup** from the **Object Designer** in the **Classic Client**.

From this page, select the **Initialize Storage & Logistics** option, as shown in the following screenshot:

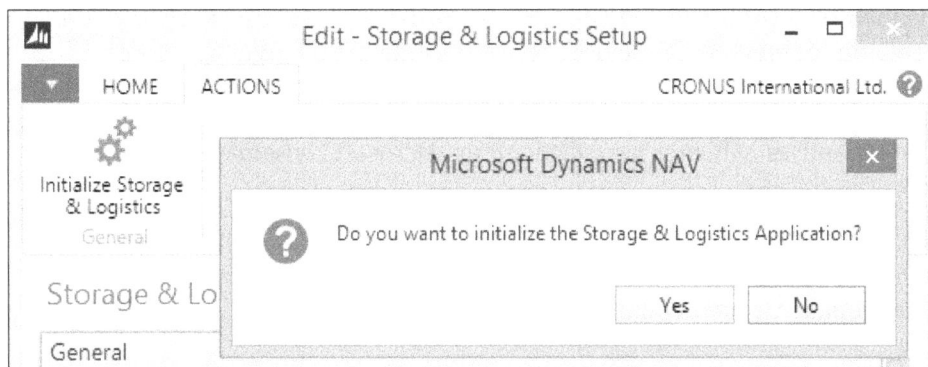

The process

To design a solid solution for a specific market, we first need to analyze the business processes and see where the fits and gaps are with the standard product.

The companies that will be using this solution are logistics providers. These companies do not buy and sell products but sell logistics services such as transportation and storage.

There can be various moments in the supply chain where these companies are required. Products are often manufactured in companies all over the world and shipped to consumers elsewhere. Products can cover great distances, as shown in the following diagram:

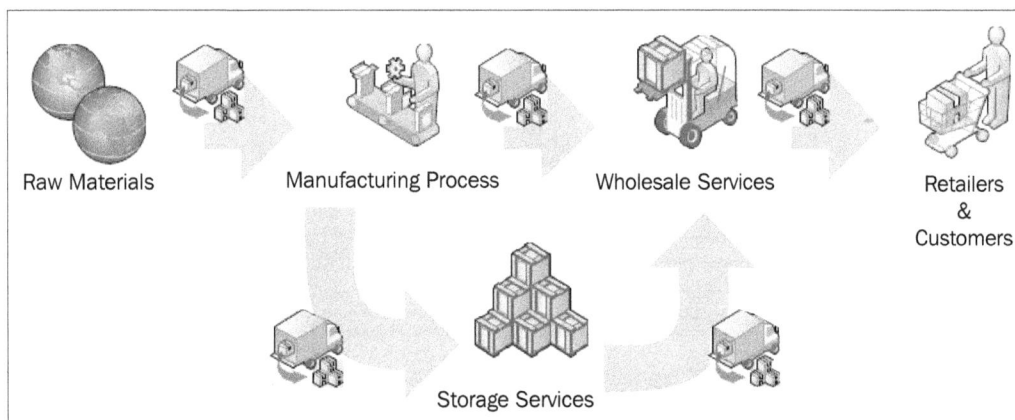

Using standard features

Microsoft Dynamics NAV, like many ERP systems, is designed for people to handle their own products and supports the process of costing as we have seen in the previous chapters. For logistics service providers, this inventory control and valuation functionality is not necessary since the products are not their property. This means that they would want to use the warehouse functionality without the item ledger entries, which is very difficult in Microsoft Dynamics NAV.

Logistics service providers also offer transportation solutions. They will pick up the products and deliver them to the customer. The process includes combining different stops in routes resulting in a more cost-efficient way of transportation. This functionality is not available in Microsoft Dynamics NAV.

Defining the modules

In this chapter, we will design three new modules on top of Microsoft Dynamics NAV that integrate with each other and could still be used separately. These modules also integrate with the standard application through **Sales & Purchase Documents**.

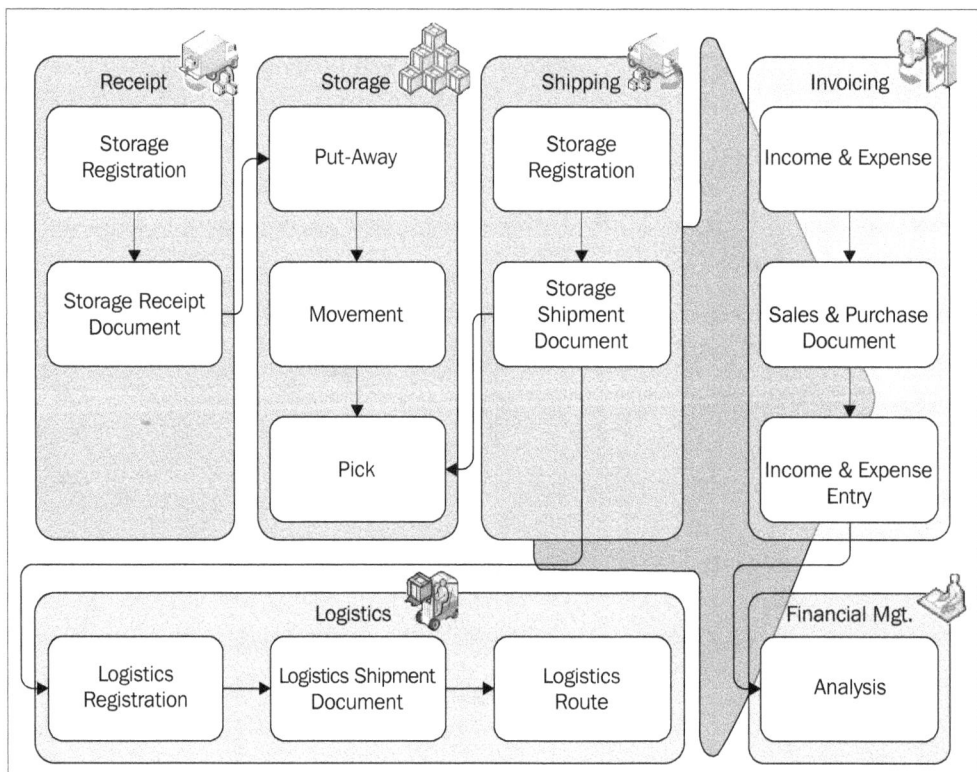

Storage

The first part of the application is the storage module. This allows us to receive and ship products and move them internally in the warehouse. The design of this module is very similar to the warehouse documents in the standard application that we discussed in *Chapter 6, Trade*.

Logistics

The logistics module supports the planning of routes, delivering the products to the consumers. This is integrated into the storage module but can also be used from sales shipment documents in the standard application.

For the design of this module, we have looked at the production orders in Microsoft Dynamics NAV that we discussed in *Chapter 5, Production*. The routes and shipments have a **Status** field that indicates the progress, similar to a production order.

Invoicing

The storage and transportation services are then invoiced to the customer periodically or when the products leave the warehouse.

For this, we will use the standard Microsoft Dynamics NAV invoicing solutions but we will add a new **Income & Expenses** module in between the logistical solution and the invoicing functionality.

We have looked at the design of Job Ledger Entries and how they are invoiced. This will be discussed in the next chapter.

The storage application

In a storage warehouse, products come and go all the time. A big difference between a storage company and a production plant is that the storage company does not care about what exact products they have; they care about the amount of space they require for storage. The business is selling storage handling, storage space, and transportation.

For our application, we'll assume that our warehouse has a receipt and a shipping region, an in-between staging region and a bulk storage region. If we simplify the warehouse, it might look like the following floor plan:

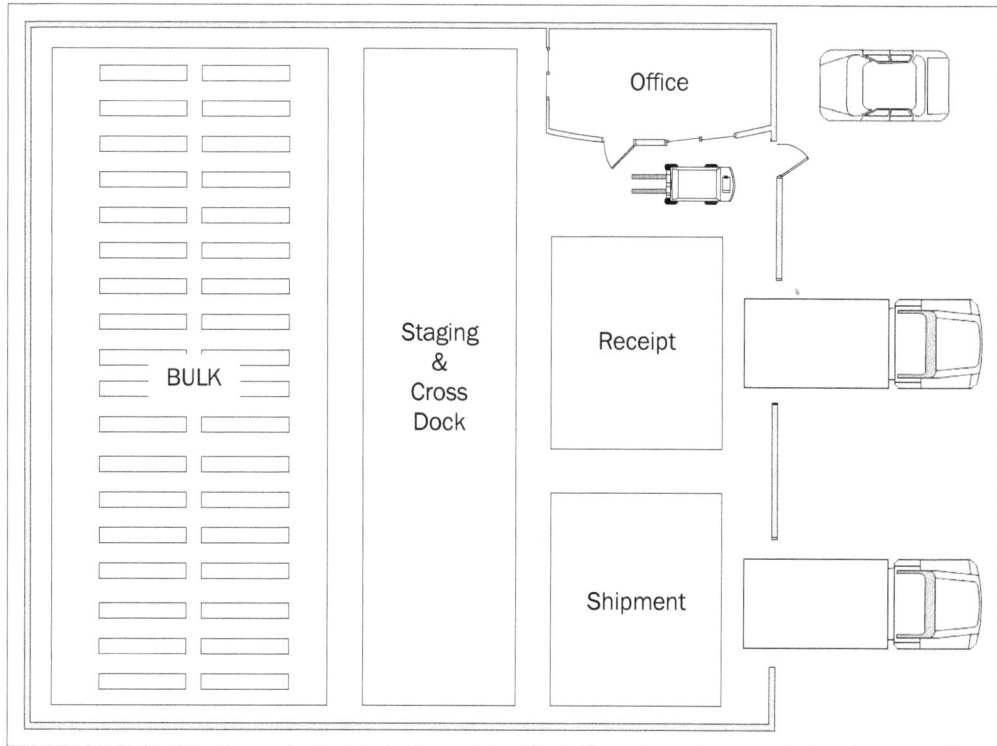

Let's look at the various sections in detail:

- **Receipt**: When products come in, they are first unloaded from the truck onto a receipt region. This is often located close to the unloading dock, so the truck can quickly move on to its next stop after the products are unloaded and the loading documents are checked. From the receiving location, the products should be stored away as quickly as possible since another truck might come and we need the space. The products can now go to either the staging region or the bulk region.

- **Staging**: The staging region is an in-between region where products can be stored but will leave the warehouse quickly when it is too busy to properly store in the bulk area and we need the space in the receipt region.

- **Shipment**: When products leave the warehouse, they will first be moved to the shipment region. This allows us to quickly load the trucks when they arrive and easily compare the loading documents with the real products.

- **Bulk**: When we expect products to be in the warehouse for a longer period, they will be stored in the bulk area where we can define shelves. A shelf can have a capacity for one or more products depending on the setup in the system.

Documents

The first step is to have a registration of what will be coming to our warehouse by creating the receipt documents. In the old days, we would often receive this information by phone or fax, but today most companies use interfaces, such as EDI and web portals for this. This keeps us from making mistakes when typing the information in the system and allows us to automatically populate the receipt document.

The receipt documents will be combined into put-away documents that register the transfer from one region to the other. The software will also suggest a shelf to store the products.

When the products leave the warehouse, our customers will also register a shipment document. On their call, we will start the order picking process and combine the shipments. The pick documents will tell us on which shelf the products are stored.

Incidentally, it may also be necessary to move the products in the warehouse. This will be registered in internal movement documents.

The storage documents are connected to the logistics document structure, which we will see later in this chapter, while discussing logistics.

Look, learn, and love

In *Chapter 2, A Sample Application*, we learned how to use a journal and entry design patterns to register usage. In this chapter, we will continue with this and add some document design pattern structures.

To design our application, we will look at how existing pieces of Microsoft Dynamics NAV are designed and reuse them.

> On https://community.dynamics.com/nav/w/designpatterns/ default.aspx, you'll find dozens of design patterns for Microsoft Dynamics NAV including many used in this chapter.

Journal

The core of our application is the **Storage Journal**, which is created from the same template as the **Squash Journal** earlier. The difference is that people in a warehouse use documents rather than journals.

Documents

We will support the five types of documents we discussed earlier, namely, Receipt, Shipment, Put-away, Pick, and Movement. The documents can be created manually by end users or created automatically. We will also provide an interface structure to allow customers to register receipts and shipments.

As all the documents have the same structure and mostly the same fields, they are in the same table to share business logic.

> Sharing the same table for multiple document types allows easier sharing of business logic across the application.

This is also done in the standard Microsoft Dynamics NAV application for sales and purchase documents as we discussed in *Chapter 6, Trade*.

Master data

To define what we are storing in the warehouse, we will use a new table called **Product**, which is similar to the Item table in the standard system. By creating a new table, we will improve upgradability of our solution, which will help us be more in control of our own application or in other words, less likely to be impacted by the changes Microsoft implements in the standard product.

Drawing the design pattern

If we combine this information into a table and transaction structure, it would look like the following diagram:

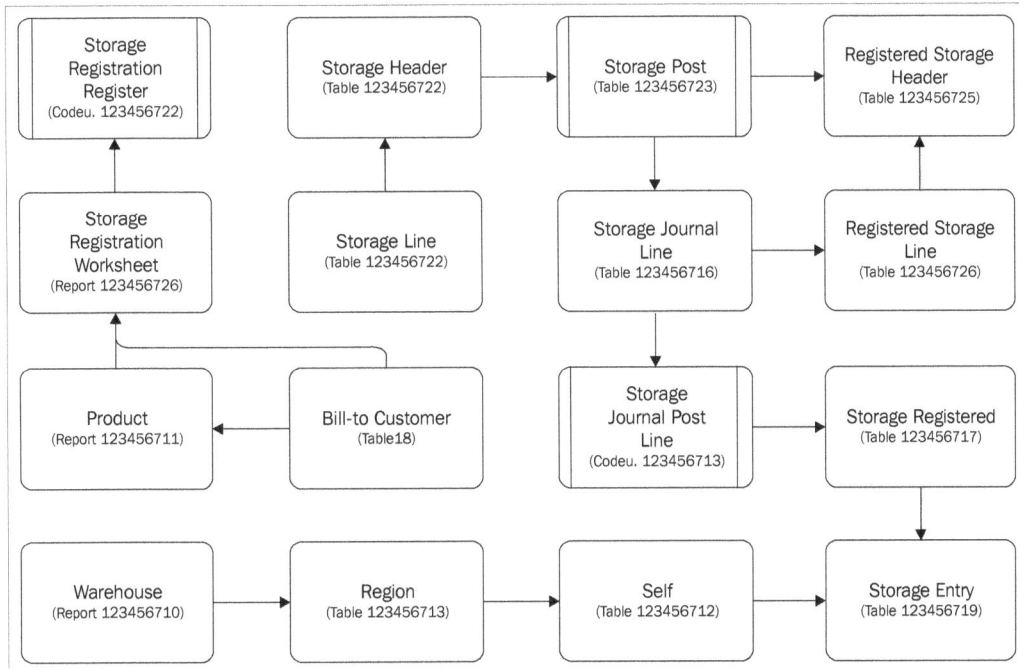

The actual inventory is kept in **Storage Entries**. By filtering on a warehouse code, region code, or shelf number, the inventory can be calculated.

Sharing tables

The **Storage & Logistics** add-on application also has some shared tables. It does not make sense to have a product or warehouse table for each part of the add-on. We choose to also share the setup and the cue tables for the Role Center definition. The Storage & Logistics application has four Role Centers.

> By sharing the cue table, it is much easier to place the same cues on different Role Centers. If we were to create one table for each Role Center, we would need to copy and paste the cue definition to the table for each change request.

Getting started

In our scenario, we'll ship and receive products for a company called CRONUS International Ltd. for whom we do shipping. We have warehouses in Austria, Belgium, Czech Republic, Denmark, Germany, Great Britain, Iceland, Netherlands, Norway, Sweden, Slovenia, Slovakia, and the USA.

Each warehouse has the same basic layout as explained earlier in this chapter. From the warehouse, we plan routes to transport the products to the consumer. After initializing the application and restarting the application, the **Role Center** should look like this:

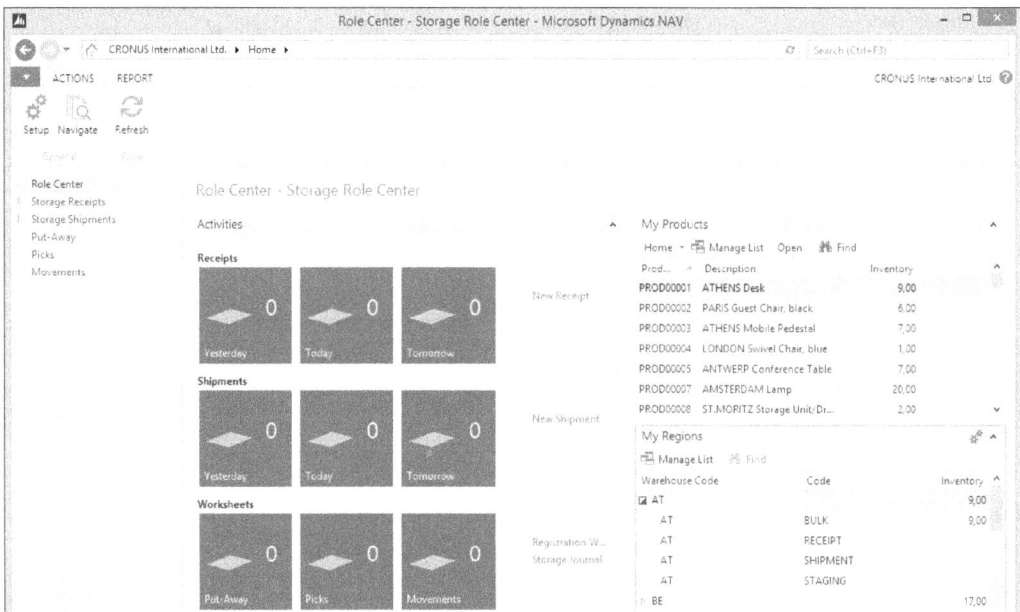

Let's look at the various sections in detail:

- **Activities**: This window shows the workflow for the warehouse floor

- **My Products**: This contains all customer products we have on inventory

- **My Regions**: This allows us to see what inventory is where in our warehouses

Opening balance

The opening balance was created using the Storage Journal. By using the journal to create opening entries, we are sure that business rules are followed.

In our design, we have decided that end users are not allowed to directly register inventory on the bulk location. We start by receiving it, and then we create a put-away document to move it to the bulk location. We'll see how this is done later in this chapter when we discuss the storage documents.

> Have a look on the **Storage & Logistics Setup (123456701)** page to see how this was done in the `CreateOpeningBalance()` function.

Products

Products are references to the items of our customers that we keep in inventory. They contain a **Bill-to Customer No.** and a **Customer Item No**. This allows us, for example, to keep the item with number **70000** for two different customers.

We can also see and set up **Storage Prices** for this product, which we will later use for the invoicing.

Warehouse

A warehouse is a physical building with an address. To move products from one warehouse to another warehouse, we would need to ship them, create a route, and then physically receive them in the other building.

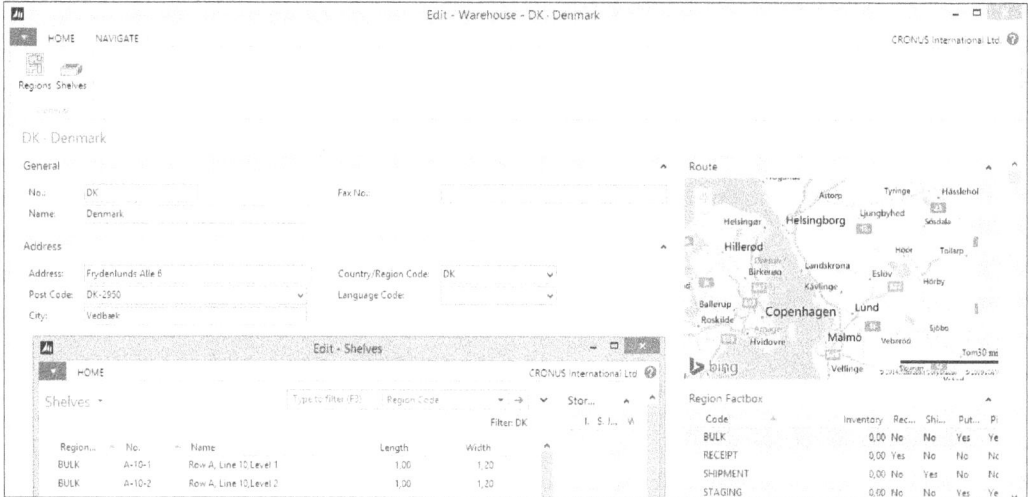

Regions

A region is a part of the warehouse that is used for a specific storage activity. In our example, we have a receipt, staging, bulk, and shipment region. To move products from one region to another, we should create a put-away, movement, or pick document.

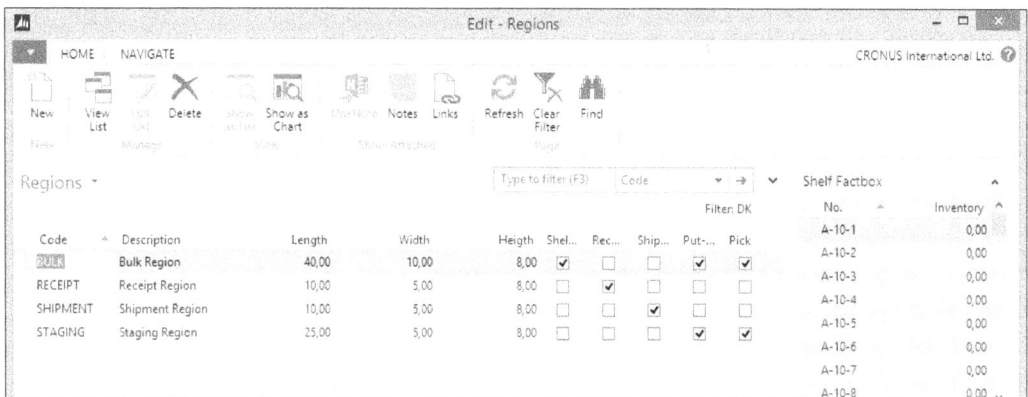

Shelves

A shelf is a specific part of a region. The specific code of a shelf often indicates its position in the warehouse. For example, our warehouses have two rows, A and B, with 18 lines and 8 levels where each shelf can contain one pallet.

Registration worksheet

The warehouse process starts with receiving products. To save time when the products arrive on the dock, we ask our customers to register their products in advance. This is done in the storage registration worksheet.

In our application, we have simulated an interface with our customer CRONUS International Ltd. We can start the interface from the Role Center directly.

1. We start the **CRONUS Storage Import Receipt** report from the **Role Center**, as shown in the following screenshot:

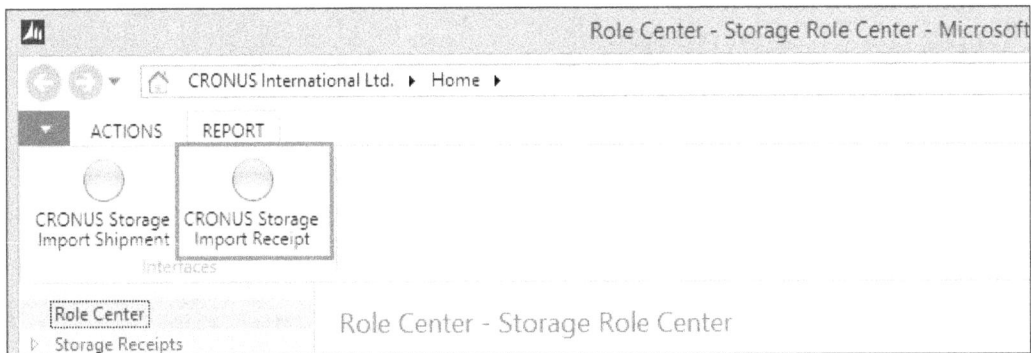

2. The system pops up and asks for a **Storage Registration Code**.
3. We will choose **CRONUS** from the list and start the import process.
4. After this, we open **Registration Worksheets**.

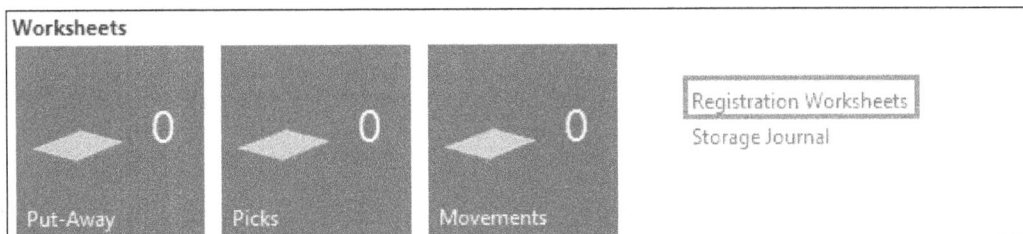

5. When we now open the registration worksheet, we see what CRONUS will send us today. This allows us to prepare our business, maybe move around some products, and schedule resources.

6. We can now register this worksheet, which will create the receipt documents for us.

Storage documents

We use documents to determine which product goes where. Creating those documents in the system manually requires a large amount of work, so in our application, this is done automatically.

Receipt

By default, all products that are received are stored in the **RECEIPT** region. This region does not have shelves. If required, we can change the region code.

After we register the receipt document, we have inventory on the **RECEIPT** location:

Since this is a relatively small region, we need to move the products to the bulk location as quickly as possible. This is done using a put-away document.

Put-away

A put-away document is used to move products from the receipt region into the bulk region. The storage entries tell us what is in the receipt region, so we copy that information into a new put-away document. These documents can be created manually, and based on the warehouse information on the document, we can pull the data into the document.

Another requirement is to have an automated process that creates put-away documents based on the entire content of the receipt region.

1. To provide for this functionality, we have created the **Receipts to Put-Away (123456715)** report. This processing-only report reads the storage entries for the receipt region, and creates the put-away documents based on certain predefined rules.

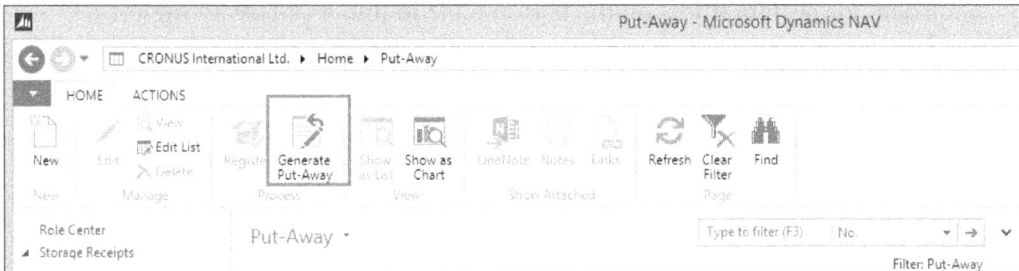

2. The report filters down the storage entries-based regions of type **Receipt** and with inventory.

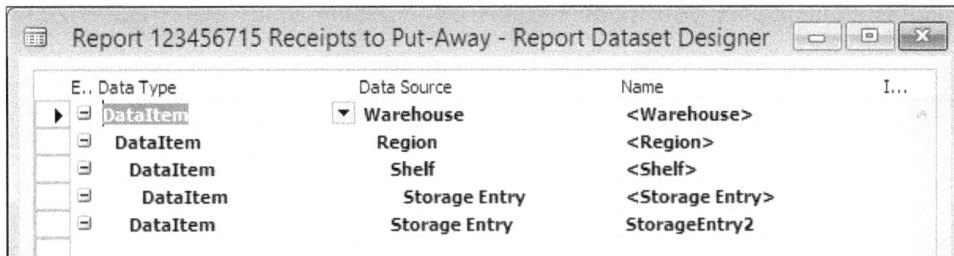

E..	Data Type	Data Source	Name	I...
	DataItem	Warehouse	<Warehouse>	
	DataItem	Region	<Region>	
	DataItem	Shelf	<Shelf>	
	DataItem	Storage Entry	<Storage Entry>	
	DataItem	Storage Entry	StorageEntry2	

3. It creates a put-away document for each warehouse suggesting the first put-away region in the warehouse. For each `StorageEntry`, the `CreateLine` function is started. Let's have a look at the C/AL code for this:

```
CreateLineCreateLine()

FindOrCreateStorageHdr;
```

```
Region2.SETRANGE("Warehouse Code");
Region2.SETRANGE("Put-Away", TRUE);
Region2.FINDFIRST;

WITH StorageEntry DO BEGIN
  NextLineNo := NextLineNo + 10000;
  StorageLn."Document Type" := StorageHdr."Document Type";
  StorageLn."Document No." := StorageHdr."No.";
  StorageLn."Line No." := NextLineNo;
  StorageLn."No." := "Product No.";
  StorageLn."Warehouse Code" := "Warehouse Code";
  StorageLn."Region Code" := Region2.Code;
```

4. The first step is to check whether it's necessary to create a new storage document. We create a new document for each `Warehouse` and `StorageDate`.

5. Then, the system filters on the region table to find a put-away region. For each `StorageEntry`, a `StorageLine` is created.

6. After running the report, our put-away document looks like this:

7. The suggested **Region Code** is **BULK** and the **Apply-to Region Code** is **RECEIPT**.

8. If we now try to register this document, we will receive an error since we did not enter any `Shelves` because this is mandatory on this region.

> This check is done in the codeunit Storage Jnl.-Check Line. By moving these checks into this codeunit, we make sure these rules are mandatory in each posting.

9. Since we rely on the system to keep track of our inventory, we can also have it suggest available shelves for us. This is also done using batch report **123456716 Generate Put-Away Shelves**. Let's design the report and look at the C/AL code in `StorageLineDataItem`:

```
Storage Line - OnAfterGetRecord()

Counter := Counter + 1;
Window.UPDATE(1,"Document No.");
Window.UPDATE(2,ROUND(Counter / CounterTotal * 10000,1));

Shelf.SETRANGE("Warehouse Code", "Storage Line"."Warehouse Code");
Shelf.SETRANGE("Region Code", "Region Code");
Shelf.SETRANGE(Inventory, 0);
Shelf.SETRANGE("Blocked by Storage", FALSE);
Shelf.FINDFIRST;

"Shelf No." := Shelf."No.";
MODIFY;
```

10. For each `StorageLine` in the put-away document, it finds another shelf by filtering on availability based on `Inventory` and `BlockedByStorage`.

11. The `BlockedByStorage` field is a flow field that returns true if the shelf is used on a warehouse document preventing two forklift trucks from stopping at the same shelf.

12. When this report is executed, we can register this put-away document and we can see the **Storage Entries** that are generated from the **Product Card** using the **Ledger Entries** action:

Posti...	Docu...	Documen...	Prod...	Storage D...	Warehou...	Region C...	Shelf No.	Description	Open
22-1-2015	Receipt	SRCPT00001	PROD00011	22-1-2015	GB	RECEIPT		TOKYO Guest Chair, blue	☐
22-1-2015	Put-Away	SPUT00012	PROD00011	22-1-2015	GB	BULK	A-12-5	TOKYO Guest Chair, blue	☑
22-1-2015	Put-Away	SPUT00012	PROD00011	22-1-2015	GB	RECEIPT		TOKYO Guest Chair, blue	☐

Storage Entries ▾   Type to filter (F3)   Posting Date ▾ → ⌄   Filter: PROD00011

Here, we can see that the put-away document has applied its entries to the receipt entries. Since we moved everything, the original entry is closed and the remaining quantity is set to zero.

This functionality is similar to what we created in *Chapter 2, A Sample Application*, when applying an invoice entry to a reservation.

Shipment

After a while when the products are in inventory, the customer may send a request to ship them. The shipping documents are sent using the same interface as the receipt documents.

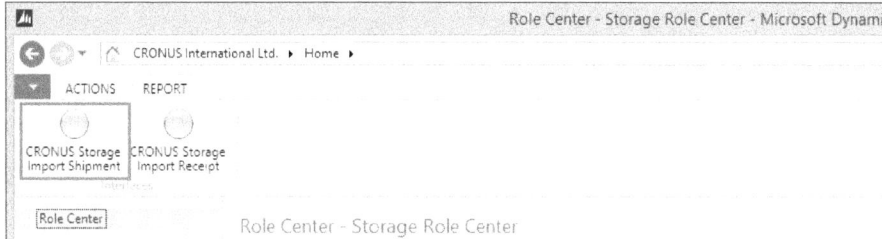

CRONUS Storage Import Shipment option

Running the **CRONUS Storage Import Shipment** report will create the **Storage Registration Worksheet**, which we can check and register to a shipment document, the same way as the receipt documents earlier.

The system creates a shipment document for each **Ship-to Address**.

Customer ...	Name	Address	City	Warehouse ...	Region Code	Shelf No.	Storage Date
70000	The Cannon Group PLC	192 Market Square	Birmingham	GB	SHIPMENT		22-1-2015
70000	The Cannon Group PLC	192 Market Square	Birmingham	GB	SHIPMENT		22-1-2015
70000	The Cannon Group PLC	192 Market Square	Birmingham	GB	SHIPMENT		22-1-2015
70000	The Cannon Group PLC	192 Market Square	Birmingham	GB	SHIPMENT		22-1-2015
70000	The Cannon Group PLC	192 Market Square	Birmingham	GB	SHIPMENT		22-1-2015
70000	The Cannon Group PLC	192 Market Square	Birmingham	GB	SHIPMENT		22-1-2015
70000	Antarcticopy	Katwilgweg 274	Antwerpen	BE	SHIPMENT		22-1-2015

We now have to start the process of moving the products from the storage region to the shipment region.

Picks

The products that will be shipped need to be picked from the bulk or staging region using a pick document. As with the put-away functionality, our application design provides an automated process that supports this process.

To create the document, we use batch **Report 123456717 Shipments to Pick**, as shown in the following screenshot:

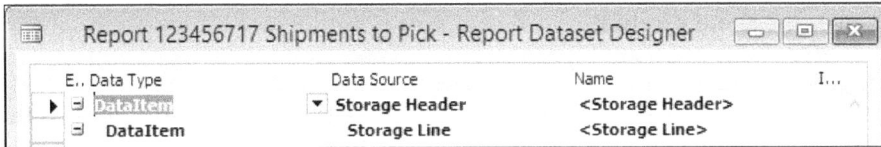

This report can combine shipments into one or more pick documents:

```
Storage Line - OnAfterGetRecord()

Counter := Counter + 1;
Window.UPDATE(1,"Document No.");
Window.UPDATE(2,ROUND(Counter / CounterTotal * 10000,1));

Product.GET("No.");
Product.SETRANGE("Warehouse Filter Code", "Warehouse Code");
Product.CALCFIELDS(Inventory);
IF Quantity > Product.Inventory THEN
  ERROR(Text001, Quantity, Product.Inventory, "No.");

QtyToPick := Quantity;

StorageEntry.SETCURRENTKEY("Product No.");
StorageEntry.SETRANGE("Warehouse Code", "Storage Header"."Warehouse
Code");
StorageEntry.SETRANGE("Product No.", "No.");
StorageEntry.SETRANGE(Open, TRUE);
IF StorageEntry.FINDSET(TRUE) THEN REPEAT
  StorageEntry.CALCFIELDS("Blocked by Storage");
  IF NOT StorageEntry."Blocked by Storage" THEN BEGIN
    IF QtyToPick >= StorageEntry.Quantity THEN
      QtyToPick := QtyToPick - StorageEntry.Quantity
    ELSE BEGIN
      StorageEntry.Quantity := QtyToPick;
      QtyToPick := 0;
    END;
    CreateLine(StorageEntry);
  END;
UNTIL (StorageEntry.NEXT = 0) OR (QtyToPick = 0);

IF QtyToPick > 0 THEN
  ERROR(Text002, "No.");
```

First, the system checks whether the products are in inventory in this warehouse. If they are here, it starts browsing through the storage entries to look for available shelves. Here, we also use the **Blocked by Storage flow** field to avoid two employees fighting over the same product.

One of the functional requirements in our application is to avoid having half a shipment to be picked and block the **SHIPMENT** region being incomplete. If there are not enough inventories available for the pick, the system will display an error.

After the pick is created, we update the **Pick Status on the Shipment** field. In the following screenshot, we can see that there are three **Pick Lines** attached to this shipment:

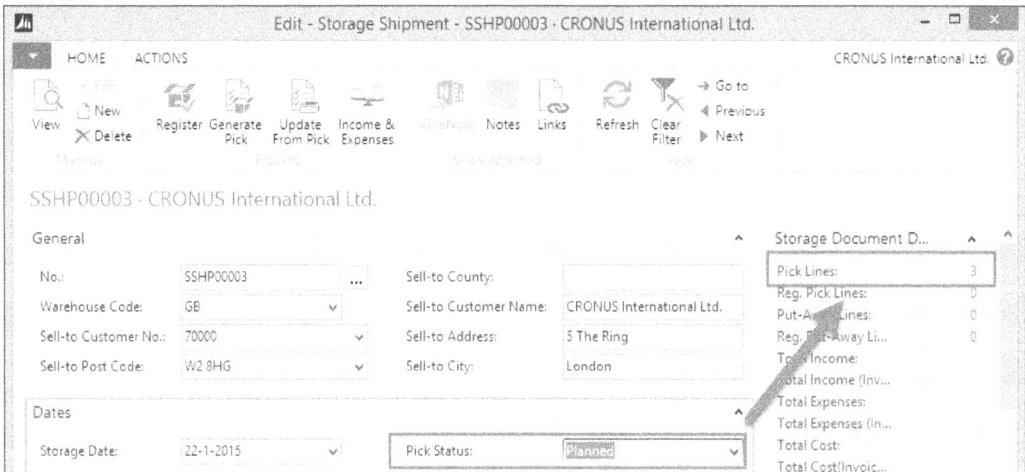

When we click on **3**, the system opens the lines. Double-clicking on the lines will open the pick document.

> To influence the double-click event, assign the **RETURN** shortcut to one of the actions on a page.

After registration of the pick document, the status of the shipment moves to **Completely Picked**. We can see that the **Pick Lines** are registered:

The last step before the shipment can be registered is updating the storage lines with the **Apply-to Storage Entry No.** from the pick document. For this step, we have designed a dedicated report **Update Storage Shipment (123456718)** that can be started from the **Storage Shipment Document**, as shown in the following screenshot:

After this, the shipment can be registered. The products have now left our warehouse and are on the road to the customer.

The logistics application

Similar to production orders in the standard application, the processes in our logistics application are status-driven rather than transaction-driven. This is why this part of the application does not have a journal with entries. The tables can have archived copies but they are not part of a normal registering or posting routine.

> For the examples in this part of the chapter, we should change the default **Role Center to Logistics Role Center (123456700)** in the **Profile table (2000000072)**.

Drawing the design patterns

If we look at the structure of the logistics application, we can see that the typical posting transactions are missing. The application uses a status-driven workflow based on events that are defined in the triggers of the tables.

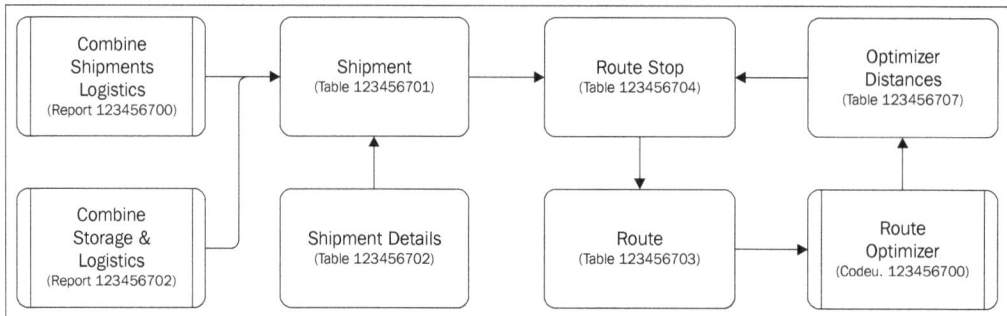

The logistics shipment and shipment details have a lot of similarity with the shipments from the warehouse. We have chosen to move them into new tables for the following reasons:

- **Security**: In Microsoft dynamics NAV, the table level is most important for security. If we share this table, it would be impossible to set up users to have access to logistics and not to the warehouse or vice versa.

- **Locking**: If two departments use the same table for different purposes, they will most likely have a different locking mechanism. For example, in logistics, shipments are bound to the route object. The warehouse shipments are bound to other shipment documents. Filtering the same table in main processes in different ways will significantly increase the probability of blocks and deadlocks.

- **Table size**: The storage documents are registered shortly after they are created. Most documents are deleted and moved to registered tables on the same day that they are created. Logistics shipments have a longer life cycle. It takes longer to take the products from our warehouse to the customer and during this process, many things can go wrong because of outside events. The transport tables may be periodically cleaned up like manufacturing or jobs in the standard Microsoft Dynamics NAV product.

Getting started

To start the logistics process, we can create some shipments manually but the application also provides an interface to the sales shipments and warehouse shipments.

Let's start the **Combine Shipments (Sales)** option from **Activities** on the **Logistics Role Center** to generate some data to work with.

Shipments

Logistics shipments are products moving from one physical address to another physical address.

In our example, the shipments are created from our warehouse to the customer but a shipment can also be from another address to a customer. Tracking the status of a shipment is very important for the planners. A shipment starts with the **Ready to Ship** status as soon as all mandatory fields are checked.

When the shipments are combined into routes, the shipment moves to shipping and the status is changed to **Shipping**. During this stage, the products are picked up from the warehouse. When this happens, the **Pickup Date Time** is populated. This is done from the route.

After delivery, the **Delivery Date Time** is populated and the status is set to **Shipped**.

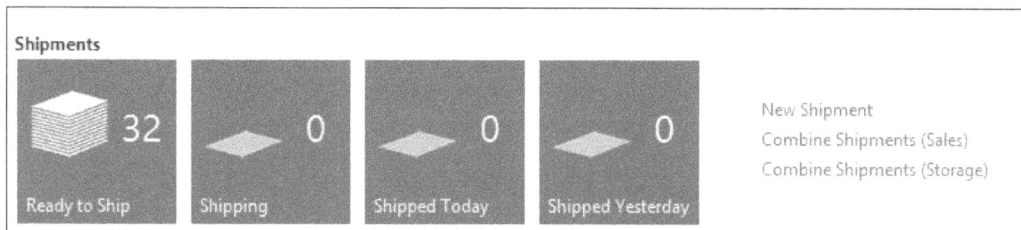

The planners can follow the shipments from their Role Centers in a workflow.

Routes

Shipments are combined into a route. For the planners to make a product planning, it is very important that the shipment details are correct. The length, width, height, and weight of the products determine whether they can fit in a truck, ship, airplane, or train.

Our example add-on system has a report to combine shipments into a route. The shipments in a route will be combined into stops if they have the same address information.

Combining shipments

Combined shipping is done in the **Shipment To Route & Warehouse (123456701)** report. The shipments are grouped per warehouse. For each warehouse, a new route is created.

For each shipment, the system creates a route stop. The stops have different types, Pickup, Delivery, Pickup Group, and Delivery Group. Each shipment then gets a Pickup and Delivery stop:

```
Shipment - OnAfterGetRecord()

IF Route.Description <> Warehouse.Name THEN BEGIN
  Route."No." := '';
  Route.Description := Warehouse.Name;
  Route."Shipment Date" := WORKDATE;
  Route.Status := Route.Status::Planned;

  Route."Bill-to Customer No." := "Bill-to Customer No.";
  Route."Bill-to Name" := "Bill-to Name";

  Route.INSERT(TRUE);
  i := 0;
END;

i := i + 10000;

RouteStop."Route No." := Route."No.";
RouteStop."Line No." := i;
RouteStop.Type := RouteStop.Type::Pickup;
RouteStop.VALIDATE("Shipment No.", "No.");
RouteStop.INSERT;

i := i + 10000;

RouteStop."Route No." := Route."No.";
RouteStop."Line No." := i;
RouteStop.Type := RouteStop.Type::Delivery;
RouteStop.VALIDATE("Shipment No.", "No.");
RouteStop.INSERT;
```

After the routes are created and the shipments are assigned to a stop, a grouping and optimizing algorithm is started. This is codeunit `Route Optimizer (123456700)`.

Route optimizer

The algorithm in our example is designed to find the optimal route to deliver the products to the addresses by calculating the distance of each address from the warehouse. The route starts from the address that is closest to our warehouse and ends at the address that is the farthest away.

This is just an example of a simple algorithm. Each company will have its own algorithm that needs to be implemented:

```
RouteStopPickup.SETRANGE("Route No.", Route."No.");
RouteStopPickup.SETRANGE(Type, RouteStopPickup.Type::Pickup);
RouteStopPickup.FINDFIRST;

RouteStopDelivery.SETRANGE("Route No.", Route."No.");
RouteStopDelivery.SETRANGE(Type, RouteStopDelivery.Type::Delivery);
RouteStopDelivery.FINDSET;
REPEAT
  Window.UPDATE(2, RouteStopDelivery."Shipment No.");

  IF NOT Optimizer.GET(RouteStopDelivery.Name) THEN BEGIN
    CLEAR(BingMapMgt);
    BingMapMgt.CalculateRoute('', RouteStopPickup.Latitude,
RouteStopPickup.Longitude,'', RouteStopDelivery.Latitude,
      RouteStopDelivery.Longitude, Optimizer."Distance
(Distance)",Optimizer."Activity Time", Optimize::Distance);

    Optimizer.Name := RouteStopDelivery.Name;
    Optimizer.Latitude := RouteStopDelivery.Latitude;
    Optimizer.Longitude := RouteStopDelivery.Longitude;
    Optimizer.INSERT;
  END;

  UNTIL RouteStopDelivery.NEXT = 0;
```

The calculation of the distance is done by calling a web service from Bing Maps. This is explained in *Chapter 9, Interfacing*.

Each distance is stored as a record into the **Optimizer** table, which is a helper table. This table is a temporary variable in this codeunit.

Temporary tables have multiple benefits that make them interesting to use. As they are not stored in the database, they have much better performance compared to real tables. This also has a benefit for concurrency since there can be no locking.

> Temporary tables are free to use. They are not checked in the license file when used. To create and modify the definition, a valid license is still required. The video at `https://www.youtube.com/watch?v=QHn5oEOJv0Q` shows how to use temporary datasets.

After generating the distances, all Pickup shipments are combined into one stop by assigning them all to the same `Sequence No.` value:

```
RouteStopGroup.INIT;
RouteStopGroup."Route No." := Route."No.";
RouteStopGroup."Line No." := 10;
RouteStopGroup.Type := RouteStopGroup.Type::"Pickup Group";
RouteStopGroup."Sequence No." := 10;
RouteStopGroup.Name := RouteStopPickup.Name;
RouteStopGroup.INSERT;

RouteStopPickup.MODIFYALL("Sequence No.", 10);
```

By sorting the distance helper table on distance, we can easily assign the correct `Sequence No.` to the delivery stops. For each `Sequence No.` value, we will also generate a group record in the stop table:

```
Optimizer.SETCURRENTKEY("Distance (Distance)");
Optimizer.ASCENDING(FALSE);
Optimizer.FIND('-');
REPEAT
  RouteStopGroup.INIT;
  RouteStopGroup."Route No." := Route."No.";
  RouteStopGroup."Line No." := Sequence;
  RouteStopGroup.Type :=
    RouteStopGroup.Type::"Delivery Group";
  RouteStopGroup."Sequence No." := Sequence;
  RouteStopGroup.Name := Optimizer.Name;
  RouteStopGroup.INSERT;

  RouteStopDelivery.SETRANGE(Name, Optimizer.Name);
  RouteStopDelivery.MODIFYALL("Sequence No.", Sequence);
```

```
Sequence := Sequence + 10;
IF (xLongitude <> Optimizer.Longitude) OR
   (xLatitude <> Optimizer.Latitude)
THEN BEGIN
   IF xLongitude + xLatitude <> 0 THEN BEGIN
      CLEAR(BingMapMgt);
      BingMapMgt.CalculateRoute('', xLatitude, xLongitude,'',
         Optimizer.Latitude, Optimizer.Longitude,
         RouteStopGroup.Distance, RouteStopGroup.Time,
         Optimize::Distance);
      RouteStopGroup.MODIFY;
   END;
   xLongitude := Optimizer.Longitude;
   xLatitude := Optimizer.Latitude;
END;
UNTIL Optimizer.NEXT = 0;
```

After optimizing the route, it should look something like what is shown in the following screenshot. We pick up two shipments at the warehouse and drive them to two addresses in the country.

Route follow up

During the route, the planner needs to follow up with the driver. This will result in the status update of the shipment.

In our solution, the planner should populate the **Date Time Completed** field. This field is automatically updated in the shipment using a flow field.

Incidents

A special status for a shipment is an incident. If, for any reason, we cannot deliver the shipment, it should be taken back to the warehouse and shipped again. Based on the reason of the incident, we might need to invoice extra services.

The incident can be on a stop group or on an individual shipment and can have status **Undeliverable**, **Closed**, or **Other**. The planner can add extra comments.

The other shipments that do not have incidents get the new status, while the incidents move to another place on the Role Center.

Follow up

The incidents can be followed up by the planner via the Role Center. Incidents that have not been handled, keep the status open until someone decides what to do with it.

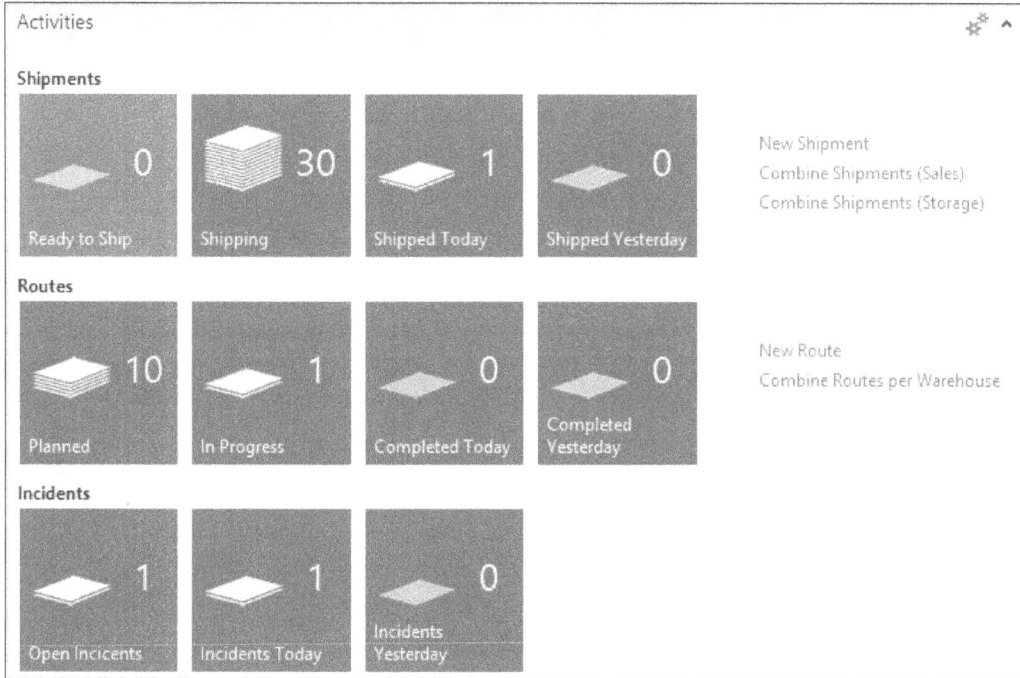

The invoicing application

In *Chapter 2, A Sample Application*, we introduced invoicing for an add-on solution. For the solution in this chapter, we'll take this one step further.

Our company is invoicing different logistics services, such as:

- Handling costs for storage receipt and shipments
- Storage costs for the period we keep the inventory
- Costs for transporting the products to the end consumer

All these costs need to be combined in one invoice. Some customers may require monthly invoicing or some weekly and for incidental customers, we invoice directly. This requires a special module to handle the invoicing.

> For the examples in this part of the chapter, the **Default Role Center** in the **Profile table (2000000072)** should be changed to **Income & Expenses Role Center (123456761)**.

Let's have a look at the process to see where the invoicing is required:

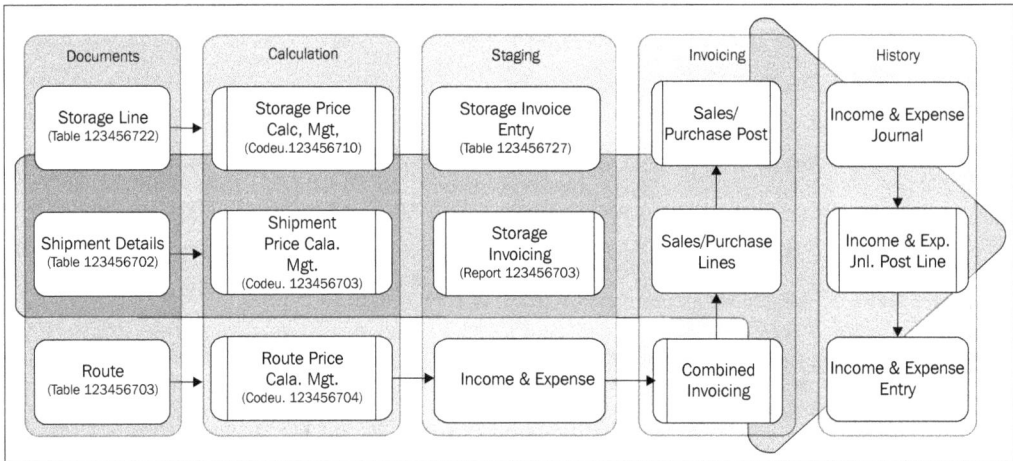

Income and expense

Everything that we want to invoice at one time to a customer, we store in a new table that we will call Income & Expense. This is a container where they will be kept until the periodical invoicing is done for this customer.

The Income & Expense records can be created manually by end users or automatically by the system. Let's have a look at them:

To create a new Income & Expense record, we need to fill in the following fields:

- **Income & Expense Code**: This is a reference to the group of Income & Expense.
- **Type**: This can be either Income or Expense. The former will be used on sales invoices and the latter is reserved for future use on purchase invoices if we decide to hire other companies to handle our logistics.
- **Description**: This is the description that will be printed on the sales invoice.
- **Quantity**: This is the number of services that we have done. For example, the number of storage days or number of kilometers or miles in a route.

- **Unit Cost/Total Cost**: This can be used to calculate the profit of a service.

- **Unit Price/Total Price**: This is the price the customer will see on the sales invoice.

- **Unit of Measure Code**: This is a reference to the calculation method such as BOX, KM, MILES, or DAY.

- **Applies-to Document Subtype**: This is a reference to Storage Header, Registered Storage Header, Logistics Shipment, or Logistics Route. If necessary, this can be expanded to accommodate other add-ons.

- **Applies-to Document (Line) No.**: This is a reference to the Storage and Logistics documents that this Income & Expense record belongs to.

- **Applies-to Entry No.**: This is a reference to the Storage Invoice Entry.

Invoicing

After the Income & Expenses are created, we can start the invoicing process. To support this, some minor changes are done in the invoicing part of Microsoft Dynamics NAV and as an example, we choose a slightly different approach compared to *Chapter 2, A Sample Application*.

Sales Line

The **Sales Line** table (37) has gotten some minor modifications. We have added an extra type for **Income** and implemented a table relation for the **No.** field:

This enables us to also create new entries on a sales invoice without having to create an Income & Expense first.

The Sales Line also has a reference to the **Income & Expense Entry No.** and the **Apply-to** fields. This enables us to create the **Income & Expense Journal Lines** in the **Sales Post Code Unit**.

Codeunit Sales-Post (80)

The sales post code unit has only one change to populate the Income &
Expense Journal:

```
OnRun()

        . . .
        SalesLine.Type::Income:              //* Chapter 7
          PostIncome;


PostIncome()

IF SalesLine."Qty. to Invoice" = 0 THEN
  EXIT;

WITH IncExpJnlLn DO BEGIN
  INIT;
  "Posting Date" := "Posting Date";
  . . .
  "Source Code" := SrcCode;
  "Posting No. Series" := "Posting No. Series";
  "Dimension Set ID" := SalesLine."Dimension Set ID";
  IncExpJnlPostLine.RunWithCheck(IncExpJnlLn);
END;
```

This is done in the same way as the Resource Journal, however, we moved the
code that creates the journal line to a function, and this improves readability and
upgradability of our code.

> As the Sales Line has all the **Posting Group** and **Amount** fields
> populated, the General Ledger Entries, VAT Entries, and Customer
> Ledger Entries are automatically generated by the standard application.

Pricing methodology

Our add-on solution has three levels of automatic price calculation that are more
or less identical. We can calculate prices for storage documents, logistics shipments,
and routes.

Let's look at the storage prices as an example of how this is done.

Storage prices

In the **Storage Price** table, we can register prices for different storage activities.

Wareh...	Type	Produc...	Shelf No.	Startin...	Income & E...	Description	Unit Price	Ending Date
	Receipt	PROD00001			21. RECEIPT	Cost of Receipt	10,00	
	Shipment	PROD00001			21. SHIPMENT	Cost of Shipment	10,00	
	Storage	PROD00001			21. STORAGE	Storage Costs	10,00	

Storage Prices — Type to filter (F3) — Warehouse Code — Filter: PROD00001

When the price is calculated, the system will filter down in this table to find the price that matches best. For example, if a product has a price for receipt without a warehouse code, this price is used in all warehouses, but if one warehouse code is populated, this warehouse has a special price.

Prices can be differentiated to receipt, shipment, pick, put-away, movement, and storage. The first options are used on the storage documents, the latter when calculating storage cost.

The **Income & Expense Code** determines which type of Income & Expense will be created for this combination. A storage document can have more than one Income & Expense, for example, a normal receipt line and a customs surplus.

Calculation

The Income & Expenses are created using a Price Calc. Mgt. Codeunit, which we are familiar with from *Chapter 2*, *A Sample Application*, only this time we will not update the Unit Price but create the Income & Expenses.

The calculation for storage is done in codeunit 123456710:

```
FindStorageLinePrice

WITH StorageLine DO BEGIN
  Product.GET("No.");
  StorageLinePriceExists(StorageHeader, StorageLine);
  CreateIncExp(StorageHeader,StorageLine,TempStoragePrice);

END;
```

The `FindStorageLinePrice` function will call the standard `StorageLinePriceExists` function to find the storage prices that match the criteria. For all the storage prices in the filter, it calls the `CreateIncExp` function:

```
CreateIncExp()

IncExp.SETRANGE("Applies-to Document Type", IncExp."Applies-to
Document Type"::"Storage Header");
IncExp.SETRANGE("Applies-to Document No.", StorageHeader."No.");
IncExp.SETRANGE("Applies-to Document Line No.", StorageLine."Line
No.");
IncExp.DELETEALL;

WITH StoragePrice DO BEGIN
  FoundStoragePrice := FINDSET;
  IF FoundStoragePrice THEN BEGIN
    REPEAT
      IncExpCode.GET(StoragePrice."Income & Expense Code");
      IncExp.INIT;
      IncExp."Entry No." := 0;                //* For Autoincrement
      IncExp.Type := IncExpCode.Type;
      IncExp."Income & Expense Code" :=
        "Income & Expense Code";
      IncExp.Description := Description;
      IncExp.Quantity := StorageLine.Quantity;
      IncExp."Unit Cost" := IncExpCode."Unit Cost";
      IncExp."Total Cost" := IncExp.Quantity *
        IncExp."Unit Cost";
      IncExp."Unit Price" := StoragePrice."Unit Price";
      IncExp."Total Price" := IncExp.Quantity *
        IncExp."Unit Price";
      IncExp."Applies-to Document Type" :=
        IncExp."Applies-to Document Type"::"Storage Header";
      IncExp."Applies-to Document No." := StorageHeader."No.";
      IncExp."Applies-to Document Line No." :=
        StorageLine."Line No.";
      IncExp."Bill-to Customer No." :=
        StorageHeader."Bill-to Customer No.";
      IncExp."Gen. Prod. Posting Group" :=
        IncExpCode."Gen. Prod. Posting Group";
      IncExp."VAT Prod. Posting Group" :=
        IncExpCode."VAT Prod. Posting Group";
      IncExp.INSERT;
    UNTIL NEXT = 0;
  END;
END;
```

Each price will create a separate Income & Expense record.

> The Income & Expense table is set to **Auto Increment**. This means that SQL Server will generate the entry number for us. This enables multiple users to generate entries in this table at the same time without blocking each other.

Result

When new documents are generated by the system or end users, the prices are automatically calculated. The user can see the total cost and price on the **Fact Box** and change, remove, or add records if necessary, as shown in the following screenshot:

Periodic invoicing

One of the services we are providing is storage. This means that sometimes products can be in our warehouse for several days or even weeks or months. Our customers will be invoiced for the time they use our warehouse space.

Each time we receive a product in our warehouse or move a product to another region or shelf, a storage entry is created to keep track. For invoicing, we also create a Storage Invoice Entry. This is mainly because the inventory handling and invoicing are done on different moments by different persons. The products can be shipped to the customer when we start the invoicing process.

The Storage Invoice Entry is created with a **From Storage Date** that is inherited from the Storage Date of the Storage Entry. The Storage Invoice Entry also has a **To Storage Date** that maintains blank until the product leaves the warehouse or moves to another location that might have another price. The Income & Expense Code determines which price will be invoiced and is determined when posting a **Storage Document**.

The batch report **Storage Invoicing (123456703)** is used for the creation of the Income & Expenses. Let's have a look at how this is done.

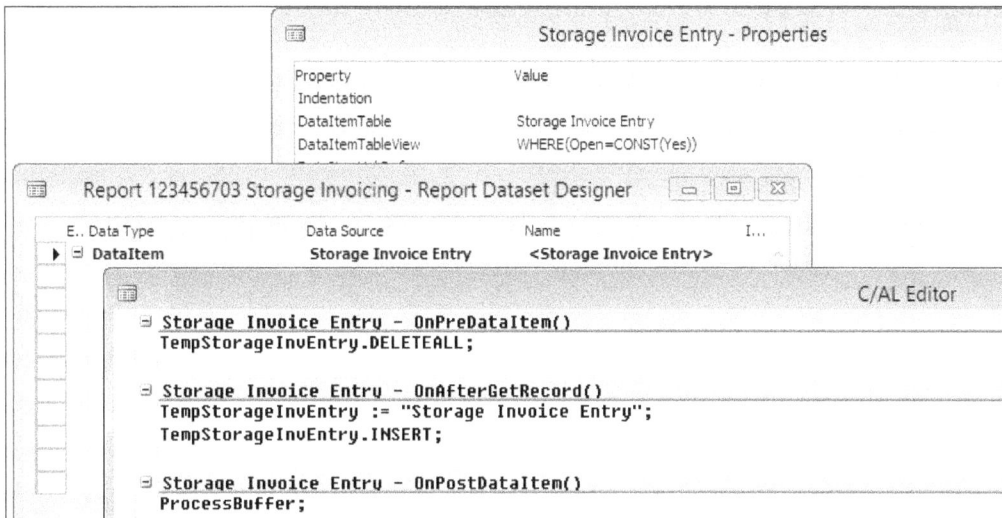

```
Storage Invoice Entry - Properties

Property              Value
Indentation
DataItemTable         Storage Invoice Entry
DataItemTableView     WHERE(Open=CONST(Yes))
```

Report 123456703 Storage Invoicing - Report Dataset Designer

E.. Data Type	Data Source	Name	I...
▶ ⊟ DataItem	**Storage Invoice Entry**	**<Storage Invoice Entry>**	

C/AL Editor

```
⊟ Storage Invoice Entry - OnPreDataItem()
  TempStorageInvEntry.DELETEALL;

⊟ Storage Invoice Entry - OnAfterGetRecord()
  TempStorageInvEntry := "Storage Invoice Entry";
  TempStorageInvEntry.INSERT;

⊟ Storage Invoice Entry - OnPostDataItem()
  ProcessBuffer;
```

The report only has one Storage Invoice Entry `DataItem`, which is filtered on **Open=Yes**.

In the report, all the Storage Invoice Entries are moved to a buffer table first and handled later. There are two important reasons for implementing a solution like this:

- **Changing Record Set**: This report filters on Storage Invoice Entries, which are open for invoicing. When the Storage Invoice Entry is completely invoiced, we want to change this value. This means that the record set we use is changing during the process. This is something the SQL Server backend cannot handle and this will result in very poor performance. By first moving all records to a buffer table, the filtering will be done on a virtual table that is maintained on the Service Tier rather than SQL Server.

- **Locking**: If we were to filter on open entries and modify our dataset, it would result in locking more records than necessary. Filtering on a non-clustered index will result in SQL Server moving to Range Locks rather than Row Locks. By reading the actual Storage Invoice Entry one by one using the clustered index, we will make sure that SQL Server only locks the records we use for this process, allowing other users to keep creating new records at the end of this table.

Processing the buffer

When processing the buffer, we first check whether this entry has been invoiced before. If this is the case, we start invoicing from the previous date, if not; we use the From Storage Date.

Then, we check whether the products have already left the warehouse or have been moved. If this is the case, we can close this entry by invoicing until this date; otherwise, we will invoice until the Workdate.

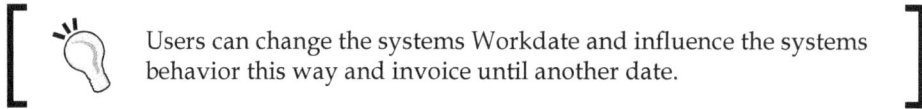

> Users can change the systems Workdate and influence the systems behavior this way and invoice until another date.

```
ProcessBuffer()

StorageInvEntry.LOCKTABLE;

WITH TempStorageInvEntry DO
  IF FIND('-') THEN REPEAT
    StorageInvEntry.GET("Entry No.");

    IF "Last Invoice Date" <> 0D THEN
      FromDate := "Last Invoice Date"
    ELSE
      FromDate := "From Storage Date";

    IF "To Storage Date" <> 0D THEN
      StorageInvEntry."Last Invoice Date" := "To Storage Date"
    ELSE
      StorageInvEntry."Last Invoice Date" := WORKDATE;

    Date.SETRANGE("Period Type", Date."Period Type"::Datum);
    Date.SETRANGE("Period No.", 1, 5);
    Date.SETRANGE("Period Start", FromDate,
      StorageInvEntry."Last Invoice Date");
```

```
IncExp."Entry No." := 0;
IncExp."Income & Expense Code" := "Income & Expense Code";
IncExp.Type := IncExp.Type::Income;
IncExp.Description := STRSUBSTNO(Text000, FromDate,
  StorageInvEntry."Last Invoice Date");
IncExp.Quantity := Date.COUNT;
IncExp."Unit Cost" := "Unit Cost";
IncExp."Total Cost" := IncExp.Quantity * "Total Cost";
IncExp."Unit Price" := "Unit Price";
IncExp."Total Price" := IncExp.Quantity * "Unit Price";
IncExp."Global Dimension 1 Code" :=
  "Global Dimension 1 Code";
IncExp."Global Dimension 2 Code" :=
  "Global Dimension 2 Code";
IncExp."Bill-to Customer No." := "Bill-to Customer No.";
IncExpCode.GET(IncExp."Income & Expense Code");
IncExp."Gen. Prod. Posting Group" :=
  IncExpCode."Gen. Prod. Posting Group";
IncExp."VAT Prod. Posting Group" :=
  IncExpCode."VAT Prod. Posting Group";
IncExp."Unit of Measure Code" :=
  IncExpCode."Unit of Measure Code";
IncExp."Applies-to Entry No." := "Entry No.";
IncExp.INSERT;

StorageInvEntry.Open := "To Storage Date" <> 0D;
StorageInvEntry.MODIFY;
UNTIL NEXT = 0;
```

The next step in our code is to calculate the number of workdays between the two dates. This will prevent our customer from paying for storage on Saturday and Sunday. We do this by using the virtual date table. This table contains all dates, weeks, months, quarters and years between January 1 0000 and December 31 9999 and can be very useful in date calculations.

With this result, we can now create the Income & Expense records that will be invoiced later. If the **To Storage Date** is populated, we close the Storage Invoice Entry.

Combined invoicing

The data model we use allows us to combine invoicing on all the services we provide for our customers. We can create one invoice that contains handling, storage, and transportation costs for our customers.

This is done by batch report 123456704 Combine Storage & Logistics, which works exactly the same as the report in *Chapter 2, A Sample Application*.

Add-on flexibility

The add-on we have created in this chapter is definitely not ready to be used by a real company but it demonstrates how to create a flexible solution that can be easily expanded by others.

Most modern logistic service providers offer other services to customers, such as value-added logistics, item tracking, and third- and fourth-party logistics.

Value-added logistics

When a company offers value-added logistics services, they not only keep products on inventory but they also offer services around this, such as display packaging.

This can be best compared with manufacturing in Microsoft Dynamics NAV. A list of items called a bill of materials is combined into a new product. This new product is then shipped to the customer.

When the displays are no longer necessary, for example, when a marketing campaign is finished, the displays need to be picked up from the customer and disassembled into the original products.

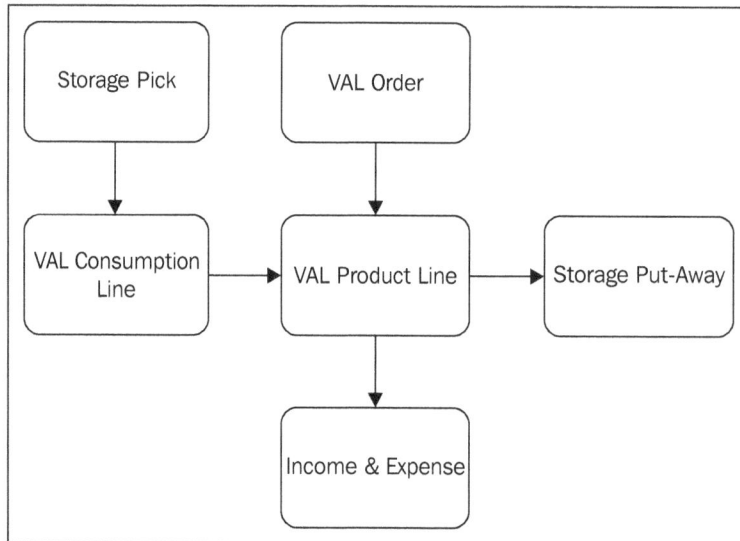

In our solution, this could be implemented by creating a VAL region where the products are moved to.

Item tracking

Our customers also want to know the whereabouts of their products, which warehouse they are in, and which product was shipped to which customer. This is especially important in the food and medicine industry to be able to call back a lot, if something is wrong.

To implement this in our solution, it requires some changes. First, we need to implement a Tracking Code in the Storage Entries, and secondly, we need to implement some kind of Tracking Entries when we ship a product outside our warehouse since our logistics solution currently does not have any entries, only status fields.

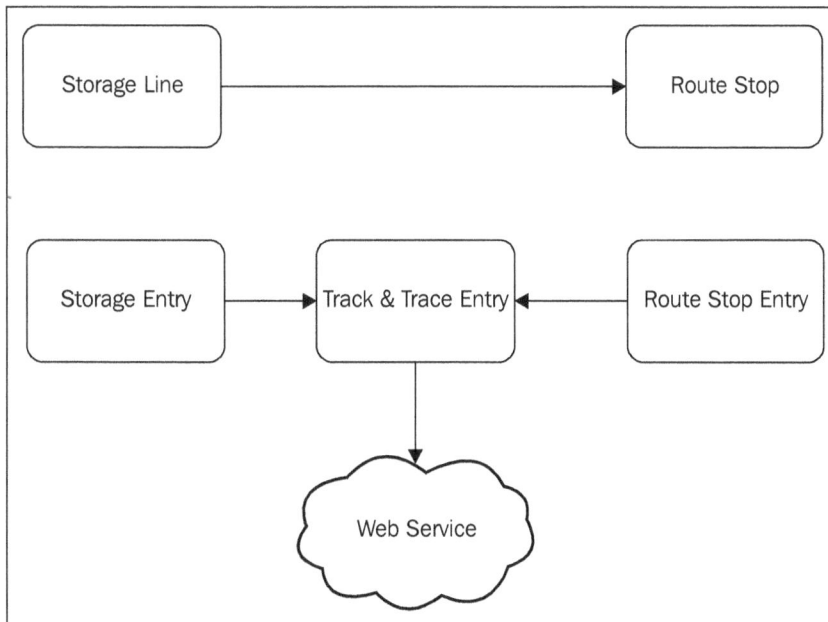

Third- and fourth-party logistics

In our example database, we plan shipments on routes and drive them to the end customer with our own trucks. This is called second-party logistics. First-party logistics would be if we were to handle our own products with our own trucks.

The following figure shows the increasing complexity of logistics if it gets outsourced and combined:

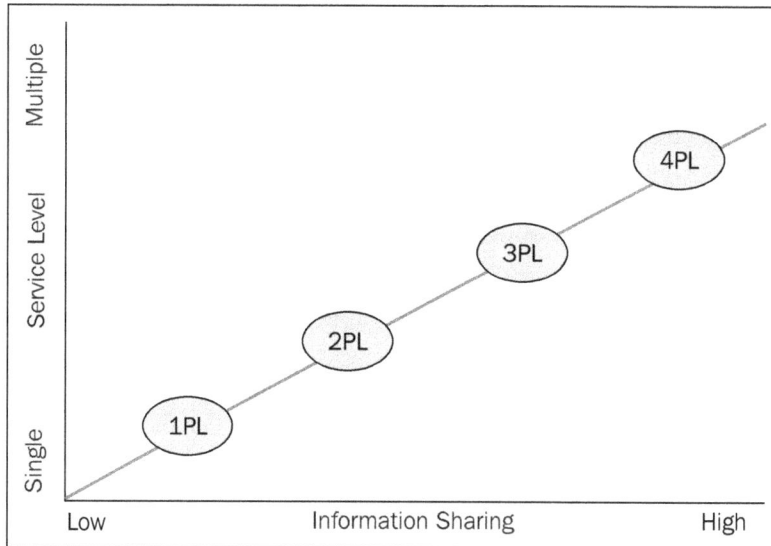

If we provide third-party logistics, we would use other companies to offer parts of the services to our customers. We will then tell them which part of the service to handle and report back to us when it is finished. The third party involved does not know the details of the complete transaction.

If we offer fourth-party logistics, we would outsource a complete warehouse or route to another company. We would only tell them which product should be moved where and they would handle it, without us knowing the details.

Very often, third- and fourth-party logistics are mixed but they are usually handled by interfaces between different companies.

Summary

In this chapter, we looked at the Microsoft Dynamics NAV product from a completely different viewpoint compared to the previous chapters.

The goal was not to design a rock-solid storage and logistics add-on solution for Microsoft Dynamics NAV as this would require much more than one chapter. The information in this chapter is intended to demonstrate how to integrate new functionality on top of Microsoft Dynamics NAV. We analyzed business processes and designed new data and transaction models to handle them in the product and implemented this.

For our solution, we designed two new document structures and two new journals and entry structures. We stayed close to the standard methodology of Microsoft Dynamics NAV by creating a framework that can easily be expanded. We also spend some time looking at how to prevent unnecessary locking in the database and how to avoid changing a filtered dataset.

Finally, we looked at some examples of how our add-on solution can be enhanced to better suit other demands in the market.

This chapter does not end here. The C/AL objects provided with this chapter can be studied in order to understand even better how the pieces are put together.

In the next chapter, we will design an application inside Microsoft Dynamics NAV. We will look at how it can be used for a consultancy company using the Jobs module and extending this with new functionality to meet specific requirements.

8
Consulting

In this chapter, we will learn how Microsoft Dynamics NAV fits a consultancy company. Most consultancy companies have project-related processes. They take on larger projects that take a certain time to complete. Some consultancy companies also purchase and sell items.

For the projects, the consultancy company needs to keep track of used resources and items. Sometimes they can invoice the resource hours they spend one-on-one but most of the time they will also take a risk in doing fixed price projects. In this case, it is even more important to know if the project was budgeted well and ensure money is not lost on the way.

There are many types of companies working this way. Examples are accountancy firms and lawyers, but also many companies in the construction business work like this.

For this chapter, we will use an example, a company we are all very familiar with, either because of working as an employee, a customer, or maybe even an owner. We will look at the business process of a Microsoft Dynamics NAV Partner.

The partner in our case sells Microsoft Dynamics NAV licenses for new projects. They also help existing customers in upgrades and support. Lastly, they are selling infrastructure solutions, assembling servers, and desktop systems in house.

We will discuss four different project scenarios and see how Microsoft Dynamics NAV can be used to support those. To do this, we will create some modifications along the way. The objects required for this chapter can be downloaded from `http://ftp.packtpub.com/chapter8.fob`. After reading this chapter, you will have a good understanding of the possibilities and limitations of the Job Module in Microsoft Dynamics NAV, how it fits in with the rest of the product, and how it can be expanded safely.

The process

The two main processes for Microsoft Dynamics NAV partners are implementing new projects and providing services such as supporting and upgrading to existing customers. A third process is selling infrastructure and assembling computer systems but this is an extra service, not the core business.

To support the projects (jobs), the company needs people, software licenses, and hardware. The people (resources) need to be carefully planned on the projects as they are the least flexible part of the company. Hardware (items) and software licenses (G/L Accounts) will be purchased from vendors like Microsoft.

The projects can be divided into large and small projects. The larger projects are new implementations and upgrades. Smaller projects are usually implementing small features and helping users with regular support issues.

Invoicing can be done in various ways. New implementations and small projects can be invoiced per billable hour while upgrades are sold at a fixed price. For hardware, we will use items. Licenses are invoiced directly to the general ledger.

Large projects also have budgets and planning that needs to be maintained. If the budget is fully used and the planning milestones have not been reached, there should be a new budget created in order to complete the project.

To support this process, we will use the Jobs functionality with some customizations. Projects are called Jobs in Microsoft Dynamics NAV so we will use that term from now on.

> The Jobs module has been completely redesigned by Microsoft for Version 5. In this chapter, we will use a lot of the new functionality where we would have done customizations in the older versions of Microsoft Dynamics NAV.

Fits

The registration of the Jobs module can be done using the standard functionality of Microsoft Dynamics NAV as well as the budgeting and planning.

The standard software also allows us to invoice Jobs both fixed price and on time and materials. We can also purchase items for our Jobs. In Microsoft Dynamics NAV 2013, a timesheet module has been added to the application, which we will use and explain in this chapter.

Gaps

The Jobs module in Microsoft Dynamics NAV is often referenced as a framework that almost always needs some changes. Fortunately, it is designed to be easily changed and we will do so to support our processes.

Resource groups

Although many companies work this way, budgeting for resource groups is not possible. We will create a solution for that. We will also make it possible to see the total number of planned, used, and invoiced hours.

Item calculation

We will create a solution calculating the system assembling. As hardware specifications are changing very rapidly, we do not want to create a new item for each system we may only sell once or twice.

Issue registration

Our support team needs a single point for registration of all support issues for all customers and to follow up their workflow. For this, we will also create functionality to register and followup issues.

Getting started

Before we start creating any new jobs, we should have a look at the following data and posting model of the Microsoft Dynamics NAV Jobs module:

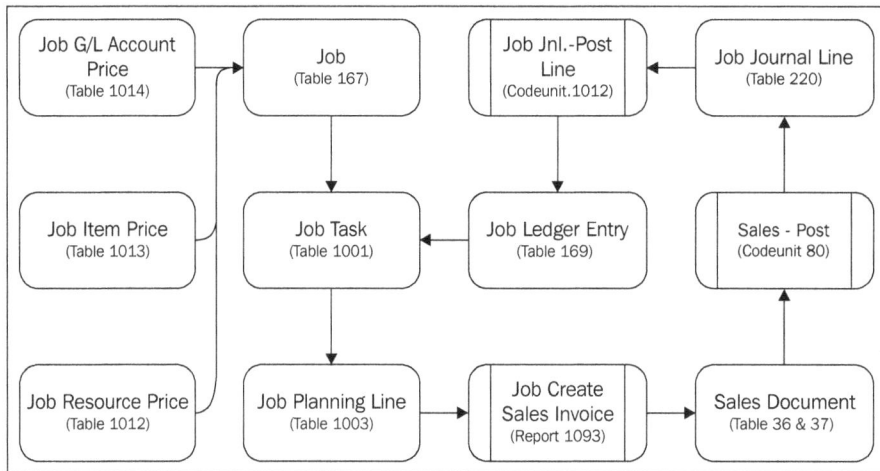

The starting point is the job table that has **Job Tasks** and **Job Planning Lines** that we can use for budgeting and planning. Each job can have its own prices.

The **Job Planning Lines** get invoiced through the standard Microsoft Dynamics NAV Sales functionality, which then creates **Job Ledger Entries**.

How many jobs

The first step is setting up a new job. There can be different angles on setting up jobs. This depends on how we want to work with the system. The minimum requirement is to have at least one job per bill to customer. This enables us to do the invoicing. Some companies use jobs this way to use it as a pre-invoice engine.

Another angle can be to set up new jobs nicely for each project that we do for the customer. In our case, this starts with the basic Dynamics NAV implementation. When this is finished, we close the job. If the customer has any new requirements, we need to start a new job. This way we can keep better track of what issues we have outstanding with each customer. The downside of this methodology is that it requires some work to set up a new job every time.

Most companies end up with a solution in the middle. It is common to set up a new job for larger jobs and to have a job for support issues. This also allows us to set up different invoicing strategies for each job. We will use this strategy.

Job Card

Let's have a look at the **Job Card** and the important fields there:

Let's see these fields in more detail:

- **No.**: This is the unique number of a job. We can use different Number Series strategies for this, from simple sequential numbering to linked Number Series for different job types or manual numbering.

- **Description**: This field should contain a logical description of the job for internal use. Most people will search in this field so make sure to have certain rules for naming. This will make searching for old jobs easier in the future.

- **Bill-to Customer No.**: Each job has one bill-to customer. If we want to invoice multiple customers for one job, we need to customize the application.

- **Search Description**: By default, this will be populated with the value of the description field but can be changed to another value if required.

- **Person Responsible**: This is an informative field indicating who is responsible for this job.

- **Blocked**: If this field is checked, it is not possible to make new entries for this job. We use this for closed jobs.

- **Job Posting Group**: This refers to the G/L Accounts that are used for the **Work In Progress (WIP)** postings. There can be different G/L Accounts for different types of Jobs or WIP methods.

- **WIP Method**: Each job can have one WIP method. We will discuss this briefly later in this chapter.

- **Status**: The jobs have a limited set of status fields. The only available status values are **Planning**, **Quote**, **Order**, and **Completed**.

> Most companies want to have more sub statuses for the order phase. The best approach for this is to add a new status field that maps with the standard status field. This requires minimum changes to the application while creating new workflow possibilities.

- **Allow Schedule/Contract Lines**: If this field is not checked, it is not possible to create planning lines that have the options **Both Schedule** and **Contract**. When planning lines are created they will be split into a schedule and a contract line.

- **Starting Date** and **Ending Date**: These are informative fields that are only used to calculate the currency exchange rates for the job.

- **Foreign Trade**: In the Jobs module, it is possible to send calculate and create invoices in another currency than the local currency. This will multiply the complexity of the implementation and should be used carefully.

Job task and planning lines

When the job is created, the next step is to create Job Tasks and Planning Lines. These can be used in different ways.

Using Job Task lines, we can divide the job into smaller pieces, which we can then schedule and invoice. The more detailed the Job Tasks, the better we can measure the progress of the job. But the amount of work required to maintain them would also be more. Balance is a keyword for success here.

Creating Job Tasks and Planning Lines

The Job Tasks can be created with the same structure as the Chart of Accounts, meaning the actual Task Lines can be grouped using Begin and End Total lines. Each level can be indented for better readability.

The Job Planning Lines are the detail lines of each Job Task. This defines what we will do and how this will be invoiced. A Job Planning Line can be linked to the master data types Resource, Item, G/L Account, or Text.

> Job Tasks and Job Planning Lines can be copied very easily from other jobs. This allows us to reuse them and even create template jobs for frequently used combinations.

The Line Type in the Job Planning Line defines how it will be invoiced. There are three types:

- **Schedule**: The amounts on this line will only be used for budgeting purposes. When invoicing, we need to post one or more job journal lines that will be invoiced or we can create another Job Planning Line with the invoice amount. Schedule lines should be used when billing for time and materials.

- **Contract**: This line will be invoiced with the exact amounts. However, the amounts do not show up in the budget. This can be used when invoicing fixed price jobs in a schedule, for example, 50 percent when signing the contract and 50 percent on job completion.

- **Both Schedule and Contract**: This line will be invoiced in exactly the same way as the contract lines but the amount will also show up in the budget.

Job journal

When the Job Tasks and Job Planning Lines are set up, we can start the job. During the job, we will consume resources and items from our company. This should be registered using the Job journal. The **Job Journal** is the lowest level of the Journal Posting diagram we drafted in *Chapter 1, Introduction to Microsoft Dynamics NAV*, and uses the other journals to create the resource, item, and general ledger entries.

When creating a Job Journal Line, the following few fields are particularly important for the process:

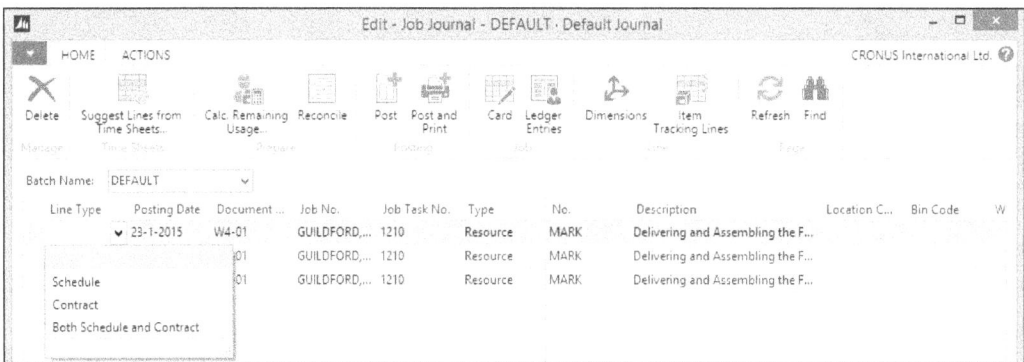

Let's have a look at the fields in more detail:

- **Line Type**: This has the same options as the **Job Planning Line**, **Schedule**, **Contract**, and **Both Schedule and Contract**. When the job journal line should be invoiced, the type should be **Contract**. When the job journal line is part of a fixed price, the Line Type should be left blank. Then the Line Type is **Schedule**, the system will create additional Job Planning Lines of this type, which may corrupt our budget for the customer since they are already created.

- **Unit Cost and Unit Price**: These fields will determine the cost of the job and price that will be invoiced to the customer if the Line Type is **Contract**. This information is also used in the calculation of the work in progress.

Job examples

Let's go through some different job scenarios to see how we can use this functionality.

Chapter objects

The chapter objects contain both the changes that we will discuss in this chapter as well as the example jobs we will use. After importing `chapter8.fob` as described in *Appendix, Installation Guide*, run page 123.456.700 **Jobs Add-on Setup** and run **Initialise Application**.

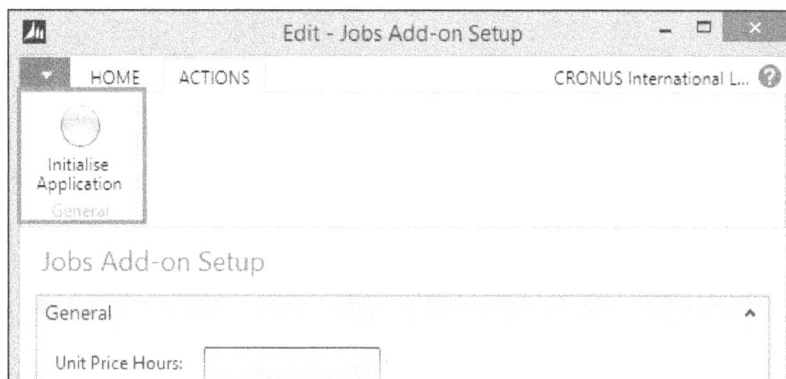

When this completes, restart the Role Tailored Client. You should now see the Project Manager Role Center.

The new implementation

Implementing Microsoft Dynamics NAV 2013 is not an easy task and many things need to be taken care of before we can use the product. We will implement Microsoft Dynamics NAV for Packt Publishing. The Job for this example is `EXAMPLE1`.

For the implementation, we will create various Job Task groups. Each part of the implementation gets a code. As the sorting is done on this field, we will create code using numbers and a logical name, for example, `0200. SETUP` and `0210. FIN`.

> Leave enough space in the numbers to add additional lines if required. This will avoid renaming, which is an expensive task for the database engine and users will have to wait until it is completed.

Our consultants will help the customer to install the system, help with the setup, and convert the data from the old system. When this is done we will help them with testing and train them using Microsoft Dynamics NAV. The consultants will be set up in the system as Resources, which are in turn entered into the Job Planning Lines.

When everything is working as expected, we can schedule a go-live weekend and help them in the first period using the system.

Job Tas... ▲	Description	Job Task Ty...	Totaling	Job Posting...	Scheduled Q...
0000.JOB	Job Total	Begin-Total			
0100. INSTA...	Installation and Setup	Begin-Total			
0110. INSTC...	Install and Setup clients	Posting		SETTING UP	4,00
0120. INSTSE...	Install and Setup server	Posting		SETTING UP	4,00
0199. INSTA...	Total for Installation and Setup	End-Total	0100. INSTALL..0199. INSTALLTOTAL		8,00
0200. SETUP	Application Setup	Begin-Total			
0210. FIN	Financilals	Posting		SETTING UP	4,00
0220. INV	Inventory	Posting		SETTING UP	4,00
0230. SALES	Sales	Posting		SETTING UP	4,00
0240. PURCH	Purchasing	Posting		SETTING UP	4,00
0299. SETU...	Total for Setup	End-Total	0200. SETUP..0299. SETUPTOTAL		16,00
0300. CONV	Conversion	Begin-Total			
0310. CONV...	Opening Balance	Posting		SETTING UP	4,00
0320. CONVI...	Inventory	Posting		SETTING UP	4,00
0399. CONV...	Total for Conversion	End-Total	0300. CONV..0399. CONVTOTAL		8,00
0400. TRAI...	Training and Testing	Begin-Total			
0410. OVERV...	Global Overview Training	Posting		SETTING UP	4,00
0420. KEYYS...	Keyuser Training	Posting		SETTING UP	4,00
0499. TOTT...	Total Training	End-Total	0400. TRAINING..0499. TOTTRAIN		8,00
0500. GO-LI...	Go-Live and support	Begin-Total			
0510. GOLIVE	Go-Live weekend	Posting		SETTING UP	4,00
0520. SUPPO...	After Care	Posting		SETTING UP	4,00
0599. TOTAL	Total	End-Total	0500. GO-LIVE..0599. TOTAL		8,00
9999.JOB	Job Total	End-Total	0000.JOB..9999.JOB		48,00

Invoicing a job like this is done using a budget. We will make a precalculation of the number of hours we think are necessary and start with that. During the job we need to measure the used budget and compare it with the progress.

Budgeting

The budget is created using the Job Planning Lines. During this phase of the job, we do not yet know which resource will be used for the Job Tasks and it might even be done by more than one resource. This is why we want to use Resource Groups in our budget.

> This is not possible in the standard application so we have created a modification, which we will discuss at the end of this chapter.

Job Planning Lines

Line Type	Planning D...	Planned De...	Type	No.	Description	Quantity	Unit Cost	Total Cost	Unit Price	Line Amou...
Schedule	22-1-2015	22-1-2015	Resource Group	TECHN	Technician	4	20,00	80,00	40,00	160,00
Schedule	22-1-2015	22-1-2015	Resource Group	TECHN	Technician	4	20,00	80,00	40,00	160,00
Schedule	22-1-2015	22-1-2015	Resource Group	CONS	Consultant	4	40,00	160,00	80,00	320,00
Schedule	22-1-2015	22-1-2015	Resource Group	CONS	Consultant	4	40,00	160,00	80,00	320,00
Schedule	22-1-2015	22-1-2015	Resource Group	CONS	Consultant	4	40,00	160,00	80,00	320,00
Schedule	22-1-2015	22-1-2015	Resource Group	PROG	Programmer	4	60,00	240,00	120,00	480,00
Schedule	22-1-2015	22-1-2015	Resource Group	PROG	Programmer	4	60,00	240,00	120,00	480,00
Schedule	22-1-2015	22-1-2015	Resource Group	CONS	Consultant	4	40,00	160,00	80,00	320,00
Schedule	22-1-2015	22-1-2015	Resource Group	CONS	Consultant	4	40,00	160,00	80,00	320,00
Schedule	22-1-2015	22-1-2015	Resource Group	PROG	Programmer	4	60,00	240,00	120,00	480,00
Schedule	22-1-2015	22-1-2015	Resource Group	CONS	Consultant	4	40,00	160,00	80,00	320,00

The **Line Type** of these Job Planning Lines is **Schedule**. This means that these lines are just for budgeting and schedule purposes. The system will invoice the actual consumption posted in the Job Journal.

The infrastructure

To use Microsoft Dynamics NAV 2013, Packt Publishing needs a new infrastructure. Their current systems do not meet the requirements for Microsoft Dynamics NAV 2013.

For this job, we could create new Job Task Lines in the implementation job, but for a clearer overview, we will create a new job, EXAMPLE2.

Our company builds and sells its own computer systems. We can build both servers and desktop systems. As none of the systems are exactly the same and available components switch regularly, we do not want to create an item and a bill of materials for each system. Instead we use a calculation system, which we add as a customization to Dynamics NAV that allows us to determine a price for a system. For other products like switches, routers, printers, and laptops, we use items that we purchase from vendors.

The Job Tasks and Job Planning Lines for this job look like this:

Job Tasks and Job Planning Lines

The installation costs in this job are **Resource Groups** with Line Type Schedule, just as in the previous job, so we invoice actual hours spent on the Job.

The other lines are of type **Both Schedule and Contract**. This means we will invoice exactly what is in the budget. The Job Journal Lines for these tasks should be posted with a blank Line Type.

The upgrade

Our customer requests an upgrade from Navision Version 3.70 to Microsoft Dynamics NAV 2013. We can do this for a fixed price but we require a fee to analyze the system.

For the EXAMPLE3 job, we can start with a limited number of Job Task Lines, just for the quote. When the customer agrees to do the upgrade, we can add new Job Task Lines.

Both the quote and the upgrade are a fixed price and posted directly to the general ledger. This does not mean we cannot have our resources register the actual hours using the Job Journal but the **Line Type** should be blank.

Another part of the upgrade is not done at a fixed price. The system needs a redesign, a conversion to SQL Server 2014, and the customer wants additional training and support.

Job Tas... ^	Description	Job Task Ty...	Totaling	Job Posting...	Scheduled Q...	Contract Qty...	WIP-Total	WIP Method
0000.JOB	Packt Publishing - Upgrade 3.70 to 2013	Begin-Total						
0100.QUOTE	Analysis	Begin-Total						
0150.QUOTE	Analisys old system	Posting		SETTING UP	1,00	1,00		
0199.QUOTE	Analysis Total	End-Total	0100.QUOTE..0199.QUOTE		1,00	1,00		
0200.UPGR...	Upgrade	Begin-Total						
0250.UPGRA...	Fixed Price Upgrade	Posting		SETTING UP	3,00	3,00		
0299.UPGR...	Upgrade Total	End-Total	0200.UPGRADE..0299.UPGRADE		3.00	3.00		
0300.REDES...	Redesign							
0310.REDESI...	Item Tracking							
0320.REDESI...	Jobs Planning							
0399.REDES...	Redesign Total							
0400.SQL	SQL Conversion							
0410.SQL2008	SQL 2014 Conversion							
0420.SQLBE...	SQL Benchmark							
0430.SQLTU...	SQL Performance Tuning							
0499.SQL	SQL Conversion Total							
0500.GOLIVE	Go-Live							
0510.GOLIVE	Training							

Edit - Job Planning Lines - EXAMPLE3 Packt Publishing - Upgrade 3.70 t

HOME   ACTIONS   NAVIGATE   REPORT

Job Planning Lines

Line Type	Planning D...	Planned De...	Type	No.	Description	Quantity	I...	...	Unit Price	Lin
Both Schedu...	22-1-2015	22-1-2015	G/L Account	6620	Fixed Price Upgrade...	1	##	##	13.250,00	
Both Schedu...	22-1-2015	22-1-2015	G/L Account	6620	Fixed Price Upgrade...	1	##	##	10.600,00	
Both Schedu...	22-1-2015	22-1-2015	G/L Account	6620	Fixed Price Upgrade...	1	##	##	2.650,00	

Upgrading for re-design

The fixed price part of the upgrade is invoiced in three phases. When the job starts, we invoice 50 percent, and when we deliver the test system, we invoice 40 percent, and finally 10 percent is invoiced three months after go-live.

This is done using lines of **Both Schedule and Contract** Line Type.

The support team

For the support team, our policy is to create one job per fiscal year per customer. We will use this job, EXAMPLE4, to invoice the maintenance of the license and all support issues.

The support issues can be both little questions customers call us for, like changing a report or a page, or implementing new features that requires only a few days' work.

Each issue and new feature will be created as a Job Task Line. The new features will be created by the account manager who sells the feature. We can then decide if the invoicing is done at a fixed price, using contract lines, or on time and materials using schedule lines.

Our support team also needs to use the job system, but we do not want them to manually create a new Job Task Line for each support call and we also want them to view all outstanding issues for all customers easily. For this, we have created a new issue registration system, which we will discuss at the end of this chapter.

Each issue in the system is linked to a Job Task. When support engineers create a new issue, the Job Task Line is automatically generated for them and they can use it in our time and billing system.

Time sheets

For all the jobs in our examples, it is critical to have a solid registration of resource hours. In the standard Microsoft Dynamics NAV Job application resources need either to post a Job Journal for each combination of job, Job Task and Posting Date or we can use the new Time Sheet application introduced in Version 2013.

> On the MSDN page at `http://msdn.microsoft.com/en-us/library/hh175112(v=nav.71).aspx`, you can find more information on how to set up and use Time Sheets in Microsoft Dynamics NAV.

Design pattern

The **Time Sheet** application is layered above the Resource Journal Line and is created using Resources and Job Tasks.

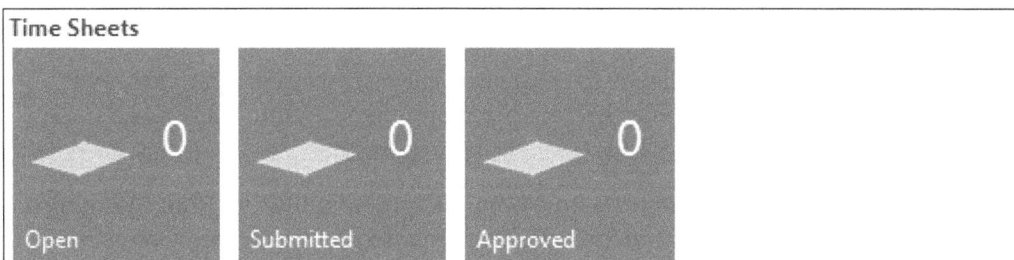

There is an approval process for the person responsible for the job allowing them to make corrections.

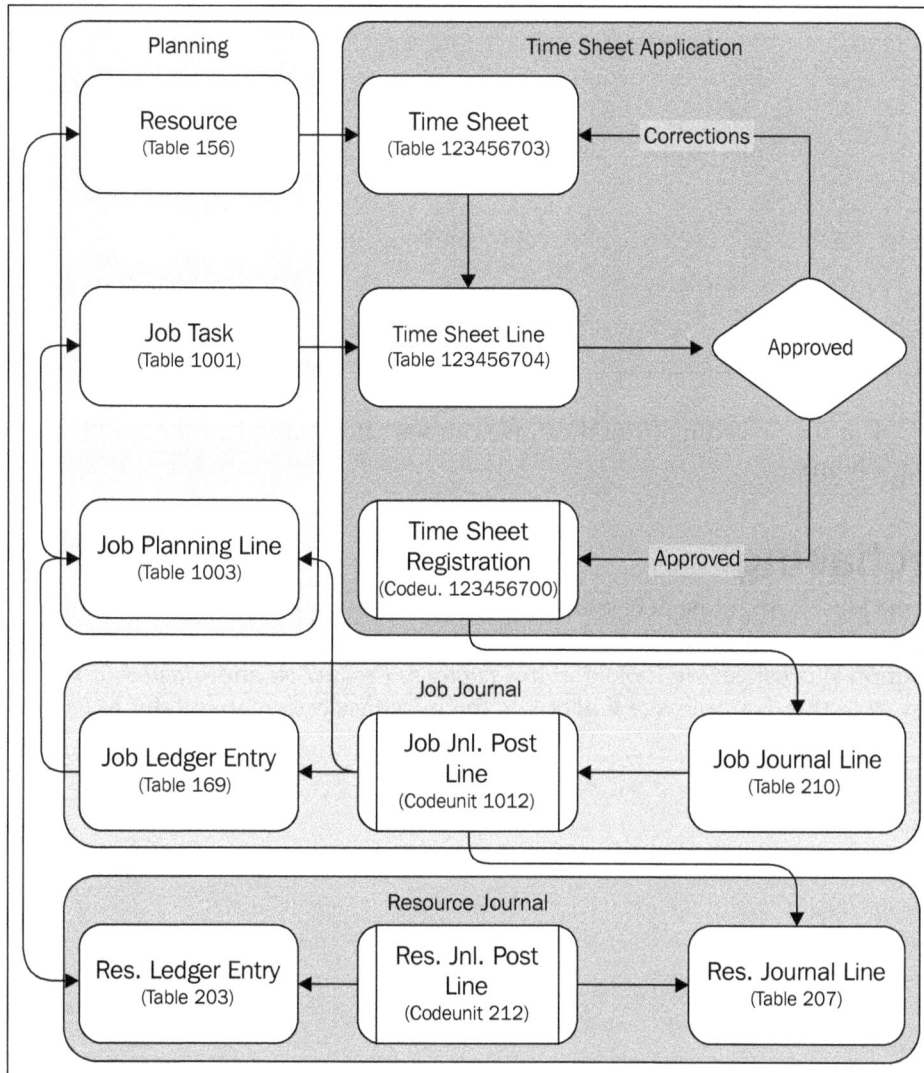

The time sheet is designed to be created for each week. The time sheets are generated using a process, not by the user. After that the resource can create **Time Sheet Line** for each Job Task Line and populate the number of hours each day of the week.

If we look at the preceding time sheet, we can see after it updated that **Wednesday** is missing 2 hours.

Purchasing

For some jobs, it might be necessary to purchase items specifically for that job. In Microsoft Dynamics NAV 2013, the Jobs module was integrated with the Requisition Worksheet we looked at in *Chapter 5*, *Production* and *Chapter 6*, *Trade*. However, in this example, we will create the purchase orders manually like this:

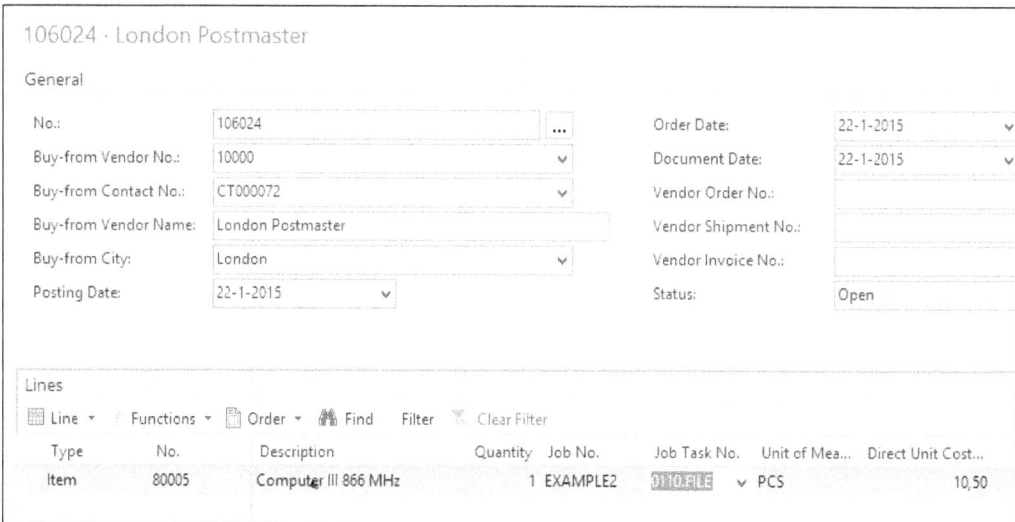

When purchasing for a job, the **Job No.** and **Job Task No.** fields should be used. If we set the Job Line Type to contract this item will be invoiced to the customer. Usually, this is not required since it should have been in the Job Planning Lines already.

Item costing versus work in progress

After we post this purchase document and navigate from the purchase invoice, we can see that the system has created two value entries for this item:

Posting D...	Item Led...	Entry Type	Adj...	Document Type	Docume...	D...	Sa...	Cost Amount (Expec...	Cost Amount (Actual)	Item Ledger ...
22-1-2015	Purchase	Direct Cost	☐	Purchase Invoice	108028		0,00	0,00	10,50	1
22-1-2015	Negative A...	Direct Cost	☐	Purchase Invoice	108028		0,00	0,00	-10,50	-1

This is very important for the costing as we discussed in the previous chapters.

> Purchased items for jobs are not calculated as inventory but used for the work in progress calculation.

Invoicing

When everything in our jobs is set up as required and the Job Journal is used to post the usage, creating the invoices is a simple task.

In the Job Manager Role Center, we can see if a job is due to be invoiced. This is done using a flow filter on the **Planning Date** field of the **Job Planning Lines**.

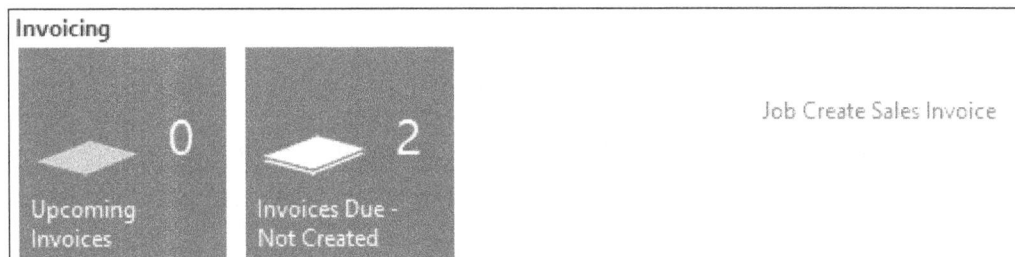

Each Job Planning Line has a planning date. This can be used to schedule our resources but is far more useful for invoice scheduling. Each Job Planning Line that is ready to be invoiced should get the invoice date in the **Planning Date** field.

The invoices can then be created using the batch report **Job Create Sales Invoice (1093)** but we can also preview the invoice by using the report **Job Suggested Billing (1011)**. This report can be started from each job.

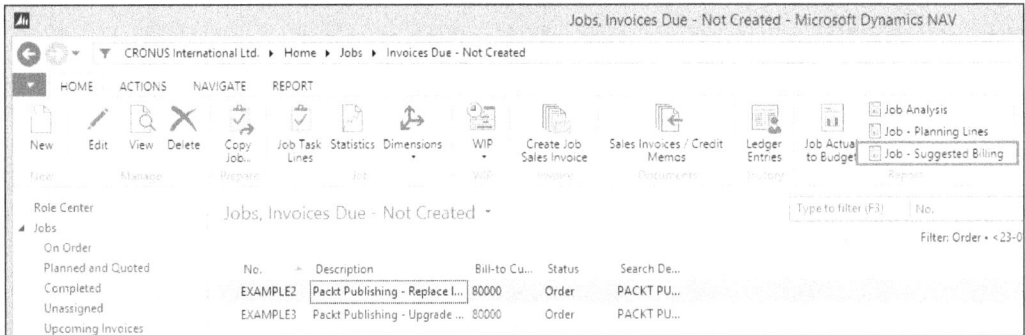

Job-Suggested Billing

The sales invoice lines are created using the same description as the Job Planning Lines. To clarify information for the customer on the invoice we can use extra text lines.

When the invoice is created and posted, the Job Task is updated with the actual invoicing information.

Calculating work in progress

Since most jobs are not completed in a day or a week, it is important to know the status of each job in time. This can be measured in quantity and financially. In quantities, we can see how much of the budget is being used by looking at the **Job Task** page. For financial progress, we can calculate the WIP.

WIP calculates the cost we made and the sales we invoiced on the job and creates Job WIP Entries for this. This can then be posted to the general ledger if required. The WIP amounts depend on the WIP method.

In Microsoft Dynamics NAV, WIP is calculated based on a combination of costs and sales as set up in the Job WIP method table.

Let's create an example and calculate the WIP for five example methods.

Code	Recognized costs	Recognized sales
COMPLETED CONTRACT	At completion	At completion
COST OF SALES	Cost of sales	Contract (invoiced price)
COST VALUE	Cost value	Contract (invoiced price)

Code	Recognized costs	Recognized sales
PERC. OF COMPLETION	Usage (total cost)	Percentage of completion
SALES VALUE	Usage (total cost)	Sales value

We created a job with a total price of 1000 and total cost of 500. We used 4 resource hours' worth 500 and cost 250. We invoiced nothing.

	Recog. cost	Recog. sales	WIP cost	WIP sales
Cost value	125	0	125	0
Sales value	250	250	0	250
Cost of sales			250	
Percentage of completion	250	250	0	250
Completed contract			250	

Now, we send an invoice to the customer for the hours spent. We invoice 500.

	Recog. cost	Recog. sales	WIP cost	WIP sales
Cost value	375	500	-125	0
Sales value	250	250	0	-250
Cost of sales	500	500	-250	
Percentage of completion	250	250	0	-250
Completed contract			250	-500

In the last example, we will use an item that costs 250 that we cannot invoice. We now have 500 costs and 500 sales.

	Recog. cost	Recog. sales	WIP cost	WIP sales
Cost value	500	500	0	0
Sales value	250	250	0	-250
Cost of sales	500	500	0	
Percentage of completion	500	500	0	0
Completed contract			500	-500

When the WIP is positive, it means that we have done more than we invoiced. When the WIP is negative, we have invoiced more than we have done.

Each company that uses Microsoft Dynamics NAV should make their own decision about what WIP method to use. WIP methods can change for each job and even change during a job.

WIP post to general ledger

Some accountants want to post the WIP amounts to the general ledger. The benefit of doing this is to have all the financial information in one place for easier reporting.

The G/L Accounts for the WIP posting are set up in the Job Posting Group. When posting WIP to the general ledger, there is always a reversal posting. When a company does monthly reporting, the WIP is posted on the last day of the month and reversed on the first day of the next month.

Changing jobs

In this chapter, we have used some changes to the Job functionality in order to make it work for CRONUS International Ltd. to sell Microsoft Dynamics NAV.

Quantity budgeting

For some companies, it is very important to know the total number of hours required for a job and the number of hours used rather than the exact amounts.

For this, we have created new flow fields in the **Job Task** table:

The flow field definition is quite special.

```
Sum("Job Planning Line"."Quantity (Base)"
    WHERE (Job No. = FIELD(Job No.),
           Job Task No. = FIELD(Job Task No.),
           Job Task No. = FIELD(FILTER(Totaling)),
           Contract Line = CONST(Yes),
           Planning Date = FIELD(Planning Date Filter)))
```

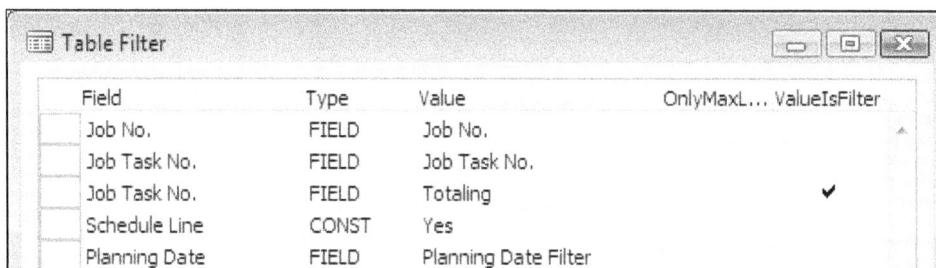

Field	Type	Value	OnlyMaxL...	ValueIsFilter
Job No.	FIELD	Job No.		
Job Task No.	FIELD	Job Task No.		
Job Task No.	FIELD	Totaling		✔
Schedule Line	CONST	Yes		
Planning Date	FIELD	Planning Date Filter		

The **Totaling** field is for the lines of type **End-Total**. The `ValueIsFilter` property ensures that the field will be interpreted as a filter instead of a value.

The result is visible in the Job Task page (1002).

Job Tas... ⌃	Description	Job Task Ty...	Totaling	Job Posting...	Scheduled Qty. (...	End Date
0400. TRAI...	**Training and Testing**	Begin-Total				
0410. OVERV...	Global Overview Training	Posting		SETTING UP	4,00	22-1-2015
0420. KEYYS...	Keyuser Training	Posting		SETTING UP	4,00	22-1-2015
0499. TOTT...	**Total Training**	End-Total	0400. TRAINING..0499. TOTTRAIN		8,00	
0500. GO-LI...	**Go-Live and support**	Begin-Total				
0510. GOLIVE	Go-Live weekend	Posting		SETTING UP	4,00	22-1-2015
0520. SUPPO...	After Care	Posting		SETTING UP	4,00	22-1-2015
0599. TOTAL	**Total**	End-Total	0500. GO-LIVE..0599. TOTAL		8,00	
9999.JOB	**Job Total**	End-Total	0000.JOB..9999.JOB		48,00	

Result of ValueIsFilter property

Resource Groups

For scheduling, we have implemented the possibility of using Resource Groups in the **Job Planning Lines** as well as **Calculations**. This is done by adding two new fields, **Add-on Type** and **Add-on No.**:

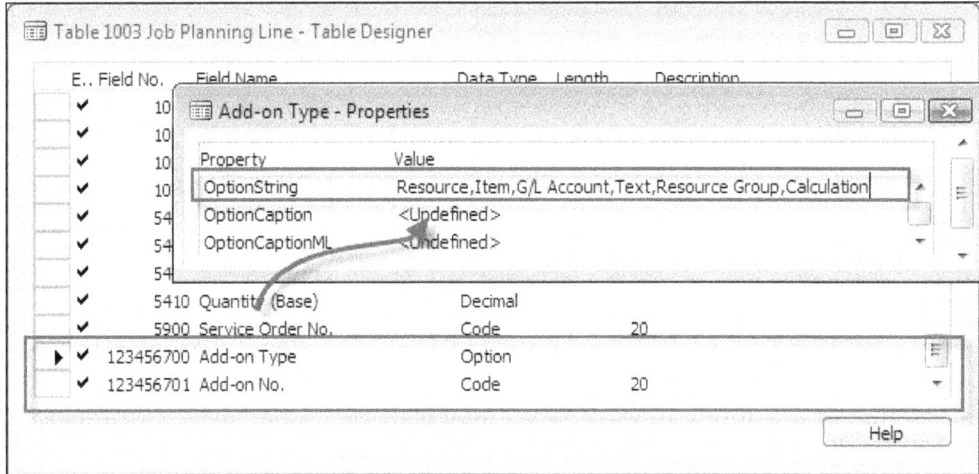

These fields replace the standard **Type** and **No.** fields on the pages allowing users to select these new options. The caption of the new fields matches the replacement fields.

```
Add-on No. - OnValidate()
CASE "Add-on Type" OF
  "Add-on Type"::Resource, "Add-on Type"::Item, "Add-on Type"::"G/L
Account", "Add-on Type"::Text:
    BEGIN
      VALIDATE(Type, "Add-on Type");
      VALIDATE("No.", "Add-on No.");
    END;
  "Add-on Type"::"Resource Group":
    BEGIN
      TESTFIELD("Line Type", "Line Type"::Schedule);
      VALIDATE(Type, Type::Text);
      VALIDATE("No.", '');
      ResGroup.GET("Add-on No.");
      Description := ResGroup.Name;
      "Resource Group No." := ResGroup."No.";
```

```
GetJob;
ResCost.SETRANGE(Type,
  ResPrice.Type::"Group(Resource)");
ResCost.SETRANGE(Code, ResGroup."No.");
IF ResCost.FINDFIRST THEN BEGIN
  "Unit Cost" := ROUND(
      CurrExchRate.ExchangeAmtLCYToFCY(
        "Currency Date","Currency Code",
        ResCost."Unit Cost","Currency Factor"),
      UnitAmountRoundingPrecision);
```

In the C/AL code, we can make sure that when users select the values available in the standard product, the normal code is executed. If a user selects a Resource Group, we execute our own business logic.

To make sure everything works as expected we use the Type Text in the background. Line Type is set to Schedule because we do not want to invoice Resource Groups, we just want them to be budgeted.

The Unit Cost and Unit Price are calculated using the Resource Cost and Resource Price tables, which support the use of Resource Groups. This is an inheritance from the previous Job functionality prior to Version 5.0.

The page Job Planning List (1007) is changed to show our add-on fields instead of the normal fields.

To completely finish this functionality, we would also need to change the reports that show the Job Planning Lines and the C/AL code that creates the Job Planning Lines when posting a Job Journal Line. This is not done in the example code for this chapter.

Calculations

Some companies using the Job functionality have a need for flexible calculations. In our example, we use it to calculate the price of a computer system but other examples are book publishers or construction companies.

They want to know what it costs to create a product without exactly knowing which screws, hinges, or color of chipboard is used. For these companies, we designed a simple but effective calculation module.

In our database, there are two example calculations: a server, and a desktop system.

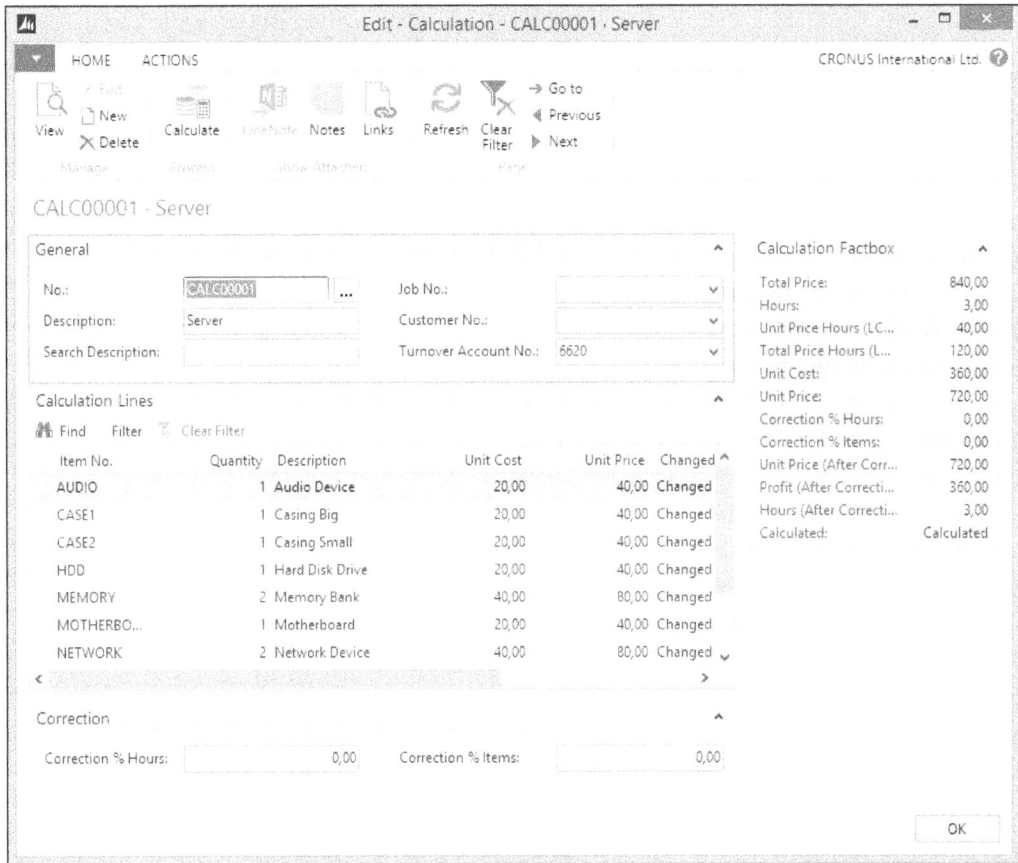

The calculation is designed using a header/line construction with a Number Series and a Line Number. The calculation lines are items.

When a new calculation is created some lines are automatically inserted. This is done in a C/AL function that is called from the OnInsert trigger.

The OnInsert trigger will also copy the default Unit Price for Hours from our setup table.

```
OnInsert()
CalcSetup.GET;

IF "No." = '' THEN BEGIN
  CalcSetup.TESTFIELD("Calculation Nos.");
```

```
    NoSeriesMgt.InitSeries(CalcSetup."Calculation Nos.",xRec."No.
Series",0D,"No.","No. Series");
END;

"Unit Price Hours (LCY)" := CalcSetup."Unit Price Hours";
InitLines;
```

The `InitLines` function creates a calculation line for each item marked as
Calculation Item. This is a new field that we added to the item table:

```
InitLines()
CalcLn.RESET;

i := 0;
Item.SETRANGE("Calculation Item", TRUE);
IF Item.FINDSET THEN REPEAT
  i += 10000;
  CalcLn."Calculation No." := "No.";
  CalcLn."Line No." := i;
  CalcLn.VALIDATE("Item No.", Item."No.");
  CalcLn.INSERT;
UNTIL Item.NEXT = 0;
```

In the calculation, we can choose how many we will use from each item and the system
will calculate the cost and price but also the required number of `Hours` that is required.
The `Unit Cost` and `Unit Price` are used from the item table. `Hours` is calculated from
a new field, and we added `Minutes` on the item table as well.

```
Calculate()
CalcLn.RESET;
CalcLn.SETRANGE("Calculation No.","No.");
CalcLn.CALCSUMS("Unit Cost", "Unit Price", Profit, Hours);
CalcLn.FIND('-');
CalcLn.MODIFYALL(Changed,Calculated::Calculated);

CalcLn.CALCSUMS("Unit Cost", "Unit Price", Hours);

"Unit Cost" := CalcLn."Unit Cost";
"Unit Price" := CalcLn."Unit Price";
Profit := "Unit Price" - "Unit Cost";
Hours := CalcLn.Hours;

Correct;
```

```
"Total Price Hours (LCY)" := "Hours (After Correction)" * "Unit Price
Hours (LCY)";
"Total Price" := "Total Price Hours (LCY)" +
  "Unit Price (After Correction)";
Calculated := Calculated::Calculated;
MODIFY;


Correct()
"Unit Price (After Correction)" := "Unit Price" + ("Unit Price" *
("Correction % Items" / 100));
"Profit (After Correction)" :=
  "Unit Price (After Correction)" - "Unit Cost";
"Hours (After Correction)" :=
  Hours + (Hours * ("Correction % Hours" / 100));
```

When we now use the `Calculate` function, the system will generate a total `Unit Cost`, `Unit Price`, and `Hours` for this product to be created. Flexibility is added to the system by allowing users to correct hours and usage with a percentage.

The calculation can be used in a Job Planning Line the same way as the Resource Groups earlier; the only difference is that we use the G/L Account type in the background to invoice a calculation fixed price. Let's look at the C/AL code in the `OnValidate` trigger of the `Add-On No.` field in the Job Planning Line:

```
Add-on No. - OnValidate()
CASE "Add-on Type" OF
  "Add-on Type"::Resource ... "Add-on Type"::Text:
    ...
  "Add-on Type"::"Resource Group":
    ...
  "Add-on Type"::Calculation:
    BEGIN
      Calc.GET("Add-on No.");
      IF Calc."Turnover Account No." = '' THEN BEGIN
        TESTFIELD("Line Type", "Line Type"::Schedule);
        VALIDATE(Type, Type::Text);
        VALIDATE("No.", '');
      END ELSE BEGIN
        TESTFIELD("Line Type",
          "Line Type"::"Both Schedule and Contract");
        VALIDATE(Type, Type::"G/L Account");
        VALIDATE("No.", Calc."Turnover Account No.");

      END;
      Description := Calc.Description;
      GetJob;
```

To complete this functionality, we will create a method to use the hours in the calculation for the Resource planning. This can be done using Job Planning Lines of line type Schedule with no unit cost and unit price.

Issue registration

For our support team, we have implemented an issue registration solution. This allows them to have a simple application where they can register issues for all customers and keep track of the status without going in and out of each job.

The issue registration is a header/line construction with a Number Series and a line number. The lines can be used to phrase questions and answers.

When a support engineer creates a new issue, the system will create the Job Task automatically. Let's have a look at the C/AL code that does that:

```
CreateJobTask()
TESTFIELD("Job No.");
TESTFIELD("Job Task No.", '');

OldJobTask.SETRANGE("Job No.", "Job No.");
OldJobTask.SETRANGE("Job Task Type",
  OldJobTask."Job Task Type"::Posting);
IF OldJobTask.ISEMPTY THEN
  OldJobTask.SETRANGE("Job Task Type",
```

```
        OldJobTask."Job Task Type"::"Begin-Total");
    OldJobTask.FINDLAST;

    JobTask."Job No." := "Job No.";
    JobTask."Job Task No." := INCSTR(OldJobTask."Job Task No.");
    JobTask.Description := Description;
    JobTask."Job Task Type" := JobTask."Job Task Type"::Posting;
    JobTask.INSERT(TRUE);
    CODEUNIT.RUN(CODEUNIT::"Job Task-Indent Direct", JobTask);

    "Job Task No." := JobTask."Job Task No.";
```

The system searches for the last `Job Task` of the type `Posting` in the Job. If that cannot be found, it searches for the last `Begin-Total` line.

Assuming this line exists, we create a new `Job Task` line using the `INCSTR` function to increment the number. The description is copied to the `Job Task`. The support engineers can now register their hours on this `Job Task`.

This piece of C/AL code is very simple but shows how effective a small solution can be without even touching any of the standard Microsoft Dynamics NAV objects. This is a very safe way of developing.

Summary

In this chapter, we have learned how to implement the Job functionality of Microsoft Dynamics NAV. We also discussed different strategies of setting up Jobs and Job Tasks.

We created several examples with different invoicing methods using the Job Planning Lines in a creative way. When purchasing items for jobs, the items are not used for costing but in the work in progress calculation we discussed in detail.

Invoicing is done automatically when everything is done as it should be done. Lastly, we designed some small enhancements for the Job module without doing big changes in the standard application. This was the last chapter about the functionality of Microsoft Dynamics NAV. We have discussed all possibilities of the application and how they should be changed without risking or breaking anything.

In the next chapter, we will look at how Microsoft Dynamics NAV can interface with other applications.

9
Interfacing

When the first version of Microsoft Dynamics NAV for Windows was released in 1995, the system was very closed. It was possible to import and export data using flat text files and that was basically it. These flat text files were placed on a floppy disk and sent by postal mail. Internet and e-mail were just coming, large USB sticks were a dream, and when the previous version of this book was released in 2009, OneDrive and Azure where being invented.

Since then, the world has changed tremendously. Internet, e-mail, SQL Server, .NET, and Azure changed the way we think about interfacing with applications and we are still changing. Today Microsoft Dynamics NAV 2013 has a completely open database and supports a wide range of interfacing possibilities, which we will learn in this chapter.

Version 1.0 of Navision ran on Windows 95, which later became an industry standard and for more than a decade, Windows was the only serious platform. Today, business people use iPads and Android tablets. Microsoft Dynamics NAV 2013 is one of few ERP platforms that can run cross-platform on all devices, even supporting login using Google or Facebook credentials.

In this chapter, we will first discuss the available interfacing technologies and the interfaces available in the standard product. Then we will talk about interfacing methodology and how to create reliable interfaces.

At the end of the chapter, we will create some sample interfaces and see how the future will further improve interfacing.

After reading this chapter, you will have a good understanding of what interfaces the product supports out of the box, what interfacing technologies to use, and how to design a solid business to business interface.

Interface types

When discussing an interface, we usually start with the technology, but before that, some other basic questions need answering, such as the following:

- Does it need to import, export, or both?
- Is it started manually or automatically?
- Is the interface timer or event driven?

Let's discuss these questions.

Import and export

The first question is whether the interface should only export data from Microsoft Dynamics NAV or whether it would also import data to the system that then needs to be processed.

When importing and exporting, the data process can be started manually by an end user using data pulling or data pushing. The interface can also be event- (real time) or timer-driven (asynchronous).

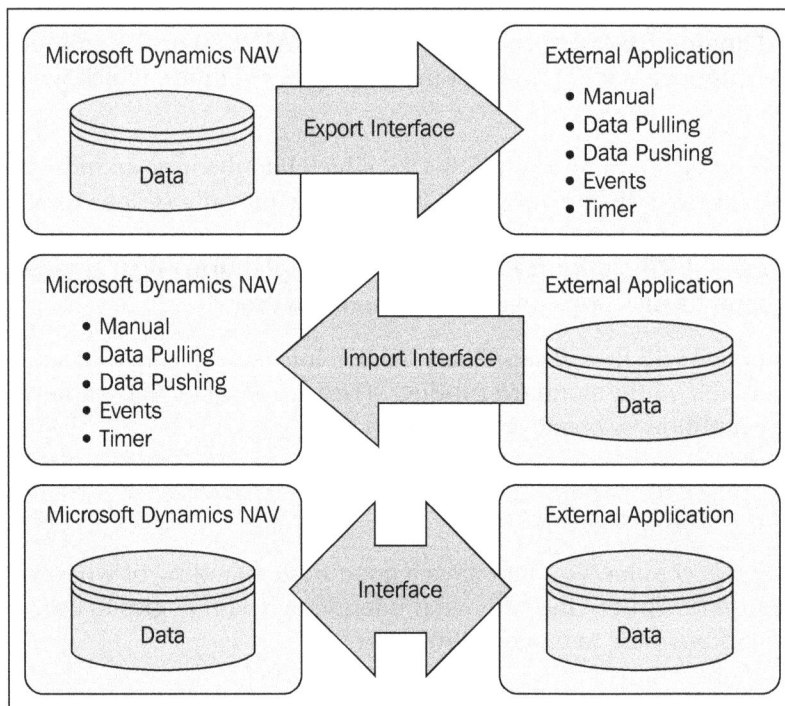

Manual

When an interface is manual, the first application has an export process and another application has an import process. The end user first manually starts the export process and then manually starts the import process in another application, usually saving the data to a flat file. This is a classic approach to interfacing.

An example of manual interfacing is exporting telebanking information from Microsoft Dynamics NAV or sending XBRL files to your accountant.

Data pulling

When using data pulling to export data, the interface is started from an external application. This application will read the data from the database and process it.

When using data pulling to import data, the interface is started from the application, which reads and processes data from another application.

Data pushing

If an interface uses data pushing, the exporting application writes the data to the other data source. This method is used when the data in the other application does not need further processing. A typical example is exporting data from Microsoft Dynamics NAV to Microsoft Office applications such as Word or Excel.

Event-driven versus timer-driven

When data pushing or data pulling is combined with the use of events or timers, there is no longer a need for end user interference. The interface will then run automatically.

We will discuss these methods in detail later in this chapter when we discuss interface methodologies.

Interfacing technologies

In Microsoft Dynamics NAV, there are a wide range of methods to interface. Each method is useful for certain types of interfacing and less useful for other types. We will discuss all available methods in the C/SIDE development platform.

File

Flat files and XML files are both supported by Microsoft Dynamics NAV. Flat files have been available since the introduction of the product in 1995 using data ports for the classic clients.

XML support was introduced in Version 3.60 as an extra option for data ports. Version 4.0 introduced the XMLPort object that replaced the data port for importing and exporting XML files.

Currently in Microsoft Dynamics NAV 2013, XMLPort objects are used both for XML and flat files. Additionally, C/AL has a FILE object that can be used to access files directly without using XMLPort objects.

Automation control

The implementation for Microsoft COM and ActiveX in Microsoft Dynamics NAV is referred to as automation control.

Automation control or ActiveX allows software applications to be reused as an embedded part of another application. Most Microsoft applications support being used in such a way. Examples are Microsoft Office, Windows Scripting Host, and **ActiveX Data Objects** (**ADO**).

Microsoft Dynamics NAV has support for automation control. Consuming automation control is done using interfaces exposing methods and properties.

The most commonly used and generic interface is iUnknown. This is also the only automation control interface supported by Microsoft Dynamics NAV. If the automation control uses other interfaces, a wrapper should be created in Visual Studio transforming the interface to iUnknown. We should also create a wrapper when the automation control needs to be embedded using a form control.

> More information about the iUnknown interface and COM technology can be found at http://en.wikipedia.org/wiki/IUnknown.

Events

Most automation controls allow data to be pushed. Using events for automation control, it is also possible to start business logic in Microsoft Dynamics NAV when something happens in the other application.

Limitations

In Microsoft Dynamics NAV 2013, automation control can only be used from the client side. All code that runs on the server side cannot use automation control objects.

DotNet interoperability

The support of .NET was introduced as a replacement for automation control. It is possible to use a wide range of .NET objects directly in C/AL programming language. They can be used in both server side and client side.

Within the standard application, most automation interfaces are replaced with .NET interfaces such as the Excel interface, which we will discuss later in this chapter.

There are limitations using .NET in Microsoft Dynamics NAV, which are typically solved by creating wrapper DLL objects in C#. The Excel interface is an example of that too.

> A good place to start learning about .NET in C/AL is www.vjeko.com. The limitations are discussed at http://vjeko.com/blog/top-10-things-i-miss-in-net-interoperability-in-nav-2013.

Client extensibility

Using the page objects, the level of allowed creativity in the user interface is very limited since the page objects do not provide WYSIWYG capabilities or allow the developer to determine control positions. Each client determines how the UI is rendered and the developer has no control. This is solved using client extensibility. This technology allows using all UI capabilities that Visual Studio and .NET offer, however, when developing for cross-platform, JavaScript should be used.

> Refer to https://www.youtube.com/watch?v=WErBd1mlZFM to learn how to get started with JavaScript add-ins for Microsoft Dynamics NAV.

Open Database Connectivity (ODBC)/ADO

Open Database Connectivity (ODBC) was developed in 1992 with the goal of allowing all types of databases to exchange data in a unified way. ADO is the successor of ODBC and was developed in 1996.

ADO and ODBC for Microsoft Dynamics NAV allows both reading and writing in the application database as well as reading and writing to other databases.

> Using ADO and ODBC more advanced requires basic knowledge of T-SQL Statements. Refer to http://www.differencebetween.com/difference-between-odbc-and-vs-ado/ for the differences between ADO and ODBC.

Reading from Microsoft Dynamics NAV

To read data from the database, you only need to have a valid ODBC driver installed on the Windows machine that you are using and credentials to log in to the database.

Let's create an example to import data from Microsoft Dynamics NAV using Excel.

1. Open Microsoft Excel and select **Data** and then select **From SQL Server** form **From Other Sources**, as shown in the following screenshot:

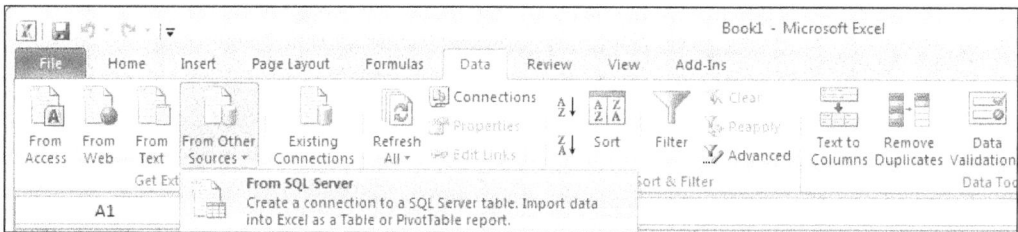

From SQL Server

2. Select a **Server name** and valid **Credentials**:

3. Select a database and the table that you want to view. In our example, we will select the **Customer** table. Then select **Finish** and **OK**.

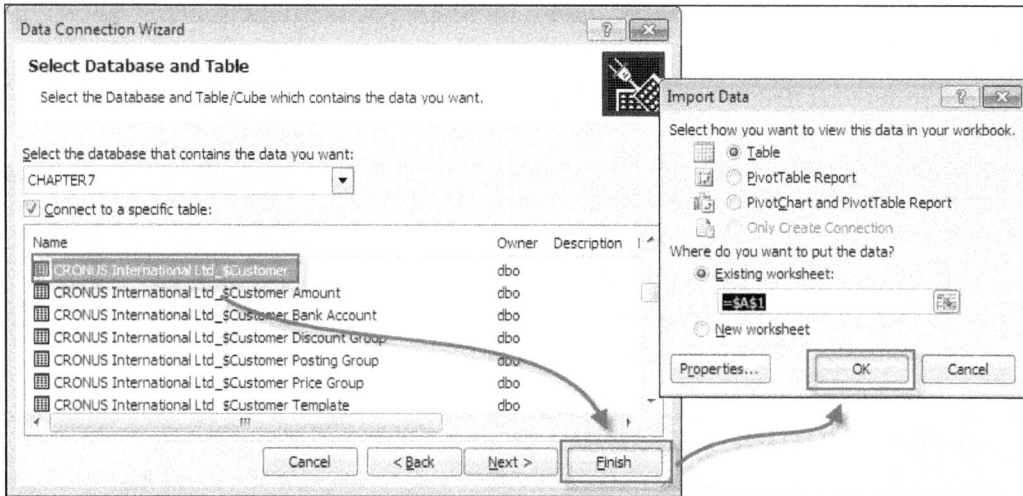

4. We now have the Microsoft Dynamics NAV Data in Excel.

Since flow fields are not actual fields in the SQL Server database, we cannot use them in ODBC/ADO.

Writing to Microsoft Dynamics NAV

Directly writing data to the Microsoft Dynamics NAV database using ODBC is not recommended as best practice. The reason for this is the missing business logic at this interface level.

When writing via ODBC, we directly address SQL Server without allowing the C/AL business logic to validate the data we create. The C/AL data normally ensures data integrity for the business rules we develop. The same applies when using the C/ODBC driver for the native database.

> To work around this issue, the data can be saved in a special interface buffer table and processed by a C/AL transaction using an application server or started from the user interface.

Talking to other databases

To use ODBC to read and write data from Microsoft Dynamics NAV to other databases, it is recommended to use **ActiveX Data Objects (ADO)**. ADO is a Microsoft technology that allows using an ActiveX interface to connect using ODBC. Using ADO allows us to both read and write to the database on the other end.

We could even use ADO to connect to the Microsoft Dynamics NAV SQL Server database and run SQL Statements from C/AL code.

> We will use ADO in the interface methodology section of this chapter.

SQL Server interfacing

Since Microsoft Dynamics NAV runs on top of a SQL Server database, we can use all available technologies in SQL Server to get data in and out. This offers a wide range of options that go beyond the scope of this book, but let's briefly discuss some of them:

- **Linked Servers**: In SQL Server, it is possible to set up linked servers. This allows us to send queries to other databases such as other SQL Servers, MS Access, or Oracle and create views based on this data.

- **Views**: A view in SQL Server is a saved query with a fixed result set that can be interpreted as a table. In C/Side, we can use a view as a data source for a table using the Linked Object property and create a page or report based on this data source.

- **SQL Server Integration Services**: This replaces DTS Packages as the primary component for SQL Server to integrate with other databases. Using SSIS requires good knowledge and skills of both SQL Server and Microsoft Dynamics NAV.

- **Reporting Services**: This is a server-based reporting platform that can be integrated with SharePoint allowing users to design RDL reports based on T-SQL queries.

- **Analysis Services**: This is Microsoft's answer to the OLAP, BI, and data mining requirements of their customers.

> Another SQL Server component we can use is the SQL Server Agent. This component allows us to schedule interface tasks that run directly on the database.

Microsoft Message Queue

Microsoft Message Queue (**MSMQ**) allows applications to integrate that run asynchronously with an unreliable connection. This interfacing technology is very popular for websites that use information from Microsoft Dynamics NAV and send information back to the database.

The introduction of .NET Interoperability made using MSMQ in combination with Microsoft Dynamics NAV much easier. Using `System.Messaging.MessageQueue` only a few lines of C/AL code are required to post a message on a queue.

Application server

MSMQ is always combined with using an application server to handle the requests sent back by the website.

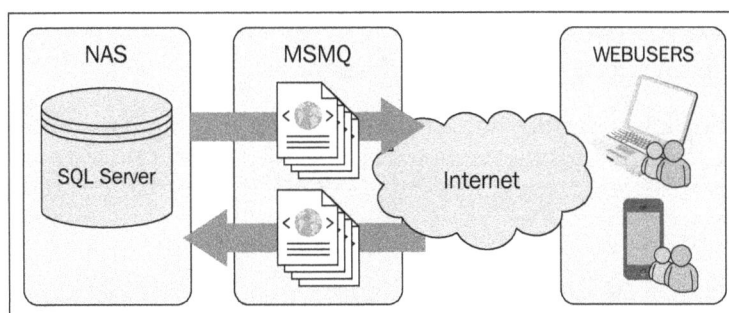

The web users can be employees from the company using a web solution for timesheet registration or a PDA or customers using a web shop.

> This blog entry at `http://mibuso.com/blogs/ara3n/2011/01/10/using-ado-on-rtc-in-nav/` explains how to get started with MSMQ using .NET.

Web services

When it comes to real-time interfacing, web services is the first technology of choice. Web services allows you to use function libraries from applications inside other applications.

Microsoft Dynamics NAV 2013 allows you to expose all C/AL code as a web service using SOAP and OData protocols.

Consuming web services is a lot more difficult than exposing one. There is no standard framework of doing so. The two most commonly used solutions are consuming using XMLDOM .NET interop objects or wrapping the web service inside a Visual Studio `.dll` using service references.

Exposing a NAV web service

In Microsoft Dynamics NAV 2013, every `Page` object and most codeunits can be exposed as a web service. This can be done using the **Web Service Table (2000000076)**.

Web Services ▾						
Object Type ▲	Object ID	Object Name	Service N... ▲	Published	OData URL	SOAP URL
Codeunit	5313	Outlook Synch. Dispatcher	Outlook	✓	Not applicable	http://MARK-PC1:7047/DynamicsNAV71/WS/CRONUS%20International%20Ltd./Codeunit/Outlook

To publish a web service, select the object type and object ID and find a unique service name. Then select the **Published** checkmark.

When publishing a web service, the URL is displayed making it easier to find it.

Consuming a Microsoft Dynamics NAV web service

To consume the web service, an address, `http://<Server>:<WebServicePort>/<ServerInstance>/WS/<CompanyName>/`, is generated that is called from the other application.

> The `SystemService` web service is always available and returns a list of available company names.

Standard application interfaces

We discussed all the available interface technologies for Microsoft Dynamics NAV. Let's have a look at how this has been implemented in the standard product.

In this book, we will not explore each interface in depth since that would almost require another book. We will just briefly discuss where to find all technologies we discussed in the standard application and indicate where a white paper or website can be found.

An example of flat file is Exporting Contacts. Microsoft Dynamics NAV allows us to export our contacts using an **XMLPort**.

The **XMLPort** for this functionality has number (5050) and uses the Format Variable Text. Other options are **Xml** and **Fixed Text**, as shown in the following screenshot:

XMLPorts have a node structure like pages. The **XMLPort** starts with integer table as the first data type followed by the **Contact table** fields.

> More information about programming **XMLPorts** can be found in *Programming Dynamics NAV 2013, David A. Studebaker, Christopher D. Studebaker, Packt Publishing.*

Office integration

Microsoft Dynamics NAV and Microsoft Office are integrated to use with Word, Excel, and Outlook. We will first discuss the standard Word and Excel integration and discuss alternatives later. Lastly, we will briefly discuss the possibilities for Outlook integration.

Word and Excel integration

In Microsoft Dynamics NAV, each form or page can be exported to Word and Excel. This built-in technology is automatically provided by the user interface and requires no effort from developers.

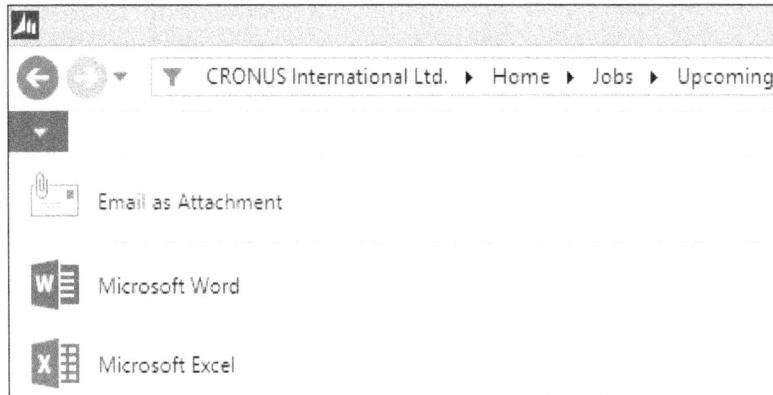

Default presence of Excel and Word

Style sheet tool

To be more flexible in the layout, Microsoft has released a style sheet tool for Microsoft Dynamics NAV and Word. This tool allows users to easily generate style sheets.

> The style sheet tool Version 3.0 can be downloaded from http://www.mibuso.com/dlinfo.asp?FileID=1543.

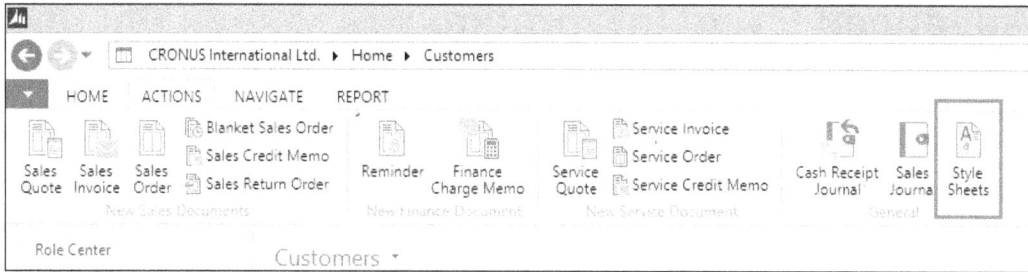

The manual provided with the style sheet tool gives a good description about how to create the style sheets.

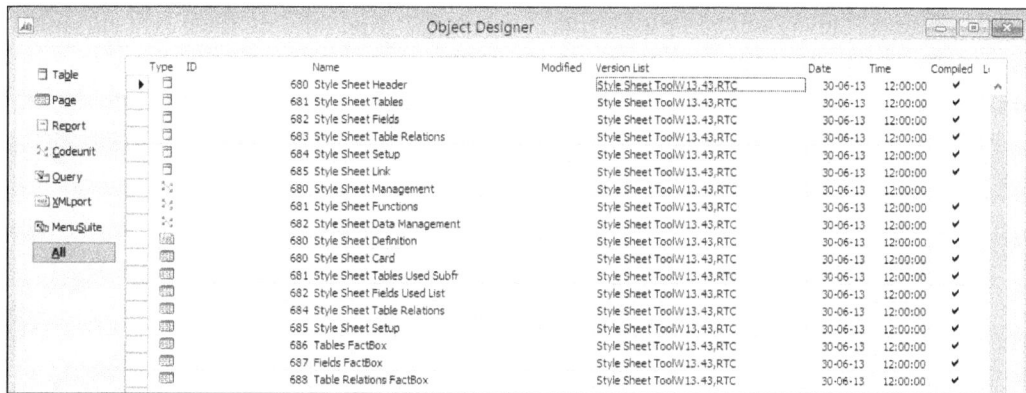

Add the action to the action designer (under the appropriate group) with the following properties:

Expanded	Type	SubType	Name	Caption
0	Action		<Action680>	Style Sheets

The OnAction trigger should contain the following line:

```
StyleSheetDataMgt.LoadStylesheetDataRTC(GETPOSITION,
    CURRENTKEY,PAGE::"<<PageName>>");
```

Here, StyleSheetDataMgt is a variable of type codeunit, 682 (Style Sheet Data Management).

> When this action is done for one page, it can be easily copied and pasted to other pages. Make sure you change the page name.

Advanced Excel integration

When exporting information to Excel that needs to be combined from different parts of the application, using style sheets is not the ideal way.

To support this, the **Excel Buffer** table (370) can be used. This table can be populated with data and then sent to Excel using a simple C/AL command.

This is used in several parts of the application, for example, to import and export the budgets we discussed in *Chapter 3, Financial Management*.

Let's create a sample codeunit that exports data to Excel using the Excel Buffer table:

1. Create a new codeunit and define a global variable of type record Excel buffer. This needs to be a temporary variable. Also, define the other variables as displayed in the following screenshot:

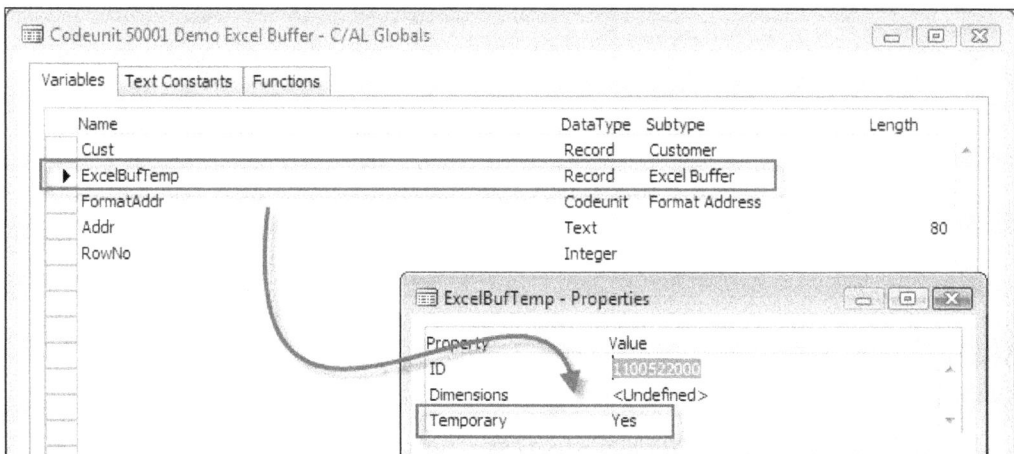

> Temporary record variables are not stored in the database; they're stored in the client memory. This allows multiple users to create the same records without blocking each other. It is also faster since all handling is done without the network and database.

2. Create a new `EnterCell` function with the parameters displayed in the following screenshot:

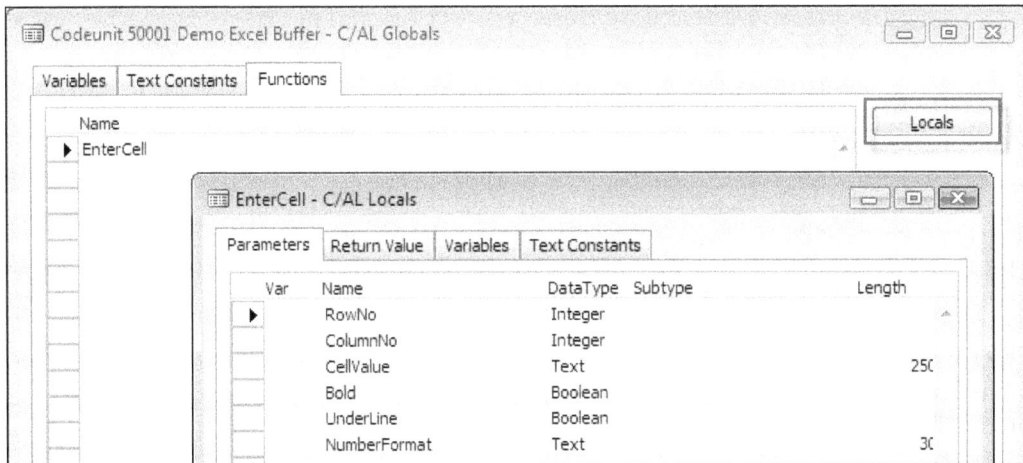

3. Put the C/AL code in place that will handle the interface:

```
OnRun()
ExcelBufTemp.CreateBook(Cust.TABLECAPTION);

Cust.FIND('-');
REPEAT
  RowNo := RowNo + 1;
  EnterCell(RowNo, 1, Cust."No.", FALSE, FALSE, '');

  FormAddr.Customer(Addr, Cust);
  EnterCell(RowNo, 2, Addr[1], FALSE, FALSE, '');
  EnterCell(RowNo, 3, Addr[2], FALSE, FALSE, '');
  EnterCell(RowNo, 4, Addr[3], FALSE, FALSE, '');
  EnterCell(RowNo, 5, Addr[4], FALSE, FALSE, '');
  EnterCell(RowNo, 6, Addr[5], FALSE, FALSE, '');
  EnterCell(RowNo, 7, Addr[6], FALSE, FALSE, '');
  EnterCell(RowNo, 8, Addr[7], FALSE, FALSE, '');
  EnterCell(RowNo, 9, Addr[8], FALSE, FALSE, '');

UNTIL Cust.NEXT = 0;

ExcelBufTemp.WriteSheet(Cust.TABLECAPTION,COMPANYNAME,USERID);
ExcelBufTemp.CloseBook;
ExcelBufTemp.OpenExcel;
ExcelBufTemp.GiveUserControl;
```

```
EnterCell()
ExcelBufTemp.INIT;
ExcelBufTemp.VALIDATE("Row No.",RowNo);
ExcelBufTemp.VALIDATE("Column No.",ColumnNo);
ExcelBufTemp."Cell Value as Text" := CellValue;
ExcelBufTemp.Formula := '';
ExcelBufTemp.Bold := Bold;
ExcelBufTemp.Underline := UnderLine;
ExcelBufTemp.NumberFormat := NumberFormat;
ExcelBufTemp.INSERT;
```

This C/AL code will browse the customers in the database and format the addresses using the Address Format (365) codeunit.

The **Customer No.** field and the result array `Addr[]` are saved in the Excel buffer table. Lastly, we start the C/AL functions to generate the Excel spreadsheet based on the data.

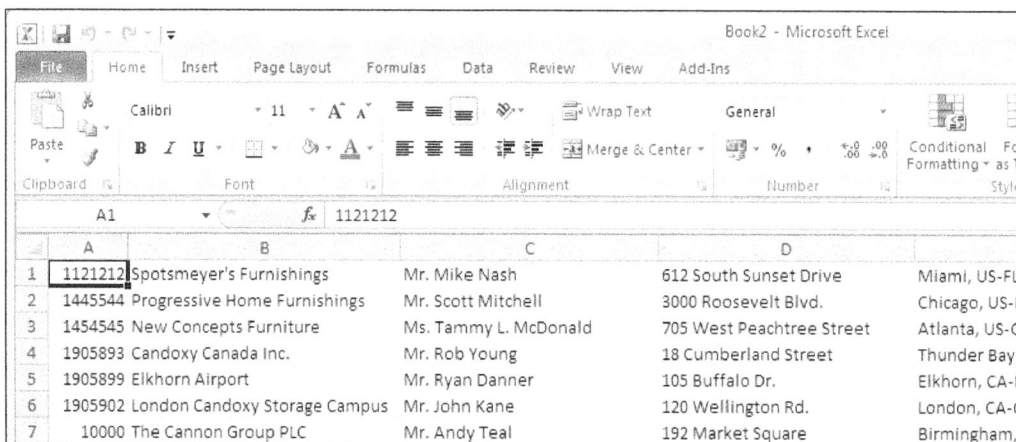

	A	B	C	D	
1	1121212	Spotsmeyer's Furnishings	Mr. Mike Nash	612 South Sunset Drive	Miami, US-FL
2	1445544	Progressive Home Furnishings	Mr. Scott Mitchell	3000 Roosevelt Blvd.	Chicago, US-I
3	1454545	New Concepts Furniture	Ms. Tammy L. McDonald	705 West Peachtree Street	Atlanta, US-G
4	1905893	Candoxy Canada Inc.	Mr. Rob Young	18 Cumberland Street	Thunder Bay,
5	1905899	Elkhorn Airport	Mr. Ryan Danner	105 Buffalo Dr.	Elkhorn, CA-N
6	1905902	London Candoxy Storage Campus	Mr. John Kane	120 Wellington Rd.	London, CA-C
7	10000	The Cannon Group PLC	Mr. Andy Teal	192 Market Square	Birmingham,

C/AL functions result

Outlook integration

Microsoft Dynamics NAV 2013 allows different levels of interfacing with
Microsoft Outlook:

1. The Outlook part on the Role Center.
2. Sending e-mails from pages using the `ExtendedDatatype` property.
3. Using the Mail (397) or SMTP Mail (400) codeunits to send e-mails.
4. Synchronize contacts and to-do's using the Outlook integration web service.
5. Reading e-mail from exchange using the **E-Mail – Logging** functionality.
6. Microsoft Dynamics NAV 2013 R2 can be connected to Office 365.

Outlook part

On a Role Center it is possible to activate the Outlook System Part. This allows users
to see their e-mail, agenda, and tasks directly on the Role Center.

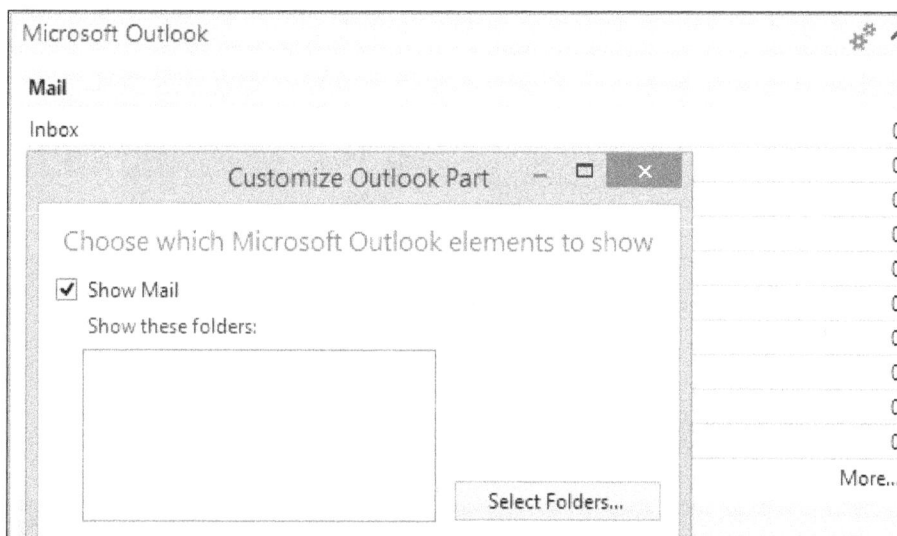

This functionality is built in the Windows client and cannot be changed using
C/AL Code.

ExtendedDatatype property

When a **Text** field in a table uses the `ExtendedDatatype` property, **E-Mail** the Windows client will automatically allow the users to directly send an e-mail to the address specified in the field.

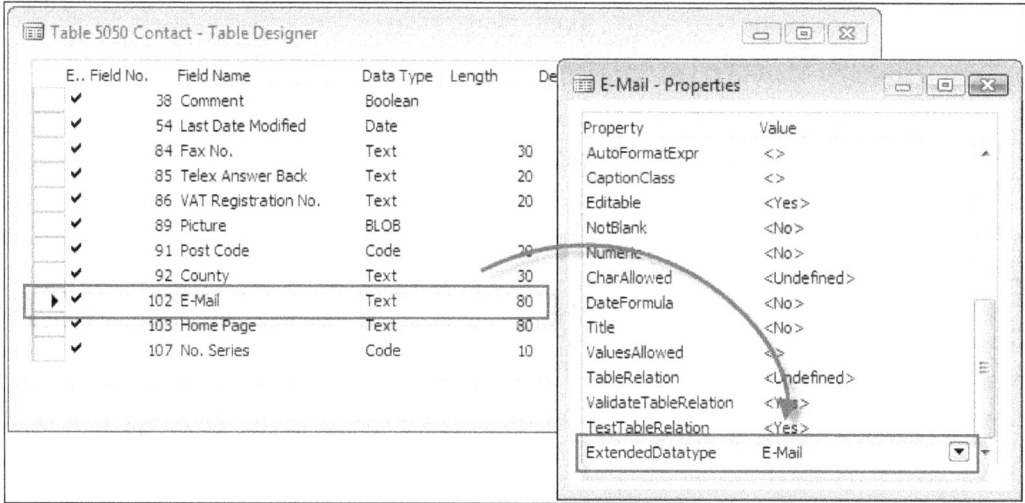

This is also built-in functionality in the Windows client that cannot be influenced by C/AL code.

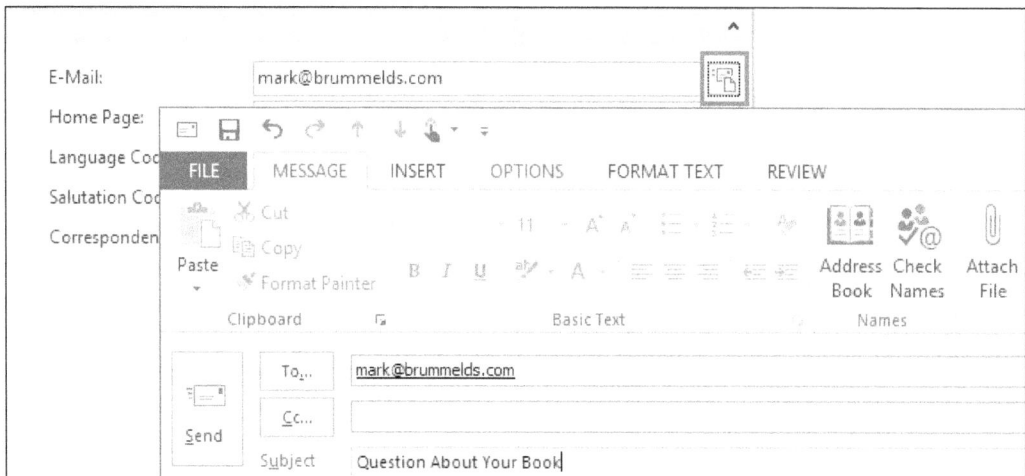

Mail and SMTP mail codeunits

Before the introduction of the `ExtendedDatatype` property, the e-mails from Microsoft Dynamics NAV were sent using an Automation Control wrapper DLL to Microsoft Outlook. This is handled in codeunit 397 and can still be used to send e-mails directly From C/AL code.

Codeunit SMTP Mail (400) allows us to send e-mails directly to an SMTP server.

Outlook synchronization

Microsoft Outlook can be used as an offline client for Microsoft Dynamics NAV. Every table can be synchronized to Microsoft Outlook when a connection with both systems is available. Using the Offline functionality in Outlook, users can view the data when they are on the road and even change the information or create new data.

This is done using the Outlook Synchronization web service that we discussed earlier this chapter.

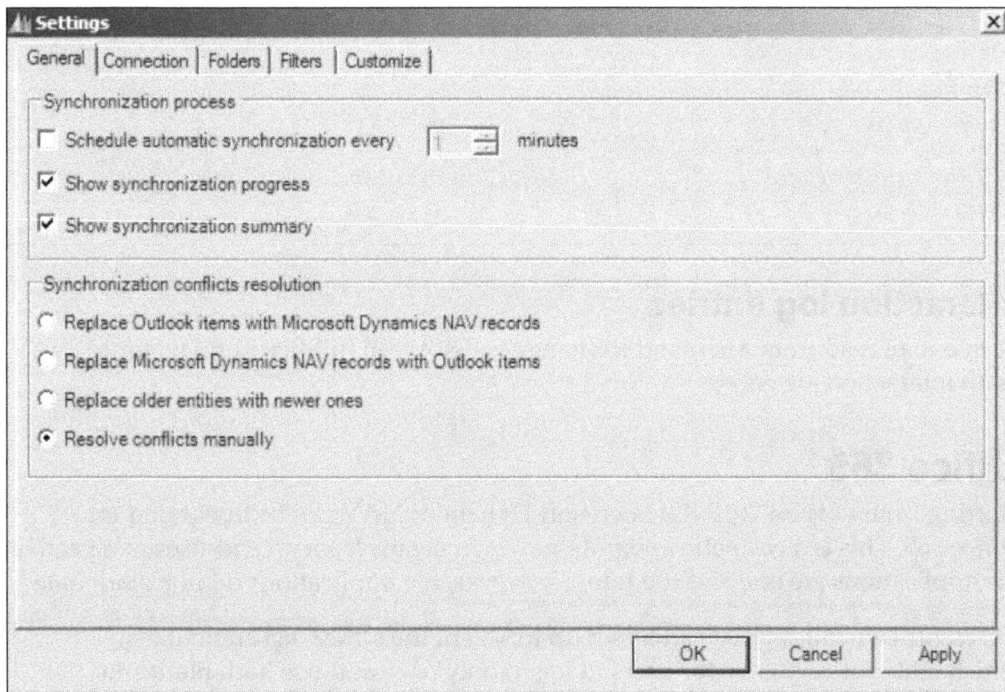

The functionality is well documented by Microsoft.

Exchange integration

To read incoming e-mails, Microsoft Dynamics NAV offers integration with Exchange Public folders. Information in these mailboxes can be read and used in Microsoft Dynamics NAV.

The handling of the interface is done using the Job Queue and the Application Server (NAS).

In the **Marketing Setup**, which we discussed in *Chapter 4, Relationship Management*, we can set up the parameters for the exchange integration.

Marketing Setup		
General		˅
Inheritance		˅
Defaults		˅
Interactions		˅
Synchronization		˅
Numbering		˅
Duplicates		˅
E-Mail Logging		˄
Autodiscovery E-Mail Address:	Queue Folder Path:	...
Email Batch Size: 0	Storage Folder Path:	...

Interaction log entries

Each e-mail read from Microsoft Exchange is displayed in Microsoft Dynamics NAV as an interaction log entry.

Office 365

Starting from version 2013 R2, Microsoft Dynamics NAV can be integrated into Office 365. This is a cosmetic integration, which means from an end-user perspective the applications are one and the same; however, the applications do not share data.

Microsoft Dynamics NAV can be set up to accept the Office 365 credentials, which makes it very easy for users to log in only once and use both platforms.

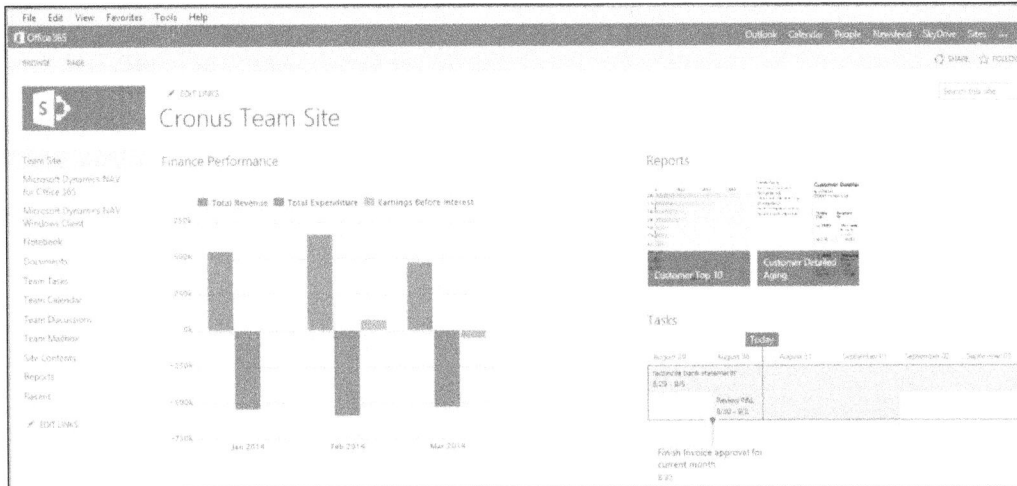

Login with the Office 365 credentials

SharePoint

Microsoft Dynamics NAV 2013 RTM was shipped with a special SharePoint client. However, since this was directly discontinued in R2 we will not discuss this.

In Microsoft Dynamics NAV 2013 R2, the web client is SharePoint-compliant. To use Microsoft Dynamics NAV 2013 R2 in combination with SharePoint, it is possible to add web parts that connect to the web client.

It is possible to connect to both the on premise version of SharePoint and SharePoint Online.

Client add-ins

Microsoft Dynamics NAV 2013 ships with one client add-in for Microsoft Connect. An example page object that uses the Connect control is Connect (9175).

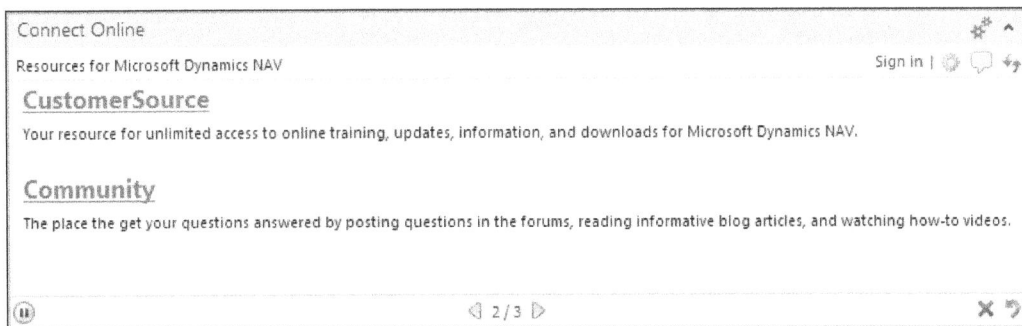

Let's have a look at how this done.

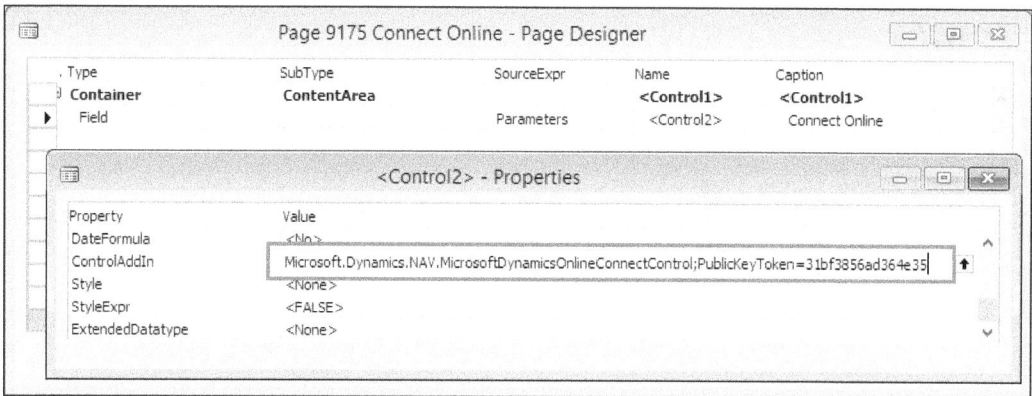

The page type of this page is **CardPart** and it has no source table. The only control on the page is **Parameters**, which is a function with a Text (350) return value.

The `ControlAddIn` property points to the add-in that will be used when this page is started. This add-in will replace the original control on the page.

In the `Parameters` function, a string is created to feed information into the connect add-in enabling it to show information that is interesting for the current role. This is done using a combination of other C/AL functions:

```
Parameters()
InitCurrentRoleValues;

EXIT(Add(Version) + Add(Locale) + Add(Role) + Add(RoleID) +
  Add(Serial));


Add()
EXIT(Parameter + Separator);


Version()
EXIT('version=' + FORMAT(ApplicationManagement.ApplicationVersion +
':' +
  ApplicationManagement.ApplicationBuild,0,XMLFormat));


Locale()
// Windows Language ID
EXIT('locale=' + FORMAT(CurrentLanguageID,0,XMLFormat));

Role()
// Profile ID (Any text entered in Profile ID)
```

```
EXIT('role=' + FORMAT(DELCHR(CurrentRole,'=',Separator),0,
  XMLFormat));
```

RoleID()
```
// Role Center ID (Page ID)
EXIT('roleid=' + FORMAT(CurrentRoleID,0,XMLFormat));
```

Serial()
```
// License ID
EXIT('serial=' + FORMAT(SERIALNUMBER,0,XMLFormat));
```

Separator()
```
EXIT(';');
```

XMLFormat()
```
EXIT(9);
```

InitCurrentRoleValues()
```
CurrentLanguageID := GLOBALLANGUAGE;
CurrentRoleID := ApplicationManagement.DefaultRoleCenter;
CurrentRole := FORMAT(CurrentRoleID);
...
```

In *Chapter 7, Storage and Logistics,* Client Extensibility and Bing Maps are used to show the stops of a route on a map.

The available libraries are stored in the client add-in table (2000000069).

Interface methodologies

So now we have discussed interface types, interface technologies, and the built-in interfaces in Microsoft Dynamics NAV.

Let's design and develop a new business to business interface. We will use the objects from *Chapter 7, Storage and Logistics,* to create the interface.

The scenario

One of our customers wants to e-mail the shipments from now on instead of faxing. The e-mail will contain an Excel file in a predefined format.

Interfacing

The design

Let's bring back the data model we designed for the logistics part of the solution in *Chapter 7, Storage and Logistics*.

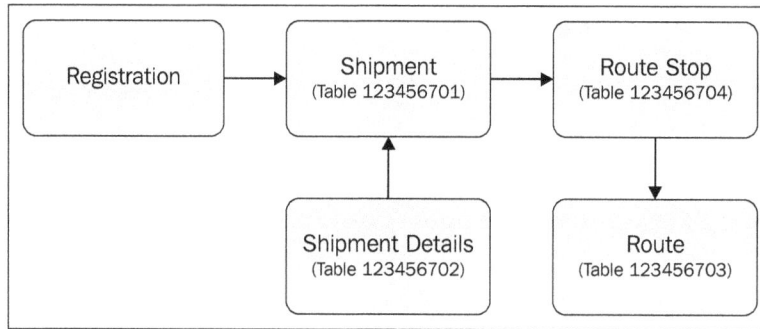

The process starts in the registration table. From a registration, we generate shipments and shipments are combined into a Route with stops.

So we need to move the data from the Excel sheet to the registration table.

The mapping

When a customer delivers us an Excel sheet with information, it seldom happens that they exactly use the same fields as our table. Therefore, we need to create a mapping. Each field in the Excel sheet needs to be mapped to a field and missing fields need to be identified and discussed.

The Excel Sheet we get from the customer looks like this:

	A	B	C	D	E	F	G	H	I	J	K	L
1	Goods Code	Description	Date	Pallets	Length	Width	Height	Weight	Delivery At	Address	Postal Code	City
2	LS1029	Loud Speaker LS 1029	10-1-2010	10	100	20	40	1000	Mr. Mark Brummel	Duivenlaan 6	7331 AS	Apeldoorn

[400]

Field number	Field name	Data type	Length	Mapped field
1	Registration Batch	Code	10	-
2	Line No.	Integer		-
6	Shipment Date	Date		Date
8	Product No.	Code	20	Goods Code
10	Description	Text	50	Description
12	Unit of Measure	Text	10	-
16	Quantity	Decimal		Pallets
20	Length	Decimal		Length
21	Width	Decimal		Width
22	Height	Decimal		Height
31	Gross Weight	Decimal		-
32	Net Weight	Decimal		Weight
36	Units per Parcel	Decimal		-
37	Unit Volume	Decimal		-
53	Ship-to Name	Text	50	Delivery At
55	Ship-to Address	Text	50	Address
57	Ship-to City	Text	30	City
58	Ship-to Contact	Text	50	-
59	Ship-to Post Code	Code	20	Postal Code
60	Ship-to County	Text	30	-
61	Ship-to Country/Region Code	Code	10	-

Most of the fields in the Excel sheet can be mapped to a field in our table.

The gaps

Some fields that are needed in NAV are not populated by the Excel sheet. For some fields this is okay, for example, the **Registration Batch** and **Line No.** fields are determined by the import.

Some other fields are more difficult. **Unit of Measure**, **Gross Weight**, **Units per Parcel**, and **Unit Volume** are left blank in the Excel sheet, but they are all needed in NAV.

For these fields, we need to come to an agreement with the customer. They need to either specify these fields or tell us whether they have default values. Let's look at our gaps and fill them in:

- **Unit of Measure**: For this customer it is always "PALLET"
- **Volume**: This can be calculated using `Length x Width x Height`
- **Gross Weight**: We agree that this is equal to net weight
- **Units per Parcel**: This is always 1

What if it does not work

Reading the external data into the database is just one step in creating a reliable interface.

But what happens if the customer contacts us and says, "We sent you a file with 10 lines and the shipment document shows 9 lines". When we check our database the shipment does show 9 lines, but there is no way to check whether we imported the original 10 lines. At this stage, the imported Registration lines are deleted and the shipments are generated.

If this happens, we need traceability. In a well-designed interface, we should always create a table that exactly matches the imported data. This allows us to first check whether everything matches.

The data from this table can be processed but should not be deleted from the database and periodically cleaned up. This allows us to check whether things go wrong.

We will demonstrate this in a more advanced example.

The scenario

The implementation of our storage and logistics add-on requires a real-time interface with a Radio Frequency application. The RF scanners are used for the pick process. The RF application uses its own database system with tables we should populate and read afterwards.

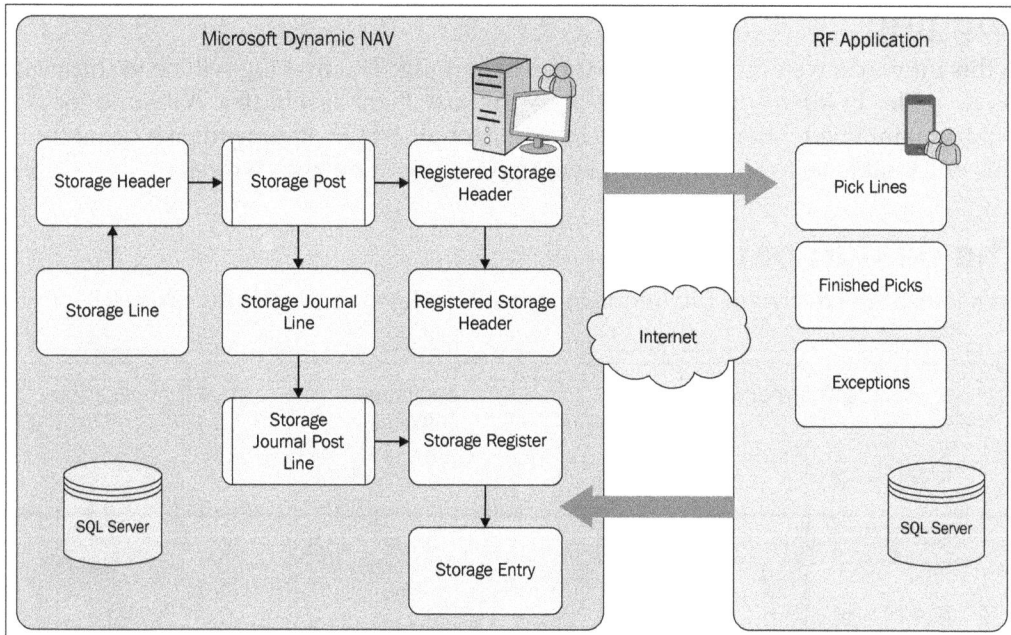

The RF application has three tables. Our interface needs to export data to the **Pick Lines** table, and it needs to import data from the two remaining tables, **Finished Picks** and **Exceptions**.

The interface type

This is an import and export interface that will use data pushing for the Pick Lines and data pulling for the Finished Picks and Exceptions. The interface will be timer-driven. Every minute we will poll for new data.

The interface technology

For this interface, we will use a combination of technologies that we discussed in this chapter. The main technology is DotNet interoperability.

Active data objects

The Picking database runs on SQL Server so we will use ADO to connect to the database and send T-SQL Statements to read and write data.

Logging

In this interface, we will enable two types of logging. The first log will be to duplicate the RF tables in Microsoft Dynamics NAV and use them as a buffer. A second log will be maintained where we will save a copy of all T-SQL statements we generate. This will enable us to see what we generated if something goes wrong.

The design pattern

Let's look at the design of the interface we will be developing for this project:

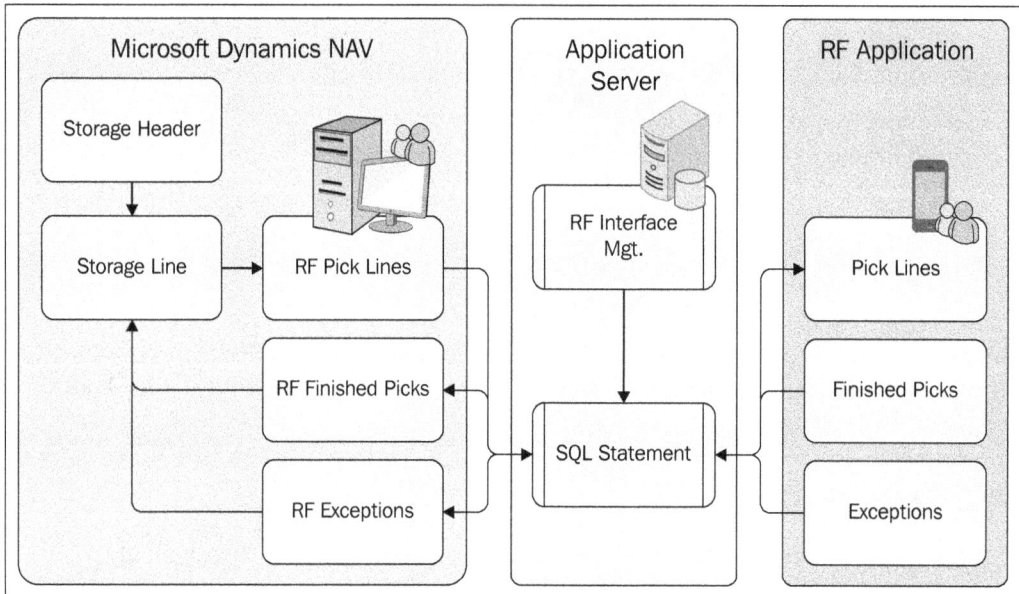

The interface will be controlled from an **Application Server**. Each minute it will execute a codeunit that checks whether there are new **Storage Lines** that need to be exported. These lines will first be moved to the **RF Pick Lines** buffer table and then moved to the RF database using ADO and T-SQL. **New Finished Picks** and **Exceptions** from the RF database will be moved to Microsoft Dynamics NAV using the same technology and can then be processed.

The solution

To run the interface, we have created three codeunits and a table. The SQL Statement table is used to log each interface session.

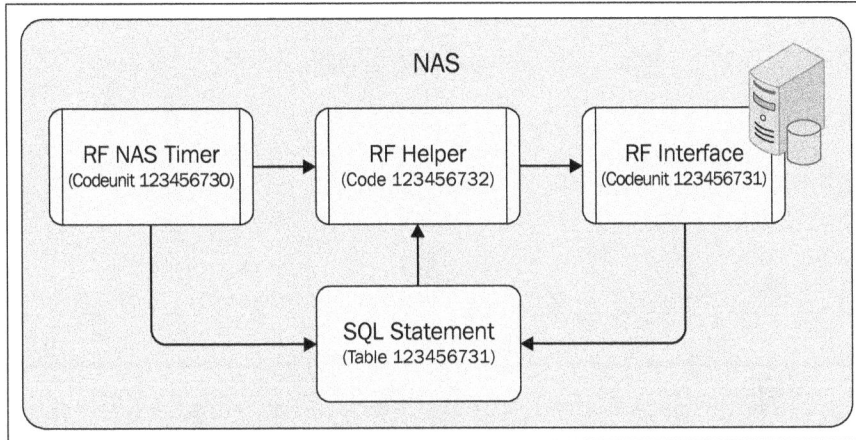

The **RF NAS Timer (123.456.730)** codeunit is started from the `NASHandler` function in codeunit `ApplicationManagement`. It uses an indefinite loop.

Let's look at the C/AL code that is required to make this work:

```
OnRun()

RFInt.CreateConnectionString;
RFLoop(600000);

RFLoop(MilisecondsBetweenPolls : Integer)
WHILE TRUE DO BEGIN
  IF NOT CODEUNIT.RUN(CODEUNIT::"RF Helper") THEN
    ParseError;
  COMMIT;
  MaxMilisecondsSleep := 10000;
  FOR Count := 1 TO MilisecondsBetweenPolls DIV MaxMilisecondsSleep DO
    SLEEP(MaxMilisecondsSleep);
```

```
      SLEEP(MilisecondsBetweenPolls MOD MaxMilisecondsSleep);
END;


ParseError()
SELECTLATESTVERSION;
RFIntSetup.GET;
SynchID := RFIntSetup."Synchronization ID";

SQLStat.INIT;
SQLStat."SQL Statement 1" := 'ERROR : ' + GETLASTERRORTEXT;

SQLStat.Bold := TRUE;
SQLStat.SessionID := SynchID;
SQLStat.Type := SQLStat.Type::Error;
SQLStat.INSERT(TRUE);
COMMIT;
```

The SLEEP function is used to make sure the interface only runs each minute. By breaking the SLEEP function into smaller intervals it is possible to stop the Windows Service that executes this C/AL code in between the SLEEP command.

> GETLASTERRORTEXT is a C/AL function that returns the last error message that was generated by the system. It can be used in combination with IF CODEUNIT.RUN syntax to catch runtime errors.

The RF Helper (123.456.732) codeunit is a wrapper codeunit that is used for error catching and maintaining readability.

During each run of the interface we create a new SQL Statement ID, which we can filter on to trace any errors:

```
OnRun()
SELECTLATESTVERSION;
RFIntSetup.GET;
RFIntSetup."Synchronisation ID" := RFIntSetup."Synchronisation ID" +
1;
RFIntSetup.MODIFY;
SynchID := RFIntSetup."Synchronisation ID";

SQLStat.INIT;
SQLStat."SQL Statement 1" :=
  '-SYNCHRONISATION STARTED- ID = ' + FORMAT(SynchID) + ' -';
SQLStat.Bold := TRUE;
```

```
SQLStat.SessionID := SynchID;
SQLStat.Type := SQLStat.Type::StartStop;
SQLStat.INSERT(TRUE);

COMMIT;

CLEAR(RFInterface);
RFInterface.SetSynchID(SynchID);

StorageLn.LOCKTABLE;
IF StorageLn.FINDSET THEN REPEAT
  RFInterface.CreatePickLines(StorageLn);
UNTIL StorageLn.NEXT = 0;

COMMIT;

CLEAR(RFInterface);
RFInterface.SetSynchID(SynchID);
RFInterface.ReadFinishedPicks;

COMMIT;

CLEAR(RFInterface);
RFInterface.SetSynchID(SynchID);
RFInterface.ReadExceptions;

COMMIT;

SQLStat.INIT;
SQLStat."SQL Statement 1" :=
  '-SYNCHRONISATION STOPPED- ID = ' + FORMAT(SynchID) + ' -';
SQLStat.Bold := TRUE;
SQLStat.SessionID := SynchID;
SQLStat.Type := SQLStat.Type::StartStop;
SQLStat.INSERT(TRUE);

COMMIT;
```

Then the three interface functions are triggered to synchronize the three required tables.

COMMIT

After each command we execute the COMMIT statement. This will make sure that everything in the database is stored up to that point. This is necessary since the ADO statements we create are outside our transaction. If our interface run rolls back, it might synchronize data that is already synchronized.

The **RF Interface (123.456.731)**. Here, the actual ADO synchronization is done in this codeunit. This codeunit is SingleInstance. This will keep the ADO connection alive during the NAS session:

```
CreateConnectionString()
IF ConnActive THEN EXIT;


RFIntSetup.GET;
Database := RFIntSetup."Database Name";
Server := RFIntSetup."Server Name";

ConnString := 'Data Source=' + Server + ';' + 'Initial Catalog=' +
Database + ';Trusted_Connection=True;';

SaveReadSQL('Connection ' + ConnString + ' opened on ' + FORMAT(CURREN
TDATETIME),TRUE,0,0,0, '');

SQLCon := SQLCon.SqlConnection(ConnString);

SQLCon.Open;
ConnActive := TRUE;

CloseConnectionString()
SQLCon.Close;

SaveReadSQL('Connection closed on ' + FORMAT(CURRENTDATETIME),TR
UE,0,0,1, '');

CLEAR(SQLReader);
CLEAR(SQLCommand);
CLEAR(SQLCon);
ConnActive := FALSE;
```

For the interface we use three DotNet variables.

		Codeunit 123456731 RF Interface - C/AL Globals	

Variables | Text Constants | Functions

Name	DataType	Subtype
SQLCon	DotNet	System.Data.SqlClient.SqlConnection.'System.Data, Version=4.0.0.0, Culture=neutral, PublicKeyToken=b77a5c561934e089'
SQLCommand	DotNet	System.Data.SqlClient.SqlCommand.'System.Data, Version=4.0.0.0, Culture=neutral, PublicKeyToken=b77a5c561934e089'
SQLReader	DotNet	System.Data.SqlClient.SqlDataReader.'System.Data, Version=4.0.0.0, Culture=neutral, PublicKeyToken=b77a5c561934e089'
SynchID	Integer	
ConnActive	Boolean	

Let's have a look at the three DotNet variables in more detail:

- SQLConnection: This is used for the connection with the database and to execute the T-SQL statements
- SQLCommand: The result sets of a SELECT statement can be read using this
- SQLReader: The reader is used to read the data and convert data types between ADO and C/Side

Writing data

The RF application needs data from the Storage Line table. We first create a mapping to the RF application as we did with the Excel interface earlier in this chapter.

This mapping is saved in a buffer table for traceability:

```
CreatePickLines()
CreateConnectionString;

SaveReadSQL('CreatePickLines',TRUE, 1, 8388608, 3, '');

PickID := COPYSTR(StorageLn."Document No." + FORMAT(StorageLn."Line
No."), 1, 20);

SaveReadSQL('Pick Document : '+PickID,TRUE,3,16711680,7,'');

WITH RFPickLines DO BEGIN
  "Pick Code" := PickID;
  Quantity := StorageLn.Quantity;
  "Terminal ID" := 1;
  "Display 1" := StorageLn.Description;
  "Display 2" := 'Warehouse ' + StorageLn."Warehouse Code";
  "Display 3" := 'Region ' + StorageLn."Region Code";
  "Display 4" := 'Shelf ' + StorageLn."Shelf No.";
  INSERT;
```

```
SQLStatement := 'INSERT INTO [RF Pick Lines]' +
                '([Pick Code],'+
                '[Quantity],'+
                '[Terminal ID],'+
                '[Display 1],'+
                '[Display 2],'+
                '[Display 3],'+
                '[Display 4])'+
                'VALUES('+
                Quote + PickID + Quote       +','+
                FORMAT(Quantity)             +','+
                '1'                          +','+
                Quote + "Display 1" + Quote +','+
                Quote + "Display 2" + Quote +','+
                Quote + "Display 3" + Quote +','+
                Quote + "Display 4" + Quote + ')';
END;

ExecuteSQL(SQLStatement);

StorageLn.Exported := CURRENTDATETIME;
StorageLn.MODIFY;
```

The actual data is moved to the RF database using an INSERT command.

> To avoid exporting the same data twice we need to keep track of what we exported. The simplest way to do this is to create a new field called Exported. Making this field a DateTime also enables the traceability of the application.

Reading data

When reading data from the RF database, we also send a T-SQL SELECT query for the data. We use the SQLReader.Read to browse through the records that are in the result set.

For each record in the result set, we create a record in our buffer table, which we then can use to update the information in the Storage Lines.

When reading data we do not want to import the same data twice. To avoid this, we need to store a unique identifier in a table that enables us to remember where we left in the last run:

```
ReadFinishedPicks()
CreateConnectionString;

SaveReadSQL('ReadFinishedPicks',TRUE, 1, 8388608, 3, '');
```

```
RFIntSetup.GET;
LastSync := RFIntSetup."Last Finished Pick";


SQLCommand := SQLCon.CreateCommand();
SQLCommand.CommandText := SaveReadSQL('SELECT ' +
             '[Reference Entry No],' +
             '[Terminal ID],' +
             '[Duration],' +
             '[Ready Date Time]' +
   ' FROM [RF Finished Pick] WHERE [Reference Entry No] > ' +
     LastSync,FALSE,2,0,2, ''));

WHILE SQLReader.Read() DO BEGIN
  RFFinishedPick.INIT;
  RFFinishedPick."Reference Entry No." :=
    ReadInteger('Reference Entry No');
  RFFinishedPick."Terminal ID" := ReadInteger('Terminal ID');
  RFFinishedPick.Duration := ReadInteger('Duration');
  RFFinishedPick."Ready Date Time" :=
    ReadDateTime('Ready Date Time');
  RFFinishedPick.INSERT;
END;

RFIntSetup."Last Finished Pick" := Quote + FORMAT(RFFinishedPick."Refe
rence Entry No.") + Quote;
RFIntSetup.MODIFY;

AdoRecordSet.Close;
```

In our example, this unique identifier is `Reference Entry No.`

Log, log, and log more

Although much of the logging is done using the buffer tables, we also want to store the general process of the interface each time it runs. This is done using the SQL Statement table. Both the SQL Statements as well as the other events are stored there.

By using the COMMIT functionality, we can exactly see where it stopped by looking at the last record in this table. We can solve the problem that caused the interface to stop and restart the interface without losing data.

> Never use the COMMIT statement unless there is a very good reason for it. C/SIDE will normally handle the transactions for you, enabling a full role back when things go wrong. Creating a COMMIT statement in a normal C/SIDE transaction will prevent C/SIDE from rolling back.

Testing

Let's test the interface we have just designed and developed. In order to do this, we need to have records in the Storage Line table and the RF database needs to exist somewhere.

The RF database

To test the objects we have created for this solution, the RF database should exist on your system. This database can be created using a T-SQL script and should be executed on a Microsoft SQL Server machine.

> The script RF database.sql is part of the object files downloaded for this book.

Open the script in SQL Server Management Studio and click on **Execute**.

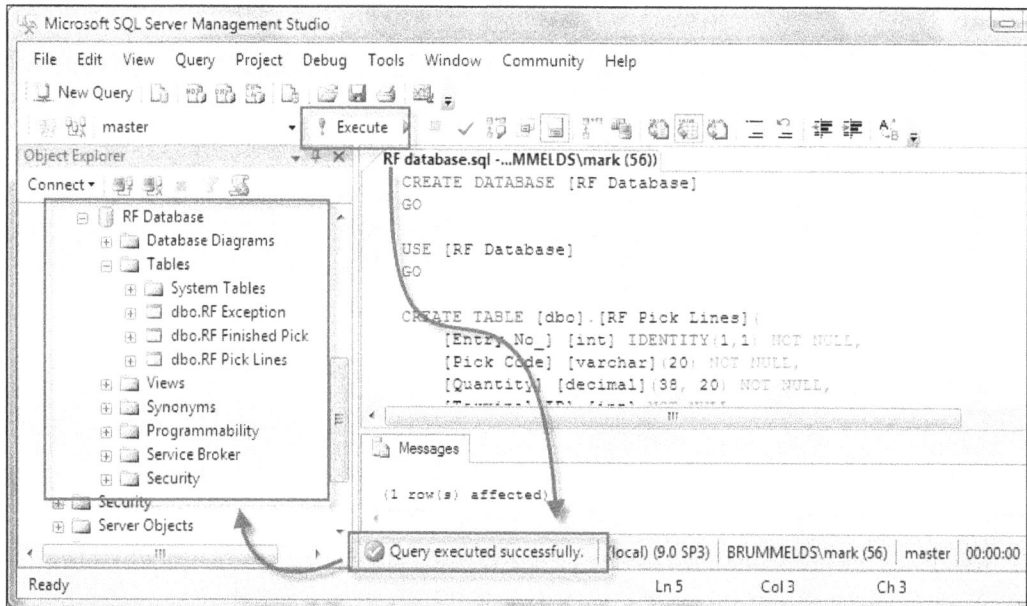

The test

Even though the C/AL code can run in the Windows client, we will run the test in the classic client. The reason for this is that the interface will run in the NAS, which will execute the C/AL code the same way as the classic client. Another reason to use the classic client is that this is the interface for the DBA to perform all their tasks.

To start a test run, open page **RF Interface Setup** (123.456.780) from the Object Designer.

Make sure that the Database and Server are correct. The server should be the SQL Server instance where the SQL Script was executed.

> The ADO connection uses the Windows Account NT AUTHORITY\NETWORK SERVICE with Trusted connection. This user should have enough rights to insert and read data from the RF database.

To start a test run, click on the **Test** button.

Viewing the results

If everything went well, the results should show both in the log and in the buffer tables and the RF database. Let's check them all.

SQL Statements

The SQL Statement log can be opened by either pushing the **Log** button on the **RF Interface Setup** form or opening the **SQL Statements** (123.456.781) form from the Object Designer.

SQL statements

The information on the form shows us exactly what the interface did during this run.

The buffer tables

When we open the buffer tables from the Object Designer, we can see that the interface moved the data from the Storage Line table into the RF Pick Lines table.

The **RF Finished Pick** and **RF Exceptions** are also populated with the records from the RF database.

The RF database

The last thing to check is the data in the RF database. The data in both databases should now be exactly the same.

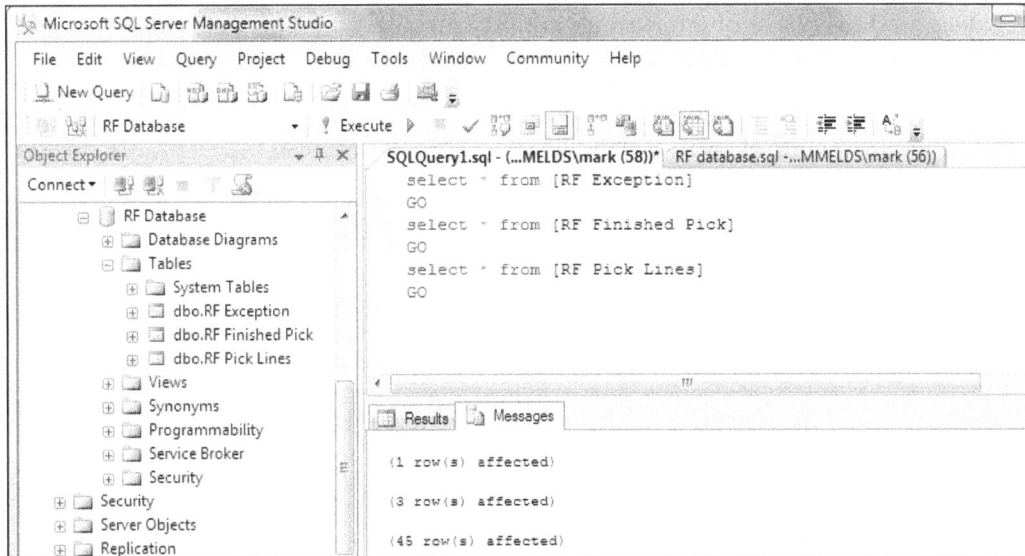

This can be checked from the SQL Server Management Studio.

Interfacing into the future

Interfacing will become more and more important in the future as technology evolves. Newer technologies and faster Internet connections will allow us to integrate our applications better but will also make it more accessible for end users.

Cloud-enabled Microsoft Dynamics NAV

With the release of version 2013 R2, Microsoft Dynamics NAV is now cloud-enabled. This means that the product is officially supported to run on the Microsoft Azure platform.

Summary

In this chapter, we looked at how Microsoft Dynamics NAV can interface with other applications.

We discussed the basics of interfacing, import versus export, and data pulling versus data pushing. An interface can be executed manually or by a timer or event.

Microsoft Dynamics NAV supports a wide range of interfacing technologies, such as files, automation control, .NET, ODBC, ADO, and web services.

It is also possible to integrate using SQL Server technologies. The Application Server (NAS) is often used for interfacing with other systems, for example, using Microsoft **Message Queuing** or **Active Data Objects (ADO)**.

The wide range of interfaces that come with the product have been discussed including all interfaces with Microsoft Office, Exchange, and SharePoint.

We designed and developed two business-to-business interfaces; one to import data manually from Microsoft Excel and the other to automatically import and export data to another database using ADO and a timer.

When designing an interface, reliability and traceability are the key elements. In the next chapter, we will talk about application design methodologies and principles.

10
Application Design

In Microsoft Dynamics NAV, technology and functionality go hand in hand. It is impossible to design a good change or enhancement to the application without thorough knowledge of how the standard pieces fit together. With this knowledge now available, we can start designing our own applications.

In this book, we talked about application design for Microsoft Dynamics NAV. We discussed the design patterns, how it works, and why it works that way. We designed several small and large changes to the system both in detailed examples and on a conceptual level.

For this chapter, we will fit all the pieces together that we have learned in this book and turn them into concepts for good application design.

We will also discuss how to approach a Microsoft Dynamics NAV implementation project and how to maintain the application. This requires a different approach depending on the level of customization the project contains.

Application life cycle

Designing an application is more than just analyzing processes and developing new objects. These phases are just the tip of the iceberg.

Once your application has been designed and developed, it is most likely that one or more companies will start using it. When this happens, your software will start a new phase in its life cycle. Let's have a look at the life cycle of a Microsoft Dynamics NAV application:

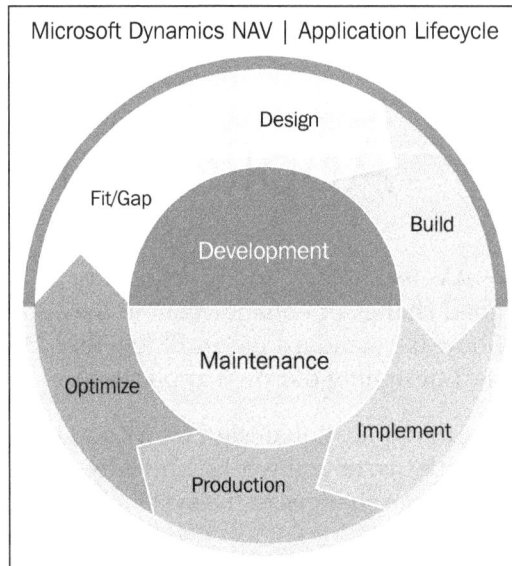

The **Development** phase of the application starts with the **Fit/Gap** analysis, followed by the **Design** and **Build** steps we did in the earlier chapters. When that is completed, the **Maintenance** phase of your application will start.

The **Maintenance** phase starts with the implementation and taking the software into **Production**. The first time this will happen, it will be the Microsoft Dynamics NAV implementation in your company. Once this is done, your system will enter the real life cycle where constant improvements will be made to the application.

With the flexibility of the Microsoft Dynamics NAV product, this is a very special procedure where it is easy to encounter the many pitfalls there are along the way.

We will discuss some guidelines that are important to follow. There are six categories: Design to use, Maintain, Support, Upgrade, Perform, and Analyze.

Design to use

Designing software is not a goal, it's a way to support companies doing their business. This makes usability one of the most important focus areas when designing your application.

The first thing that pops in mind when talking about usability is the user interface. Microsoft Dynamics NAV 2013 has two interfaces that are commonly used, the Windows Client and the new Web Client.

Pages

Page objects are used to define the user interface. They are very strict in how they are displayed. However, they have a lot of advantages. Let's go through some of the design options:

- **Tabs**: Pages have vertical tabs that can be opened at the same time, making it less desirable to move fields to the first tab.

- **Embedded Lists**: Another advantage of pages is that the users always get to see an embedded list page first and then continue to the card, which opens in a new Windows control after selecting a record.

- **Importance**: On pages, it is possible to promote controls to be displayed when the tab is closed or made additional so the end users have to specifically make them visible. Use this functionality carefully when designing your application.

- **Personalization**: If not restricted, all pages can be personalized by the end users, even card pages. This makes it easier to customize pages during an implementation for a company, department, or end user. Personalization does not change the object definition and does not require a developer.

Let's walk through the elements of a page as shown in the following screenshot taken from the example add-on solution in *Chapter 7, Storage and Logistics*:

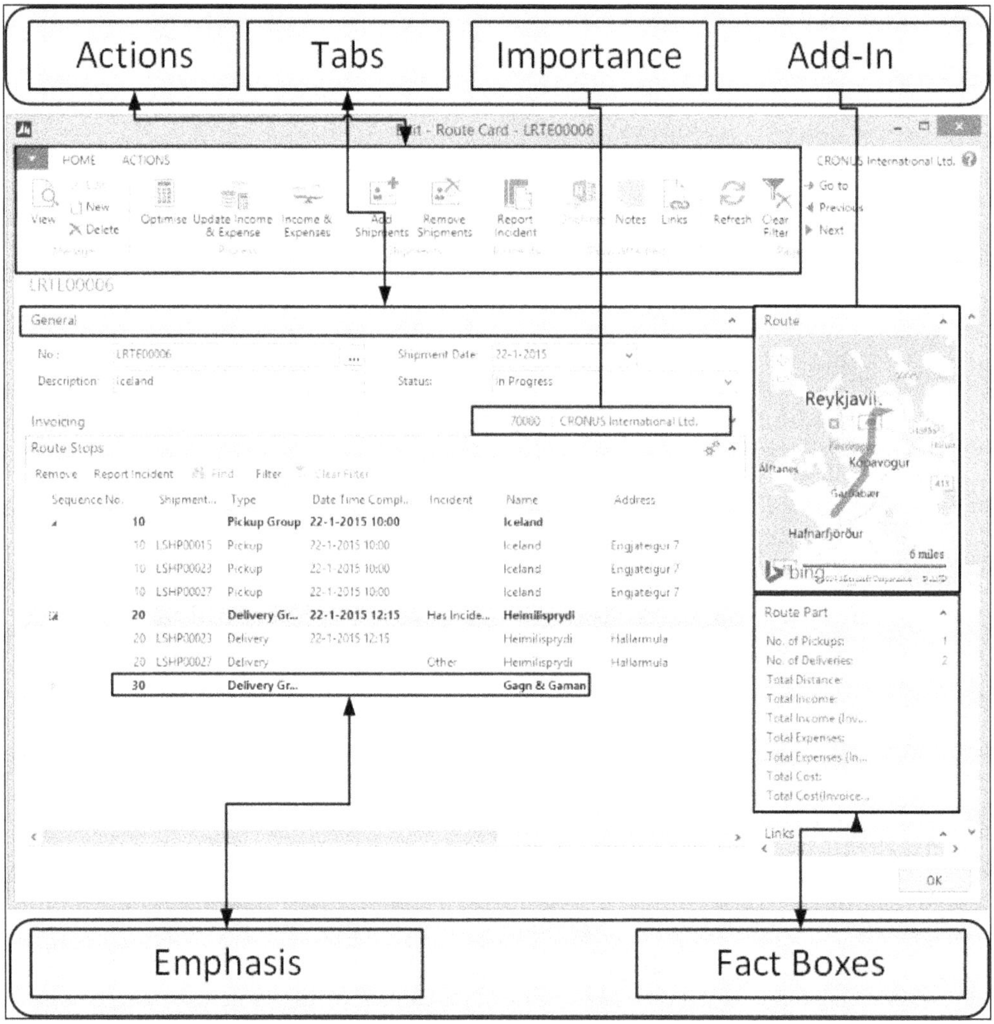

Let's have a look at the fields in more detail:

- **Actions**: All transactions that can be performed on a page are actions. Some actions are generated by the system while other actions are defined by the developer. Users can select which actions they want to emphasize, making it easier for them to get started with the application.

- **Fact Boxes**: Each page can have an unlimited number of fact boxes attached. Fact boxes can be used to show detailed information about a record. The **Route** page in *Chapter 7, Storage and Logistics,* is a good example where we can see the route in Bing maps and the details of the stops.

- **Emphasis**: A control on a page can be emphasized to a limited combination of colors, bold, and italics.

- **Client extensibility**: A control on a page can be taken over by a `.net dll`. The .NET control will use the content of the `.dll` and render the information. We discussed Client extensibility in *Chapter 9, Interfacing.*

- **Web Services**: All pages can be exposed as a web service. This makes it possible to create your own user interface in Visual Studio, Borland Delphi, or another development tool that can consume web services.

Role centers

When it comes to usability in Microsoft Dynamics NAV 2013, the Role Centers are the heart of the application. The Role Center is the place where the end users starts their working day and returns to regularly. Let's discuss the Role Centers we created in this book.

Squash application

The Squash Court Role Center was created in *Chapter 2, A Sample Application,* and looks like this:

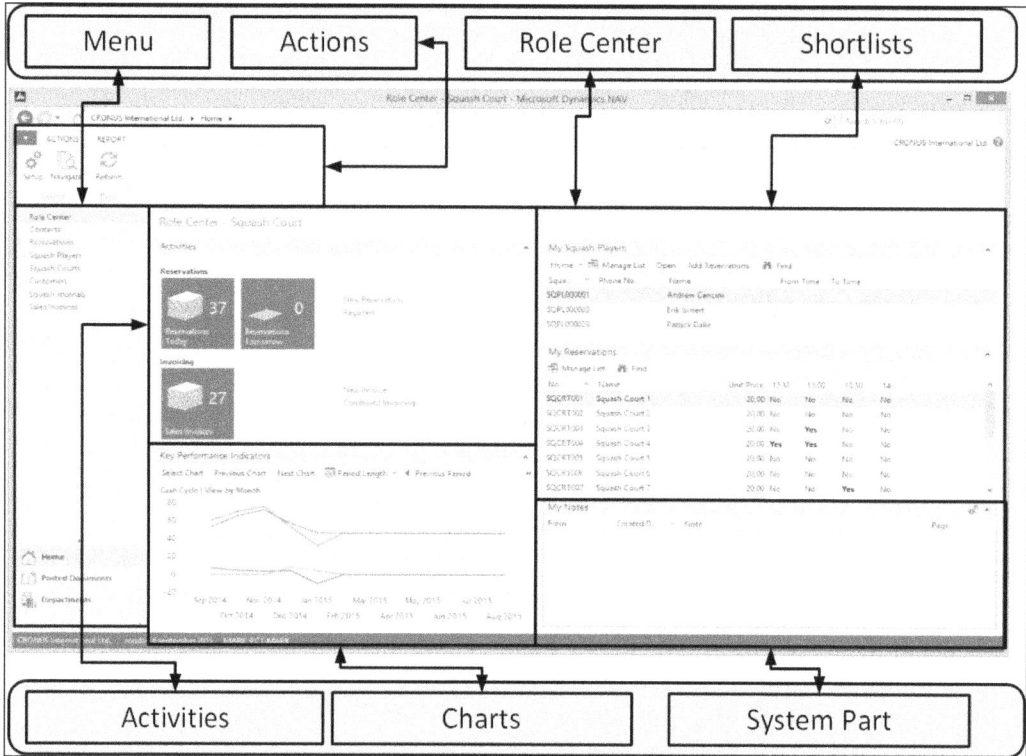

The purpose of the screenshot is to just familiarize with the different sections in an application

The **Application** screen has two sections, the **Menu** section and the **Role Center** section.

The **Menu** section is created by merging actions from the Role Center with the main menu. By clicking on **Departments** in the left-hand side corner, an end user can access the entire application depending on the security setup.

> More information about the home items can be found on the blog at https://marijebrummel.blog/2014/07/02/tip-26-grouping-in-the-homeitems/.

The Role Center has a left and right part. The left part usually contains the activities and a shortcut to Microsoft Outlook. The right part contains shortlists to the **My List** pages that show frequently used records and notes. An end user can customize the Role Center and move the parts around.

Storage and Logistics

This application has four different Role Centers. We will discuss the Storage Role Center (123.456.726). Other Role Centers are Logistics Role Center (123.456.700), Manager Log. and St. Role Center (123.456.756) Income and Expenses Role Center (123.456.761).

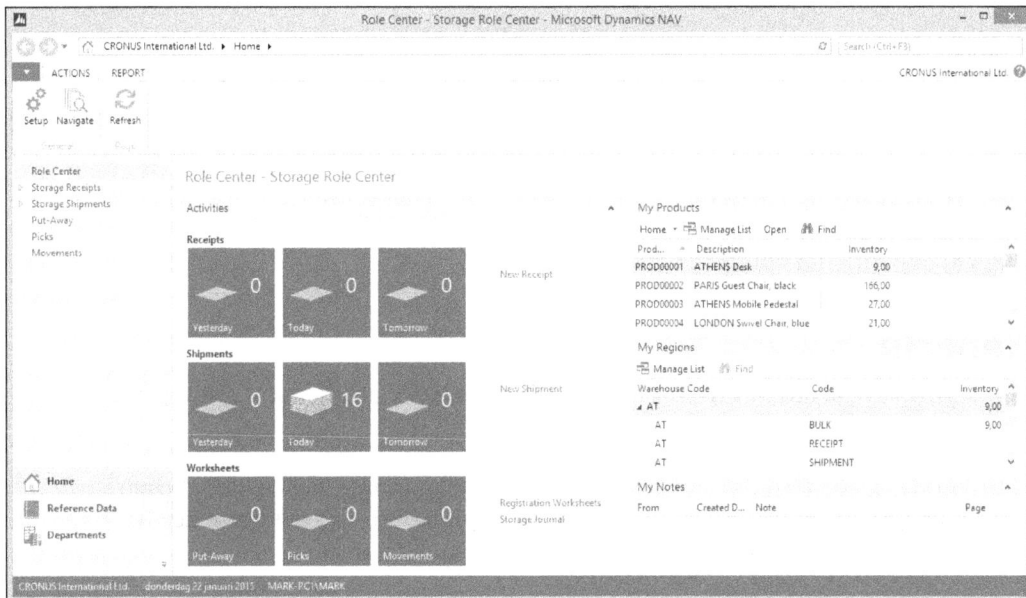

On the **Activities Storage** page, employees can directly go to the documents filtered on dates from the stacks. From the **Menu** options, users can create new documents or open worksheets and journals.

We have designed two shortlist pages, **My Products** and **My Regions**. **My Products** can be changed by the user by clicking on the small lightning button and select **Manage List**, as shown in the following screenshot:

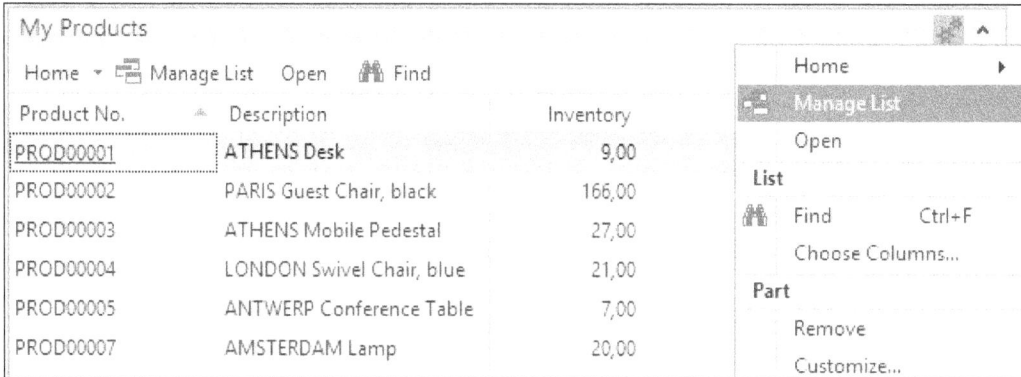

The **My Region** page is built on the Region table. Users cannot change this list. The page uses the `SourceTableTemporary` property and `ShowAsTree`. This allows users to expand and collapse warehouses.

Reports

The reports in the standard Microsoft Dynamics NAV application are typical ERP reports that show the required information and that's it.

Designing reports requires special skills and is not as easy as it seems. When changing a report layout from the standard application, it is best practice to leave the original report as it is and modify the saved copy.

We will discuss more about reports in the *Design to analyze* section.

Design to Maintain

It seldom happens that software is designed and developed, never to be changed. The objects created are usually changed many times in the lifetime of the application.

The changes to an existing object may be done quite a while after the object's original development. At this time, even if the changes are done by the original developer, it will be difficult to remember how and why some changes are done.

Hence, it is important to develop in a unified way. This will make it easier for developers to read each other's code or to understand their own code after months or years.

Written external documentation is a no brainer at this point but we should realize that this is not always done and focus on more obvious and easier ways. A well designed and built application should be self-documenting. This is done by following some simple guidelines.

Naming

While creating new objects, it is important to follow the naming guidelines of the product. Field and variable names should explain themselves.

> This MSDN article at `http://msdn.microsoft.com/en-us/library/ee414213.aspx` describes more details on naming conventions in Microsoft Dynamics NAV.

Singular and plural

Table names should be singular. This will make the C/AL TABLECAPTION command return a usable value. Let's look at an example in the Item table (27):

```
OnDelete()
...
ItemJnlLine.SETRANGE("Item No.","No.");
IF ItemJnlLine.FIND('-') THEN
   ERROR(Text023,TABLECAPTION,"No.",ItemJnlLine.TABLECAPTION);
```

The preceding command will generate the following error message with the table caption singular:

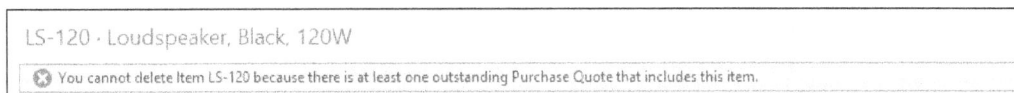

> LS-120 · Loudspeaker, Black, 120W
>
> ⊗ You cannot delete Item LS-120 because there is at least one outstanding Purchase Quote that includes this item.

List pages should be plural as they contain more than one record while card pages are singular.

Reserved words

Reserved words should not be used in objects as name for fields, variables, and functions.

> Microsoft has published a list of reserved words at `http://msdn.microsoft.com/en-us/library/ee414230.aspx`.

One very important reserved word, which is missing in that list is **Action**. This is reserved for using `IF Page.RUNMODAL = ACTION::OK then`.

Names and abbreviations

Using standard naming and abbreviations is one of the strong points of the application that makes it easy to learn for new developers.

Here are some examples:

- **<<Table name>> No.**: This is the standard reference to a field in a table relation. If the field has a relation with the customer, the field is called **Customer No.** and if the relation is with vendor, we use **Vendor No**. In our example application, we have used **Product No.**, **Squash Player No.**, and so on.

- **Line No.**: This fieldname is always used in the popular Header/Line and Journal constructions. This field always uses the auto split key property in pages.

- **Entry No.**: This fieldname is always used for entry and register tables such as G/L Entry and Customer Ledger Entry.

- **Name and Description**: This is the standard naming for persons or products.

- **Quantity/Qty.**: This is the standard name and abbreviation to measure quantity.

- **(LCY)**: This is the abbreviation for Local Currency.

- **Duty Due** %: When the field represents a percentage, this sign should be in the field name.

A list of naming conventions can be found on MSDN at
`http://msdn.microsoft.com/en-us/library/ee414213.aspx`.

Quantity versus quality

There is a general rule that can be applied to the quantity and quality of software that says that when more functionality is added to the product, it is difficult to maintain a certain level of quality.

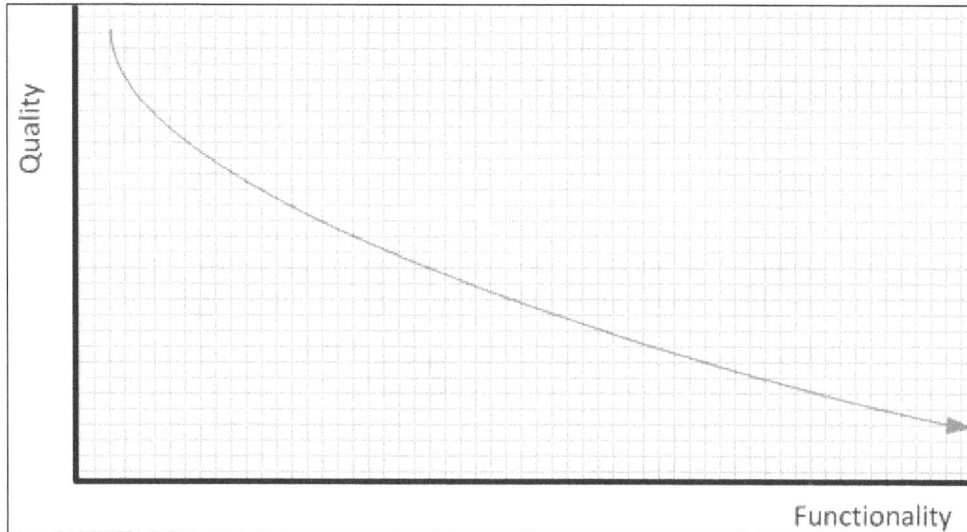

To avoid this in your solution, make sure you don't just add all the requirements from your prospects into the product in one release and instead use a release policy that ensures small pieces of functionality to be developed, tested, and implemented each time.

Loosely coupled

When developing an add-on product, it is important to divide it into smaller parts. This will make it easier to have several developers work on the application and release parts of the application. Each part of the add-on has its own framework that interacts with other pieces of the add-on or the standard product.

This is exactly what we did in the storage and logistics example add-on application. The add-on has three main functional areas: Storage, Logistics, and Income and Expenses. These three areas share the same master data.

Each area interacts with other parts of the application using mini interfaces. Using this concept will also have great benefits when upgrading to newer versions, which we will discuss in the *Design to upgrade* section.

Design to support

There are different levels of providing support. First-level support is usually done by someone at the customer site that works in the IT department or someone that has a feeling for IT. The general first line support questions are about filters, missing data, and so on.

Second-level support is usually a small bug in the software or something missing in the setup or master data. Depending on the customer, this will be solved by the internal IT department or escalated to the partner.

As a developer, you will most likely employ third-line support where something needs to be debugged or reverse engineered in order to find the bug.

So before a bug reaches the developer, other people have already spent time in analyzing the issue without success. The development of the software should be done in such a way that third-line support makes a minimum change or occurrence.

When the guidelines discussed in the *Design to use* and *Design to maintain* sections are used, it will already be easier for the second-level support to analyze the issue.

Second-level support

Most problems in support occur in the second level. The first-level support engineers are often very familiar with the system and the third-level support engineers are often the original developers of the software.

Second-level support people need to be able to go in a database and analyze the issue without having to change their way of thinking.

Let's briefly summarize the general guidelines for this specific topic:

- **Shortcuts**: Use standard shortcuts as much as possible. For example, use *F9* for posting and registering, and *Ctrl + F7* for ledger entries. Avoid using reserved shortcuts such as *F8* (copy previous) and *Alt + F3* (filter to this value).

- **Screen Layout**: Avoid screen layouts that are too creative. Too much information on a screen is often an indication of a bad design and will be difficult to support. Typical examples are multiple subpages and hiding elements based on business logic subpages.

- **Variable Naming**: As discussed in the *Design to maintain* section, good naming will make a huge difference when looking at someone else's design. This starts with trying to use Microsoft's naming conventions for the standard application.

- **C/AL Placement**: Microsoft Dynamics NAV is very flexible when it comes to placing C/AL code in objects. Pages support using C/AL code to the extent that it is possible to write an entire posting routine there. C/AL coding should be done in tables or codeunits unless this is not possible.

- **Using Functions**: When your C/AL code exceeds the size of your screen, it is best practice to create a function. This will make the original code more readable for others. Use a name for your function that makes sense so the code will document itself. An example for this can be found in the codeunit Register Time Sheet (75000) we discussed in *Chapter 8, Consulting*.

- **Global versus Local Variables**: Variables can be both global and local in C/AL. Microsoft does not have strict guidelines on which to use when. The general rule when looking at the standard application is to use global variables unless the variable is only used in a function — then it can be local.

> The compiler does not give a warning when using a local variable with the same name as the global variable. The system will always use the local variable first.

Design to upgrade

It might not be the first thing to realize when designing your application but there will come a time when it needs to be upgraded to a newer version.

When upgrading your application, we can split this task into two parts. Part one is the part of the add-on that is written on top of the standard application, that is, new tables, pages, and codeunits that are loosely coupled with the standard application. This part is often easily upgraded. The other part is the changes done in the base application. These changes are often more difficult to move to a newer version.

Has Microsoft changed my (referenced) object

Whether or not Microsoft has changed your referenced objects is the question it comes down to when analyzing the upgrade task. If the object you modified has not been changed by Microsoft, the upgrade is easy. If Microsoft has changed the object slightly, we might need to analyze the changes to see whether we need to change something as well.

With each release, Microsoft tends to redesign a part of the application. If your solution is integrated with the part Microsoft has redesigned, it will be a bigger task to bring the add-on forward.

> To see the design changes made by Microsoft in a new release, analyze the upgrade toolkit objects to see what it hits.

Here are a few examples of some common redesigns.

CRM (Version 2.0)

In Version 2.0, Navision introduced the current CRM application we discussed in *Chapter 4*, *Relationship Management*. The most important change was to merge company contacts and persons into one table while implementing new functionality.

Dimensions (Version 3.x)

In Version 3.0, Navision introduced the dimension solution that we know today. Before this, the current Global Dimensions 1 and 2 were called **Department Code** and **Project Code**.

Bin code (Version 3.x)

With the introduction of WMS, the usage of the Bin Code field changed. The Bin Code used to be a field in the Item Ledger Entry table (32) and moved to the Warehouse Entries.

Inventory valuation (Version 3.x)

No single piece of code in Microsoft Dynamics NAV has changed as many times as the inventory valuation solution. Try to avoid changing this in your add-on application.

Item tracking (Version 3.6 and 4.0)

As with inventory valuation, item tracking has been changed many times. Where older versions had Item Tracking Entries and Item Ledger Entries, they are merged into one table in newer versions as discussed in *Chapter 6*, *Trade*.

MenuSuite (Version 4.0)

Although it is not a functional change, the introduction of MenuSuite in Version 4.0 caused a lot of work to upgrade to.

MenuSuite do not support C/AL code. This means that all Journals need to be changed for this version.

Jobs (Version 5.0)

As discussed in *Chapter 7*, *Storage and Logistics*, the Jobs functionality has been changed in Version 5.0. The budgeting in the previous version was done differently using Budget Entries and Phase, Task, and Step tables.

The Job Journal Line and Job Ledger entries have not changed, but the new Job Task table has become a mandatory field when posting on a job.

When there is no other way, it is possible to take out the Job Objects and renumber them to be customized tables. This allows you to upgrade to a newer version with minimum impact. After the upgrade, a new project can be started to move to the new Job functionality completely.

Dimensions (Version 2013)

Version 2013 introduced a new design pattern for storing dimensions. Although the design is a much better one, it requires a lot of redesign to implement this new pattern.

Item costing (almost all versions)

The item costing has been improved in almost every new version of Microsoft Dynamics NAV. Changes in item costing is difficult to upgrade to newer versions and almost always need to be redesigned.

Documentation

While many parts of the application will have no issue in the upgrade, it is useful to have external documentation when there is a need to redesign.

This documentation should contain information about the business reason for implementing the feature. With that information, it is possible to do a new fit/gap analysis.

> External documentation such as Microsoft Word and Visio files can be linked to C/Side objects. This way it is easy to find the documentation when a developer needs it.

Split operational and financial information

In the Storage and Logistics application, we chose a data and transaction model that can be easily upgraded to a newer version of Microsoft Dynamics NAV.

This is achieved by creating separate modules that move data to each other.

Design to perform

All good applications are useless if the performance is not adequate. Performance is very important to keep in mind when designing your application.

When talking about performance, there are two typical issues. The first issue is an application with an overall slow performance, and the latter is an application with good performance but where users block each other or create deadlocks.

Both issues have their own approach to be analyzed and solved. We will not talk in detail about this process but rather explain how to avoid these situations in general.

OLTP versus OLAP

In any ERP system, it is important to balance **Online Transaction Processing** (**OLTP**) with **Online Analytical Processing** (**OLAP**). This is especially important when working with Microsoft Dynamics NAV. The reason for this is its unique data and posting model, which creates the analytical data while processing the transaction.

Creating this analytical information in real time can have advantages, but when posting the transactions take too much time, it might not be worth it.

Examples of analytical information are dimension information and analysis view entries, but also VAT Entries and Value Entries. Although they give us important information about the business, we do not always need them instantly when processing the transaction.

Other examples of analytical information are secondary keys and `SumIndexFields`. All this information will be created when creating the master record. If a Ledger Entry table has 32 secondary keys and 15 `SumIndexFields`, it will take a considerable amount of time to write this information to the database.

Fast transaction posting

Good performance starts with fast transactions. There are several ways to achieve this. The major ones being: cleanup unused indexes and application setup.

Cleanup unused indexes

Each secondary `SumIndexFields` field in the database needs to be maintained whether it is used or not. Microsoft Dynamics NAV allows end users to create their own schedule to maintain this.

Creating such an index schedule is quite a complex task and so should be done by experienced functional developers.

> In versions prior to Microsoft Dynamics 5 SP 1, the overhead of unused `SumIndexFields` was substantially higher compared to newer versions.

Application setup

It all starts with a solid application setup. Some setup features in Microsoft Dynamics NAV will cause the system to create more analytical information when posting transactions.

An example is **Update On Posting** for **Analysis** Views. This feature will update the Analysis View Entries at the same time as the General Ledger Entries are created.

Other examples are the **Automatic Cost** options in the inventory setup. When they are activated, the cost is adjusted each time an Item Ledger Entry is created.

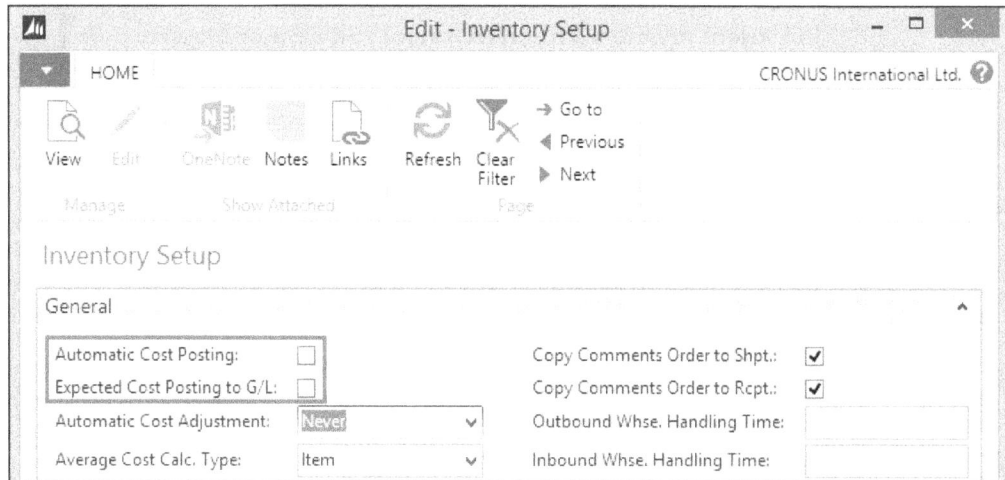

Job Queue

Microsoft Dynamics NAV is shipped with an excellent multithreaded Job Queue system. This process is called an Application Server and can execute C/AL code in report and codeunit objects.

Examples of Job Queue tasks are creating the Analysis View Entries, Posting the Adjust Cost for Inventory Valuation or even Posting Sales, and Purchase documents.

Background posting

Background posting was introduced in Microsoft Dynamics NAV 2013 and allows you to post documents using a Job Queue. This means that the user who starts the posting routine does not need to wait until this process has been completed before starting a new task.

Date compressing and cleanup

When the number of records in a table exceeds normal proportions, it might be useful to start thinking about doing data maintenance. This is a normal procedure in all ERP systems, and Microsoft Dynamics NAV has the capability to do that.

Date compression

Most Entry tables in Microsoft Dynamics NAV can be compressed by date.
This means that all entries with the same values will be replaced by one new
entry. The detailed information is lost afterwards.

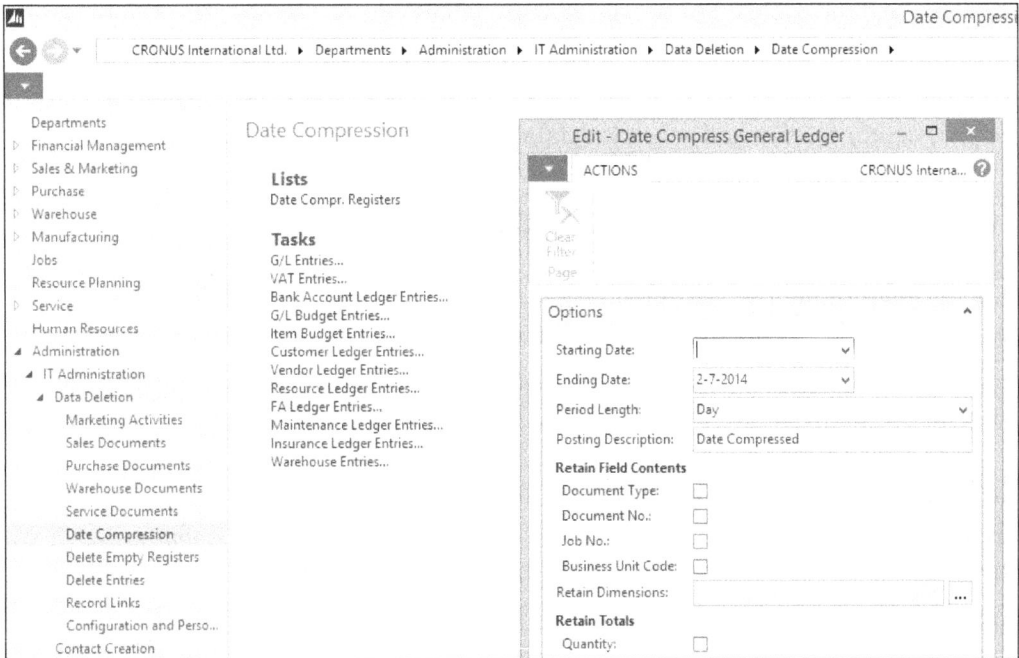

Data compression

Saving the detailed information can be easily implemented by changing the
compression report. The detailed information can be saved in a copy of the
original table.

> The total size of the database has minimal impact on the
> performance. More important is the size of the tables we are
> writing to during a transaction.

Data cleanup

Microsoft Dynamics NAV allows most data to be deleted when the fiscal year it was created is closed.

Examples of data that can be deleted are Sales Shipments and Purchase Receipts. They can be either deleted or moved to copy tables.

Cleaning up data will prevent the transactions to be slower when your company uses Microsoft Dynamics NAV for a longer time. Data cleanup generally starts after using the product for 5 years and when the database exceeds 100 gigabytes in size.

Locks, blocks, and deadlocks

The Microsoft Dynamics NAV product is very sensitive for blocking and deadlocks. This has everything to do with the posting model, the inheritance of the Native database, and the numbering used in entry tables.

Blocks and Deadlocks are caused primarily by Locks in the database. Locking is a mechanism databases use to ensure consistency of the data.

Native server versus SQL Server

Originally, Microsoft Dynamics NAV had a proprietary (Native) database. This database did not support row-level locking, only table locking.

Microsoft Dynamics NAV 2013 no longer supports this database and only runs on SQL Server, which does support row-level locks. However, the current data and transaction model is designed for table locking.

The benefit of row-level locking on SQL Server is best experienced in systems with many users creating documents in the same database. Most posting transactions in the database are isolated, meaning only one user at a time can post a document from anywhere in the application.

Locking is always done for a single company; unless tables are shared as explained in *Chapter 4, Relationship Management*, a user from company A cannot lock a user in company B.

Locking principles

In Microsoft Dynamics NAV, locking starts with the LOCKTABLE command. Using this command will generate the T-SQL statements that are generated by the application to issue a UPDLOCK hint where without the statement, READUNCOMMITED is issued.

Let's create an example that shows how locking is done.

1. For this example, we create a new codeunit Locking A (60000). The codeunit has a global variable Cust of type Record 18:

```
OnRun()
Cust.LOCKTABLE;
Cust.GET('10000');
IF CONFIRM('Maintain Lock in database') THEN;
```

2. We start this codeunit and leave the confirmation window open.

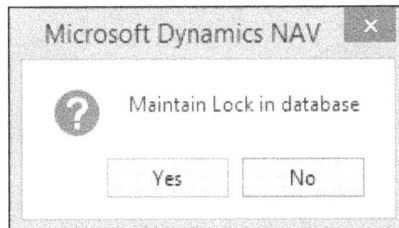

3. Now, we go to the Windows client, open the **Customer Card** for customer **10000** and try to change the name. After 10 seconds, we will get the following message:

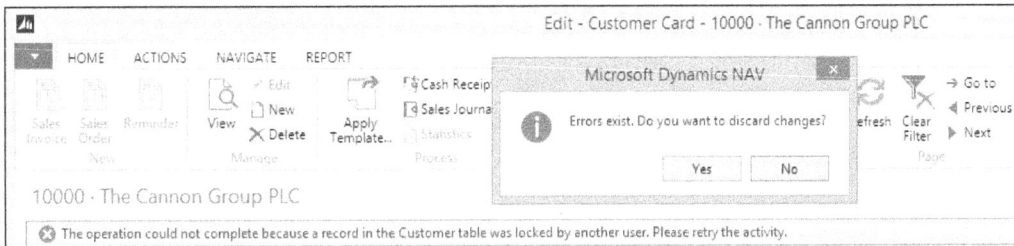

The reason for this error message to pop up is that the other user issued an exclusive lock on the record. If we move to customer **20000**, which is the next record in the database, we can safely change the name. This record is not locked.

Deadlocks

Let's take this example one step further and simulate a deadlock. Deadlocks happen if users try to lock each other's record in a different order.

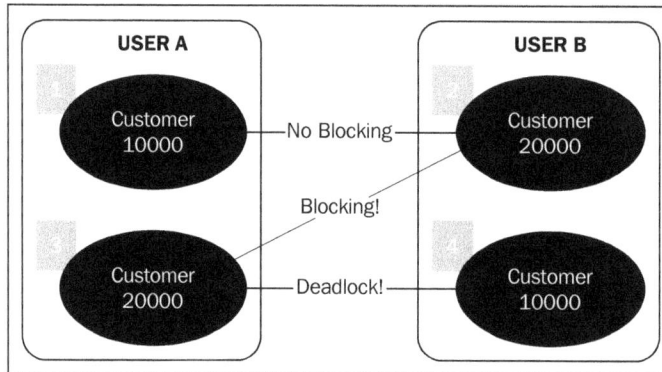

Let's see this in more detail:

- User A reads and locks Customer 10000
- User B reads and locks Customer 20000
- User A tries to read and lock Customer 20000, a blocking event starts
- When user B now tries to lock Customer 10000, a deadlock occurs

To demonstrate a deadlock, we have created two Codeunits Deadlock A (60001) and Deadlock B (60002). We need two sessions on the same SQL Server database to do this. Start Deadlock A on one client:

```
OnRun()
Cust.LOCKTABLE;
Cust.GET('10000');
IF CONFIRM('Start another client and run codeunit 60002') THEN
  LockOtherCust;

LockOtherCust()
Cust2.GET('20000');
IF CONFIRM('Maintain Lock') THEN;
```

Start Deadlock B on the other:

```
OnRun()
Cust.LOCKTABLE;
Cust.GET('20000');
IF CONFIRM('Select Yes on the other client') THEN
```

```
    LockOtherCust;

LockOtherCust()
Cust2.GET('10000');
IF CONFIRM('Did the deadlock happen?') THEN;
```

Then, select **Yes** on both the confirmation boxes. One of the clients should now deadlock.

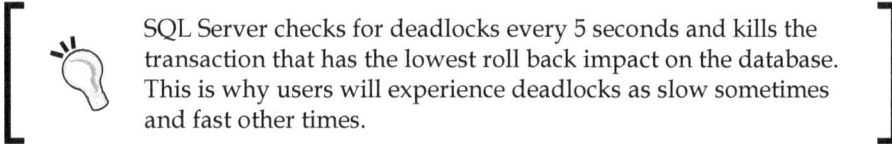

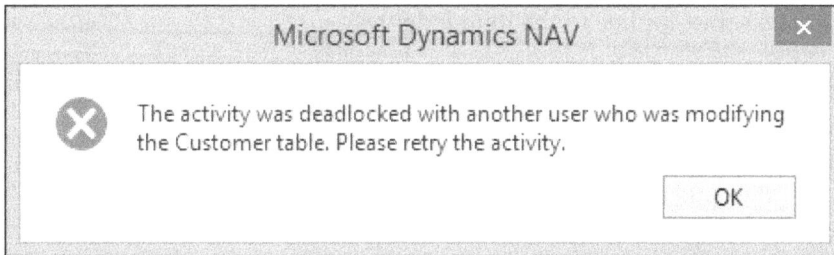

> SQL Server checks for deadlocks every 5 seconds and kills the transaction that has the lowest roll back impact on the database. This is why users will experience deadlocks as slow sometimes and fast other times.

Microsoft Dynamics NAV

The activity was deadlocked with another user who was modifying the Customer table. Please retry the activity.

OK

The error message is confusing since it lets us to believe we have locked the entire table, which is not true.

The `LockOtherCust` function reads a record from the customer table with another variable. This new variable `Cust2` does not explicitly issues a `LOCKTABLE` command. This proves that `LOCKTABLE` is a transaction command that is valid for all variables of this type.

Blocking and deadlocks in Microsoft Dynamics NAV

The standard application has several built-in blocking events by design. This is to ensure the database integrity and to avoid deadlocks.

The two main isolating tables in Microsoft Dynamics NAV are the G/L Entry table (17) and the Item Ledger Entry table (32).

Codeunit 12 shows these lines of code before creating G/L Entries:

```
StartPosting(GenJnlLine : Record "Gen. Journal Line")
WITH GenJnlLine DO BEGIN
  GlobalGLEntry.LOCKTABLE;
  IF GlobalGLEntry.FINDLAST THEN BEGIN
```

Both Codeunit Sales-Post 80 and Purch.-Post 90 that we discussed earlier have optional isolation on the G/L Entry table.

```
LOCAL LockTables()
SalesLine.LOCKTABLE;
ItemChargeAssgntSales.LOCKTABLE;
PurchOrderLine.LOCKTABLE;
PurchOrderHeader.LOCKTABLE;
GetGLSetup;
IF NOT GLSetup.OptimGLEntLockForMultiuserEnv THEN BEGIN
  GLEntry.LOCKTABLE;
  IF GLEntry.FINDLAST THEN;
END; .
```

In real life, this means that no one in a company can post to the general ledger at the same time. The same applies to the item ledger.

> This blog entry at `https://blogs.msdn.com/b/nav/archive/2012/10/17/g-l-entry-table-locking-redesign-in-microsoft-dynamics-nav-2013.aspx` explains the usage of the optional G/L locking while posting documents.

This emphasizes the importance of fast transactions and generating analysis data in separate batches.

Impact on development

If we summarize the impact of all this knowledge on your development, it emphasizes the importance of designing your own application structures that interface with the standard application.

When changing and implementing the standard application, try to reduce the overhead during posting as much as possible.

Create compression routines and allow end users to periodically clean up records. In the next section, we will talk about how to design to analyze and allow end users to generate analysis data in batches separate from the posting transactions.

Design to analyze

Analysis in Microsoft Dynamics NAV should always be done on (ledger) entry records. There are many types of entry records that are either created during a transaction or in batches.

Avoid building analysis on document tables. It should always be possible to delete old data in the database without losing the essential information for data analysis.

Report design

Designing a report in Microsoft Dynamics NAV starts with generating a Data Set. This is built using table relations and can get quite complex.

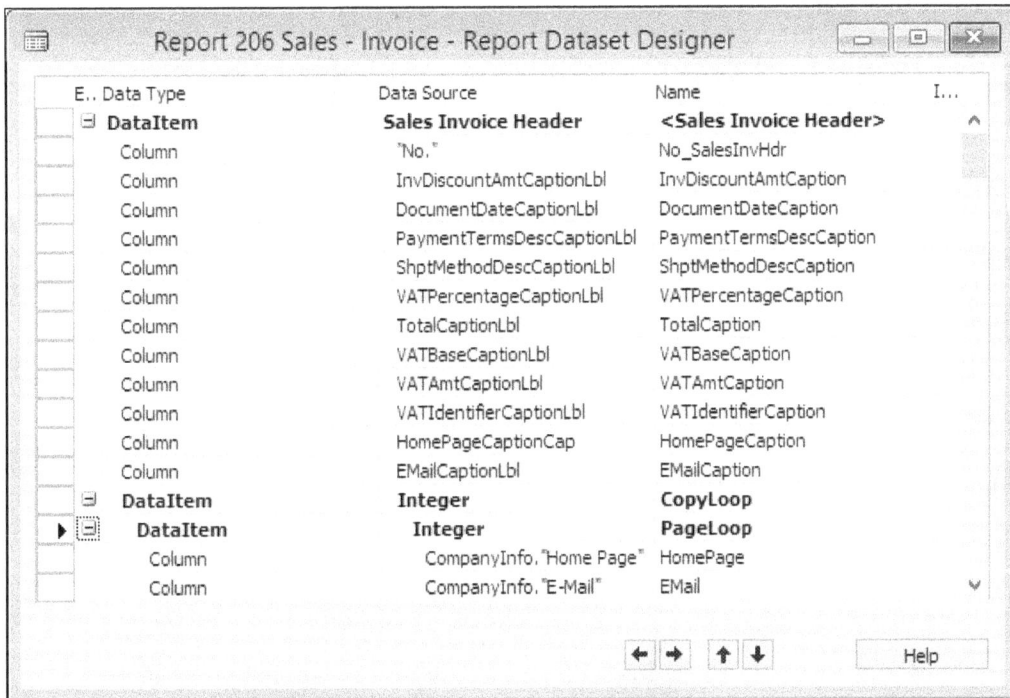

When the Data Set is defined, the second step is to define the layout. Creating report layouts is beyond the scope of this book.

Reports with a large Data Set are complex to maintain and have a risk of being slow in performance since the database engine needs to read all the information before combining the information into a view.

This can be solved by preparing the data first and running the report afterwards. This approach is quite common in data warehousing. The preparation of the data can be done in scheduled batches running in the Job Queue.

Version and object management

When doing software development, discussing version management is unavoidable. Microsoft Dynamics NAV is flexible in this and allows developers to make their own decisions on this subject rather than forcing them to one way of versioning.

What is a version

In Microsoft Dynamics NAV, there are two ways of determining what a version is. The first and easiest approach is to change the version of an object each time it changes. The initial released Version is 1.00 and each change increments to 1.01, 1.02, and so on. A big change will lead to Version 2.00.

Another more common approach in Microsoft Dynamics NAV is to group version numbers in releases of a group of objects together. When this is applied, the application gets a version number that is incremented each time we release. This means that an object with version number 1.01 can jump to 1.04 if it was not changed in releases 1.02 and 1.03.

Version numbering

There are rules in Microsoft Dynamics NAV for version numbering, although the rules have changed over the years.

The current version principle allows us to use letters and digits. The letters indicate the product and country code, the digits the version, subversion, and service pack number.

Let's look at an example object to clarify this. Codeunit Whse.-Printed (5779):

NAV	W1	3.	70.	01
				The last service pack this object was changed
			The last subversion this object was changed	
		The last version this object was changed		
	The Localization Version			
The Product Name				

If Microsoft change this object in Service pack 1 for 2013, the new version number would be NAVW17.00.01.

Combining versions

An object can have multiple versions, but only one version for each product or country. A localized object gets version NAVW13.70.01, NAVNL6.00.01. This means that although the global product team has not changed the object, it has been changed by the Dutch localization team.

Creating a version

Versioning in Microsoft Dynamics NAV is done manually. The version number is an editable field in the Object table (2000000001) that can be freely changed. Developing a tool to do this is easy and has been done by many partners in the channel.

The Data and Transaction model of such a solution should look something like this:

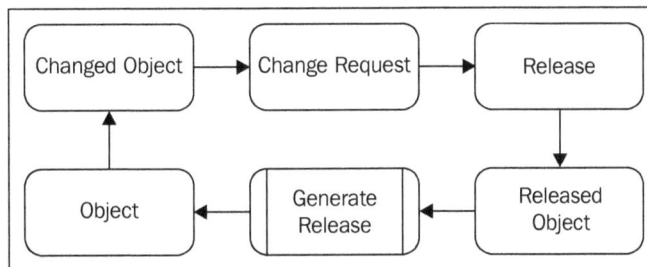

The process starts with a change request. This can be fixing a small bug or creating a new functionality. For this change request, objects need to be modified.

Each modified object is attached to the change request. We can release several change requests at the same time. All objects in the release will get the version number from the release, which can be automatically updated in the object table.

By saving the change request and release information in the database, we will also generate documentation that will help future developers to find information on why objects were changed.

Tracking object changes

Object changes can be tracked using triggers in SQL Server. All the C/Side objects are stored in the Object table (2000000001).

To connect an object change to a change request, the developer should tell the system the request they are currently working on. This will enable us to have a failsafe tracking mechanism to perform version management.

> To view the complete solution for tracking object changes
> visit `http://dynamicsuser.net/blogs/stryk/`
> `archive/2009/05/18/object-auditing.aspx`.

Saving older versions

In order to look at the changes, saving a copy of a version can be very useful. Besides
the obvious possibility of saving the files on a disk, we can also use an external tool.
One of these tools is Microsoft Team Foundation Server. This is a part of the Visual
Studio family and from Version 2013, it is available in the cloud, making it very easy
to set up and use in combination with Microsoft Dynamics NAV.

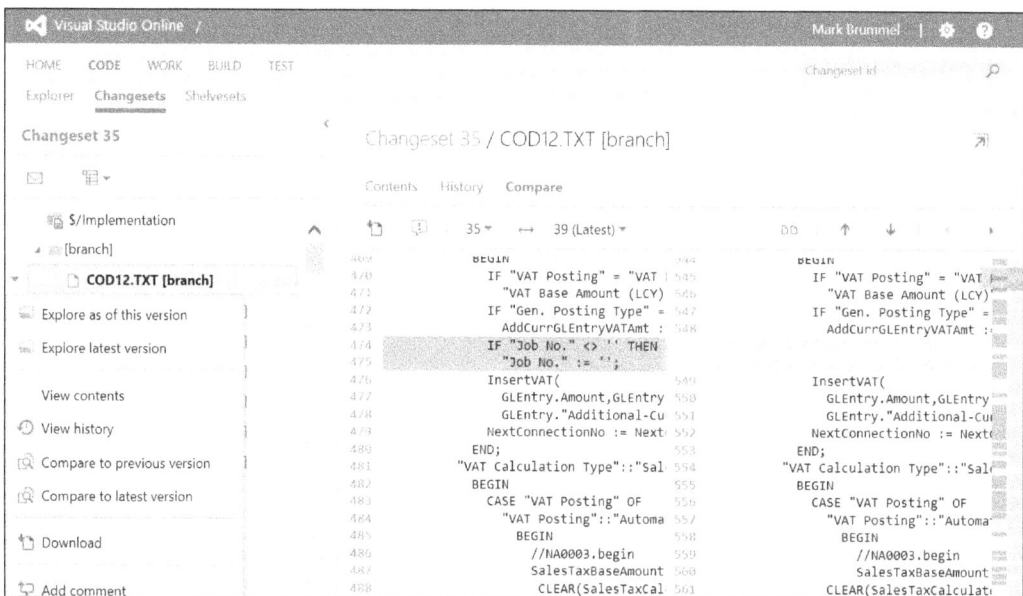

> The video blog at `https://www.youtube.com/user/`
> `SorenKlemmensen/video` demonstrates how to start using
> Visual Studio online combined with Microsoft Dynamics NAV.

Development methodology

To develop software, there are many methodologies such as Prince2, Extreme
Programming, or the Microsoft Solutions Framework.

Most of these methodologies are suitable to be applied to Microsoft Dynamics NAV but they should be used properly. Because of the flexibility of the product, it is easy to leave out steps in the process that should be there.

In Microsoft Dynamics NAV, it is easy to quickly create and modify business software. This is by far the strongest selling point for the solution, but also the biggest pitfall.

A sample approach

When an end user requests a change to the application, it is tempting for most experienced developers to go into the application and create it, preferably in the production database without documentation. This is not the desired way of doing software development.

However, Microsoft Dynamics NAV is a very suitable design environment for prototyping and Rapid Application Design. All the example applications in this book are first built with prototyping and later finalized using testing.

If we design a suitable development methodology for Microsoft Dynamics NAV, we can see that the application life cycle perfectly fits our methodology.

When implementing Microsoft Dynamics NAV, it is very important to involve the end users in each step of the development process.

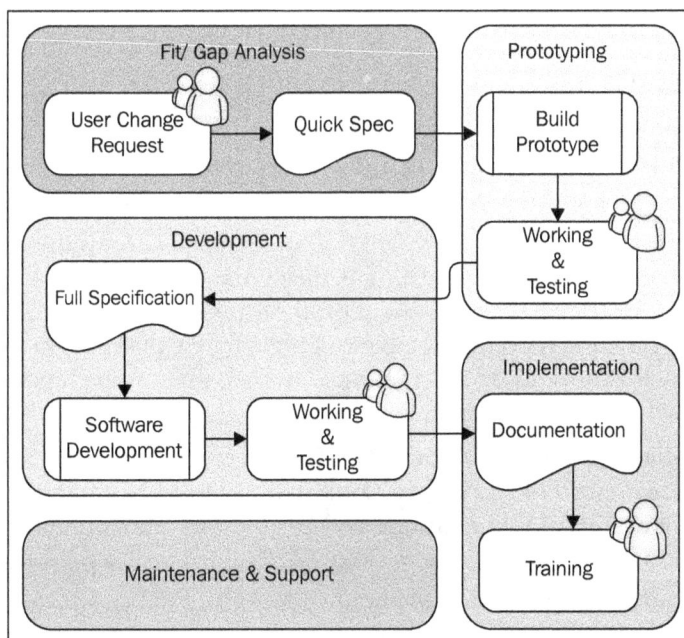

Fit/gap analysis

At the fit/gap phase, usually a quick specification is enough to describe what the user would like the system to do and a possible solution is generated in the application. This document should not count more than two or three pages. During the prototyping phase, it is very normal to come across advanced understanding. It would be a waste of valuable time to find this during the initial analysis with the risk of not finding them anyway.

Prototyping

With the **Quick Spec**, a developer creates the solution as a draft without going into too much detail. This should be enough to show the end user what the solution will look like when it is finished. Very often, this will lead to new questions and ideas that should be carefully considered and put into the full specification, or a new prototype should be built first.

Development

Depending on the amount of changes after the prototype, development can often start with the work done already. At this stage, all the details should be worked out and tested.

There is no complete checklist for developers to use when developing in Microsoft Dynamics NAV, but let's try to create one with the following fields:

- **Captions/Translations**: Make sure all objects have the required captions and translations populated.

- **Table Relations**: Make sure all Table Relations are in place, and check the Ledger Entry and Line tables as well since they are frequently forgotten.

- **Modify And Delete Triggers**: What happens if a user modifies or deletes the record. Make sure that everything is nicely handled in the `OnModify` and On Delete C/AL triggers. `OnRename` should be automatically handled by C/Side. Renaming a table with many table relations may cause severe locking in the database. If users should not rename a record, this can be blocked by placing an `ERROR` command in the `OnRename` trigger.

- **LookupPageID** and **DrillDownPageID**: Even when running the Windows client, it is important to assign a Lookup and Drilldown page ID. Lookup pages are used for table relations and Drilldown pages are used when drilling down from a SUM flow field.

- **CardPageID**: The Windows client always starts a list page when a user selects a menu item or a cue. Double-clicking a row will open the associated card page. This is controlled by the **CardPageID** property on a list page.

- **Field Groups**: To show records from a table relation when entering values, the Windows client does not directly use **LookupPageID** but first shows a **DropDown** list. The fields in this list are defined in the associated tables **Field Groups**. Each table can only have one **Field Group** called **DropDown**, as shown in the following screenshot:

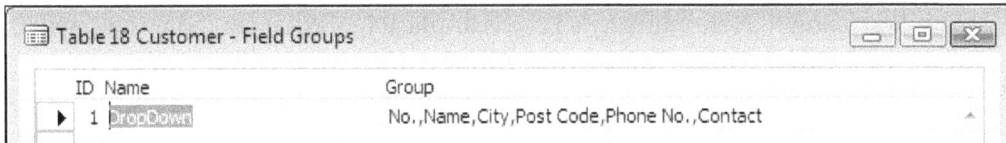

ID	Name	Group
1	DropDown	No.,Name,City,Post Code,Phone No.,Contact

Table 18 Customer - Field Groups

- **Actions**: Actions should make sense to end users. Make sure you use logical names and avoid creating menu buttons and actions that are solely for super users and just confuse end users. Actions should be placed in the correct container. Only promote actions that will be frequently used by all end users.

- **Shortcuts**: Always assign ampersand (&) shortcuts and avoid double shortcuts. When using function keys such as *F3* and *F9*, follow the Microsoft standard conventions.

- **Compression** and **Posting**: If your solution will generate a potentially large amount of data, be sure to provide compression, posting, or cleaning up routines so end users can periodically maintain the data.

- **Permissions**: Does your solution require additional permissions to be set up in the system? Make sure to document this when delivering the solution.

- **Unused Variables**: Make sure you don't leave unused variables in the C/AL objects. Although they won't break the functionality, it will make future maintenance of the software more complex.

- **FIND Commands** and **Locking**: Double check the usage of the correct find commands before you ship the software. Using the wrong commands and leaving locking to the database engine may cause extra performance overhead.

More detailed information about these features is explained in the book *Programming Microsoft Dynamics NAV 2013, David A. Studebaker, Christopher D. Studebaker, Packt Publishing*.

Testing

Testing is probably one of the most important but undervalued tasks of application design.

Testing involves the following three conditions:

- Does the software meet the original requirements? If this is not the case, it does not make sense to continue testing.

- Does it work as expected? This includes trying to deliberately break the solution. If the software is not monkey proof, things will certainly go wrong when using it. Here Murphy's Law is applicable, "What can go wrong, will go wrong."

- Does it fit the rest of the application? Is the software usable and intuitive? A solution that is bug free but difficult to use will be expensive to maintain.

Testing should be automated using the Testability Framework. This allows developers to rerun complete application tests each time they make a change.

> The blog at `http://blogs.msdn.com/b/nav/` `archive/2012/11/07/application-test-toolset-for-` `microsoft-dynamics-nav-2013.aspx` explains how to install and use the Testability Framework for Microsoft Dynamics NAV 2013.

The testing should be also done manually, performed by someone who likes doing it and has the available time. If someone is asked to test the software who is buried in normal work, the chance of bugs slipping in is quite high.

> Testing using the Testability Framework is a mandatory part of the Certified for Microsoft Dynamics process.

The cost of fixing a bug increases as the software evolves. The sooner a bug is fixed, the better.

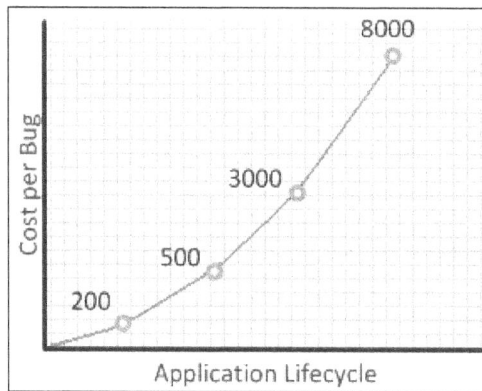

Implementation

When the changes are developed and tested, the documentation should be finalized. This can be either a manual for end users or a technical reference for future developers and support engineers.

The end users should be trained to use the software.

Maintenance and support

After the software is implemented and users are trained, the solution goes into the maintenance and support stage. During this stage, the application manager needs to take care of the data generated by the solution, analyze it, and clean up the data periodically.

If the end users request a change on the solution, the cycle starts again.

The project

Implementing an ERP product like Microsoft Dynamics NAV is not just installing a software package and starting to use it. Each part of your company will have to make decisions how to integrate their work with the software. This very often leads to an interesting new look with respect to your company's way of work.

Standard, customized, or both

There are several ways of implementing Dynamics NAV. It is highly important to make a decision what kind of implementation you want and adjust the implementation accordingly.

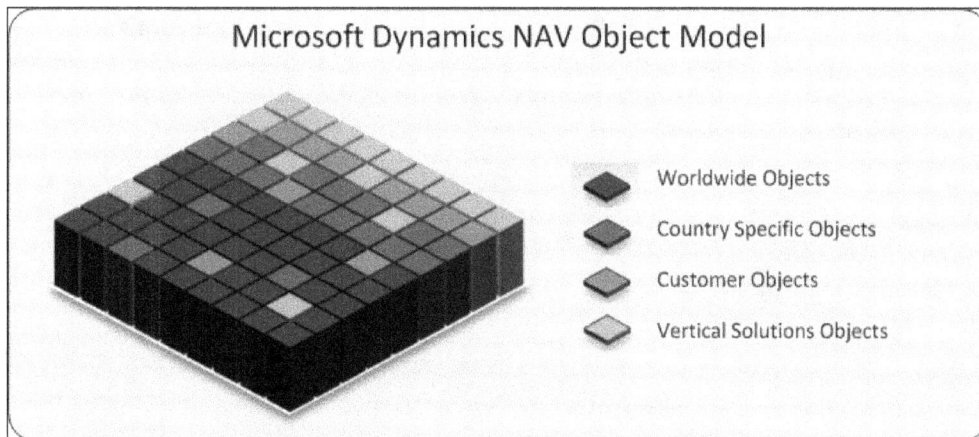

Microsoft Dynamics NAV Object Model

- Worldwide Objects
- Country Specific Objects
- Customer Objects
- Vertical Solutions Objects

Compared to when it was introduced in 1995, Microsoft Dynamics NAV 2013 is a mature ERP package with all the built-in functionalities we discussed in this book. On top of this standard product, resellers have built horizontal and vertical solutions called add-on products. These two combined offer powerful solutions for companies that cannot work with the standard product but are flexible enough to use a vertical solution.

Add-on products

Vertical solutions have started years ago as a customized solution for a company who decided to implement Microsoft Dynamics NAV. Together with the implementation partner, these companies have customized the product to meet their requirements.

Many of these add-on products are now grown up software solutions that fit a vertical industry.

When buying an add-on solution, it is good to ask the reseller some questions:

- What is the release procedure? A solid add-on solution has a release procedure. Most resellers have periodical release every half year or maybe sooner. If a bug is found in the software, there should be a hot fix. Most resellers have releases they support. Make sure to know what versions are still supported.

- How do I upgrade to a new version of the vertical solution? If a new version of the vertical solutions is released, there should be an upgrade procedure. This should be clearly documented and tested by the reseller.

- Am I allowed to make changes to the software? Most add-on resellers do not recommend their customers to change the software. The reason for this is the increased complexity of bug fixing and upgrading.

- What if I do change the software? If an add-on solution is customized anyway, it is basically downgraded from being a supported add-on solution to a customized database. For most resellers, it is difficult to support these customized solutions.

Customizing

Although customizing an add-on solution is not always recommended, customizing Microsoft Dynamics NAV should not be considered a bad practice.

The impact of customization in Microsoft Dynamics NAV can make a difference that can be compared to a suit that is confection or tailored to fit. The benefits of having an ERP package that exactly fits the organization can be more important than the increased cost of ownership of the solution.

Total cost of ownership

The total cost of ownership of Microsoft Dynamics NAV depends highly on the level of customizations. A non-customized implementation with one or two good add-on products done by experienced consultants will have a low impact on your company and will be easy to maintain and support.

The higher the level of customizations, the more it will cost to keep the application running. This is not a bad thing per se. If your company has a unique way of doing business, it might need an ERP package that supports this uniqueness.

The Road to Repeatability program

The **Road to Repeatability (R2R)** was introduced by Microsoft to help partners to be more repeatable. Although the program is primarily marketing-focused, it illustrates the trend of reselling the same Microsoft Dynamics NAV package to multiple customers.

Roadmap to success

Designing a solid application in Microsoft Dynamics NAV starts with a thorough knowledge of the standard application functionality and its design philosophy.

Secondly, we need to carefully analyze the business process we want to support and implement new functionality step by step to ensure good quality, as the solution grows bigger and mature.

Use data and posting models that are similar to Microsoft Dynamics NAV and try to maintain a similar user interface. This will make it easier for end users to adopt your solution and more likely for the software to be easy to maintain and support.

Last but not least, carry out good housekeeping in your database. Compress and clean up data periodically to guarantee a stable performance of the system now and in the future.

Summary

In this book, we have covered functional and technical design of both standard Microsoft Dynamics and how to extend the application to succeed.

This book is not finished. After the publication, we will periodically write articles, tips, and tricks based on the information in this book on `http://www.brummelds.com`.

Any questions or comments regarding the information published in this book can be posted and discussed there as well.

Installation Guide

With this book, we provide development examples that can be installed using the demo version of Microsoft Dynamics NAV 2013 Release 2 W1.

This demo version can be downloaded from `msdn.microsoft.com`.

Licensing

Microsoft has very strict licensing regulations for using and developing in Microsoft Dynamics NAV.

For educational purposes, you are allowed to use the MSDN license to develop new objects with number 123.456.700 to 123.456.799.

Installing Microsoft Dynamics NAV

After downloading the product CD from the MSDN website, start the `setup.exe` file. From the installation options, select **Install Demo**, as shown in the following screenshot:

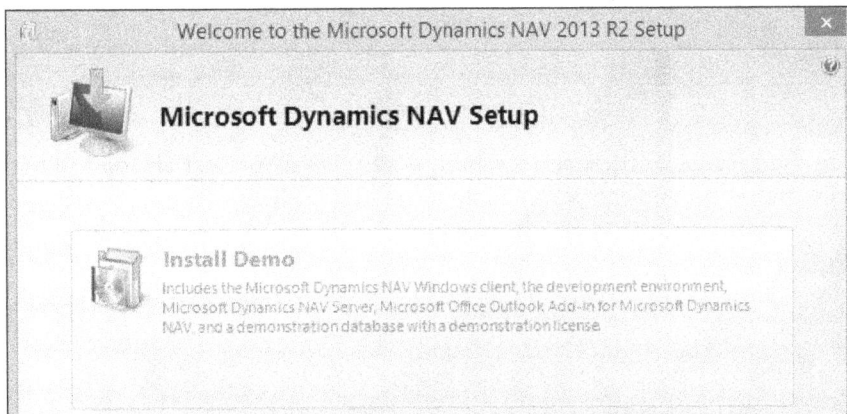

Changing the license

After the installation, we can use both the Development Environment and the Windows client. We use the Development Environment for administration purposes and development. The user interface is created using the Windows client.

Each server instance of Microsoft Dynamics NAV runs on a license file. This file determines what access we have in the system. The demo license that is installed allows us to access all functionality but not the C/AL code.

To access all the C/AL code, we need an official partner development license. To get this license, we would have to register as a partner and start being a reseller. If this is not what we want, we can use the MSDN license.

The MSDN license will allow access to all the new objects developed for the book. Access to the base application change examples is not possible with this license.

To change the license, navigate to **Classic Client**, open the **Tools** menu, and select **License Information**, as shown in the following screenshot:

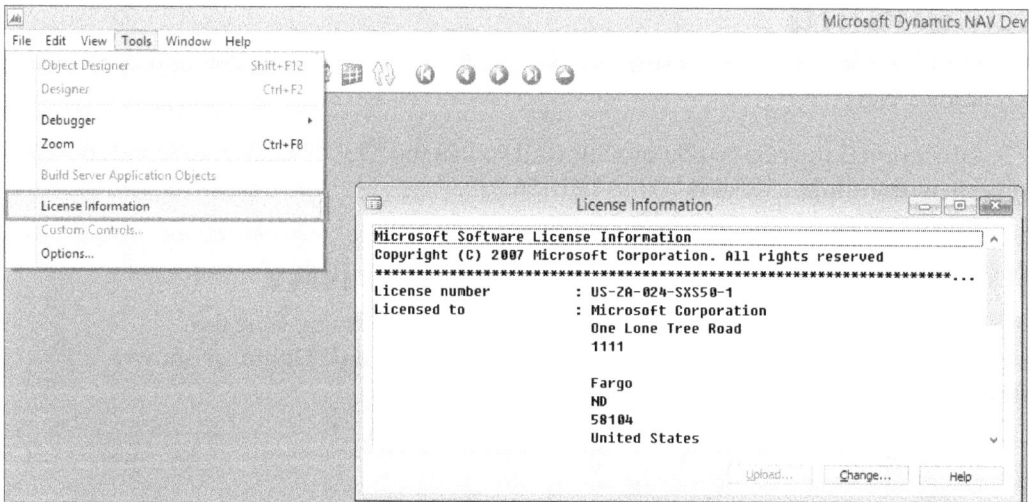

License Information

This opens the **License Information** screen where we can select **Upload**, which opens a file dialog box where we can select the MSDN license.

> To enable the license file on the Classic client, restart the application.

Restarting service tier

To enable the license file on the Role Tailored Client, we need to restart the Service Tier. This can be done from the **Services** window in the Windows **Control Panel**, as shown in the following screenshot:

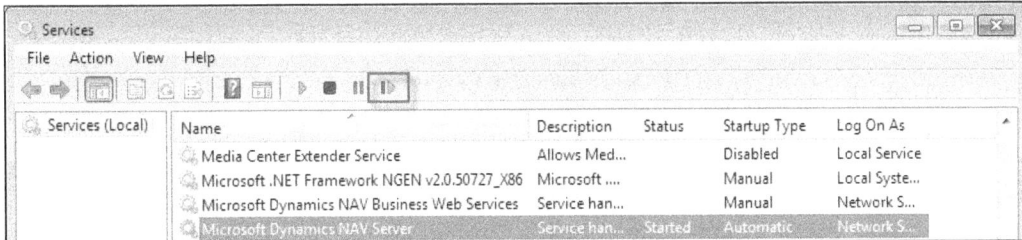

Installing the objects

This book has three Microsoft Dynamics NAV object files, two DLL files, a SQL Server script, and some helper files for the installation. They are as follows:

- `Chapter2-4.fob`: This file contains the squash court examples used in *Chapter 2, A Sample Application, Chapter 3, Financial Management*, and *Chapter 4, Relationship Management*.

- `Chapter7-9.fob`: This file contains the Storage and Logistics application used in *Chapter 7, Storage and Logistics*, and the sample interfaces for *Chapter 9, Interfacing*. We need the additional SQL Server scripts to get the ADO examples to run.

- `Chapter8.fob`: This file contains the Job extensions for *Chapter 8, Consulting*. This chapter also requires the additional DLL files to be installed.

- `RF database.sql`: This is the SQL Server script that is used in *Chapter 9, Interfacing*, to create the RD Database and create the demo data.

- `MSDN.flf`: This is the MSDN license we can use to access the custom objects numbered from 123.456.700 to 123.456.799.

- `NavMaps.dll` and `VEControl.dll`: These are the Dynamic Link Library files we need for *Chapter 7, Storage and Logistics*.

- `Pin1.gif` - `Pin5.gif`: These are the icons displayed on the Bing Map.

Importing a FOB file

To install the objects, first open the Object Designer in the Classic Client by selecting the **Object Designer** (*Shift + F12*) option from the **Tools** menu, as shown in the following screenshot:

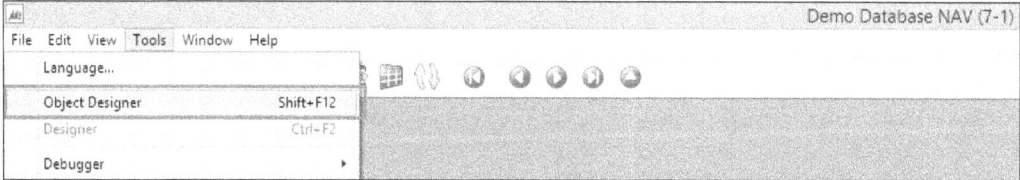

When the Object Designer is active, the **File** menu shows some additional options:

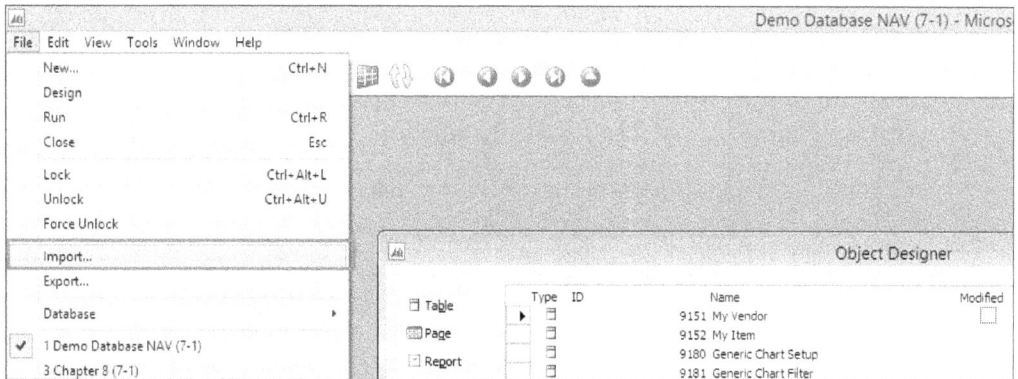

File menu options

We select **Import**, which opens a file dialog window. Now, select the `.fob` file you want to import.

If everything is as it should be, the following dialog should appear:

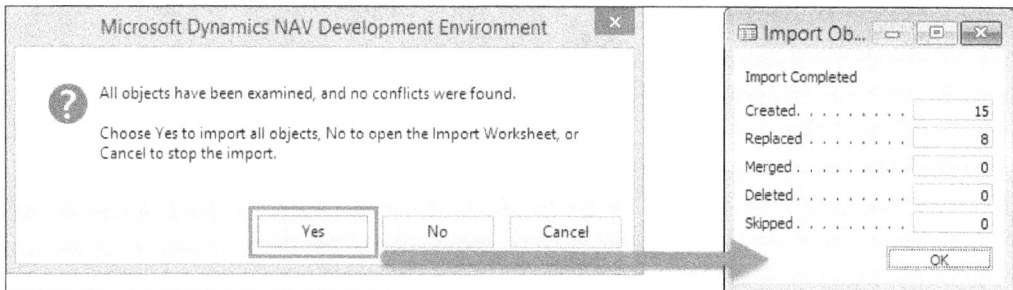

Select **Yes** and this dialog box confirms the import.

Installing the Dynamic Link Library files

To support the Bing Maps Client Add-in, Geocoding, and the distance calculation we ship the following two DLL files, five GIF files, and some supporting files for the installation:

- `NavMaps.dll`
- `VEControl.dll`
- `pin1.gif`
- `pin2.gif`
- `pin3.gif`
- `pin4.gif`
- `pin5.gif`
- `RegisterDll.bat`

These files should now be placed in this folder:

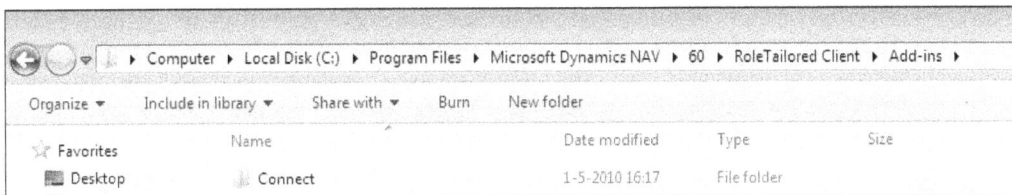

Registering NavMaps.dll

To register this DLL we use `RegAsm`. The command is predefined in the `RegisterDll.bat` file that we can execute.

Registering VEControl.dll

To register the visual map control, we add the reference to the **Client Add-in** table (2000000069). To do this, we can run the table from **Object Designer**, as shown in this screenshot:

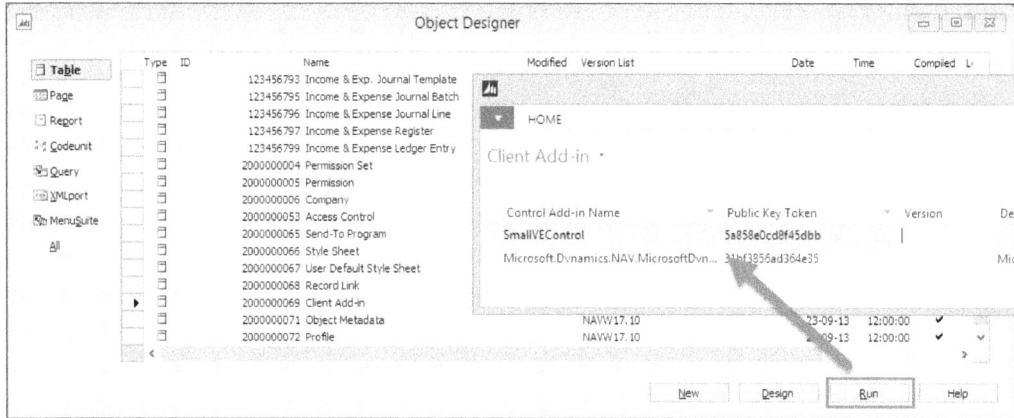

Running table from Object Designer

Index

combined invoicing,
      invoicing application **343**
COMMIT **408, 409**
CommitTracking function **227**
consolidation **118, 119**
consulting process
  about 350
  fits 351
  gaps 351
Consumption Journal **217**
contact card, Microsoft Dynamics NAV
  fields 143-145
contact information,
      sharing across companies
  about 186
  alternative approaches 190
  business relation 187
  C/AL code modifications 188
  Number Series functionality 189
  objects, implementing 190
  tables, sharing 186, 187
contacts
  about 142
  alternative addresses 148, 149
  duplicates 149, 150
  mailing groups, applying to 174
  relationships with customer
      and vendor 149
  salutation codes 146, 147
contacts, adding to segments
  about 191
  criteria filters, implementing 193
  report, expanding 191-193
  solution, testing 194
ContBusRel function **54**
ControlAddIn property **398**
costing methods
  average 204
  FIFO 203
  LIFO 203
  specific 204
  standard 204
CreateIncExp function **339**
credit memo document **244**
currencies **116**
Customer and Vendor Ledger
    Entry tables **37**

customer ledger entry **38, 101**
customers
  direct creation, disabling 185
customization, relationship management
  contact information,
      sharing across companies 186
  contacts, adding to segment 191
  customer numbering 185
  salutation formula types 181
  vendor numbering 185

D

data
  reading 410, 411
  reading, from
      Microsoft Dynamics NAV 382, 383
  writing 409, 410
  writing, to Microsoft Dynamics NAV 384
data analysis **120**
data and posting model, Jobs module
  Job Ledger Entries 352
  Job Planning Lines 352
  Job Tasks 352
data pulling, import and export **379**
data pushing, import and export **379**
date cleanup **436**
date compression **434**
DemandtoInvProfile function **226**
design, interface methodologies
  about 400
  gaps 401
  mapping 400, 401
  working 402
design patterns, Microsoft Dynamics NAV
  about 13
  Application programming
      interfaces (APIs) 13
  architectural patterns 13
  implementation patterns 13
  types 13
design to analyze guidelines
  about 440, 441
  report design 441
design to maintain guidelines
  about 424, 425
  naming 425

N

naming conventions
URL 426
naming guidelines
naming and abbreviations 426
plural 425
reserved words 425, 426
singular 425
Navigate functionality 23
navigation, squash court application
about 94
FindRecords 94, 95
ShowRecords 95
testing 96
Navision 10
Navision Financials 1.0 9
Navision Software A/S 9
NavMaps.dll
registering 457
NAV web service
exposing 386
Number series, basic design patterns 21, 22

O

object management
about 442
object changes, tracking 443
objects installation
about 455
Dynamic Link Library files, installing 457
FOB file, importing 456
ODBC
about 381
data, reading from Microsoft
Dynamics NAV 382, 383
data, writing to Microsoft
Dynamics NAV 384
interacting, with other databases 384
Office 365 396
Office integration
about 388
Excel integration 388
Word integration 388
Online Analytical Processing (OLAP) 432

Online Transaction Processing (OLTP) 432
Open Database Connectivity. *See* **ODBC**
opportunities
about 160
deal, closing 170, 171
sales quote, assigning to 169
sales stages 162
workflow 160-162
opportunity
creating 164-168
Order 244
Outlook integration
about 178, 393
e-mail logging 178
Exchange integration 396
ExtendedDatatype property 394
mail codeunit 395
Office 365 396
Outlook part 393
Outlook synchronization 395
SMTP mail codeunit 395
Outlook part 393
Outlook synchronization 395
Output Journal 217, 230

P

pages
about 419
actions 421
advantages 419
client extensibility 421
embedded lists 419
emphasis 421
fact boxes 421
importance 419
personalization 419
tabs 419
web services 421
periodic invoicing, invoicing application
about 340-342
buffer, processing 342, 343
pharmaceuticals/medicines industry
about 300
invoicing, contributing 300
medication card 300

[PACKT] enterprise
PUBLISHING
professional expertise distilled

Thank you for buying
Microsoft Dynamics NAV 2013
Application Design

About Packt Publishing

Packt, pronounced 'packed', published its first book "Mastering phpMyAdmin for Effective MySQL Management" in April 2004 and subsequently continued to specialize in publishing highly focused books on specific technologies and solutions.

Our books and publications share the experiences of your fellow IT professionals in adapting and customizing today's systems, applications, and frameworks. Our solution based books give you the knowledge and power to customize the software and technologies you're using to get the job done. Packt books are more specific and less general than the IT books you have seen in the past. Our unique business model allows us to bring you more focused information, giving you more of what you need to know, and less of what you don't.

Packt is a modern, yet unique publishing company, which focuses on producing quality, cutting-edge books for communities of developers, administrators, and newbies alike. For more information, please visit our website: www.packtpub.com.

About Packt Enterprise

In 2010, Packt launched two new brands, Packt Enterprise and Packt Open Source, in order to continue its focus on specialization. This book is part of the Packt Enterprise brand, home to books published on enterprise software – software created by major vendors, including (but not limited to) IBM, Microsoft and Oracle, often for use in other corporations. Its titles will offer information relevant to a range of users of this software, including administrators, developers, architects, and end users.

Writing for Packt

We welcome all inquiries from people who are interested in authoring. Book proposals should be sent to author@packtpub.com. If your book idea is still at an early stage and you would like to discuss it first before writing a formal book proposal, contact us; one of our commissioning editors will get in touch with you.

We're not just looking for published authors; if you have strong technical skills but no writing experience, our experienced editors can help you develop a writing career, or simply get some additional reward for your expertise.

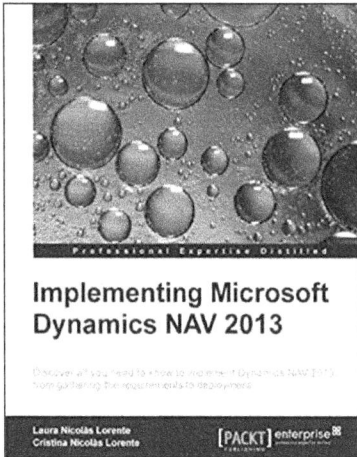

Implementing Microsoft Dynamics NAV 2013

ISBN: 978-1-84968-602-0   Paperback: 554 pages

Discover all you need to know to implement Dynamics NAV 2013, from gathering the requirements to deployment

1. Successfully handle your first Dynamics NAV 2013 implementation.

2. Explore the new features that will help you provide more value to your customers.

3. Full of illustrations and diagrams with clear step-by-step instructions and real-world tips extracted from years of experience.

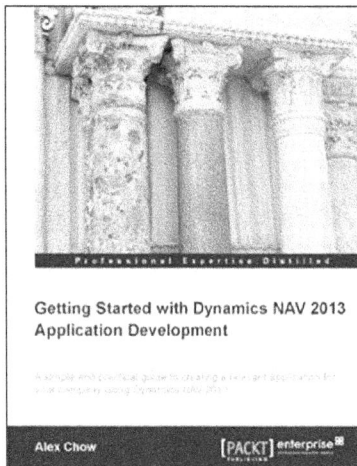

Getting Started with Dynamics NAV 2013 Application Development

ISBN: 978-1-84968-948-9   Paperback: 230 pages

A simple and practical guide to creating a relevant application for your company using Dynamics NAV 2013

1. Understanding user requirements and drawing inspiration from existing functions.

2. Creating the application and integrating it into standard Dynamics NAV.

3. Presented in a simple tutorial style with a resource to get a free trial full version to help you get started.

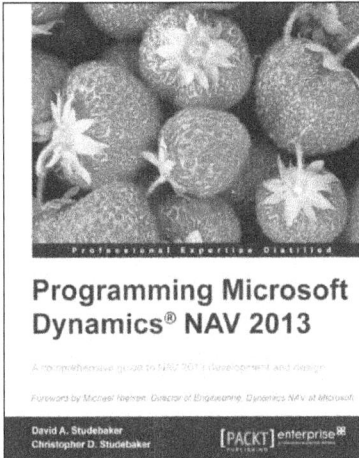

Programming Microsoft Dynamics® NAV 2013

ISBN: 978-1-84968-648-8   Paperback: 630 pages

A comprehensive guide to NAV 2013 development and design

1. A comprehensive reference for development in Microsoft Dynamics NAV 2013, with C/SIDE and C/AL.

2. Brimming with detailed documentation that is additionally supplemented by fantastic examples.

3. The perfect companion for experienced programmers, managers, and consultants.

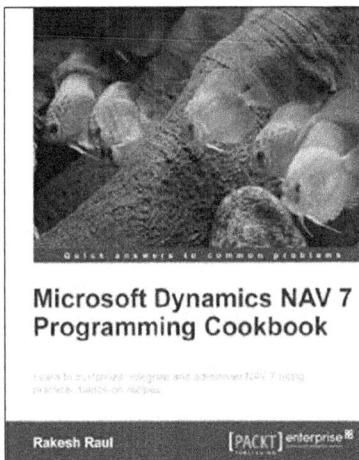

Microsoft Dynamics NAV 7 Programming Cookbook

ISBN: 978-1-84968-910-6   Paperback: 312 pages

Learn to customize, integrate and administer NAV 7 using practical, hands-on recipes

1. Integrate NAV with external applications, using the C/AL or SQL Server.

2. Develop .NET code to extend NAV programming possibilities.

3. Administer the Microsoft NAV 7 server and database.

Please check **www.PacktPub.com** for information on our titles

www.ingramcontent.com/pod-product-compliance
Lightning Source LLC
Chambersburg PA
CBHW080120220326
41598CB00032B/4908